# Cow Boys and Cattle Men

# Cow Boys and Cattle Men

*Class and Masculinities on the Texas Frontier, 1865–1900*

Jacqueline M. Moore

*Published in cooperation with*
*the William P. Clements Center for Southwest Studies,*
*Southern Methodist University*

NEW YORK UNIVERSITY PRESS
*New York and London*

NEW YORK UNIVERSITY PRESS
New York and London
www.nyupress.org

Library of Congress Cataloging-in-Publication Data

Moore, Jacqueline M., 1965–
Cow boys and cattle men : class and masculinities on the
nineteenth-century Texas frontier / Jacqueline M. Moore.
p. cm.
"Published in cooperation with the William P. Clements Center
for Southwest Studies, Southern Methodist University."
Includes bibliographical references and index.
ISBN-13: 978-0-8147-5739-0 (cloth : alk. paper)
ISBN-10: 0-8147-5739-1 (cloth : alk. paper)
1. Cowboys—Texas—History—19th century. 2. Ranchers—Texas—
History—19th century. 3. Masculinity—Texas—History—19th
century. 4. Sex role—Texas—History—19th century. 5. Ranch life—
Texas—History—19th century. 6. Frontier and pioneer life—Texas.
7. Texas—Social life and custom—19th century. 8. Cattle trade—Social
aspects—Texas—History—19th century. 9. Social classes—Texas—
History—19th century. 10. Texas—Social conditions—19th century.
I. William P. Clements Center for Southwest Studies. II. Title.
III. Title: Cowboys and cattlemen.
F391.M934    2009
305.33'6362130976409034—dc22          2009026858

New York University Press books are printed on acid-free paper,
and their binding materials are chosen for strength and durability.
We strive to use environmentally responsible suppliers and materials
to the greatest extent possible in publishing our books.

Manufactured in the United States of America
10  9  8  7  6  5  4  3  2  1

*For my mother, who walks in tallgrass prairies*

# Contents

# Acknowledgments

No author writes alone, and in producing this book I have been especially grateful to receive input from a large number of scholars, as well as help from archivists and courthouse staff. Ultimately, of course, any responsibility for errors and misinterpretations lies with me alone. I am particularly grateful to my colleague, Light Cummins, who has been encouraging at all times, has helped me tremendously with the historiography and contextualization, and who generously read and commented on both the initial proposal and the first complete draft of the book. He has been truly valuable. I am very grateful for the financial support Austin College's Richardson endowment has given me to carry out the early research, as well as for my fellow faculty members' continuing interest in my topic and their moral support. I am also greatly indebted to the Summerlee Foundation, which enabled me to spend a year-long sabbatical at the excellent William P. Clements Center for Southwest Studies at Southern Methodist University as the 2007–2008 Summerlee Foundation Research Fellow in Texas History. The fellowship generously funded me to finish my research travel and also to present my findings at an international conference on the history of masculinity at Birkbeck College, University of London, in May 2008.

The Clements Center staff and faculty have helped me to see my work from a variety of perspectives and have significantly enhanced my book through their hosting of a manuscript workshop in January 2008. Two excellent outside historians, Louis Warren and Robert L. Griswold, were kind enough to take part in this workshop and offered close readings and excellent suggestions for improvement. Thanks also to Benjamin H. Johnson for chairing the workshop so admirably and to Edward Countryman, David D. Doyle, Clark Pomerleau, Glen Ely, Julia Schiavone Camacho, Joaquín Rivaya-Martínez, Tim Bowman, Christy McPherson, Dale Topham, and Andrea Boardman for participating in the workshop and for giving me so many good comments to help improve and tighten up my work and situate it within existing scholarship. David Doyle was good enough to read a rewrite of chapter 2 and made excellent suggestions for improvement. I am especially grateful to Ed Countryman for sharing his wisdom on Western film and art and also for agreeing to write a book for the series, I hope it's not too much! Sherry Smith has been a joy to office next to this year, and also gave me great comments on the first draft as well as the insights of her incredible professional expertise. Julia, Joaquín, and Dan Herman, as fellow fellows, have been great sounding boards and good colleagues to get to know. Andrea Boardman's attention to detail is astonishing, and I always knew I was in good hands. Hope you liked the postcards! RuthAnn Elmore earns a medal for supplying me with the necessary candy to go on and for allowing me to bore her endlessly with excerpts of some of the terrible writing I encountered in the course of research. That—*and* she provided great administrative support as well!!

I have benefited tremendously from conversations with a number of scholars and individuals. Panhandle historian Frederick W. Rathjen very patiently listened to me explain my thesis and sources and suggested others for me while I was in Canyon, Texas. Robert Griswold put me in contact with cowboy historian William W. Savage Jr., who kindly identified a number of factual errors in my first draft and gave me good suggestions for sources. While I know he does not agree with all my interpretations, I hope that at least I have no longer misrepresented any facts, and I wish to thank him for being so gracious. Homero S. Vera, Museum Coordinator of the Kenedy Ranch Museum in Sarita, Texas, helped me greatly by advising me on area archives and what to look for there. He also helped me think more clearly about the vaqueros on the South Texas ranches and the Anglos that live among them. Caleb Roach also offered good suggestions for specific collections in Alpine. I have also been helped in informal or brief discussions with a number of people, including an anonymous audience member at the very first paper I gave on the topic at the Texas State Historical Association in 2001, who first helped me to think about how the work made the man, and the owner of the Maverick Inn in Alpine, Texas, who told me about cowboys' macho attitude toward hardship. Thanks also to Sean Brady, the convener of the London conference, for giving me a forum for my research, and to Harry Brod who, along with many other excellent scholars in attendance, gave me confidence in my work's place in the historiography of masculinity.

Not surprisingly, I have visited many archives in the process of researching this book and have incurred debts at all of them. Lacking organization, moreover, I usually showed up with little to no notice and proceeded to run through a significant portion of their holdings, so I am especially grateful for their patience and help. I have probably spent the most time over the years at the Center for American History at the University of Texas in Austin. I wish to thank the excellent staff as a whole there, most of whom I have troubled at one time or another. As I did the bulk of the pulls over two weeks nearly ten years ago, the graduate student workers who did the most physical labor have now no doubt gone on to their own careers, so I thank them and wish them well. The staff at the Southwest Collection at Texas Tech University in Lubbock also graciously put up with me romping through their records several years ago. They were superb help and their finding aids were wonderful. I also thank the archivist for letting me bring in a pillow to read microfilm more comfortably and then letting me call her at home and arranging for security to let me in to retrieve the pillow when I left it there! Becky Livingston, acting archivist of the Panhandle Plains Historical Museum in Canyon, was a great help to me finding boxes in yet another romp through the records, as was Emily Armer. The staff of the highly efficient Archives of the Big Bend at Sul Ross State University in Alpine patiently helped me to search their catalogue and then equally patiently brought out the reams of files I needed and suggested other collections. Sara Schueneman at the South Texas Archives on the campus of Texas A & M University, Kingsville, allowed me to abduct her desk while I searched the catalogue and found all the tapes and files I needed, despite the fact that they were getting ready to move the Archives to the new location. Jesenia Guerra, archivist at the Corpus Christi Museum of Science and History, also took a morning to help me look at some King-Kenedy correspondence and records, although unfortunately all predated my period of study. Finally, Jim Bradshaw, archivist at the J. Evetts Haley Memorial Library and History Center in Midland, provided great help as well as encouragement going through Haley's interview files as I finished up my last day of research at the end of a 2,500-mile trip. He truly tempted me to stay longer, and I only wish I had had more time to do so.

In addition to visiting archives, I also made a number of unannounced visits to county and district courthouses, looking for criminal records. While not every courthouse I visited had records dating back as far as I needed, a surprising number did, and the staff almost always had a good idea where to find it. I would therefore like to thank specifically: Gayle McCollum, from the Donely County Clerk's Office; Terresa Collins,

Armstrong County Clerk's Office; Carol Miller and Janelle Craven, Gonzales District Clerk's Office; Ashley Reyna, Atascosa County District Clerk's Office; Lydia Steele, Uvalde County District Clerk's Office; Rose Pietsch, Bastrop County Clerk; Estella Carrusco, Josie Flores, and Dianne O. Florez, Reeves County Clerk; Mary Lou Chavez, Reeves County District Clerk's Office; and the staff of the Guadalupe County District Clerk's Office. In the process of looking at court records, I encountered an incredible number of highly competent women who were running these offices and keeping track of everything. Although I was researching masculinity, these women also reminded me that Texas women are far stronger and more capable than any stereotypical "southern flower."

Finally, I would like to thank Deborah Gershenowitz and Despina Papazoglou Gimbel of NYU Press for their help, encouragement, and patience, as well as April Montgomery, my student, who kindly proofread the introduction on a bus in the middle of Malaysia.

Jacqueline Moore
April 2009

# Introduction

*The West, the Man, and the Myth*

We paint the history of the West, particularly Texas, in traditionally masculine terms. Men tamed the frontier, broke horses, subdued Indians, and dominated the landscape, forcing it to yield to their needs. The Old West made men. In the 1920s and 1930s, old-time cowboys looked back fondly to a time when "men were men and women weren't governors," and argued that the movie cowboys had been over "prettified."[1] One chronicler from the 1940s went as far as to proclaim, "The history of West Texas is essentially the history of men."[2] The cowboy has become an icon of Anglo masculinity to generations of Americans. From John Wayne to the Marlboro Man, Teddy Roosevelt to George W. Bush, men have been "cowboying up" to tame both literal and figurative frontiers, and to prove their manhood and that of their country.

The masculine cowboy hero depicted in film and literature is usually a figure straddling the frontier between civilization and the wilderness, sometimes siding with the townspeople against the wilderness and sometimes with the equally mythical noble Indian savage against civilization. Whether he accepts or rejects white society, his manhood is clear, and often superior to those of the so-called respectable men around him. In real life, the historical cowboys in the early cattle industry did not conform to movie cowboy masculinity, nor did their employers and the surrounding townspeople share this image of the manly cowboy.

To examine the ways in which cowboys and cattlemen themselves defined their masculinity, we must look at the Texas cattle frontier in the late nineteenth century. Texas was the birthplace of the modern cattle industry as well as the birthplace of the cowboy. While large-scale cattle ranching spread across the Great Plains in the thirty-five years following the Civil War, it was Texans who first adapted Mexican techniques of caring for cattle from horseback, and who were some of the most prominent cattle barons. Texas cowboys moved around the country working on ranches in Colorado, Montana, and the Dakotas, and many took cattle—and cowboy culture—up the trail through Oklahoma, Kansas, and Nebraska. Thus, Texas is a good arena in which to examine ideals. The period from 1865 to 1900 is particularly interesting. The end of the Civil War and the opening of the railheads in Kansas and the meatpacking plants in Chicago made cattle raising a profitable investment, leading to the rise of long cattle drives north. Although there were always a few absentee owners, many of the early cattlemen worked the ranches themselves, often operating on a small scale. As the industry attracted more investors in the early 1880s, however, many of the smaller ranches sold out to neighboring larger land-holders or corporate syndicates. The cattle industry, like other industries in this period, turned to mass production and systematic approaches to earning profit. These changes significantly affected the men who worked on the ranches.

What complicates any analysis of Western history is the tradition of American exceptionalism based on the "taming of the frontier," that both popular and scholarly sentiment have perpetuated, which has contributed to many myths about the West. This exceptionalism is perhaps even stronger in Texas, which has the historical distinction of being an independent republic. The Texas cowboy is surrounded by mythic images (knight of the prairie, symbol of freedom, masculine icon, or sentimental poet). The iconic cowboy is independent, unaffected by society's suffocating rules and etiquette; free to go where he wants, when he wants; and answers to no man but himself. His is a life of high adventure on the trail, fighting off Indians and desperadoes, performing physically daring feats on a daily basis, and protecting women and children from harm. The early Texas cattlemen, particularly the so-called Cattle Kings, have also earned a somewhat iconic status as the down-to-earth builders of Texas in contrast with the later foreign corporate investors who allegedly cared little for frontier hospitality and were mainly concerned with the bottom line.

Dime novelists and Wild West show promoters in the late nineteenth and early twentieth centuries created romanticized images of the cowboys and cattlemen. Anxious about their own masculinity in the face of new immigration and women's encroachment into the workplace and voting booth, late nineteenth-century Anglo-American men from the middle and upper classes exalted these images. As sociologist Michael Kimmel describes it, "the vast prairie [was] the domain of male liberation from

workplace humiliation, cultural feminization, and domestic emasculation."[3] The historical truth is less romantic. Most historians now recognize
that at base, cowboys were essentially working-class men who, far from
being free, were subject to the same restraints that late nineteenth-century
workers faced across the country. They defined masculinity as their ability to perform their work, to control their own lives, and to respect other
men who did the same. Cowboys did physically demanding work and experienced their share of stampedes and bucking horses, but most of the
time they were simply hard-working hired hands. They lived outside of
"civilized" society because of the nature of their work. Theirs was an all-
male fraternity and they prized male camaraderie and friendships above
most else, but it is also true that their economic and social circumstances
often prevented them from pursuing other paths. They relished their freedom, but they also read the Montgomery Ward and Sears & Roebuck
"Wish Books" in their free time while dreaming of settling down.[4]

The large ranch owners and cattlemen, who employed the majority of
cowboys after the mid-1880s, often came from similar middle-class backgrounds as the later corporate investors, and had different ideas about
what was masculine. They saw themselves first and foremost as businessmen, tamers of the frontier. Moreover, as the business world as a whole
became more corporate in the late nineteenth century, many cattlemen
adjusted to the new style of business themselves and adopted the methods
of the corporations. The cattlemen's goal was to bring civilization to the
West and to profit from it. Civilization meant steady economic growth
and the foundation of stable community institutions. While cattlemen
may have disliked settlers filing claims on open land within their range,
they still wanted to build up towns and realized that a larger population
raised the value of the land they did own. They enjoyed their interaction
with civilized society and believed that the true mark of manliness was
exercising moderation, which was essential to maintaining social order.
Their brand of masculinity emphasized responsibility, and restrained behavior within proper boundaries.[5] Their concept of civilization was also
based in part on a female presence. They hoped to create an environment
for a stable family life and all the social niceties that came with what they
referred to as the feminine touch. The usual prerequisite for the presence
of respectable women was law and order, something which the cowboys
often resisted.

Thus, there was a clear class distinction between cowboy and cattleman. A cowboy was a hired hand who worked cattle on horseback on the

ranch and/or up the trail, but who occasionally did other work on foot for the ranch such as repairing fences. Conversely, a cattleman was simply a ranch owner or manager who employed cowboys. While some early cattlemen certainly started life working on ranches as cowboys, they were usually the ranches that their family owned and they could later inherit. Samuel Burk Burnett of the 6666 Ranch, for example, however much he identified himself as a cowboy in later life, was the son of a rancher who learned his trade on his father's small but successful ranch. Moreover, those cattlemen who continued to behave like cowboys, such as Burnett and Will Hale, were exceptions; as a rule, cattlemen adopted a more genteel lifestyle. Most ranch owners sent their sons to work beside their men to teach them the business and to learn the importance of hard work. The sons might even go off to other ranches to see some of the country and to gain new experiences. But they always knew they were training to run their own business, whereas the hired hands could seldom aspire to own the ranch without independent financial resources.

In truth, while there were certain conditions unique to the frontier, social and economic relations differed little from those elsewhere in the country. Scholars have challenged historian Frederick Jackson Turner's view of the frontier as an incubator of democracy. Settlers imported class and social hierarchies wholesale into the region along with gender and racial biases, and social conflict.[6] Attitudes about masculinity on the frontier did not differ substantially from the rest of the United States, either. Starting in the decades after the Civil War, as the Texas frontier became more settled and the open range disappeared, the real cowboys faced increasing demands from the people around them to rein in the very traits that many Americans considered the most masculine.

The term "manhood" has several meanings, but two main connotations exist. The first is a distinction between manhood and boyhood; in other words, manhood equates with those qualities that distinguish a male adult. The second sense of the word refers to distinctions between men and how one defines the qualities of being a man, that is, his manliness. I use the term "manhood" in this book to refer to both senses of the word, based on the understanding that standards for manhood are fluid and that even within certain groups, individual standards may vary.[7] I use the terms "manliness" and "masculinity" to refer to the second sense of manhood, that is, the qualities of being a man, with the same understanding.

Both concepts of manhood rely on subjective qualifications that vary according to historic, social, cultural, and economic circumstances. Some cultures require formal rites of passage such as circumcision rituals or bar mitzvahs to mark when a boy becomes a man, for example. But since many boys undergo these rituals at the onset of puberty, and maturity levels vary among boys, few would argue that boys literally become men through such a ritual. There are usually other subjective considerations that allow others to recognize when a boy has "grown up." Manhood, in this sense, is not necessarily age-dependent. Similarly, there are subjective considerations as to what makes a man masculine. Some may believe certain character traits such as self-reliance or self-control denote masculinity, others believe physical strength or achieving material success are signs of manhood. A long-haired surfer dude from San Diego, California would likely have different ideas of masculinity than a high school football player in San Diego, Texas. What a metrosexual professional New Yorker sees as enlightened manly behavior, a New York cabbie might see as ridiculous. In the same way, what people thought was masculine behavior in 1870 is not necessarily the same as what we think it is today. My purpose is not to judge or rank different ideals of manhood, or even to contrast them with contemporary standards. Instead, I hope, first, to identify what cowboys and cattlemen themselves thought was manly; second, to use manhood as a new prism through which to illuminate the history of the cattle industry; and third, to determine how differing standards of manhood reinforced social hierarchies.

Historians recognize that there has been more than one model of masculinity operating at any given time, and the efforts of cattlemen to control cowboys in Texas in the late nineteenth century clearly illustrate this point. Between 1865 and 1900, ranchers and cowboys and the people around them expressed the hierarchy between owners and employees in terms of manhood. No one would call a *cowboy* a *cattleman* unless he owned the ranch. Men have used the term "boy" in both positive and negative contexts with a variety of meanings attached to it. Calling a man a "boy" can deny him his status as an adult or imply immaturity. Former trail driver Jeff M. White recalled a trip to California during the Gold Rush: "I was the youngest in the outfit, being only 20 years old, and was called a 20-year-old-boy."[8] In the nineteenth century, whites referred to black males as "boys" regardless of their age, expressing both a belief that they were a "childlike race" and an understanding that they were not the social equals of white men. But "boy" can also be a term of endearment, implying camaraderie. Walter Smith attended an Old Trail Drivers Reunion in the 1920s and met a lot of his cowboy friends, "many of them

I had not seen in forty-five years, boys that I had been associated with during the early days of the frontier."[9] Men also referred to each other as boys out of habit. "One peculiarity about the cowboy . . . was that he was always called a 'boy,' no matter how many years he had lived."[10]

Some cowboys resented the term. Jim Shaw objected that cowhands were always described as cow boys on cow ponies when "they were horses and men."[11] Other men embraced it as a way of creating fraternity. For many working-class men, "boy" was a preferred choice of terms as it invoked the solidarity of boyhood friends when they were free of responsibility, and it also had an air of anti-authoritarianism about it.[12] Some cowboys preferred the term "cowpuncher," and in the northern ranges, they used this term almost exclusively.[13] Others believed the term, which came from the cattle prods the cowboys used to get the cattle to stand up on train cars during shipping, belittled cowboy skills, reducing them to manual laborers. But all agreed that the term "cattleman" or "cowman" was reserved for the ranchers. A visitor to the XIT Ranch in the 1890s observed the distinction within a few days: "'Cow' is the name for all kinds of cattle, and every man is a 'boy' in Texas until he is an old man. Sometimes men are spoken of as 'cowmen' but they are dignified *owners* of cattle, not their care-takers."[14] When future cowboy Hubert Collins first came to the frontier, his brother defined a cattleman as "an owner of a herd on any given range or trail. . . . Generally they are the older men of any outfit which passes here. The cow-boys call them the bosses."[15] Thus, ownership implied a greater sense of manhood, at least linguistically.

The cattle industry is an integral part of the history of American expansion in the nineteenth century. On the edges of the frontier, cattlemen were the forerunners of Anglo civilization, and were responsible for building new towns and ensuring economic growth. They were useful citizens. But the cowboy was a nostalgic figure from the start. In the nineteenth-century view of the inevitable March of Progress, his job was to tame the frontier for the next wave of productive farmers, and then fade away into history.[16] He was a man outside of time. Teddy Roosevelt described his ranch in the Dakotas as one where "Civilization seems as remote as if we were living in an age long past."[17] Novelist Owen Wister called the cowboys "a queer episode in the history of this country. Purely nomadic and leaving no race or posterity, for they don't marry."[18] But in Texas in the late nineteenth century, when the settlers came, the cowboys did not fade away, a fact that made them out of place and inconvenient. Even twentieth-century historians could not understand why they had not faded sooner and asked incredulously: "How and why did this cattleman's frontier last so long?"[19] Unable to ignore the cowboys, the townspeople tried to rein them in and make them invisible, and by the turn of the century they had largely succeeded. The cattlemen, always businessmen, adapted to new conditions, and joined in the efforts to regulate the cowboys.

Much of this regulation of employees was economic in nature and reflected larger trends in the rise of corporate industry elsewhere in the United States. Nonetheless, the language that cowboys, cattlemen, and townspeople used makes it clear that they saw the differences between them partly in terms of manhood. A cowboy was always a boy; a cattleman was always a man. Real men restrained themselves, boys acted without restraint. These contrasting ideas of proper manly behavior correspond with the differing ideals of manliness that middle- and working-class men have historically described for themselves. In general, middle-class men have placed value on the ability to provide for their families and restraint of baser appetites. With fewer resources and opportunities to support their families, working-class men have often turned to public rituals of manhood such as drinking, fighting, and swearing to demonstrate their manliness, behavior which shows a decided lack of restraint.[20] Cowboys' ideals of manly behavior matched those of working-class men elsewhere in America, and cattlemen regularly counseled and enforced middle-class values of restraint as the manly ideal. Like other working-class men, cowboys found that greater regulation of their work and leisure activities restricted their opportunities to demonstrate their manhood, and that increasingly, society defined true manhood by economic success and social restraint, two options they either could not, or would not, embrace.[21] Cowboys, for the most part, resisted attempts to restrain them, but just as the cowboy himself was supposed to fade away, so his ideas of manly behavior came to seem old-fashioned and out of step with modern society to the people around them.

The primary sources I have used for this book are not all new ones as far as cowboys go; indeed, in most cases they are part of the established canon. However, I have asked new questions of these sources and examined them for different types of evidence that has allowed me to draw new conclusions. I have relied extensively on firsthand accounts for my research, both from cowboys and cattlemen. The majority of the accounts come from two main sources. *The Trail Drivers of Texas* (1925) is editor J. Marvin Hunter's collection of 325 anecdotes and memoirs from the members of the Old Time Trail Drivers' Association, established in 1915. These accounts range in length from one to twenty-eight pages and come from a variety of perspectives. The other main source is the Works Progress Administration's Life Histories, 445 of which are available online through the Library of Congress's American Memory Project. Most historians are familiar with the interviews that the WPA did with former slaves in the 1930s. In Texas, they also interviewed old-time cowboys and other pioneers. In addition to these main sources, there are numerous published and unpublished memoirs of cowboys available in libraries and manuscript collections around Texas. The two most useful and best-known of the published cowboy memoirs are Charlie Siringo's *A Texas Cowboy*, and E. C. "Teddy Blue" Abbott's *We Pointed Them North*.[22] While Abbott was mostly a cowboy in the northern ranges and Nebraska, he worked extensively with Texas cowboys and did brief stints in Texas himself. Moreover, in later years, many Texas cowboys worked the northern ranges too; therefore, his experiences were ones they shared.

As with all firsthand accounts, however, it is necessary to take many of them with a grain of salt. The date of the Old Time Trail Drivers' accounts and WPA interviews, for example, meant that many of the cowboy experiences they recalled were at least twenty or thirty years earlier, and thus their memories might not be accurate. In his introduction to the 1985 reprint of *Trail Drivers of Texas*, historian B. Byron Price acknowledges that the book often "reeks of 'good old days' sentimentality."[23] In addition, by the twentieth century there was a very strong heroic myth of the cowboy in the public mind that many cowboys were no doubt happy to validate. After being the source of scorn and disrepute in the late nineteenth century and in early film depictions, cowboys clearly wished to rehabilitate their reputations. Therefore, I have treated each source as critically as possible, verifying facts when possible and comparing accounts. It is fairly easy to distinguish those narrators whose goal is self-promotion from those who simply are telling their experiences, and when possible I have given more credence to the latter. I have also placed more emphasis on ideas that multiple cowboys expressed in the same way. For my purposes, the veracity of the stories the men told was often less important than the way in which they told them. For example, it mattered less to me whether or not the narrator was actually there when they captured Billy the Kid than it did the way in which he described the heroes and villains of the story and what qualities he admired in them. Nonetheless, whenever possible I have supplemented and verified these sources with newspaper accounts, ranch records, and court records.[24]

The overwhelming majority of these primary sources come from Anglo cowboys, despite the fact that many cowboys from this period were black or Hispanic. The WPA narratives include a few from African American cowboys, and there are quite a few Anglo cowboy narratives that detail interaction with black cowboys, if sometimes in a racist manner.[25] However, Hispanic cowboys seem to all but disappear from the documentary record for this period. Everyone agrees that vaqueros taught the Anglo cowboys many tricks of the trade during the antebellum period, that Anglos adapted the vaquero dress and gear to their purposes, and that much of the cowboy terminology such as *rodeo, remuda,* and *riata* come from Spanish. However, in accounts of the period after the Civil War, there is next to no mention of vaqueros in any detail outside of the King or Kenedy ranches except to say that they were there. The standard cowboy narrative usually starts with a list of men who were in the same outfit, with Anglos listed by their full names or nicknames, and then "two negroes and a Mexican," or some variation thereof. WPA interviewers recorded the story of only one Hispanic cowboy and likely did not interview more due to a language barrier. The only published narrative I have found written by a Hispanic cowboy comes from a Uruguayan with French and Spanish parents who obviously looked down on the Mexican cowboys as much as the Anglos did. Lastly, while there has been some excellent recent scholarship on Indian cowboys, most notably Peter Iverson's *When Indians Became Cowboys*, this topic is beyond the scope of my work.[26] Most of the Indians who ranched worked in Oklahoma, and many of these ranches date from a later period than my research. I was only able to identify one Indian cowboy in the Texas narratives, and his story was no different from those of the Anglo cowboys.[27] Thus, while I would have liked to have done more analysis of the experiences of nonwhite cowboys from their own perspective, it was not possible to go into as much detail as I have for Anglo cowboys.

Nonetheless, it is clear from late nineteenth-century sources that race played a role in the hierarchy of masculinities. In the opinion of the white majority, white manhood was the epitome of virility and masculinity; thus, being a minority automatically meant a man was less of a man. In part white workers retained a sense of masculinity by considering themselves superior to blacks, Hispanics, and certain immigrant groups. White supremacy ensured instant and often violent retaliation in the South and Southwest when a black or Hispanic man tried to assert himself. Ironically, the most common justification for lynching in the 1890s was that a black man had sexually assaulted a white woman, a justification that revealed anxiety on the part of whites that perhaps black men had superior physical masculinity. Social scientists and politicians at the end of the century both worried that white men were becoming weakened by over-civilization and argued that it was the duty of whites to put their superior manhood to good uses such as conquering the "childlike" races of Africa and Asia. The cattlemen perhaps similarly feared that the cowboys' physicality proved their manhood was more potent than their own and so downplayed physical strength in favor of strength of character.

I have discussed the unique situation cowboys of color faced whenever relevant, but I do not wish to imply that they did not share the same experiences that other cowboys faced, and indeed, I have tried to use examples that show those common experiences throughout the book, preferring not to segregate them completely in the narrative. In most ways, outside of the South Texas large ranches, black and Hispanic cowboys experienced the same treatment as Anglo cowboys on the job, and there are enough instances of friendships between whites and nonwhites to suggest that they shared many of the same values. Moreover, they were held to the same standards of manhood, whether or not Anglos believed they could meet them.

I have benefited tremendously from the work that others have done in both Western history and the history of masculinity. There is a vast repository of secondary sources on cowboys and the West, as the subject has provided endless fascination to both serious historians and buffs. There are a large number of coffee table books on cowboys as well as a number of antiquarian sources whose goal is to enumerate their clothes, technical skills, and language in a mostly celebratory fashion. However, there are also a number of excellent scholarly works on the cowboys, cattlemen, and ranching industry in general. One of the earliest of the reliable sources is Philip Ashton Rollins' *The Cowboy* (1922), which details all aspects of the cowboys' work and leisure although still tends a little toward the cowboy-as-bringer-of-progress-to-the-West narrative. Another excellent early source of information on the grazing industry is Edward Everett Dale's *The Range Cattle Industry* (1930). There are several histories of individual ranches that are useful, including Cordia Duke and Joe Frantz's *6,000 Miles of Fence: Life on the XIT Ranch of Texas* (1961); William C. Holden's *The Espuela Land and Cattle Company* (1970); an expanded version of *The Spur Ranch* (1934); and Tom Lea's *The King Ranch* (1957), although each of these sources is somewhat dated in its approach and interpretation.

Beginning in the late 1960s, revisionist historians began to reexamine the traditional narrative of Western expansion in which Anglo cowboys and cattlemen were the equal torchbearers of progress, defending Christian womanhood, taming the frontier, and cleansing it for development by white Americans. From this reevaluation came new awareness of the roles of women and different ethnicities on the frontier as well as a Marxist reinterpretation of labor relations that firmly established the cowboy as part of the working class. As the sources provided in the notes indicate, I have drawn on the work of many of these scholars, including William Savage, David Dary, Arnoldo DeLeón, Susan Armitage and Elizabeth Jameson, Clifford Westermeier, Richard Slotkin, Ann Butler, Kenneth Porter, Philip Durham and Everett L. Jones, Robert Hine, Byron Price, Richard Slatta, and Elliott West. Their work has enabled a new wave of scholarship on cowboys and frontier life that presents a more complete, if less shiny, picture of their circumstances, as evidenced by the work of Paul Carlson, Susan Lee Johnson, Lawrence Clayton, Richard Etulain, Louis Warren, Dee Garceau, Peter Iverson, Sara Massey, and Paul Reddin.

Given the universal acceptance of the cowboy as a masculine icon, surprisingly few scholars have applied the lens of masculinity studies to the late nineteenth-century cowboy. Almost all of the major histories of masculinity in this period note that the cowboy was an ideal for anxious East Coast middle-class men (and Teddy Roosevelt), but none of these look at the cowboy's experience himself. Moreover, most work on cowboy masculinity has tended to focus on the twentieth century and images in film and popular culture rather than the historical cowboy. The sources that have most directly analyzed historical cowboys in light of the new masculinity studies are literary scholar Blake Allmendinger's book, *The Cowboy*; and the essays of historians Karen Merrill and Dee Garceau in Matthew Basso, Laura McCall, and Dee Garceau, eds., *Across the Great Divide*. These works have charted a path for this study, as have most of the essays in the latter volume.

The field of masculinity studies is a relatively young one but incredibly rich. The groundbreaking work of Peter Filene, Michael Kimmel, E. Anthony Rotundo, Elizabeth and Joseph Pleck, Peter Stearns, Harry Brod and Gail Bederman has led to a flourishing of new scholarship, particularly for the Gilded Age and Progressive Era. The work ties in with other new studies of homosexuality by George Chauncey, Martin Duberman, John D'Emilio, and Jonathan Katz to create a revolution in our understanding of gender in all its forms. This has had particular implications in the study of nineteenth-century "Victorian America," as it has led to a reevaluation of the concepts of separate spheres, sexual identity, moral reform, imperialism, and social control. The better of these studies, like much of the new social history, have focused on the intersections of class, race, and gender and how they tend to reinforce one another. They understand that there has been no permanent model of masculinity and that gender identity is dependent on a wide variety of factors. Most of the scholarship has focused on middle-class masculinity, but more recently, historians such as Chauncey, Elliott Gorn, Susan Johnson, Peter Boag, and Craig Heron have begun to investigate working-class masculinity. It has been my intention to investigate all these issues in the context of the Texas frontier from the beginning of the trail drives in the late 1860s to the end of the nineteenth century.

The parallels between cowboy values and those of frontier miners, railroad workers, Northwest loggers, or East Coast factory workers are remarkable, and I have drawn extensively on these parallels to situate my own conclusions. I have recently had opportunities to hear work from scholars on similar conflicts between sailors and officers in the British navy; Mormon settlers and Arizona cowboys; and Klondike miners and Christian reformers, all of which stressed almost the exact same issues between social class and competing ideals of masculinity.[28] What has become increasingly clear to me from this work is that cowboys were not only like their working-class counterparts in terms of economic and social relations, but that even their cultural values were far less unique than traditional proponents of cowboy exceptionalism have assured us. In *Life on the Mississippi*, Mark Twain described Mississippi boatmen in terms that could just as easily have described the cowboy: "Rude, uneducated, brave, suffering terrific hardships with sailorlike stoicism; heavy drinkers, coarse frolickers in moral sties, . . . heavy fighters, reckless fellows, every one, elephantinely jolly, foul witted, profane; prodigal of their money, bankrupt at the end of the trip, fond of barbaric finery, prodigious braggarts; yet faithful to promises and duty, and often picaresquely magnanimous."[29] The cowboy was no more "knight of the prairie" than the boatman was "prince of the river." Like all regular working men, he lived a complex life with both hardship and pleasure and made the best of his situation.

Not surprisingly, very few hired hands went on to become cattlemen themselves. Most cowboys ended up leaving the profession to become merchants or farmers, as there was little opportunity within the cattle industry itself. Some retired from the work due to injury, which was common. A few stayed on into their forties and beyond, but the majority were between the ages of twenty and forty. And although some cowboys came from genteel backgrounds themselves, while they were cowboying, they had to conform to working-class standards of behavior or risk ridicule. Cowboys in the late nineteenth century were thus, in the words of anthropologist Beverly J. Stoeltje, "an age graded, all male, occupational group, associated with animals and mobility, representing a variety of ethnic and class backgrounds, permanently situated at the bottom of the economic scale, and often temporarily cast in the role."[30]

Two competing images of the cowboy emerged in the late nineteenth century. He was either a miscreant—if sentimental—boy who could not adapt to modern times; or a manly hero, fulfilling America's destiny of taming the continent. By local standards, cowboys were a throwback to a more primitive time. However, for middle-class men outside the West, who worried they had become over-civilized, the cowboy became a symbol of masculinity at this time precisely *because* of his "primitive" masculinity. To Teddy Roosevelt, for example, the cowboy possessed "few of the emasculated milk-and-water moralities admired by the pseudo-philanthropists; but he does possess, to a very high degree, the stern, manly qualities that are invaluable to a nation."[31] By the 1920s, his image had gained heroic proportions even among Westerners themselves. Editor J. Marvin Hunter dedicated the *Trail Drivers of Texas* (1925) to "the old trail drivers . . . to the young and the brave who fought manfully for proud, imperial Texas" and who made possible "the development of an empire so vast in its possibilities as to excite the envy of the world."[32] Founder of the Old Time Trail Driver's Association, George W. Saunders, went even further with his praise.

It is plain that all commercial achievements, civilization, good government, Christianity, morality, our school system, the use of all school and state lands making them revenue-bearers, the expansion of the stock business from the Rio Grande to the British possessions, which is producing millions of dollars; the building of railroads, factories, seaports, agricultural advancement and everything else pertaining to prosperity can be traced directly to the achievements of the old-time trail drivers.[33]

The myths that surrounded the cowboy painted him as a perfect balance of aggressive masculinity and civility. "They may be boisterous and uncouth in some respects, yet, at heart they are 'diamonds in the rough,' while for charity, manhood and chivalry they stand erect—the peers of any bearer of shield and lance 'when knighthood was in flower.'"[34] They envisioned him as an ideal boy and sort of noble savage, wise, not through formal education, but because he was close to nature.[35] They even held up his faults as somehow virtuous. Folklorist John A. Lomax opined, "There is a certain wholesome strength, cleanliness and variety in his profanity, and even in his vulgarity, that I do not believe is equaled by any other race of men."[36] In her description of "The Real Cowboy," Bulah Kirkland claimed she could pick out a cowboy instantly on the street, not because of his clothes, but because "he has a very open countenance and almost innocent eyes and mouth. He is not innocent of course; but living in the open, next to nature, the cleaner life is stamped on his face. His vices leave no scars, or few, because old mother nature has him with her most of the time."[37] Ironically, if a cowboy had read such descriptions of himself in the 1870s, he might have cringed at such a childlike picture. As historian William Savage has pointed out, the B movie cowboy that evolved from these images preserved heroes in a state of arrested adolescence.[38]

But the cowboy was always subject to other peoples' definitions and redefinitions. Some recognized the irony of these descriptions, since just a few years earlier they had been the object of public scorn. In 1881, President Chester Arthur warned America about the dangers of the vicious, lawless cowboys roaming the Arizona countryside. While Arthur's comments were meant to refer to a spate of outlawry in Arizona, many Americans did not make a distinction between criminal and cowboy.[39] Lee D. Leverett described himself and his fellow cowboys quite humbly: "Fact is, we were all as strong as a hoss in power, and in smell as well."[40] As historian Dee Garceau has quoted cowboy Bruce Siberts (or perhaps his ghostwriter): "Owen Wister hadn't yet written his book, *The Virginian*, so we cowhands did not know we were so strong and glamorous."[41]

I have divided the book into two parts, roughly corresponding to work and leisure. I begin part I with a brief summary of the so-called crisis of masculinity that occurred in the late nineteenth century and an overview of the history of the cattle industry, particularly the shift to more corporate methods of ranching in the 1880s. I examine how boys became men on the frontier in part by taking on a man's workload and in part by their acceptance from men of their respective social classes. I then explore in detail the ways in which cowboys expressed masculinity through control of their working environment and their work skills, and the ways in which cattlemen increasingly limited their opportunities to do so.

In part II, I look at how cowboys increasingly turned to their leisure activities to define and display their manhood, only to find, once again, that cattlemen and other respectable townspeople tried to limit these activities as well. I look first at how the men themselves defined masculinity through their friendships and associations. Cowboys used humor against their employers and racism against nonwhites to bolster their own masculine identity as they lost opportunities to display it elsewhere. The relationships that cattlemen and cowboys had with women also led to differing ideas about manhood. The cattlemen often had their choice of respectable women to marry, and thus defined marriage and the ability to provide for a family as essential markers of manhood. As social outcasts, cowboys had few opportunities to meet with "good" women, and had mixed feelings about the prostitutes who would associate with them. Given the difficulties cowboys faced in their relationships with women, it is not surprising that they preferred socializing with other men. They performed public rituals that displayed their masculinity through drinking, gambling, and fighting. Cattlemen, while recognizing the element of honor involved in such rituals, by and large rejected them as irrational and detrimental to their main project of bringing civilization, law and order to the frontier. The cowboy thus became a pariah in the cow towns he had helped build. The Epilogue briefly traces the evolution of this historical cowboy to the mythic hero through dime novels, literature, art, and film.

In 1892, the *San Antonio Daily Express* published one of the earliest correctives to the negative image that people had of cowboys as gunslingers and outlaws. Cowboys were often wild, the editor noted, especially when they drank, but they were never murderous. Besides, the cowboys had all become mellower than they were in the days of the early frontier.[42] In many ways, this defense accurately reflected a process that was taking place. In the course of taming the frontier, the cattleman tried to tame the cowboy and impose his own standards of behavior on him, including ideals about masculine behavior. Not surprisingly, the new heroic image of the cowboy reflected a restrained and virtuous ideal of masculinity that still celebrated the "boys" for being somewhat wild. The cattlemen ultimately maintained social hierarchies in part by asserting their own version of masculine behavior as being superior to that of the cowboys. By the twentieth century, the cowboys themselves embraced their heroic mythical image, perhaps in part to counter the attacks on their ideals of masculinity. How all this happened is the subject at hand.

# PART I

# Doing the Job

# 1

# Of Men and Cattle

In order to understand ideals of masculinity among Texas cowboys and cattlemen in the late nineteenth century and the ways in which these ideals evolved and conflicted, it is first necessary to examine the intersections of the history of the cattle industry and the history of masculinity during this period. Between 1865 and 1900, the years this book covers, there were tremendous changes in American society, primarily as a result of industrialization, the rise of corporate monopolies, and the development of the industrial working class. The cattle business was no exception. Large private and corporate ranchers fenced in their lands in the 1870s and 1880s, ending the era of the open range and driving smaller ranches out of business. The large ranchers then modernized their practices to incorporate both corporate management techniques and scientific breeding measures. These latter developments ultimately both led to some de-skilling of ranch work and changed the nature of the relationship between ranchers and employees. There were regional differences in the timing of these changes, but general trends were consistent across the board.

In the nineteenth-century United States, a dramatic redefinition of manhood also occurred as a result of the rise of industrialization. In many ways, this hit the working class first, as they came into the new factory system and had fewer opportunities to control their own work or the products of it. Since the American definition of masculinity had always included some measure of independence and ability to control one's own life, working-class men struggled to redefine their masculine identities.[1] Many labor organizers tried to counteract the prevailing competitive model of manhood by emphasizing manhood through solidarity against the factory owners and managers in the form of labor unions.[2] This rhetoric achieved only limited success, however, and most working-class men simply chose to express their masculinity in a world of all-male unrestrained social bonding and ritual. Meanwhile, by the late nineteenth century, middle-class men were facing challenges to their own ideals of manhood. They had traditionally based their identities in part on their economic success as well as their commitment to a patriarchal, but moral, social order. When this order began to collapse, and their ability to succeed financially became subject to a highly competitive market, they needed to rethink masculinity. With women entering the public spheres of work and politics, unscrupulous entrepreneurs becoming millionaires, and working-class men—including a huge influx of poor immigrants— uniting in opposition to their control, these men felt under attack.[3]

Social scientists and commentators began to worry that elite men had become "over civilized," in a society in which culture was feminized and white Anglo-Saxon Protestant men seemed outnumbered by "swarthy" immigrants. Men were in danger of falling prey to "neurasthenia": a nervous condition that produced effeminacy and sapped men of their virility. A loss of masculinity could put the whole nation at risk. Teddy Roosevelt argued that if George Washington or Abraham Lincoln had shown "the least touch of flabbiness, of unhealthy softness . . . [it] would have meant ruin for this nation."[4] The solution to these problems seemed to be what Roosevelt termed the Strenuous Life. Boys should be encouraged to break away from overprotective mothers and to cultivate aggression. This aggression was essential to preparing them for the competition they would face in the business world and they could avoid the curse of feminized culture. However, there was a thin line between aggressive behavior and savagery. Thus, as boys grew older, they also needed to learn to restrain their passions and channel them into productive behavior. The new ideal man was physically fit but could control his aggression. He could channel his passion into righteous causes, but unbridled emotion was a sign of weakness.[5]

The latter ideal of restraint was key to middle-class manhood, both in the sense of differentiating from boyhood, and in the sense of masculinity in comparison with other men. Working-class men were physically fit and far from feminine, and thus on the surface might fit this new ideal if it was not for the concept of restraint. Middle-class men could still claim superiority over their working-class counterparts by showing a superior form of masculinity. They classified working-class men, who defined their own masculinity in part through unrestrained social activities, as both childlike and savage. Gradually, middle-class men began to see regulation of working-class masculinity as essential to achieving proper social order, and to creating a new employee who would identify his interests with those of his employer.[6] In some ways they did so by linking the concept of success with masculinity, arguing that any man could achieve success through willpower and manly self-assertion that was "forged in the battle of life."[7] By implication, workers who did not improve their situation were not real men, and were "best viewed as children."[8] Clearly, there were competing ideals of masculinity in the late nineteenth century.

Cowboys and cattlemen modeled their respective class ideals. Cowboys saw their masculinity in terms of their skills on the job, their control over their working conditions, and their ability to make independent decisions. They spent their leisure time in boisterous behavior designed to show masculinity through public drinking and sexual prowess. Cow towns like Dodge City at the railhead in Kansas and smaller towns like Tascosa in the Texas Panhandle gained sordid reputations as the playgrounds of drunken cowboys who gambled, consorted with prostitutes, and rode through town on their horses shooting their guns wildly in the air. While historians such as Robert R. Dykstra and Robert C. Haywood have shown that some of these descriptions were exaggerated or that they overlooked the more respectable permanent cow town residents, it is clear from cowboy narratives, criminal records, and newspaper accounts that the cowboys played as hard as they worked and that drinking, gambling, and fighting were key parts of cowboy identity.[9]

Cattlemen, however, typically enjoyed a different lifestyle. They saw their masculinity in terms of their ability to provide for their families while building civilization on the frontier. They prided themselves on supposedly superior morals to those of common men such as the cowboys, and they saw drunken violence and gambling as signs of a lack of restraint. Cattleman George W. Littlefield, for example, never drank or gambled, and Mifflin Kenedy built a church on his ranch for his cowhands, encouraging them to maintain moral behavior. Most cattlemen viewed themselves as father figures to their employees and felt they had every right to control them. Richard King, the patriarch of the King Ranch in South Texas, took on the role of a *patrón* with complete control and authority over his employees and the families that lived on his *encomienda*-style ranch. Charles Goodnight of the JA Ranch in the Panhandle assumed the right to set whatever rules he liked for his employees on the ranch, including regulation of his cowhands' personal behavior. Colonel Joe C. Miller, founder of the 101 Ranch in Oklahoma, played patriarch to all who came to the ranch. He welcomed all visitors and employees with the phrase "Come in, children."[10] Cowboys and cattlemen were clearly considered two different classes of men. Cattlemen owned the ranch, cowboys were just employees.

While shipping cattle on the Northern Pacific Railroad, the cattlemen and bosses got free passes to travel with the regular passengers, but the cowboys had to stay in a special car attached to the end of the train.[11]

The development of the Texas cattle industry before the Civil War was a result of the efforts of both Mexican and Anglo ranchers and workers as well as black slaves. In the seventeenth and eighteenth centuries, the Spanish brought cattle and horses to the New World to supply both the military and the Catholic missions. When the missions began to secularize in the 1790s, lands and cattle were dispersed to private individuals. In the system that evolved, workers lived on the self-sufficient ranches and were bound to a *patrón* for protection and employment. Vaqueros developed methods of roping from horseback, branded cattle to designate ownership, and helped drive the cattle to market. By 1800, there were several million cattle grazing on Spanish lands in California and Texas.[12] But by 1830, while most Texas cattle were descended from Spanish stock, about 20 percent of the cattle were "American native" stock that had come with Anglo settlers in the Austin region.[13] The blending of this stock with the Mexican cattle, as well as with cattle from Western Louisiana and elsewhere, led to the creation of the Texas Longhorn, the tough and somewhat wild cattle that could handle the heat of Texas and were equally at home in coastal prairies in Gulf Coast Texas and the brush country along the Rio Grande.[14] Additional human migrants also came to Texas, many from the Southern United States, and brought with them livestock herding practices that had developed there. Historians have debated whether these practices originated from Scots-Irish herding techniques that immigrants brought to the United States, and indeed many Texas settlers were of Scots-Irish descent. Livestock raisers in Scotland and Ireland used many of the techniques associated with Texas ranching, including open range grazing, seasonal roundups, branding, and professional drovers. It is most likely, however, that the style of ranching that developed was less a result of ethnicity than that it was best suited to the geography of Texas.[15]

Much of the cowboy's rough reputation in town came from Anglo cowboys who worked in the frontier period, when part of the job description was defending ranch property from Indian and Mexican attacks and "confiscating" cattle from neighboring herds.[16] Anglo ranching in Texas often developed at the expense of Mexican ranchers. During the Texas Revolution, Texas soldiers began stealing cattle from the Mexicans to feed the troops and driving them north. Following the war, soldiers continued this practice. Indeed, until the 1870s, raiding on both sides of the border was common, and border hostilities often revolved around cattle thefts.[17] Many Mexicans who owned land grants were intimidated into leaving or selling their land to the Anglo ranchers in the region after the Texas revolution. Others were forced out later when Anglo ranchers such as Richard King and Mifflin Kenedy fenced in their land and blocked access to water sources, some of which did not actually belong to them.[18] On the Gulf Coast, intimidation also displaced a number of black landowners. Aaron Ashworth owned over 3,000 head of cattle in Jefferson County in 1850 but was driven off by envious Anglos.[19] There were a few black cattlemen, such as Silas Jackson, who owned a large ranch near Goliad, or D. W. "80 John" Wallace, who eventually amassed over 10,000 acres in Mitchell County in north central Texas. Black owners were rare, however, as it was difficult for African Americans to purchase land in the years after the Civil War due to racial prejudices.[20]

Throughout the period leading up to the Civil War, Mexican vaqueros passed their skills on to Anglo settlers, who adapted their clothing and equipment to meet the needs of the job. In addition, some of the Anglo ranchers hired vaqueros to work for them, especially in South Texas, where they often hired the Mexican ranchers they had displaced.[21] In the most direct transfer of customs and skills, in the 1850s, Richard King, a former riverboat captain, secured a large parcel of land in Southern Texas and persuaded an entire Mexican village to relocate to his ranch and take him as a *patrón*. King's vaqueros or *kineños*, as they were called, lived on the ranch for generations with their families, and the job became an inheritance they passed down from father to son.[22]

By the 1850s, Texas ranchers had established markets for their cattle, which they drove up the Shawnee Trail to Kansas City and Sedalia, Missouri as well as New Orleans and Shreveport, Louisiana. A few even drove cattle to California to feed the Gold Rush migrants. However, most still shipped their cattle via steamship from Brownsville and Galveston to the Caribbean. During the Civil War, the Union blockade stopped both shipping and drives, and with many men off fighting, the herds went largely untended for five years. At the end of the war, there were an estimated five to six million wild cattle in Texas. In the next few years, ranchers began to round up all unbranded cattle, known colloquially as mavericks, to rebuild their herds. With the Southern economy in shambles, however, there was no demand for beef in the old markets. In 1866, Chicago opened its stockyards and the ranchers realized that if they could get their cattle to a railhead they could potentially sell to a national market. In 1867, the Kansas

Pacific Railroad established such a railhead at Abilene, Kansas, and a few ranchers began the long trail drive north.[23] Meanwhile, other ranchers had discovered during the Civil War that they could make money with government contracts to supply beef for the military, and later, for Indian reservations, so they drove cattle west to New Mexico and California, and north to Nebraska and the Dakotas.

The first cattle drives to the north after the Civil War started in 1866, with ranchers employing a few men to accompany them and their herds to the Mississippi to ship up the river. Faced with unfamiliar territory, and problems with outlaws, Indians, and settlers who objected to thousands of cattle driving across their land, the ranchers got very few cattle to market that year. In the following years, tick fever from Texas cattle caused the farmers in Illinois to block passage to the herds, and both Kansas and Missouri passed quarantine laws requiring cattlemen to leave their cattle in stock pens until it was determined they did not carry the fever.[24] These early drives up the Chisholm Trail were not without difficulty but could be very profitable. Jonathan Hamilton Baker, a rancher from near Graham, Texas, took a herd up the trail in 1870, a banner year for cattle, earning enough profit to buy his wife a sewing machine, washing machine, and a carpet for the house. Nonetheless, in 1871, he suffered an overall loss on the drive.[25] In general, those cattle that got to market showed a promising profit, and ranchers were not deterred. While they faced opposition from settlers in Kansas, they avoided most conflicts by moving the trails further west through the Panhandle opening the Western Trail. By 1872, an estimated 1.5 million cattle had come through the pens in Abilene, Kansas, and the invention of refrigerator cars enabled the stockyards in Chicago to begin shipping dressed beef to the East Coast markets.[26] The recession of 1873 led to a drop in prices, and the number of cattle going up the trail dropped by over half the following year. While the numbers of cattle never matched the 1871 peak, the average drive between 1870 and 1890 was between 250,000 and 500,000 each year, although many of these cattle went up to pastures on the northern ranges rather than to the railheads. In addition, prices rose again, and up to the 1880s, cattlemen generally earned profits on their herds.[27]

One reason for the declining numbers of cattle on the trail had less to do with prices than with the arrival in Texas of the railroads. In 1873, the Missouri, Kansas, and Texas railroad reached Denison, Texas on the Red River and extended to San Antonio. Other railroads followed and extended down through Fort Worth, connecting to railroads in Galveston and Houston. As the railroads got closer to the ranches, the cattlemen discovered they could apply new ranching methods. Previously ranchers had preferred the rangy Texas longhorn cattle, as they could survive the heat and lack of water on the trail better than most thoroughbred cattle. Now they began to breed different types of cattle, bringing in Hereford bulls and experimenting with new hybrids that could result in maximum weight. Whereas the early cattle drives had passed through open prairie and could afford to fatten cattle along the trail, the closing of these lands as the lines of settlement moved West made the practice harder. The railroads enabled the ranchers to fatten their beef on the home range before shipping it north. The opening of Armour packinghouse in Kansas City in 1871 and the advent of the refrigerator car again made shipping fat slaughtered beef the most profitable. In 1876, the *San Antonio Express* even predicted that the year's overland drive would probably be the last of the great ones and advised cattlemen to let their cattle grow as big as possible on the range to make the most money.[28] By 1879, however, cattle prices were on the rise again to around $18 a head and the drives picked up again, although mainly to the northern ranges in Colorado, Montana, and the Dakotas, as open grassland became scarce in Texas.[29]

Around the same time ranchers began experimenting with better stock in the mid- to late 1870s, more settlers moved into the region and the era of uncontested open range grazing soon came to an end. Unsettled land in Texas was divided up into parcels with different designations. The Texas legislature set aside some of these parcels specifically as "school lands" and earmarked them for homesteaders to purchase, with the proceeds going to support the state school system. These parcels were scattered around the state and often were in the middle of cattle ranges. As it could require up to fifty acres a head to graze cattle, early ranchers did not usually own all the land they ranched but claimed grazing rights on open land. When settlers filed on school lands within their ranges, the cattlemen did not respond well. They accused settlers of stealing their cattle (sometimes accurately). In addition, they tried to block access to water sources for smaller ranchers to discourage them from settling. The larger ranches in South Texas were some of the first to begin fencing. Hipolito Garcia, owner of the Rendado Ranch in Zapata County, fenced in 90,000 acres of his ranch with wooden poles.[30] In the early 1870s, Mifflin Kenedy fenced in his ranch, including a lake that allegedly belonged to a neighbor.[31] The Coleman, Fulton and Mathis Company constructed plank fences around its Aransas Bay property in 1871 and 1872.[32]

Ultimately, many of the cattlemen turned to fencing their ranges as the best solution, especially with the invention of barbed wire, which made fencing cheaper. Joseph F. Glidden first patented barbed wire in 1874, and within a few years it had reached Texas. Glidden's sales representative Henry Sanborn arrived in Sherman, Texas in 1875 and set up a demonstration ranch in Grayson County. He only sold a small amount of wire at first, but anticipating a large market among ranchers, he ordered more shipped to Texas and imported an additional salesman, Jud Warner, based in Austin. The following year Sanborn and Warner began to push sales further south in the state and brought in more help.[33] Salesman John "Bet-A-Million" Gates came to San Antonio and built a cattle corral constructed of barbed wire in the middle of the city, proving that his product could hold Texas cattle, and taking in a large number of orders.[34]

Ranchers in South Texas were quick to see the advantages and fenced in many of their ranges in the next few years. Mexican land grant owners often had complicated land tenure and could not fence off their land, but the Anglo ranchers had no qualms about fencing off water supplies. By 1883, almost all ranch land in South and Southwest Texas was converted to enclosed ranches, and most of the small Mexican ranchers were driven off the land by drought and lack of grazing land. Some Mexicans tried to move into sheepherding instead but faced similar issues. In the drought of 1893, many sold out at bargain prices to the Anglo ranchers around them, such as Edward C. Lasater of the Falfurrias Ranch and Robert Kleberg of the King Ranch. The Texas Rangers helped Anglos enforce their claims against the Mexicans so that South of Corpus Christi they were known as *los rinches de la Kineña*, or "the King Ranch Rangers."[35]

Nonetheless, barbed wire did not catch on immediately elsewhere in Texas, although John Gates himself went on to earn a fortune. In 1881, to boost sales, Glidden and Sanborn decided to set up the Frying Pan Ranch in the Panhandle, under Sanborn's management, to demonstrate the advantages of barbed wire to cattlemen. The ranch had 120 miles of barbed wire enclosing from fifteen to twenty thousand cattle. Although the ranch itself was cut in two by the arrival of the railroad and part of it became the new town of Amarillo, the demonstration was effective, since other large ranches in the region soon adopted barbed wire. Fences not only kept out settlers, they made it easier for cattlemen to control their breeding program. The SMS ranch built its first barbed wire fences in 1882, and other ranches followed. The Matador Ranch installed its first barbed wire in its horse pasture and by 1883 was proposing more interior fences. The most notorious fencer was the XIT, which installed nearly 800 miles of barbed wire in its first year alone. With his profits from barbed wire manufacturing, Isaac L. Ellwood bought the southern division of the Spade Ranch, which had also served as a demonstration ranch in the Panhandle.[36]

But barbed wire could be both an ally and an enemy to the cattlemen. In 1883, a drought made smaller ranchers and farmers whose water supply was cut off fight back. In what was known as the Barbed Wire War or the Fence Cutting War, small groups of men called "nippers" went around at night in secret, cutting wire fences to allow access to public roads and water. Sometimes they left threatening notes with political overtones, reflecting a larger awareness of the antimonopoly Farmer's Alliance movement of the 1880s, which got its start in Texas. Ranchers fought back through stock associations and by offering large rewards for capture of the fence cutters. They also used their influence in the state legislature, which in 1884 passed a law mandating one- to five-year prison sentences for anyone who cut a wire fence. As a concession to the small farmers, however, the law required gates in fences at regular intervals to allow access and instated fines for illegal fencing of public land.[37] Wire cutting was not a factor for all ranchers. In the Big Bend region the fencing came later, with the Gages being the first to fence their land in 1886, and in general, the ranchers in the area faced few problems with wire cutters.[38]

In Kansas and other points north of Texas, farmers installed their own barbed wire fences to keep cattle out of their crops and to block passage across their land. In 1884, in response to more tick fever in Texas cattle, the Kansas legislature passed a stronger quarantine law banning all Texas cattle except between December 1 and March 1—in other words, no cattle during the drive season. In response, cattlemen called the first National Cattle Growers Convention and called for the establishment of a National Cattle Trail. However, the plan never came to fruition. People were still worried about fever, the northern plains were now becoming well stocked, farmers opposed closing land to settlement, and, most of all, the railroads did not want the competition.[39]

While many ranchers were already shipping via railroad, there had been complaints that the railroads overcharged. In 1880, the *Fort Griffin Echo* editorialized that it was cheaper to drive cattle than to ship them and that the cattle arrived at market in better condition from the drive.[40] Such anti-railroad sentiment was increasingly common in agricultural states in the late 1870s and 1880s with the rise of the railroad monopolies, and in this case, large cattlemen felt the pinch as much as small farmers did.

Nonetheless, while drives to northern ranges continued into the 1890s, by 1885, the railroads had reached the Panhandle and ranchers could ship almost directly, and in 1887, the trail though Kansas closed completely.[41] From the mid-1880s on, as cattle prices settled around $18–$25 a head, at least one newspaper urged the development of slaughterhouses and refrigerator companies in Texas to recoup some of the money going to Kansas City and Chicago meatpacking companies.[42] In 1886, cowboy Charlie Siringo estimated the cost of raising a 950-pound steer for three years plus transportation to Chicago to be $10.50, and with cattle selling at three cents a pound, the steer would sell for $28.50, leaving a profit of $18.[43] This estimate was undoubtedly optimistic, however, and based on optimal conditions.

The winters of 1885–86 and 1886–87 were far from optimal with the arrival of a series of blizzards in the Panhandle. In previous difficult winters, cattle had drifted south across the open range, but by this time the big ranches had installed a series of barbed wire drift fences to stop cattle from drifting onto neighboring ranches, and cattle were trapped against these fences, resulting in what became known as the Big Die-Up. In the 1886 blizzards, some ranches lost as much as three-fourths of their herds.[44] A similar catastrophe hit the Gulf Coast in 1895, leading to the deaths of thousands of cattle. The destruction was so severe that when Alf Truitt and his family traveled through the region seven years later, they still saw piles of bleached cattle bones over 100 feet wide all along the road.[45] In both the Panhandle and South Texas, many small ranchers could not absorb the loss and were forced to sell out, often to their larger neighbors, who consolidated their holdings. Other enterprises, such as the Coleman-Fulton Pasture Company or the Spur Ranch, passed into the hands of corporate investors.[46] Thus, after the mid-1880s, the majority of ranches in these regions were large enterprises, often owned by absentee investment corporations and run by professional managers, or large, almost feudal, *patróns*.

There were of course many regional differences in the Texas cattle industry. While a few ranches continued to operate in East and Central Texas after the Civil War, many of the ranches in these areas had converted to cotton by the 1870s. The postwar ranching industry was thus concentrated in one of four regions—the Gulf Coast, the South Texas Plains, the Panhandle and West Texas, and the Big Bend—and developed over different periods of time. Some of the oldest Anglo ranches were on the Gulf Coast prairie, which stretched from roughly Corpus Christi

east to the Louisiana border and beyond. The ranching heritage of this
region lives on in the chain of Saltgrass Steakhouses, so named for the
salt grasses on which the cattle fed, supposedly producing superior quality meat. The area is home to numerous river deltas, including the Guadalupe, Colorado, Brazos, Trinity, and Sabine Rivers. In the 1820s, Stephen
F. Austin established one of the earliest Anglo settlements in Texas in this
region with the encouragement of the Mexican government. Many other
Anglo settlers entered the region illegally. The main group of settlers first
pursued agriculture rather than ranching, following traditional Southern plantation practices. They brought their slaves with them and thus
there was a large black population along the coast. By 1840, cattle had
become more numerous, with many herds over 500, especially concentrated around the Sabine, Trinity, and Brazos rivers. Farther west, around
Galveston, some ranchers amassed larger herds in the thousands. The first
cowboys in this region were usually slaves, who were the regular workers,
as well as some Mexican and Louisiana French laborers from the region.
However, it was the young Anglos, who entered the area in the 1830s and
1840s to round up their own herds from the strays and Mexican cattle
near the Rio Grande, who allegedly first earned the term "Cow-Boys." By
1850, 30 percent of all Texas cattle were located in the Coastal Prairie. It
was these early ranchers who began driving cattle to Louisiana and established the hide and tallow industry in Galveston.[47]

One of the leading cattlemen of this region was Abel "Shanghai" Pierce,
who started as a cowboy himself on the Grimes Ranch before the Civil
War and built up his fortunes trailing herds in the years immediately after. By 1867, he had amassed $100,000 and left the business briefly to live
in Kansas City, where he went into banking. In the 1870s, he returned to
Texas, trailing cattle, and began buying up land around Matagorda on the
Tres Palaces River, establishing Rancho Grande. Pierce spent the next two
decades building up Galveston and looking for the best way to rid Texas
cattle from tick fever. Like other cattlemen, he suggested crossbreeding
Texas cattle with tick-resistant Brahman bulls from India.[48] Other ranchers expanded their holdings in the years after the Civil War and many
employed former slaves as cowhands, leading to the creation of some all-
black outfits. A few blacks also managed to purchase land in this area, but
Anglos often drove them off the land through intimidation, as they had
Aaron Ashworth.[49]

Southwest of San Antonio and Corpus Christi, and reaching to the Rio
Grande, the South Texas Plains were home to a number of large ranches

modeled on a Mexican *encomienda* style, with generations of vaqueros and their families living on the ranch under the protection of an Anglo *patrón* who provided them with food, housing, and clothing. These ranches were largely self-sufficient. La Parra, the ranch Mifflin Kenedy established south of Corpus Christi, was 325,000 acres, had 300 employees, and a church and school.[50] The King Ranch encompassed 500,000 acres, houses for 500 workers and their families, a commissary store, a blacksmith, and a wagon shed. The relationships on these ranches were familial and paternalistic. The *patróns* expected complete loyalty, and the vaqueros identified their success with that of the ranch. Unlike most cowboys, the vaqueros on these ranches were often married, and the presence of their wives and children created a strong sense of community and family responsibility.[51]

The vaqueros on the King and Kenedy ranches and others like them thus could gain a sense of manhood from their role as husbands and fathers in a way cowboys elsewhere could not. They also did not spend the same time in town carousing that the other cowboys did. Nonetheless, like other cowboys, the *kineños* and *kenedeños* saw their work as a defining part of their masculinity, and spent a good portion of their workweek away from their families in all-male cow camps. The Anglo cattlemen on these ranches, moreover, resembled their counterparts in the rest of the state in almost every way, and took the same measures to improve their ranches and control their men. While a few members of the first generation might have had a rough edge to them, the second generation that took over in the 1880s and 1890s was made up of modern cattlemen who were as concerned with the latest scientific techniques and efficiency as their northern compatriots. However, these men often depended on traditional and familial loyalties from the vaqueros to minimize conflict with them.[52]

The Llano Estacado, or Staked Plains, on which most of the Panhandle and West Texas ranches were located, stretch from the Canadian River north of Amarillo, Texas, to the Concho River around Midland/Odessa and from the Pecos River in New Mexico to the east of Lubbock, Texas.[53] The Panhandle was first settled by Hispanic sheepherders from New Mexico who came to graze there seasonally in the 1860s and 1870s. In 1876, Casimero Romero led a group of settlers and their families along with some hired hands and nearly 5,000 sheep to what would become the town of Tascosa, in the northwest Panhandle. They built a few adobes and were later joined by several other families so that by 1880, the Hispanic population was over 350. Sheep vastly outnumbered cattle in the early days, but after Charles Goodnight and John Adair set up the JA Ranch in Palo Duro Canyon in 1876 and began a settlement plan for the surrounding area, Anglo cattle ranchers soon rushed in.

Seventy miles east of Palo Duro Canyon, the Christian colony of Clarendon was established in 1878 in what would become Donely County three years later. Nicknamed the "Saint's Roost," the town was slow to develop at first, but as enthusiasm for the cattle industry took off, the settlement ultimately evolved into the Clarendon Land Investment and Agency Company with backing from New York and British investors. In 1879, the state created Wheeler County to administer the region around Mobeetie, the town that had developed around Fort Elliott; and the following year Oldham County was established around Tascosa.[54] Railroads did much to promote Panhandle development. With the end of the buffalo herds and removal of Comanches from the Panhandle in the 1870s, they found a demand for their excess land holdings in the region. In 1879, they sold 5 million acres to the New York and Texas Land Co., Ltd., and an additional 630,000 acres to The Francklyn Land and Cattle Company in 1884 which founded the T-Anchor ranch.[55] In 1887, the Fort Worth and Denver Railroad reached Clarendon, and its subsidiary, the Texas Townsite Company, began actively developing towns in the east Panhandle.[56] The entire Panhandle soon opened up for grazing, leading to the establishment of some of the largest ranches in the state. As more Anglo cattle ranchers entered the area, the Mexican sheepmen stopped coming to the Texas Panhandle to graze. As the son of one of the earliest Mexican settlers recalled: "Sheepherders did not want to have any fights."[57] Casimero Romero himself sold his land and sheep interests in 1882 and began a successful butcher shop in Tascosa, and a freighting business between the Panhandle and Dodge City, Kansas, where he opened a hotel and restaurant. Eventually even Romero bought a ranch in New Mexico, and moved out of the state completely in 1896.[58]

With less rainfall than the rest of Texas, however, the Panhandle took longer to settle, and many counties had populations of fewer than 1,000 well into the 1890s. The Panhandle ranches were some of the largest, in part due to geography. Since most of the water was from 300 to 800 feet below the surface, ranchers needed to have enough money to dig wells and erect windmills. In addition, once the large ranches started fencing in their property, smaller ranchers could not gain access to existing water sources. The result was that few small ranchers survived for long in the

Panhandle, which became one of the main centers of corporate investment.[59] The first larger ranches were concentrated in three main areas,
along the Canadian River in Oldham County centered on George W.
Littlefield's LIT Ranch, around the JA and LX in Randall and Armstrong
counties, and in Hutchinson County, where Thomas Bugbee and his wife
established the Quarter T Circle. In the 1880s, these were joined by the
Spur, Pitchfork, T-Anchor, Frying Pan, and Matador, which bought up
many of their surrounding smaller neighbors with the help of British and
Eastern investment corporations.[60]

The scale of the ranches in the Texas Panhandle was enormous. The
first of the great Panhandle ranches was the JA Ranch, founded by the
partnership of Goodnight and Adair, which, financed in part by British
investors, eventually leased or owned over a million acres in and around
Palo Duro Canyon. Even as early as 1879, the Millett Brothers ran 40,000
head of cattle and employed forty or more full-time hands.[61] The Kerr
Land and Cattle Company and Francklyn Land and Cattle Company each
ran over 70,000 cattle in 1884.[62] Many of these ranches eventually sold to
foreign syndicates. The Matador Ranch established by the Motley, Floyd,
Cottle and Dickens Company in 1879 sold to a Scottish syndicate in 1882.
The Spur Ranch was an amalgamation of several small ranches that sold
out in 1883 to the Espuela Cattle Company, founded by A. M. Britton of
Denver and S. W. Lomax, who had just sold the Matador to the Scottish
syndicate. The company purchased additional land from the New York
and Texas Land Company, and in 1884 reorganized as the Espuela Land
and Cattle Company, selling out again to a group of English and Scottish
investors in 1885.[63]

The biggest and most well known of the corporate ranches was the
XIT Ranch, established in 1882. After the old state capitol burned down
in 1881, the Texas legislature decided it wanted to build a new one that
was larger than the National Capitol. To finance the building, the state
gave 3 million acres of land from nine adjoining counties in the panhandle to the Capitol Syndicate, an investor group based in Chicago. The
investors planned to ranch the land until settlement moved farther west
and they could sell it for profit. In order to raise the money to stock the
ranch, the Capitol Syndicate went to London to find more investors and
formed a new investment company. The chairman of the board of directors was the Marquis of Tweesdale, governor of the Commercial Bank of
Scotland. The Capitol Syndicate ran the day-to-day affairs of the ranch,
but historian J. Evetts Haley reported that "The XIT was often thought

of as a British institution." The name XIT supposedly stood for "Ten in Texas," meaning it covered ten counties, but as the ranch actually only covered nine it was just an easier and better-looking brand.[64] At its peak, the ranch ran around 150,000 cattle and employed up to 150 hands. The XIT had a finishing ranch in Montana that could accommodate an additional 10,000 head a year to fatten for sale. It also eventually had over 6,000 miles of fences.[65] While the Panhandle ranches were not the only large-scale ranches in Texas, by the 1880s they dominated the industry, and it was in the Panhandle that the cowboys first began to feel challenges to their independence.

The last ranching region to be settled was the Big Bend, centered on the town of Alpine. As this area is somewhat mountainous, most of the ranches tended to be smaller, although a few, like the Gage and Kokernaut interests, were on a par with the corporate ranches. Aside from a few pioneers like Milton Faver, who established a ranch which straddled the Mexican border in the 1850s, the majority of Anglo ranchers came to this area in the mid- to late 1880s, mainly from around San Antonio, particularly Gonzales County. Unfortunately, they did so just as drought and severe winters crippled the industry and many were forced to sell out at a loss.[66] Vermonters Edward L. Gage and his brother Alfred managed to grow their ranching interests in Marathon in the 1880s by establishing two joint-stock corporations: the Presidio Cattle Company and the Santiago Cattle Company, inviting foreign investors to purchase stocks and bonds. Alfred, who had briefly trained as a cowboy, took over the management of the ranch in 1882 while his brother took care of investments. However, drought and poor economic conditions nearly killed off both companies, and while Edward tried to create a third corporation to offset their losses in 1891, he was unsuccessful in attracting investors. Faced with financial insolvency, Edward, described by one former employee as a "high nervous man," committed suicide in a train station washroom in Chicago. His brother Alfred, however, continued to keep the ranch going, eventually merging all the various corporations and interests into the Alpine Cattle Company in 1897.[67]

Lee Kokernaut came to the Big Bend in 1883 from Gonzales County, the same year the railroad came to Pecos, about 100 miles north of Alpine. His father was a Texas pioneer who fought under Sam Houston in the Texas Battle for Independence, so Lee was already a wealthy rancher and able to survive economic downturns. Kokernaut also helped set up the First National Bank of Alpine and became a prominent figure in the region, as did succeeding generations.[68] Because of the lateness of settlement and the economic problems, however, the Big Bend was one of the few areas where cowboys were able to buy up ranches and become cattlemen themselves. Gene Parr, for example, came to Brewster County in 1888 with only his saddle and bridle and worked breaking horses and as a cowhand for three ranches in the Big Bend, before turning to trail driving from 1895 to 1901. In 1903, he bought out his boss's interests and set up his own ranch.[69] Other cowboys bought up land in the late 1880s following the prolonged drought of 1885–86.[70] Elsewhere, where the large ranches prevailed, however, few cowboys could afford to become cattlemen themselves.

The development of the cattle industry thus often proceeded at a different pace in the different regions of Texas. Fencing occurred in South Texas in the 1860s even before barbed wire, reached its peak in the Panhandle in the mid-1880s, but did not start in the Big Bend until 1886. The railroads arrived in different parts of the states at different times, changing shipping as well as breeding practices at different times. Richard King developed his own breed, the Santa Gertrudis, by breeding Indian Brahman bulls with Texas longhorn cattle, but other ranchers simply imported Herefords. Corporations took over most of the ranches in the Panhandle, but in the Big Bend ranching was mixed private and corporate, and in South Texas the ranches remained mostly family-owned. Some ranches installed the latest technology such as branding chutes, while others did not mechanize until after World War II. Thus, it is often difficult to give specific dates for "the end of the open range" or corporatization of ranches, as it happened at different times. Similarly, the population of counties on the Gulf Coast and around San Antonio increased much sooner than in the Panhandle or Big Bend, so it is difficult to make blanket assertions about what years townspeople began regulating cowboys' social behavior.

Yet there were clear trends that cut across the industry. By the mid- to late 1880s, all ranches worried about low prices and tried to increase their profits through efficiency measures and scientific methods, whether family-owned or corporate. There were other constants across Texas. The wages cowboys earned stayed basically the same from the 1870s to 1900, in part because the labor supply increased, in part because the ranches tightened their belts. Moreover, there were not always as clear distinctions between the corporate and family-owned ranches as the myths perpetuated. The King Ranch remained a family-run business until the 1980s, but from the late nineteenth century on, its owners and managers made use of the latest techniques the corporations used and the ranch was far more than just a family business.[71] Almost all ranches developed rules restricting cowboys' behavior on the ranch and all cow towns began passing laws to restrict the cowboys as soon as they reached a critical population mass.

All of these changes in the cattle industry and settlement had a direct impact on the workers. As markets tightened, jobs became scarcer. As fences came onto the range, the cowboy became a fence rider and had to repair them as part of his work. Ranching in the Panhandle also meant that cowboys had to help dig wells, build windmills, and grow hay. In the South Texas Plains, the vaqueros built dipping tanks and grew a variety of crops as the ranches diversified. The installation of new equipment on some ranches and emphasis on breeding led to tamer cattle and tended to minimize the need for the cowboy's roping skills, similar to the way mechanization in the East lessened the need for skilled factory workers. The rise of the corporate ranches and corporate methods on family ranches also led to the more impersonal management style and greater emphasis on cutting costs. The ranch accountant had surprising power throughout Texas.

Cattlemen shared similar characteristics across the state. Some of the largest cattlemen were either already wealthy before they came to Texas or found wealthy backers.[72] Of the fifty-nine men profiled in the 1914 yearbook, *History of the Cattlemen of Texas*, over half got their start with the assistance of a relative.[73] Lee Kokernaut and C. C. Slaughter both grew up in the family business. Slaughter, founder of the Long S Ranch and later a banker, bought his first herd from his uncle. He was one of the first ranchers to breed shorthorns, and in the 1890s began breeding purebred Herefords. He became one of the largest individual land and cattle owners in Texas. George W. Littlefield grew up on his family's plantation in Gonzales County and inherited six slaves, four mules, eight horses, and his share of 1,760 acres of land. He unsuccessfully tried his hand at cotton farming after the Civil War, but raised additional money through partnership in a dry goods store, and in 1877 bought the first land for the LIT Ranch in the Panhandle. From there he kept buying up other ranches. Littlefield's nephews also benefited from the family connection, as by 1884, he had placed them on ranches around the Panhandle and West Texas as managers or owners.[74] Ike T. Pryor also benefited from family connections. Although he was orphaned at a young age, he got a job on his brother's ranch and learned the trade through him. After serving as a manager on another

Anonymous cowboy outside the LS Ranch dugout in the Texas Panhandle. The arrival of barbed wire made cowboys into line riders. Winter dugouts such as this one were far from luxurious accommodations for the workers. Courtesy Panhandle-Plains Historical Museum, Canyon, Texas.

ranch, he borrowed money to buy his own herd. Richard Robertson Russell of San Antonio got started with his first herd at age twelve when his uncle branded a calf for him. Russell later went on to become a cattleman in his own right as well as banker and sheriff.[75] William Peryman of Frio County worked his father's herds for one-third of the annual increase in stock and eventually earned enough to buy out his father's interests and 25,000 acres of land.[76]

A number of cattlemen raised their funding through investors. The Gage brothers created a number of joint-stock corporations and solicited funds from all over the country and Europe for their Big Bend ranch. Charles Goodnight started from relatively modest beginnings, but his first venture into the cattle business was as an owner of a small herd with his stepbrother. In the years before the Civil War, he began trailing his herds to New Mexico and Colorado and worked with other ranchers such as

John Chisum and Oliver Loving. When the cattle industry went into decline in New Mexico and Colorado, he established his ranch at Palo Duro Canyon in 1876, helped in part by a loan of $30,000 from Denver broker John Adair, with whom he eventually formed the JA Ranch.[77] In 1899, Edward C. Lasater depended on a $200,000 loan from an investment company that handled British mortgage lending to purchase acreage surrounding his Falfurrias Ranch.[78] H. H. Campbell got money from investor A. M. Britton of Chicago to buy a herd, and then Britton and Campbell entered a second partnership in 1879 to start the Matador Ranch.[79] John Chisum, founder of the Jingle Bob, started with an investment of $6,000 from a New York speculator and, after securing lucrative government contracts during the Civil War, was able to build up one of the largest cattle empires that stretched from Texas to New Mexico, which he ruled with an iron fist.[80] The typical investors in the cattle industry were from Boston or New York and were largely self-made men who, like Isaac Ellwood, the barbed wire magnate, often started in another related industry such as the railroad or land sales. Some, like Nelson Morris, a Chicago meatpacker who owned a 250,000-acre ranch in Texas, were absentee owners who never visited their ranches.[81]

The earliest cattlemen like Goodnight and Campbell often trailed their first herds themselves and knew the skills necessary for handling cattle, but they were still businessmen with an eye to the future. Quite a few of them had attended college, and some of them came from ranching backgrounds. Ranching was as much an investment as a calling for them, and many had reputations for being strict with their men and ruthless with business competition. Most of the successful cattlemen experimented with breeding techniques and invested heavily in land. Typically, they had business interests outside the cattle industry. Thomas Atlee Coleman of the Coleman-Fulton Pasture Company was president of the Southwest Casualty Insurance Company and the General Livestock Agent of the International and Great Northern Railroad. J.H.P. Davis of Richmond, Texas, who amassed 60,000 acres of ranch land in Fort Bend County, founded a private bank in 1892 and served as president of the Fort Bend Cotton Oil Company and Rosenberg Elevator Company. William D. Reynolds, who trailed herds with Goodnight and Oliver Loving in 1868, also had a hand in cottonseed oil, banking, and real estate.[82] J. Evetts Haley wrote in his biography of George W. Littlefield that "The bankers spoke of him as a cowman; the cowmen referred to him as a banker—both thereby conferring unintended compliments."[83]

Cattlemen in the 1860s and 1870s used a paternalistic manner with their employees, but even this style was not entirely uncalculated. Richard King, the son of Irish immigrants who made enough money in the shipping business to establish his ranch, became *patrón* in part because it was the custom of the region and in part because it gave him a stable workforce. Land in Texas was relatively cheap before the Civil War, and those men who invested in land were able to make a good profit on it. The King Ranch remained in the family to a large extent because of King's emphasis on buying up all the land the ranch occupied.[84] To King, the ranch was first and foremost an investment rather than a family. Even though he referred to the vaqueros on his ranch as his "friends," he also was heard to complain on more than one occasion about "the damn Mexicans always wanting higher pay."[85] While King and his son-in-law, Robert J. Kleberg, continued paternalistic relations into the twentieth century, nonetheless, by the 1880s and 1890s, many ranchers outside of South Texas had dropped this style.

Cowboying, with a few exceptions, was not a lifelong career, and few stayed on one ranch for very long. As historian Byron Price has noted, of the cowboys in editor J. Marvin Hunter's *Trail Drivers of Texas*, most started range work as soon as they could sit in the saddle, but only 20 percent drove cattle as full hands for more than five years, and only 5 percent for more than ten years.[86] Many young men who came West to become cowboys, as well as farm boys from Texas, signed up for the adventure of the trail or the romance of the range. The younger ones wanted to prove their manhood by showing their prowess at riding and roping. They wanted to break free from their families and the restrictions of childhood. Many read stories of adventure fighting Indians and cattle rustlers and wanted to get in on the action. Some were former soldiers who were not ready to settle down in "civilized" society after their war experiences. Some of them were orphaned or forced to leave home at a young age and went to work on a ranch, with the rancher playing the role of substitute father. Cowboys were aware of the low social status they had in the eyes of "respectable folk." But they relished the all-male camaraderie of the cow camp, and developed a culture that scorned propriety, religion, and social niceties: the world they often associated with women. A number of cowboys from middle-class or even aristocratic backgrounds also came West for the adventure, but these integrated into the cowboy lifestyle and adopted its ways while they were cowboying or else faced ridicule and isolation.

There are no clear statistics as to how many cowboys there were in total. While the cattlemen and newspapers counted cattle almost obsessively,
they did not count cowboys. Historian William Savage has argued that
there is no clear way to count them, despite George W. Saunders' widely
quoted but grossly exaggerated claim that 35,000 men went up the trail in
the late nineteenth century. Even with an extremely generous estimate of
6 million cattle with ten men to each herd of 2,000–2,500, the maximum
number of cowboys would be 30,000, but Saunders himself claimed that
one-third of the cowboys made more than one trip, which would bring
the maximum number significantly lower. Savage also points out that
based on a minimum of 4 million cattle with eight men per herd, there
would have been only of 12,800 cowboys (minus the one-third who made
more than one trip) but reiterates that even the estimate of number of cattle is in dispute. Yet other historians have claimed there were as many as
40,000 cowboys. Ultimately it is only clear that these higher numbers are
not accurate.[87] There are also no clear statistics as to the cowboys' origins.
Of the accounts in the *Trail Drivers of Texas*, most were born in Texas or
the South, but 40 percent of the entries do not list their birthplace, and
the accounts are not comprehensive.[88]

Anglo cowboys probably earned almost twice as much as most farm-
hands or unskilled factory workers, but in comparison with other skilled
workers who could earn as much as $1,200 a year, their wages were low.[89]
The wages for Anglo hands on the Spur Ranch were fairly typical for the
1880s. A beginning hand earned $20–$25 a month, a regular hand earned
$30, top hands and cooks got $40–$45, and trail bosses, $50–$65. Range
bosses who supervised home ranches earned around $125.[90] Frank Col-
linson earned $60 a month for trail work in 1873, but only because he
brought his own horses with him—the rest of the hands earned $30.[91]
In the mid-1880s, former cowboy Charlie Siringo estimated the cost of
what a cowboy would need to outfit himself for ranch work at around
$77, including a pony and saddle, but noted that starting wages were often
as low as $15 a month. He added that beginning cowboys who worked
the northern ranges earned up to $40 a month, but their initial expenses
were higher since they needed warmer clothes and bedding.[92] On the
South Texas ranches, wages were closer to $10 a month for the vaqueros,
although they received housing and some food supplies for their families.[93] In 1893, cowboys on the Coleman Fulton Pasture Company ranches
earned fifty cents a day.[94] Moreover, with the exception of the vaqueros
on the South Texas ranches, most cowboys were employed seasonally and

laid off each winter so that they would only be paid from 6 to 9 months of the year. Wages such as these made it difficult for the men to save up any money or to start their own herds, except by branding mavericks, a common practice in most of Texas in the 1860s and early 1870s, but restricted by the 1880s.

While once again there are no clear figures, some historians have estimated that one-quarter to one-third of all cowboys was black or Hispanic.[95] Whatever the total, a typical outfit included from eight to ten men and usually had at least one Hispanic or black worker, either as a cook, horse wrangler, or, occasionally as a regular hand. These figures varied within different regions of Texas. On the upper Coastal Prairie, where there was a strong slave plantation tradition, there were more black cowboys and even a few all-black outfits. Similarly, near the Mexican border and on the King and Kenedy ranches, Hispanic cowboys predominated. Typically, on Panhandle ranches such as the IOA Ranch or the T-Anchor there might be two or three African Americans in each outfit, often in the position of horse wrangler or cook.[96] Black cowboys were attracted to the work for much the same reasons as Anglo cowboys. Will Crittenden's father was a schoolteacher and an unsuccessful rancher on the side, but Will learned to ride horses early, and like many young boys, "I shore hankered some to be a cow puncher."[97] If a black cowboy had exceptional skills, moreover, he could earn respect at a time when African Americans faced increased hostility in other fields. Tom Garrett learned to ride when he was three from his father, who was an expert horse wrangler and top hand, and Tom wanted to be just like him when he grew up.[98]

Tejano cowboys were most in demand in South Texas, especially in the early years of the ranching industry. Will Hale's father's ranch was on the border with Mexico, so he hired many Mexican vaqueros to help him round up his cattle after the Civil War.[99] John Longworth, the foreman of the Slaughter ranch in southwest Texas, went to San Antonio in the late 1860s to hire men to round up cattle in the brush, and returned with almost all Hispanic cowboys. Longworth spoke Spanish fluently as a result of his experiences with vaqueros and knew their worth.[100] But while most associate Mexican vaqueros with working on the unique system of the large South Texas ranches, many outfits elsewhere in Texas had one or two Tejano cowboys who participated in the life of the cow camp with the other men. Indeed, it was a vaquero, Nicholas Martine, who first showed Charles Goodnight the Palo Duro Canyon and recommended it as a site for a ranch.[101] Race relations were not always negative. There are examples of tri-racial communities in which Anglos, Mexican Americans, and African Americans coexisted peacefully. In the first half of the 1880s in Presidio County, near Fort Davis where a unit of the so-called Buffalo Soldiers was stationed, of a population of 3,000 mostly small ranchers, 73 percent were Mexican, 16 percent black, and 9 percent whites. Moreover, one-half of all Anglos there had Mexican wives. Such a population distribution was typical of towns in this part of Texas. The intermingling was short-lived, however, as social segregation soon evolved after the black soldiers left in 1885 and more Anglos moved into the area.[102]

Racism was certainly not absent on the frontier. Cattlemen often hired black and Hispanic cowboys because they were cheaper. One of the selling points that advertisers made to potential settlers was that there was an abundance of cheap Mexican labor.[103] After the Civil War, Anglos became increasingly paranoid that Mexicans and African Americans would try to get revenge on them for the way the Anglos had treated them in the past. In the 1870s and 1880s, there was almost racial warfare in the Nueces Strip near the border with Mexico over cattle thievery on both sides. Anglos mostly attacked Mexican nationals, but they targeted Mexican Americans as well in their zeal. Elsewhere in the state, Anglos kept Mexican Americans racially subordinate through violence, including using the Texas Rangers to harass them, as well as vigilante lynchings.[104] The same was also true for African Americans who faced increasing numbers of lynchings in the 1880s throughout the South and Texas.[105]

Despite the hostilities and racism, it is clear that Mexicans and African Americans were an integral part of the development of the West and of the ranching industry. Mexican cowboys and ranchers brought the terms rodeo, buckaroo (a corruption of the word *vaquero*), lasso, and corral to the cowboys. They developed the methods and system of ranching in the Southwest and were part of the labor force and business community in small towns across the frontier. There were also many Mexican American sheepherders competing for grass ranges. African Americans worked as cowboys, cotton farmers, and soldiers. They established all-black communities across the West. Black soldiers defended whites against Indian raids, held the border against Oklahoma Sooners who were trying to cross the line before the territory opened officially, and surrounded Billy the Kid when he was arrested. As scholars Philip Durham and Everett Jones note, "The point of their history is not that they were different from their companions but that they were similar. They had neither peculiar vices or virtues to be glorified or condemned."[106]

Thus, a variety of social hierarchies came to the frontier along with the men who supposedly tamed it. Gender was clearly part of the social hierarchy in the West, and paternalism part of social control. When the cattlemen couched social distinctions in paternal terms, the cowboys generally agreed with them. But as ranching became more corporatized, and profits harder to gain, the cattlemen increased their attempts to regulate their employees, and many saw the paternal approach as an old-fashioned way of doing business. While some continued to use a familiar style with their men, other owners and managers, particularly on the corporate ranches, took a more impersonal approach, concerned more with the bottom line than with the comfort of their workers. Efficiency became the new watchword, and in this environment, cowboys who acted too independently threatened the smooth functioning of the ranch. Thus, employers began to rein in the cowboy both at work and in town, and in the process, intentionally or not, began limiting the ways in which cowboys could express their manhood. Cattlemen tried to ensure they had both higher profits on the ranch and social order in town by tying the cowboys' jobs to what they considered "proper" behavior, both on the job and in their leisure time. Ironically, by the end of the century, as the mythic heroic image of the masculine cowboy was becoming widely accepted, cowboys themselves found their masculinity challenged and restricted on all sides.

# 2

# From Boys to Men

The boys who became cowboys and cattlemen drew their ideas of what it meant to be a man from the men they grew up around. Childhood experiences varied widely depending on their geographic origins or economic circumstances, but all looked to easily identifiable personas they could try on for themselves. The heroes they chose were often active ones to match their own energy and rough play. It was much easier for boys from any social class to play Indian scout or explorer than lawyer or accountant, and far more fun.[1] Most Texas boys, like boys elsewhere in the country, idolized the cowboys they saw on the ranches or that they read about in dime novels and believed they embodied the very ideal of manhood. With their devil-may-care attitude toward society, cowboys mirrored the freedom that all young boys wanted from their parents, and they seemed to live an ideal life without responsibility. They performed dazzling feats of skill riding and roping that boys longed to be able to do themselves. Moreover, the hazing rituals cowboys used emphasized that acceptance among them was a privilege, and provided an irresistible challenge. Cowboys offered a clear path to manhood that boys could understand: master the skills and gain acceptance and you were a man.

Boys on the Texas cattle frontier thus measured their manhood in their abilities to perform the jobs the cowboys did and to act as much like them as they could, even as many adults worried that cowboys were poor role models. As a result, parents tried to ensure their sons would have at least a basic education to serve them later in life and to prolong their sons' departure from home. Cattlemen encouraged their sons to learn the skills of the cowboys as part of the business, but also instilled in them a sense that they were a part of something greater than the cow camps. They judged whether their sons had achieved manhood by whether they understood this larger role and acted in a way consistent with it. For cattlemen, the steps to acceptance were marriage and land ownership rather than hazing rituals, steps that increased their sons' responsibilities, rather than leading them away from them. But while boys assumed that passing basic mile-stones like going up the trail was a sign of manhood, both cowboys and cattlemen also looked to subjective qualifications such as maturity levels that usually came with experience alone. In the end, both future cowboys and sons of cattlemen absorbed ideas of manhood based on their social class that made it easy for the rancher to play father to his cowboys, but which could lead to tensions between them in later life.

● ● ●

Cowboys and cattlemen alike revered the role of mothers in a young boy's life. In the late nineteenth century, American popular wisdom said that children formed their basic character during their earliest years. Consequently, children up to the age of five or seven came under close female supervision, since people also thought women, through their natu-ral "tender affection and moral suasion," were most likely to create a sense of conscience in them.[2] Old trail driver C. H. Rust bemoaned the loss of the old-fashioned boy who, when confronted in a lie "resolved to ask his mother's pardon" and obeyed her from then on.[3] Cattleman George W. Littlefield advised a widow to keep her sons with her as long as possible. "I don't think a Boy should leave his mothers home. No [influence] on a boy like that of a Mother. . . . Give me the boy that loves his mother[,] one who fills with tears when he bids her good bye."[4] Hiram G. Craig took his eight-year-old son with him up the trail and later regretted his choice. "This was an exceptional trip and I was very foolish taking my child along at his age. The trip kept him away from his mother for two months."[5]

Nonetheless, at the same time American men as a whole believed that unless boys turned away from their mothers, they would never grow up. Many middle-class childrearing books stressed the importance of an un-fettered boyhood in creating men. Parents should encourage boys to be wild and aggressive. Boys needed to learn the value of both sports and academics so that they would not become feminized or over-civilized.[6] T. E. Hines blamed his early failures as a cowboy on his coddled upbringing: "Well you see I'd never been from behind my ma's apron strings and re-ally didn't know how to make it around."[7] Four years after he had advised the widow to keep her sons at home, George Littlefield told her not to hold the older one too close "for it often makes the young fellow timid and want of confidence in himself."[8] Of course, the stereotypical patri-arch of the nineteenth century was never completely devoid of sentiment for his children; indeed, one mid-century model for genteel fatherhood was popularly produced paintings of fathers surrounded by doting children at the hearth.[9] Many wealthy fathers were just as indulgent of their young sons as were their mothers. Richard King, by all accounts a somewhat rough man, was nothing but affectionate toward his children, calling them his "Pets," and would likely have spoiled them greatly were it not for the influence of his Presbyterian wife, Henrietta.[10] There is no evidence to suggest that working-class fathers were any less affectionate than their middle-class counterparts. But self-reliance was an important part of a masculine identity and it was essential for boys to break away from the sentimental relationships of the home.

In general, boys who grew up on the frontier in the late nineteenth century had an easier time developing independent identities as their early play and chores took them into wilder territory than their settler parents had known growing up, giving them opportunities to gain self-confidence and become self-reliant. Growing up in the individualistic West, the games that most boys played emphasized aggression and individual achievement more than teamwork, and rewarded those who were willing to risk more. As young children, boys often were left alone to watch family livestock or went out to hunt by themselves, and depended on their nerve and wits to face any threat, real or imagined. The stories men related of their childhood often emphasized such experiences and boasted of, in the words of historian Elliott West, "earning the self-respect that came with being intimate with the alien and fearsome."[11]

Frontier parents encouraged gendered play, giving girls sewing kits and boys guns and lassos. Boys were supposed to go out and explore, girls were supposed to stay in the house or near it.[12] At age thirteen, Troy B. Cowan went on his third short cattle drive with members of his family. His sisters also roped and rode, but since they were in charge of the cooking they did not have a chance to do very much, whereas Troy rode night herd and worked with the other hands.[13] Of course, many girls preferred hunting and exploring with their brothers, and on occasion boys did "girl work" such as washing dishes or babysitting because there was no one else to do it, but boys tended to cross gender roles far less than girls.[14] In general, middle-class fathers also emphasized different values for boys and girls. While they taught both of them obedience, honesty, and thrift, they stressed patience, kindness, and affection for girls; and courage, industry, loyalty, and perseverance for boys. They also discouraged their sons from crying or showing fear as they grew older and instilled in them the importance of maintaining their honor, even to the point of fighting.[15]

By the age of seven or eight, most boys looked more to their fathers than their mothers for models of behavior. Many men encouraged their sons to develop work skills, teaching them to ride and giving them increasing responsibility. John James Haynes' father gave each of his sons a gun and a Bowie knife at an early age and taught them to ride, hunt, and shoot as well as herd wild cattle.[16] Walter R. Morrison got a lariat from his father, a sawmill owner, when he was ten. He practiced roping from his father's saddle horses until he was good enough to get a job as a novice trail hand.[17] David and George Christie's father gave them scraps from his work so they could build their own miniature log cabin.[18] When he was eight, S. A. Wright's father bought him a shotgun to scare off squirrels and raccoons from the crops.[19] Auberry Aikin worked next to his father as a cowhand learning the business: "In fact he was my father, mother and teacher."[20] A few boys had the chance to go on the trail with their fathers at a young age, although usually only for short trips. George W. Saunders moved to a new county with his family when he was five, but remembered only riding sidesaddle with his sister in the drag, or rear of the herd.[21] The best fathers helped to shape their sons into productive and independent men by giving them more responsibility as they grew older. When he was ten, James E. Schultz's father gave him an opportunity to show what sort of a cowhand he would make by looping a few yearlings from horseback. Not long afterward he gave James a rifle and the responsibility of hunting wild game for the family, and by age twelve he sent James out alone to kill steers on the range that were too old to be beef. At thirteen, he made his son a full hand at the roundup.[22]

Not all frontier boys had such supportive parents, however. Some left home to escape abuse. Charlie Siringo's father died when he was a baby, and when he was twelve his mother remarried to an alcoholic who gambled away all of the family's money and then abandoned them, leaving Charlie to pay off his debts. Charlie believed that his leaving "made me a better boy, and no doubt a better man than I should have been had it never happened," but he himself had to leave his mother and sister at age sixteen to find work.[23] Jim Gober suffered at the hand of his neighbor, who had married into the family. Gober's father sent him to work on Bob Wright's farm in return for favors Wright had done for his family. Wright drove him relentlessly and submitted him to verbal and possibly physical abuse, but Gober did not tell his father as it would have caused a family rift.[24] Teddy Blue Abbott's father had had a poor relationship with his own father and treated Teddy accordingly. "He was overbearing and tyrannical—and worse with me than the others." Not surprisingly, he looked to the cowboys for inspiration: "All the time I was living with Texas cowpunchers, the most independent class of people on earth, and breathing that spirit." Teddy ran away when he was fourteen and would not have returned except for his mother.[25] Sam J. Rogers' father also used a heavy hand with his son. He taught Sam to ride a horse by first threatening to whip him if he fell off and then tying his feet to the stirrups when he kept falling. As Sam recalled, his father only wanted him to ride so that he take over some of the chores his father had to do around the place. Despite the abuse, Sam admired his father and wanted to be as good a horseman as he was "because he was looked up to by the other cow pokes and ranchers" for his skill in busting broncos.[26] Father-son relationships could be complicated at best.

Orphans and runaways could face problems on the frontier as well. Tejano orphans fared best as they were instantly adopted into other ranch families in the area and faced no social stigmas, even inheriting the ranch if they were older than natural sons in the family.[27] For Anglo orphans, the situation was often harder. In the 1890s, special trains came to the Midwest and plains states, including Texas, bringing orphans from East Coast cities. Families in need of extra help adopted them as workers and sometimes abandoned them in the off-season.[28] Wirt W. White's neighbor raised mules and liked cheap labor, so he brought two small orphan brothers back from Arkansas. He was supposed to feed and clothe them and send them to school, but they only went for three months and he worked them long hours and gave them few clothes. The oldest died of typhoid at age fourteen. The youngest went on to become a good ranch hand, but died swimming a river with his horse when the horse sank and he did not know how to swim. Such a death perhaps reflects the lack of childhood play in his life, when he would normally have learned those skills.[29]

Even without the orphan trains, frontier conditions produced their share of homeless children on a daily basis, and many of these boys went on to work on the ranches. Albert K. Erwin of Burnet County was fostered out to a nearby rancher from infanthood after his father's death. By age twelve he was working the cattle, and by age fifteen he had hired on to a cowboy outfit in Llano County.[30] In an unusual fostering situation, after Sioux Indians killed Harry Buffington Cody's parents in 1861, they raised him and taught him riding and hunting skills that he put to use when he escaped from them at age eleven. Cody lived off the land for the next four years, and then at age fifteen took on cowboy work for a year to support himself.[31] In 1883, a group of cowboys on a drive to the Panhandle kidnapped a thirteen-year-old black boy named Birl Brown after he followed the cattle outfit too far from home. They brought him with them for amusement, but when Birl realized his predicament he put up such a fuss that the cook sedated him with whiskey to keep him quiet. The men possibly "sold" the boy to Bill Koogle's ranch but finally abandoned him on William Lewis's uncle's ranch. As he was unable to say where he had come from, the uncle kept the boy on as labor and agreed to raise him. The white cook ultimately felt sorry for Birl and took him in as his own son and taught him to read and write. Birl insisted on learning to ride like the rest of the cowboys, however.[32]

Many of these young boys, like Birl Brown, found a surrogate father figure on the ranch, most frequently the ranch owner. Gaston Fergensen's father died when he was two years old and the family was desperately poor, so at age seven, Gaston went to look for work on a ranch. He was hired on for $10 a month to look for injured animals. Looking back nearly sixty years later, however, he believed that the ranch owner and foreman "sort of took me to raise."[33] At age ten, Henry Young ran away 200 miles from home to become a cowboy when his father would not give him more responsibilities. Luckily rancher Bill Adair took him in, hired him, and bought him clothes (on account for his wages). He also taught him skills and life lessons so that when Young finally returned home four years later, his parents did not recognize him at first. Young's story implies that the experience had made a man of him, as his father was proud and put him to work on a few trail drives.[34] Whether Adair actually thought of Young as a surrogate son or cheap labor we do not know, but it is apparent that he treated his "employee" paternalistically, and Young certainly looked up to him like a father. Jim Gober found a similar father figure in a ranch owner he applied to when he was sixteen. Informed he would have to break a horse before getting the job, he was relieved that the rancher made sure he had a proper saddle and another cowboy to help him. "My courage was bolstered considerably when I realized [he] had a greater interest than I expected in protecting my life." The cowhand also protected Gober by taking him out of sight and breaking the horse for him, telling him to get back on after he had broken it and pretend he had done the job.[35]

As admirable as their behavior was, the cattlemen's paternalism had the side effect of maintaining gender and social hierarchies. Ranch owners who raised young boys treated them as sons, but in return, expected filial obedience and loyalty when they became workers. While the ranchers had emotional ties to the boys they raised, they also recognized that creating close bonds would make a happier and more compliant workforce. The "boys" who grew up with the ranchers developed sentimental attachments to the men who raised them, and the ranchers saw them in this sentimental perspective as well.[36] The cowboys were perpetually children, in need of protection and teaching for their own good. When other hands saw the ranch owner acting paternally, they accepted it as natural, and may even have wanted that kind of a figure in their own lives. By taking on the father role, the rancher both reinforced his power and softened resistance to it. He was the one who knew what was best for the "boys," and he had the right to tell them how to behave. Many cowboys, having grown up in similar environments, did not disagree. While fathers and sons did not always see eye to eye, they generally saw themselves as working for a common cause, and cowboys similarly identified with their bosses in the early years of the cattle industry. Cattlemen perhaps counted on such loyalty to control their men. But when corporate methods of doing business replaced the paternalistic style in the 1880s, this control was less acceptable to the cowboys.

Most young boys found multiple father figures on ranches, especially among older bachelor hands who taught them skills. In some ways, these men were closer to the boys than their own fathers or the ranchers because they could spend more time with them and give them more attention.[37] Teddy Abbott grew up among Texas cowboys on his father's ranch in Lincoln, Nebraska and saw them as role models and extended family. In the summer, he camped out with them and cooked his own food "just like a man."[38] J. P. Benard looked up to "Gable," a hand with a mysterious past whom his father hired to work on the ranch. Gable taught him how to ride and rope despite his father's caution. "Old Gable was better to me th[a]n my own parents, and acted like a dad to me at all times. He let me hang around when he was busting wild ones, and taught me the tricks of the trade."[39]

Gable was not alone in the cowboy community when it came to looking after boys. In the 1860s, Sam Fawcett's outfit of cowboys raised Sam Lancaster, a nine-year-old orphan, as if he was their own child. They made him a desk out of a canned tomato box, bought him paper to write on, and gave him assignments to copy. Two of the hands in particular really kept him hard at work and made him study spelling out of a dictionary one of the other hands owned. "They taught me good, and always took care of me."[40] Older cowboys took on responsibility for young boys they worked with and were very protective. When Richard Murphy took his first trip up the trail, "the older waddies took charge of me so I wouldn't get taken in or get in wrong, and the boys held me down to earth."[41] Older boys took their cue from their elders. When Rollie Burns was nineteen, he and a twelve-year-old neighbor's son went in to Fort Worth while the neighbor ordered lumber. Burns wanted to let loose in the saloons "but I had the kid with me, and I kinda felt responsible for him."[42] Part of being a man, to Burns, was taking on responsibility for others, a lesson he no doubt learned from observing other men around him. Surrogate parents also took on disciplinary roles at times. On the King Ranch, a young boy was often separated from his vaquero father during the week while he was out at another cow camp, but the other vaqueros stepped into the role in his place, even spanking him if he did something wrong. As *kineño* Alberto Trevino recalled, "I had a father wherever I went." Such discipline by proxy did not just apply to the sons of vaqueros. When rancher Robert Kleberg sent his sons out to the vaqueros for training, they also were subject to a spanking if they misbehaved.[43]

By taking on paternal roles themselves, cowboys found ways to assert their own masculinity. If becoming a man meant taking on social responsibility, there were limited opportunities in a cowboy's daily life for doing so. Work provided the men with many duties and responsibilities to the cattle and other ranch property, but they were isolated from the rest of society as a rule. When a young boy came among them, they developed great sentimental attachments, remembering their own boyhoods and homes. However, when, as surrogate fathers, they passed on lessons they learned, they also highlighted that they were no longer boys themselves. They imitated the father figures they had known and thus created their own hierarchies in the bunkhouse, as they did with naïve tenderfeet and city-bred dudes. In cowboy society, however, once a man had proven himself, he became part of the group, accepted as an equal. Cowboys saw themselves as men, so making a boy into a man meant making him their equal.

For young boys, cowboys were irresistible, and tangible, heroes. They rejected all the forms of civilization that boys felt stifled by, such as proper manners, regular bathing, and churchgoing. They lived what seemed like independent lives, moving from ranch to ranch and working out on the range by themselves. They appeared to have no responsibilities outside their work and spent their money freely, without thought of the future. They told exciting stories of stampedes and fighting Indians. They maintained an all-male environment that was also appealing to boys who had not yet discovered female charms. And they had technical skills of riding, roping, and shooting that boys wanted to try and ways of hazing tenderfeet that made boys want to test themselves against them. All of these traits made cowboys ideal heroes for a boy who was trying to negotiate a path to manhood. In the cowboy model of manhood, growing up meant you did not have to listen to adults, especially women, fussing constantly about proper behavior and responsibility anymore. Moreover, the path to becoming a cowboy seemed simple. First you learned how to ride, and then to rope. You learned the brands and the skills of handling cattle and the routes to drive them north. You learned the songs the cowboys sang and the jokes they told. And lastly, you had an adventure or two of your own to tell around the campfire. When the cowboys accepted you as one of their own, you would be a man.

As Teddy Abbott said, "There was other people besides cowboys . . . but they was not the kind that could influence a boy." Teddy looked up to a man named Ace Harmon, a trail boss of one of the Texas outfits that came through Nebraska "and a god to me." When Teddy was fifteen, he heard Harmon say, "'In a year or two Teddy will be a real cowboy.' And I growed three inches and gained ten pounds that night."[44] V. H. Whitlock recalled the "utter joy" he felt as a small child in the Panhandle when one of the cowboys passing by with a herd would sweep him up to sit in the saddle for a while. "I longed for the time when I would be big enough to straddle a horse and ride out with them." As a young boy, Whitlock liked to hang around the ranch store listening to "old Jeff," a former cowboy who had been shot in Dodge City, Kansas. Jeff took him under his wing and told exciting stories about fighting Indians, but got Whitlock in trouble by teaching him vulgar graces to say at meals and to count 8, 9, 10, Jack, Queen, King. "Mother thought Jeff was wild and she didn't like me to be with him so much," but Jeff told him, "Us menfolks have to stick together, else the womenfolks will be running the country."[45]

Many parents fought a losing battle to keep their sons sleeping in the house instead of the bunkhouse with the "boys." F. J. "Sam" Wootan begged his mother to let him stay there, and she finally gave in. Boys like Sam and V. H. Whitlock loved staying up listening to the men's tall tales and stories about women in Old Mexico and watching them play cards.[46] Susan Newcomb's five-year-old son often left his mother alone to go to the bunkhouse to hear one of the cowboys play his banjo.[47] Branch Isbell's desire to be a cowboy came when he was twelve, and he briefly followed a group of Confederate soldiers who had driven a herd across his family plantation in Alabama singing cowboy songs.[48] C. P. Benedict admired the range boss and Cal Lowry, both older hands. "The Boss had a certain air of dignity, and a steady look in his clear grey eyes, that made me wish I could be a man like him, some day."[49] The Kleberg children grew up side by side with the vaqueros on the King Ranch and rode with them as soon as they could sit up in the saddle. Bob Kleberg in particular loved life on the ranch more than life in town.[50] John Gregory Kenedy and his sister Sarita grew up with the children of the vaqueros on the ranch and, like the Klebergs, he spoke Spanish almost as early as he spoke English.[51] Such contacts made boys long to grow up and become cowboys themselves. Even parents outside the West had a hard time convincing their sons that cowboys were not role models. As a boy in St. Louis, Charlie Russell was so fixated on going West to have an adventure that his work at school suffered.[52]

The romance of the outlaw, like the cowboy, in part perpetuated by dime novels and stories of Jesse James, was also such that parents did their best to shield their sons from it. Frank March camped out with the cowboys on the family ranch and discovered that his grandfather had warned the hands not to talk about outlaws, rustlers, and different places so that he would not get impatient to go out himself. But his grandfather's ploy backfired. Hearing the men talking about these things when they did not know he was around, and knowing he was not supposed to hear about them, just made March want to go out on his own even more.[53] "Idaho Bill" Pearson's father was so worried he would get in with a group of "wet ropers" (i.e., rustlers) that he bribed him to stay on the family ranch by offering him a trip to Europe if he would agree. Pearson took the trip and stayed with his father until 1886, when he left to look for a bigger ranch with more adventure.[54]

Parents at times had reason to worry about bad influences on their sons. Brook Campbell of San Angelo met with several outlaws in town who took a liking to the twelve-year-old and "hired" him to exercise their horses for nickels and dimes. One of them in particular, Charley Pierce, who "took a great fancy" to Campbell and paid him to deliver messages, left a strong impression. Pierce tried to "go straight" by hiring on with an outfit outside San Angelo, but he was not used to the hard work and eventually left town with his old gang, leaving Campbell his spurs to remember him by. "I cried myself to sleep that night. To a young boy, kindness and attention mean more than anything else in all the world and I could not think of Mr. Charley as being bad in any way. He was my hero and my heart was crushed." Not long after, Campbell was doubly devastated when the sheriff asked him to identify Pierce's bullet-riddled body in a photo.[55] At age fourteen, Teddy Abbott helped a member of his outfit escape from the sheriff after he had killed someone in town while on a drunken spree. He dressed up as the man and rode off, leading the sheriff on a wild goose chase while the outlaw escaped. Teddy reflected in later years, however, that "He was a killer, that fellow. He had killed a man before that, and he killed one after. At the time, though, he was a hero in my eyes. You know a kid looks at things differently, I thought a cowpuncher couldn't do wrong, and the sheriff was the enemy."[56]

Perhaps recognizing the allure of the outlaw to boys, people on the frontier could be more lenient with young outlaws than their older counterparts. In 1884, the *Austin Statesman*, reporting on a rash of fence cutting, blamed the old hands for corrupting innocent youth. Their "nefarious" plot was to involve the young boys so that citizens would be deterred from shooting at them in the dark for fear of shooting the boys.[57] When William Owens ambushed a group of rustlers on the trail, he discovered that the three remaining alive after the ambush were under twenty years old. Normally the punishment for rustlers was swift and final—they would be hung from the nearest tree. But Owens explained: "there are exceptions to all rules, and the age of the fellows provided the exception."[58] He bandaged their wounds and let them go.

It was not surprising, given encounters such as these, that many parents tried to stop their children from leaving too soon. They also hoped to prepare them for a different kind of life. Sending their children to school thus served a dual purpose. In the years immediately after the Civil War, schools were few and far between in frontier areas, but ranchers placed a high value on education. Irvin Bell of Palo Pinto recalled the ranchers' families who built Davidson Schoolhouse in 1860 and who, from 1861 to 1870, would "fort up" during the school year with an armed guard accompanying the children to school to guard against Indian attacks.[59] Most families could not afford to provide such support, however. Thus cowboy and future U.S. congressman Claude Hudspeth's early education was probably typical, consisting of "three months in a log cabin . . . where I thoroughly mastered the contents of Webster's Blue-back speller and reader combined. This constitutes the curriculum and the extent of my literary studies."[60] Auberry Aikin never attended school, but his father tutored him in the "Three R's."[61] But by the 1890s, most Texas towns had a school. Tom Boone lived close enough to town in Coryell County that he could both work on the ranch and go to school. He preferred work but "it never entered my mind not to go to school because I knew that dad wanted us kids to go."[62]

Educational experiences in the West varied widely depending on economic and geographic circumstances, and Texas had great diversity in this regard. But there were some general patterns to children's education. Girls tended to go to school earlier than boys as the families could spare them more easily, but most left by age sixteen or seventeen, at which time they often married or took on full domestic responsibilities. Most boys had more scattered educations and often were out of school throughout the year to tend to harvests and do other work.[63] Boys who came from families who lived in town, especially middle-class and wealthy families, had fewer chores and more time for education. While many of them were as eager for adventure, they had more supervision than their rural counterparts. They also had greater access to schools themselves and greater financial resources to attend. In the 1870s, Edward E. Jones was able to attend school in Fort Worth regularly until he was fifteen, which was longer than most boys in the United States at this time.[64] Vaqueros in South Texas, on the other hand, had less access to schools. Most sons of vaqueros got their education from their fathers and mothers, or on the job. From the time they were eight, the *patrón* on the Kenedy Ranch would expect the sons of vaqueros to work for the Ranch and was "not interested in the boys going to school."[65] Even as late as 1939, Alberto Trevino, a fourth- or fifth-generation vaquero on the King Ranch, learned his alphabet and numbers from the running irons used for branding on the ranch. Each cow had several brands which not only identified it as King Ranch property but showed what pasture it was from and whose calf it was, so the boy vaqueros had to be able to locate specific cows through their brands. Both of Trevino's parents were illiterate.[66]

A few cowboys did have superior educations. "Should you require any more hands, I should be glad if you could give me employment when the work commences," wrote Alf Matthews to Rollie C. Burns in perfect spelling and penmanship.[67] Congressman Hudspeth reported that some of his fellow cowboys had college educations.[68] Cowboying could even be a means to attaining an education. Spence Hardie and his brother Alva paid their way through Austin College in Sherman in the 1890s with a part-time job at Jot Gunter's ranch during the school year, working full-time in the summer.[69] Hillard J. Hay, a cowboy in Culberson County, like Hudspeth, had only had three months of formal schooling at age twenty. A representative from a local academy proposed he go back to school and Hay accepted. "I was a matured man and realized I would have to start in the soph[o]more class with classmates that were children, but I went on and graduated in four years time." He received his teaching certificate and became a teacher.[70] Hay's situation was not unusual, and it was common to have men in their twenties and even older in the schoolroom, making up for missing years of their education.[71] But his observations also highlight one of the problems with school for rural boys: it was a child's world, not a man's. Boys studied, men worked; and most cowboys had not spent many years in school.

In contrast, second-generation cattlemen were among some of the best-educated men in Texas. Whereas it was not typical for cowboys to have more than a basic education, cattlemen insisted that their sons, as future cattlemen, have proper schooling to prepare them to take over the business. Most sent their sons away to nearby cities or the East Coast to private schools and then to college. Will Hale, like many early ranchers' sons, attended boarding school. He went first to a school in New York in the 1850s and then, after getting in a fight with a boy there, switched to a school in St. Louis.[72] Milton Faver, who ranched in Presidio County on the border with Mexico, was perhaps concerned that his son by his Mexican wife would suffer from social stigma. Wanting Juan to have all the advantages that money could buy, in the late 1860s he sent him to school in San Antonio, then college in New York, and then to England, France, and Germany for several years. The plan backfired to some extent. Juan returned to the Big Bend, but it looked rather primitive in comparison to Europe, and perhaps for this reason, Faver decided to sell out his ranching interests in 1886.[73] Although Herbert L. Kokernaut grew up with the cowboys on his father's ranch near Alpine, Lee Kokernaut also wanted his son to have the sort of education he would need to run a business. He sent Herbert to private schools at Moultin and Victoria, Texas and then to Southwestern University in Georgetown, Texas, where he graduated in 1888. Herbert in turn sent his own son, Herbert Jr., to San Marcos Academy and Texas A & M University. Both sons came back to Alpine and managed the ranch interests as well as the First National Bank that Lee Kokernaut had founded.[74]

Richard King sent his sons, Richard Jr. and Lee, to Centre College in St. Louis for their main education. His son-in-law, Robert J. Kleberg II, also plotted the educational strategy of his sons carefully. Henrietta King even moved to Corpus Christi with her grandchildren to ensure that they would attend proper schools. Richard Mifflin Kleberg, "Dick," had a gregarious personality and good intelligence that his father saw as natural qualities for a leader of men. He sent Dick to university and later law school. He planned to send Bob, his less studious younger son, to school to become an agronomist, informed on the latest scientific techniques of farming. Sons did not always go along with their father's visions for them, however. Lee King chose to finish his education at a business college, and Dick Kleberg, while he completed a law degree, never became the lawyer/rancher that his father had hoped he would be, although he did supervise the Laureles Ranch. Bob also initially resisted the field of education his father had chosen for him, but he went along with his father's plans and discovered he really enjoyed it. Ultimately it was Bob who took over control of the King empire. Nonetheless, the boys still recognized that they needed an education to help them succeed, and this concern for proper education continued into the next generation.[75]

While cattlemen's sons generally agreed with their fathers' educational goals for them, most future cowboys did not share their parents' estimation of the value of an education. Many wanted to be out hunting or roping instead of sitting in the schoolhouse, which they saw as irrelevant to their future lives. As a child, black cowboy Ben Kinchlow went with his mother to Mexico after she was freed. His mother sent him to school but "after I got to ridin', I forgot all I ever knowed about school."[76] Hilory G. Bedford preferred hunting wild game, rounding up loose stock or "just anything for fun" to school, despite his older siblings wanting him to get an education.[77] W. B. Mitchell begged to be allowed to join the 1886 general roundup near Marfa. "I was determined to go but my mother did not wish for me to miss school."[78] Notwithstanding that their school year lasted only three to five months, Ernest Marshall and his childhood buddies disliked it so much, they used to break the schoolhouse windows and knock down the brick flues when no one was watching them.[79]

But for boys of any class, going to school often meant submitting to a degree of control and restriction that boys who lived in open country were not accustomed to. Lizzie Crossen, one of the few women to run a ranch in the Big Bend region, received regular reports on her son's progress at boarding school which documented a struggle to get him to behave. "Johnies temper is quick & at times he used incorrect language so that at times we had to be strict with him for his own good & now he

is quite over it & a nice boy."[80] When cattleman Charles Goodnight offered to pay for school for a boy he had taken in on the ranch, the boy
objected, saying it would be a prison, and wondered why it was necessary
when Goodnight himself "read but slowly and wrote illegibly."[81] Despite
Goodnight's own lack of schooling, it is clear he valued education, as it
was he who began a campaign to build public schools in the Panhandle
and coerced the other cattlemen into donating funds. But he may have
had additional motives as an employer. He also saw education as instill-
ing discipline and a sense of propriety, noting that college men were more
deferential than uneducated men.[82]

Restrained at home by mothers and at school by society's rules, boys
longed to be free and independent. Teddy Abbott chafed as his mother
continued to try to run his life even after he was out doing cowboy work.
"I was her pet and all that, but she was always bullyragging me about
drinking and spending my money in town, and so on—afraid I was going
to turn out bad. I thought I knew more than she did."[83] Like Huck Finn,
the eternal image of this type of boyhood, they often shunned all civilizing
efforts, however well intended, seeing in maternal tenderness an underly-
ing threat of rigid piety and petty discipline.[84] Yet while they complained
about their mothers' restrictions, sons of all ethnic backgrounds generally
followed their father's wishes out of respect. Tejano ranchers instilled deep
respect in their sons at an early age, so that even as they grew older they
would not go against them. Indeed, many Tejano men would not smoke
or drink in front of their fathers even as adults.[85] Every boy looked forward to the day his father considered him a man in his own right.

Boys played at being men and saw workload as a measure of their
manhood so were happy to take it on. From an early age, the line between
play and work was not clear. Charlene Sackett and her brother practiced
their roping skills on chickens in the yard and did mock branding.[86]
Young vaqueros played *correr el gallo* (running the cock) in which they
buried a rooster up to its neck in sand and then competing riders would
try to grab its head as they went by.[87] Young boys in training for bronco
busting rode calves or even steers, preferably mavericks, so if they killed
them there would be no harm to the ranch.[88] Hunting was a fun pastime
for many boys, but it was also an essential family function in some cases,
as the men were too busy working to hunt and there was not always meat
for the table otherwise. Children learned to ride so they had freedom to
go about on their own, but parents also needed them to deliver messages
and other goods.[89] When Marvin Powe was nine, his father sent him out

to round up some runaway horses. As Powe did not want to come back without them, he lived off the land for a week and stayed with other cowboys in camps until he found them all. When he returned, his father did not seem worried about his absence, expecting him to have completed his task.[90] When W. H. Childers' father purchased the Turkey Track Ranch, he left his thirteen- and nine-year-old sons behind at the stock farm with a few hands to "work it like it belonged to us. And, that we done. . . .That was the way of the old timer days though. Kids got to be men a heap quicker'n they do nowadays, and Cy and me went in the roundups just like we were men." Still, Childers reported, "I was just a happy-go-lucky kid on the stock farm."[91]

For many boys, however, work was not a choice; it was a fact of life. Ironically, at a time when child labor laws were coming into effect in the East, children's work on the frontier increased, especially in times of hardship. Sometimes families hired out children to shorthanded neighbors to earn a little extra cash for the family.[92] The death of a parent often necessitated boys working at young ages. Elario Cardova of Nacogdoches left home at age ten after his father died and his mother remarried. He claimed no special skills beyond horse riding but told the ranch owners that he was twelve years old, and they hired him to do the usual work watching for bogged cattle. Cardova did "boy work" for two years, during which time he learned the cowboy skills of roping and bronco busting. He began at $15 a month and then by age twelve was earning $25 a month as a regular cowhand.[93] William Owens of White Settlement reported that at age twelve, one year after his father died, he went out on his own. He could ride a horse well, as could most boys at that age, but he was not skilled with a rope or much else. He recounted that he was set to work helping to gather cattle for a roundup under the watchful eye of a rawhide, Baldy Jones, who "took me in charge."[94] Other boys of similar ages who had left home often worked on ranches doing "boy work" of helping to free bogged cattle and applying salve to injured animals to avoid screwworms.[95] Remuda wranglers were often young boys, as horse wrangling was considered an apprenticeship for going up the trail as a hand. But the horse wrangler was also often the butt of many jokes and had the worst horses to ride. Perhaps the low place of this position in the hierarchy explains the seeming predominance of black cowboys who worked horses rather than cattle. The view of blacks as children current in the late nineteenth century must certainly have added to the perception that horse wrangling was not really man's work.

From a young age, boys who grew up on Texas ranches worked with cattle and saw their skills as a sign of their passage to manhood.

Black families had a harder time earning enough money to survive. Black sharecroppers were often stuck in a cycle of debt to their landlords, who sold them supplies against their expected income from their crops. At settling time each year, they learned that the cost of the supplies they had purchased not only meant they had to give over their entire crop to their landlords but that they owed more money and were bound over to work another year. Blacks who worked in towns in general, earned much lower wages than their white counterparts. African American future cowboy Matthew "Bones" Hooks started working at age seven driving a meat wagon for the butcher and was a teamster by age nine. He also looked after his younger siblings when he was home.[96] Many Mexican families faced similar circumstances. It was common for young black or Hispanic boys to work outside the home to help support their families.

But whether working out of necessity or for fun, boys who started working at the ages of seven or eight progressed to more difficult tasks within a few years. In the words of A. P. Townsen, "I didn't have to learn to be a cowboy, I just growed up being one."[97] In 1874, at age eleven, W. A. Tinney drove a family herd from McKinney to the Red River, a ten-day drive of three to four miles a day, for the princely sum of $5.[98] Richard Murphy rode fence on the T-Diamond Ranch after leaving home at the same age, and by age twelve, Bill Dobbs was participating in roundups.[99] Nine-year-old Cliff Newland hauled supplies from the neighboring ranch house out to the cowboys in the line camps, a seventy-five-mile round trip, for fifty cents a day.[100] Boys seemed to long for opportunities to work like the men they knew. Tom McClure enjoyed busting broncs at age nine and was proud to become a regular hand at thirteen, although he recognized that "Of course, I saved dad some money on another cow poke's salary so he made [more profit] by letting me go ahead with the work."[101] Vaqueros on the South Texas ranches trained Tejano boys from age eight or nine to take on the family business. These boys took pride in the work their fathers did and wanted to imitate them.[102]

In order to do a full man's workload, however, the boys had to have a basic level of physical maturity. At fifteen, after Indians killed his father and older brother, Joe Chapman started working the roundups, as he was considered physically big enough to help with the cattle.[103] However, Fred S. Millard "tried to get work" after running away in 1878 when he was fifteen, but "everybody thought that I was too small to do anything." Eventually he found work on a farm doing chores such as milking cows, cutting wood, and helping out the wife when the farmer was away from home.[104] A. M. Garrett began rounding up mavericks with the hired hands during the late 1860s when he was eleven "and large enough to help ride the range."[105] But H. P. Cook claimed to be working as a full hand at ten and surely could not have been full size at that age.[106] Such unusual boasts stretch the readers' credulity but also emphasize the equation between workload and manhood. It was an important step for boys to take on a full workload, as it marked a progression away from boyhood.[107] Sam Rogers recalled, "I know I could do a man's work when I was about 12, because I went on the round ups with the rest of them."[108] By the age of fifteen or sixteen, most boys were usually working as full hands and doing "man's" work. Frank March's grandfather even enticed him to stay on the ranch rather than go to town by telling him that they needed men to take care of the cattle and "I was a man now."[109] Thus, manhood was at least in part measured in terms of being physically able to do the job.

Nonetheless, however much the boys would like to think of themselves as men, workload alone did not make it so. There were other, more subjective, rituals boys had to undergo. Middle-class town boys might show they had reached manhood by participating in rituals such as debating at a lyceum or entering a fraternal organization.[110] Rural boys in Texas (and some town boys), however, aspired to acceptance in the cowboy fraternity, which they saw as a real marker of manhood. Skills on the job and shrewd judgment were part of what cowboys thought made a man, as we shall see in the next chapter, but experience was also important. The one experience young men most desired was a trip up the trail, as they believed a cowboy could go up the trail a boy and come back a man. G. W. Mills reported that younger boys saw those who had been up the trail as heroes and stated that "You were not a graduate in the cowboy's school until you had been."[111] Charlie Bargsley related that even though his father only had a few cattle it was enough to make a cowboy of him "and like most young boys of that day and time, the dream of my life was to go 'up the Trail' with a big herd of cattle."[112] George W. Saunders, the founder of the Old Time Trail Drivers Association, had two older brothers who went up the trail before him, "and their reports of thrilling encounters with Indians, stampedes, buffalo chases, and the like, filled me with a wild desire to go on the trail, too."[113] However, not all cowboys saw the trail as an adventure. H. P. Walker, of Hood County, and his friend Buck had passed muster as ranch hands by performing daily work, but they still believed there was more to do and see to become real cowboys. When it came time for his boss to drive his herd up the trail, he and his friend "were raring for the chance" but "Truth of the matter was, that all the boys there had gone up one trail or another at some time or other" and "Most of the boys didn't want to go."[114]

In truth, most cowboys had had a chance to showcase their skills on the ranch. Some boys had done shorter drives before they left home. At around age eleven, William Dayton joined other neighbors' sons driving a herd of 3,000 longhorns from Williamson County to the ranch in Llano County, a distance of about 100 miles. The oldest boy in the group was around eighteen, but all the boys had been doing regular work in roundups by this time. "We lads drifted out with that he[r]d . . . fe[e]ling more important [than?] the P[r]esident of the United States."[115] Even short trails such as these could be exciting. J. M. Brown made regular drives with his father from their home about twelve miles outside of Fort Worth in to the stockyards there. "That was the high light of my kid experiences. Those trail drives. Some people would laugh at them because they were so short, but to me as a kid, they were something." According to Brown and many other sources, it was the first fifty miles that were always the hardest on the drives because the cattle were close to their home ground and reluctant to leave. So even on short drives such as this one, stampedes were not uncommon.[116]

Younger boys were not always ready for the experience, however. Ellis Petty made his first drive from Bell County to Brady County at age twelve with his father's outfit. He remembered he had a grand time, "but I sure got tired, and sometimes scared."[117] Buster "Dad" DeGraffenreid hired on with an outfit at age fifteen and suffered a rough first few months while the old hands made him do all their chores. Then one night someone who knew him gave him news of his family, who he had not seen in eight months, and he suffered a severe attack of homesickness. "I slipped off by myself that night and had a good cry for my ma."[118] Sam Rogers started off on the trail to Mexico because he "was always anxious to do something different," but once away from the ranch he began to think of how different Mexico was and "what could happen to a boy[,] a stranger away from home, so I folded up and went back."[119] When a trail boss questioned whether George W. Saunders would sleep on night watch since most boys seemed to need more sleep and were not reliable, Saunders replied that he would not sleep during stampedes and Indian fights. The boss agreed to take him on, which made George "exceedingly happy." But when he was too sleepy and hungry to keep trailing a steer after a stampede, the boss told him to get some rest because he needed it, and was not angry with him as George had expected.[120] Trail bosses who agreed to take young boys with them most likely expected to accommodate youthful behavior.

For most older boys, however, it was the adventure that called them as much as the chance to showcase their skills as cowboys.[121] E. A. "Berry" Robuck, who, in 1873, did his first drive at the age of sixteen, related stories of danger from storms, high water, hail, and stampedes, while experiencing the trials of cold, hunger, and sleeping regularly on wet blankets. "But," he explained, "it was all in the game, and we were compensated for the unpleasant things by the sport of roping buffalo and seeing sights we had never seen before."[122] F. M. Polk, who went up the trail at eighteen, concurred. "The boys had a rough time, but we certainly had lots of fun. Nothing ever happened that we didn't get a good laugh out of it."[123] But the adventure did not necessarily depend on exciting events. C. M. Crenshaw vowed never to forget his first drive at age sixteen, despite the fact that they had not even encountered a stampede along the way. As he later explained: "it was my first trail drive and I had realized my ambition to

'Go up the trail.'"[124] C. W. Ackermann's father asked a group of cowboys, including his son, if they thought they could take his cattle to Kansas. "As we were all young fellows between the ages of eighteen and twenty-two, eager for adventure, we willingly consented."[125] The trip itself was often the adventure for young men who had not been far from home. Teddy Blue Abbott recalled that cowboys who drove cattle to Montana always hoped to go just one river farther north to see what was there.[126]

Boys undoubtedly were capable of doing many of the tasks associated with trail driving even in their early teens, and many had at least been on a short drive before going up the trail to Kansas or the northern ranges in Montana and the Dakotas. When Joe Jackson bossed a herd up the trail at age eighteen the older men complained, but Joe knew exactly what he was doing and managed to lead the herd safely to water after a dry drive.[127] Boys could just as easily prove their skills on the ranch as on the trail, and many had already done so. While some scholars have identified a trip up the trail as a sort of rite of passage, historian William Savage has downplayed its significance, arguing that the drive served only as an initiation into a restricted society of trail driving cowboys, and in only a limited way prepared the boys for their role in a larger society.[128] Nonetheless, the issue is slightly more complex when viewed in terms of gender identities. Not all boys who went up the trail had the same experience, and thus it is difficult to generalize. What the trip up the trail did do for boys, however, was provide an opportunity for independence from families as well as a chance to view the larger world. In this sense, the trail gave them an occasion to develop the individual identities that distinguished men from boys, and marked part of the passage from adolescence to manhood. This passage might occur at different times for different boys, and could happen from simply moving away from home to work on another ranch, but undoubtedly the trail provided a unique opportunity for this growth.

For those who did not go up the trail, and even for some who did, there were other signposts to manhood. Owning the requisite tools of cowboying was one of them. Frank March's parents finally agreed he could take a job on another ranch if he did not take anything with him that belonged to the family ranch, so he saved up $40, bought his own horse and saddle, and left home.[129] Fred W. Whetaker remembered that as a boy his ambition was "to own a saddle hoss, saddle, bridle, chaps and a six-gun. When we were so able to be equipped, we considered that we had reached [a] man's estate."[130] Other rituals were social in nature. Teddy Abbott "sure felt big" after he stood at the bar and bought drinks for the other hands for the first time.[131] Abbott not only paid for something with his own money, but he was also participating in the bonding ritual of treating, long considered a way in which working men gained at least some power over their lives.[132]

Of course, the ritualistic nature of these behaviors meant it was possible for a boy to adopt the trappings of adulthood without actually reaching manhood. Rollie Burns used to strut around the streets of Denison at age fourteen showing off his six-shooter, but all the time he was scared he would run into his disapproving father.[133] In fact, overconfidence seems to have been a clear marker of immaturity. Teddy Abbott recognized such false bravado: "A kid is more dangerous than a man because he's so sensitive about his personal courage. He's just itching to shoot somebody in order to prove himself."[134] Again, age was not necessarily a factor. T. E. Hines, who left his home in North Carolina at twenty-one to come to Texas and be a cowboy against his parents' wishes, thought his father expected him to come back home "like a whipped pup. If he did, I told myself that's where he's going to be fooled a plenty because I was a man and could act like a man." In reality, however, Hines was ill prepared to leave home and only resisted going back to prove a point to his father. "All I had was the will not to go back, and you can't eat that."[135] More importantly, the ranch managers and bosses noticed when the boys were too cocky, as it could be detrimental to their work. Spur ranch range boss W. Dawson reported to the manager on the successful recapture of a stray cow and commented on the hand who he sent to find her. "Brand got her alright . . . he did not meet with any badger fight or any other jokes. He seems to have steadied up since I left him six years ago and I think he will be alright. He was quite a boy then but is quite mannish now."[136] "Steadying up" was an important sign of maturity.

Unlike cattlemen, most cowboys could not afford to marry or own property on their wages, so there was no opportunity to demonstrate manhood by setting up their own household. Ultimately, it was mainly their judgment and acceptance of each other that defined their masculinity. To become part of cowboy society, a newcomer usually had to undergo some form of hazing activity. Like all initiation rituals, the general rule was that anyone who was truly qualified to enter their group would have no difficulty with the ritual, whereas those who failed were not worthy of inclusion. The initiation rite did not confer manhood per se but showed that the participant was manly and could succeed in other manly pursuits.[137] Many boys who grew up in the West were accustomed to playing games with standard rules that allowed newcomers to adjust easily to a new place and enter into new friendships, and in a sense these hazings were similarly formulaic.[138] Most involved some display of physical prowess such as riding a bronco or roping a steer, while others tested nerve and self-reliance by leaving "greeners" alone to find their way home or hold a herd in a storm. Other rites of initiation involved pranks and jokes around the campfire to test a man's sense of humor and level of gullibility. Stories of hazing are legion in all the literature. Rollie Burns reported that all "tenderfoots" expected to have to ride a bronco before they could be accepted, and many accounts back up this supposition.[139] But cowboys had many ways of testing the mettle of the new arrivals. Pat Bullis believed that hazing was not just for fun but was necessary to see if the new man could do the job. Hazing changed depending on local conditions, for example, if the men had to ride unfamiliar ranges, they would test a cowboy's navigation skills to see if he got lost easily. They could also test the intangible qualities of a man through such hazing. "Under the guise of 'fun' you can find out a lot about a man. When we pulled a shenanigan everybody laughed like it was a joke, but back of that laughing and carrying on every mother's son was watching the tenderfoot."[140] Vaqueros on the King and Kenedy ranches did their own kind of weeding out process. If a newcomer was not a good worker or did not "contribute to the *esprit*" of the ranch, he would find himself assigned to the most disagreeable of jobs, facing ostracism, or open ridicule. Such men did not stay long.[141] These and similar hazing practices protected the outfit from men who could not handle the workload or could not take a joke, both important to being part of the group.

One way cowboys hazed tenderfeet was to carry out mock court trials. At age sixteen, Avery N. Barrow arrived on a horse ranch as a greenhorn but passed the test they gave him of riding a pitching horse. That evening the hands "arrested" him and held a "prairie-dog court" complete with sheriff, judge, and prosecutor. They read him a set of rules for behavior around camp and the fines associated with breaking such rules, and then charged him with failure to fall off a horse like a greener was supposed to. He chose a "mouth-piece" to defend him from among the cowboys and the two "lawyers" argued the evidence for over an hour before the court found him guilty as charged. Barrow's sentence was to buy a round of drinks for the men, payable in town.[142] These kangaroo courts were common in the cow camps and provided great entertainment for the men as well as serving as initiation rituals.[143] By mocking "civilized" behavior, the cowboys both satirized society's rules and defended their own code of behavior.

Another favorite hazing tactic was to scare the new man through stories of dangers he might face. On his first trail drive, greenhorn F. M. Polk was so scared by stories the other hands told him of Indians being nearby that he left the drive and went back home.[144] It was common for the cowboys to pretend to be bad men to scare off newcomers, with the result that many Eastern boys who ran off went back home to tell their friends that cowboys were all criminals.[145] Henry Steele's fellow cowboys warned him to look out for a man in the outfit named Hill, who they claimed would steal anything and kill him if he was not careful. They stole his matches and other small items and claimed that Hill had taken them. Gradually they deprived Steele of all his possessions, even forcing him to use prickly pear skin to roll his cigarettes. Eventually Hill, who was in on the joke, told him what had been happening. The men all had a good laugh about it and, in Steele's words, "from that time forward harmony reigned in camp."[146] This harmony was undoubtedly the result of Steele's response to the pranks. While he had not caught on to the joke and was scared to confront Hill, he nonetheless had not complained about the situation and even tried to make do without his possessions, thus showing his self-reliance, a quality essential to any man worth his salt. That he could laugh with the other men about the jokes was also part of the hazing process; if he could not take the joke, he would not have stayed with the outfit very long and the other men would have given him the cold shoulder.[147] The hazing rituals thus emphasized skill and the more intangible qualities that cowboys considered manly, and full acceptance into the cow camp was a clear sign that a boy had achieved manhood.

For cattlemen, however, acceptance by the all-male cowboy society was only one step toward true manhood. Cattlemen's sons demonstrated that they had achieved manhood by taking on greater social responsibility and economic power. Cattlemen often measured their sons' manhood through rituals such as marriage, which brought independence from the family and made them the head of their own household. Marriage often led to a gift of property, another marker of manhood. Richard King gave his son a $40,000 ranch as a wedding present, and many other ranchers made similar gifts to their sons as they grew to adulthood.[148] To be a man, a cattleman had to contribute to society as a whole, not just to the camaraderie of the cow camp.

The passage to manhood for cowboy or cattleman was not a sudden one but a gradual process. Most boys marked their independence from their parents and moving away from home as a key part of the process, but it did not change them overnight. Their lives as boys had prepared them for a competitive world, but as historian Anthony Rotundo notes, the chasm between carefree and spontaneous boyhood and manhood with all its responsibilities loomed large.[149] Many probably felt as Jim Gober did when he left home. "I had mixed emotions about the step I contemplated taking. The chance to leave a disappointing life was an exciting and refreshing idea, but the thought of leaving home, my loving, caring family, had a finality about it that was unsettling." Gober's father gave him a Colt revolver and some cartridges, warning him that it was "a mean world out there, Son. [But] You're sixteen now and old enough to keep this and use it with responsibility." Gober had tears on his departure and was homesick for a while but was also happy to start his new life.[150] Such partings were dramatic, but the boys soon grew into their new adult roles. Will Crittenden's father told him, "Well son. You wanted to get out, now be a man where ever you go and you'll always end up right by doin' so." Despite Will's mother's tears: "After de herd got started, I forgot all about my folks and went to riding herd."[151]

# 3

# At Work

As industrial capitalism rose in the late nineteenth century, economic success became far less certain and fortunes far less stable than before. Workers had less choice over their working conditions and had fewer opportunities to rise above their situation based on hard work. Many clung to older artisan ideals of manliness which emphasized independence, hard work, and pride in one's labor, all of which were challenged by modern corporate methods. Businessmen faced increasingly competitive markets in which stock speculation, labor protest, and the whims of a consumer public could shape their fortunes more than their own behavior. In this environment it was more important than ever to them to be strong, and manhood became an important source of self-worth. Writers of the period portrayed class differences in terms of manhood; those who succeeded did so through manly aggression, those who did not were men of show, rather than substance.[1] Indeed, success became the main goal for middle-class men, but given the uncertainty of achieving it in the new economy, success itself was often defined in terms of manly behavior. According to one of the many success manuals that were popular at the time, it was "not the most successful life in which a man gets the most pleasure, the most money, the most power of place, honor, or fame; but that in which the man gets the most manhood, and performs the greatest amount of useful work and human duty."[2]

Cowboys and cattlemen felt the same pressures as their counterparts on the East Coast, and sought to show their respective ideals of manly behavior through their work. Cowboys did not respect all their fellow workers equally. Western author Wallace Stegner observed that "what they most respected, and what as a boy I most yearned to grow up to, was . . . courage, competence, [and] self-reliance, and they honored them tacitly. . . . It was their absence, not their presence that was cause for remark."[3] Cattlemen, however, were facing a highly competitive marketplace with manliness defined by a balance between risk and calculation. Being a man meant showing shrewd judgment, handling men as well as cattle, and incorporating the latest techniques to keep up with an industrial society. They could no longer rely only on the traditional artisan values of hard work that the cowboys embraced.

Cattlemen, like most middle- and upper-class men in the late nineteenth century, tied their manliness to their economic success: all men worked, but only the manliest would get ahead in business. In their view, manly behavior meant controlling their passions and channeling them to benefit society. Masculinity involved responsibility and morally upright behavior, and those who could not follow these rules were like children indulging their worst impulses. Cowboy manhood, in contrast, depended less on controlling passions than controlling their own lives. Denied the cattlemen's markers of manhood in terms of providing for a family and owning property, they were more concerned with working on their own terms and asserting independence to show their own brand of manhood. These competing definitions of manhood led to tension on the ranches on a daily basis which increased as the ranches became more corporatized and cowboys had fewer and fewer opportunities to show their independence.

• • •

Cowboys measured their manliness in large part by their skills on the job and their competence to "get the job done." As cowboy Hubert Collins believed, working on a ranch was "a man's work, and the *only work* for a man to devote his life to."[4] One observer concluded in similar terms that "ranch life in those days was what was required to test the nerve and endurance of a man, and if a man could stand up to the real ranch life he was a real man."[5] So for cowboys to treat a newcomer as a man, he first needed to prove he had both the skills and the self-reliance to handle the job.[6] When Rollie Burns joined a buffalo hunting and surveying party as a young man, he did not earn the full trust of the leader of the expedition until he had ridden a wild bronco and killed his first buffalo. He continued to prove his reputation as a man by standing up to a drunken bully in a fight. These credentials were important, but did not transfer to cowboying, and when Burns got his first job on a ranch he had to prove himself all over again by breaking fifty horses for the owner in a period of three months. Since it took three to ten days of riding for the horses to become tame, Burns had to ride several of the unbroken ones each day, a feat which confirmed his skills as a rider and showed his dedication, but which convinced him never to willingly ride a bronco again.[7] George W.

Saunders proved his mettle to his fellow cowboys by taking a rope across the flooded Washita River to ferry a raft across when four men before him had failed. "I felt very proud of myself, and I think I added several inches to my stature right there."[8]

William Lewis, as the son of a ranch owner, faced a great deal of prejudice from the ranch foreman in his first months as a cowboy and had to continually prove his worth. He had to teach himself to ride broncos through trial and error, but "his determination not only amused the other hands, especially the older ones, but aroused their admiration." It helped Lewis that he never complained about his treatment and did not expect help in his task. In this way he gradually earned acceptance as a working part of the outfit, and as an equal.[9] Charlie Siringo underwent a similar hazing process even after being hired as a trail boss for the LX Ranch. He had proved his skills enough trailing other herds for the ranch owner to hire him, but the local foreman told him that since he looked too young to most of the other hands, it would be best if he just roped with them on an even basis for a while. The local expert roper, African American and former slave Ike Word, refused to work with Siringo until forced to, as he thought the new man was a greenhorn. He earned Word's respect only by showing his roping skills and breaking a horse that the others had considered too wild to ride. "From that [time] on, old Ike recognized me as a genuine cowpuncher."[10]

Word's actions showed that in the hierarchy of skills, race was less of a factor than one might expect. Mark Withers went up the trail with more than eleven different black cowboys over the years and remarked, "A good negro is a mighty good hand."[11] While black cowboys were often limited from rising to positions of authority, a number of them earned respect through their skills. Matthew "Bones" Hooks earned a reputation as one of the best bronco busters around and made a living going from ranch to ranch in West Texas and the Panhandle breaking horses. When his name came up, another old cowboy praised him, remarking, "Yes, Bones is a Negro, but those who know him say he is one of the best riders the United States has ever known." Ironically, Bones had learned his skill so well because the white cowboys had tried to embarrass him by making him ride tough horses all the time. As Bones put it: "They made me the best rider in the country, but they weren't trying to make me a rider." Bones gained such a solid reputation based on his skills that when Clarendon area cattlemen formed a vigilante committee to track down cattle rustlers, they made him a part of it.[12]

To some extent, ranchmen were willing to recognize skill wherever it existed. On at least one trip to bring a herd from Mexico, the Mexican vaqueros and Anglo cowboys fraternized easily and the Anglos learned a few tricks from the vaqueros. On another occasion, a black cowboy proved his worth by sticking with a herd through a bitterly cold night despite having few clothes to stay warm. He reportedly told the other men, "I can stand it if the rest of you can," and when he froze to death in the process the men buried him on the highest hill around with the respect they would have accorded any man in the outfit. Bose Ikard, a former slave and hand for one of Charles Goodnight's partners, hired on with Goodnight in the 1870s and became his right hand man, guarding his money and saving his life and herd on several occasions. Whatever Goodnight's personal feelings about race, he trusted Ikard completely.[13] When cattleman A. J. Clinton brought 22,400 head of cattle up the trail, only losing twenty-one on a five-day dry drive through the Nueces Canyon, the *Texas Livestock Journal* credited his entirely Mexican outfit for the success of the drive.[14] It is clear that Anglo cowboys and cattlemen alike recognized skill regardless of color, which provided exceptional men of color a chance to gain some respect.

In general, most outfits had two or three black workers, usually in the position of horse wrangler or cook. While horse wrangler was the lowliest position within an outfit, horses were an essential part of cattle work, and a good wrangler was extremely valuable. Some African Americans, such as "Nigger Jim Kelly" who worked for Print Olive, or "Nigger Frank" who worked for John Chisum, gained reputations as horse experts and often the admiration of their fellow cowboys as a result. Blacks also earned some authority in their position as cooks, who by tradition had absolute control over everything within a hundred-yard radius of the chuck wagon. Black cooks also frequently doubled as extra hands in emergencies. Historian Kenneth Porter has speculated that without the opportunity to become ranch foreman or trail boss (except in exceptional circumstances or with all-black trail outfits), being a cook was one of the few ways blacks could gain a promotion on the ranches as well as a higher salary than they could ever expect as a regular hand.[15] The cowboys in Addison Carter's outfit (who knew him as "Nigger Ad") recognized his skill as a cowhand but, "because of the custom in those days [he] never became what was known as a 'top' hand."[16] Still, repeated references to talented black cowboys throughout many cowboy narratives reinforce the idea that having strong skills could significantly raise one's social standing.

It was much harder for vaqueros to gain recognition on Anglo ranches. Typically there were one or two "Mexican" cowboys in each Anglo outfit at least, perhaps more on the trail. But while they were willing to give credit and sometimes list names for talented black cowboys, Anglo cowboys almost never name the vaqueros in their accounts and give little to no praise of any individual Hispanic cowboy's skill, despite several generic assertions that Mexicans were good ropers and riders.[17] Ironically, the term vaquero implied a certain knowledge of cattle work so that even Anglo cowboys co-opted it at times. The South Texas hero of J. Frank Dobie's 1929 *A Vaquero of the Brush Country* is in fact John Young, an Anglo cowboy, who in his description of his outfit names every Anglo cowboy individually and then says, "There were two Mexican vaqueros in the crowd, and two negroes." While in subsequent stories Young provides the names of the black cowboys, he never gives the individual names of the Mexicans.[18] Teddy Roosevelt wondered at the fact that cowboys came from every different national background and yet blended in so well that they all resembled each other with one exception. "Some of the cowboys are Mexicans, who generally do the actual work well enough, but are not trustworthy; moreover they are always regarded with extreme disfavor by the Texans in an outfit, among whom the intolerant caste spirit is strong."[19]

While vaqueros earned the respect of their employers on the South Texas ranches where they made up the majority, it was still hard for Hispanic cowboys, like black cowboys, to rise to a position of authority, particularly in the early years of the industry. On the Kenedy Ranch, Jose Maria Morales earned the trust of his employer through his long service, almost fifty years, on the ranch. As a result, he was entrusted with carrying the payroll from San Antonio. But there were no Mexican American *caporales* on the ranch until 1916.[20] On the King Ranch, Robert Kleberg did have two Hispanic horse bosses—Luís Robles and Julián Cantú—and Ramón Alvarado served as cattle boss, but all foremen and ranch superintendents were Anglo before 1926.[21] Richard King's trail crews were all vaqueros who worked for pennies a day, but he contracted with white trail drivers to boss the herds, offering them a share in the profits. Anglo cowboy Jeff Connally remembered driving a King Ranch herd up the trail with a white boss and "the balance of the bunch being Mexicans—he had them do the work and let the white man do the bossing."[22] Kenedy also contracted with outsiders to take his herds up the trail to Kansas, including at least one all-black outfit. When the vaqueros themselves took the herds up the trail, however, they were under Anglo supervision.[23] Moreover, while King and Kleberg rarely fired any vaquero who had grown up on the ranch, they would not tolerate any insubordination.[24] Thus, for Hispanic cowboys it was possible to make a basic living as a cowboy or cook, but even where they had relative freedom on the South Texas ranches they still stood in a subordinate position to the Anglo boss. *Kineños* were buried on the King Ranch in a separate cemetery in unmarked graves, while the King Ranch thoroughbred racehorse Peppy San Badger earned a huge memorial plaque with an engraved picture.[25]

Nonetheless, although cowboys of color in general had a much harder time gaining respect from Anglos for their abilities, they still measured their own self-worth in part by their work skills. The vaqueros on the Rincón Ranch, in Starr and Hidalgo counties in South Texas, "did their job regardless of time and took pride in their work. Out at cowcamp they would willingly suffer such hardships as heat, hunger, and thirst in following their daily work. . . . their patience was endless."[26] The ability to carry out this work was also part of their masculine identity. As historian Tom Lea claimed, work on the King Ranch was "a source of virile, energetic, open-air pride. . . . Men made the ranch and the ranch made men."[27]

To many observers, the type of work that the cowboys engaged in showcased their masculinity both physically and symbolically. The strength required to wrestle a steer to the ground or ride a bucking horse was the most obvious manifestation of masculinity to American society, especially in an era in which social scientists were lamenting the "over civilization" of men and advocating strong physical activity as a cure. The YMCA emphasized manly exercise as a way to reinforce moral character, the Boy Scouts encouraged boys to be boys without feminine constraints, and the new ideal man was a fine physical specimen such as Teddy Roosevelt personified, rather than the "prosperous" (i.e., somewhat portly) ideal of manhood perhaps personified by Grover Cleveland. Symbolically, cowboys were also carrying out a masculine activity through their domination of the land. To men like Teddy Roosevelt, the frontier itself was a metaphor for the forging of the manly white American race, which tested its mettle against the savage Indians and tamed the wild land, proving its superior spiritual strength. "The most ultimately righteous of all wars is a war with savages. . . . The rude, fierce settler who drives the savage from the land lays all civilized mankind under a debt to him. . . . It is of uncalculable importance that America, Australia, and Siberia should pass out of the hands of their red, black, and yellow aboriginal owners, and become

Cowboys needed strength to throw cattle, although some cattlemen believed their handling of the livestock was unnecessarily rough. Flanking a calf at branding time. Two cowpunchers are ready to hold it down for the branding, one flips him high off the ground. Spur Ranch, Texas, 1905–1910. LC-S611-701, Erwin E. Smith Collection of the Library of Congress on deposit at the Amon Carter Museum, Fort Worth, Texas.

the heritage of the dominant world races."[28] In this sense, Teddy's Rough Riders were simply a blend of cowboys and virile men from the East engaged in another act of domination and imperialism on other frontiers, racial and geographic.

Whether cowboys themselves placed as much emphasis on physical strength as a sign of manhood is questionable, however. Most cowboys were medium-sized, wiry men, since muscle-bound types would be too hard on the horses.[29] They recognized that strength was a necessary component of some aspects of the job but did not particularly think less of a man if he was not as strong as other men. Not every cowboy could wrestle a steer, but as long as he could cut it from the herd, rope it, and brand it without incident and could repeat the action several hundred times each year, few would question his abilities to do his job. As for the symbolic aspects of their work, again, perhaps Easterners and subsequent scholars have read too much into their actions. Literary scholar Blake

Allmendinger has argued, for example, that cowboys were able to assert their masculinity through their castration of bulls and subsequent eating of the "prairie oysters." While such acts certainly had aspects of domination about them and provoked much cowboy humor, they likely were not consciously "transforming the bulls' castrated testicles into signs of their own male dominance" to counteract their own symbolic castration by the ranchers.[30]

To be competent, a man needed basic skills. Riding ability was primary, as "in the cowboy's code, a man who fails to ride his animal might as well retire from the business."[31] G. F. Boone recalled that men who were not such good riders were still allowed to watch the cattle, but since the horses usually pitched a little each morning they had to learn to ride fairly quickly or have a friend to help them out, as "you had to be man enough to ride the horse that was given you. If you didn't, you los[t] the job; and that's where I made a lot of friends for life because I'd warm their horses up for them."[32] Competency also implied good roping skills and knowledge of the country and cattle brands. Without such abilities a cowboy could never expect to pilot a herd or participate in a roundup.[33] Still, there seemed to be a belief that there was an additional intangible quality that distinguished a good working cowboy. As a stage driver told young William Lewis, most people could learn to ride and rope: "But the fello' that does it good does it because he's got somethin' in here the others aint— a sort of feel that tells you what to do and when."[34] Joseph Mora simply called it good horse and cow sense, saying that some of the best cowboys he knew were only mediocre riders or ropers but could get the livestock to do just what they wanted nonetheless.[35] Frank Hastings believed that the best cowboys grew up in the business, and would not hire any students or young men who wanted to learn the job unless they demonstrated a clear understanding of it.[36]

What made cowboys men, in their own judgment in terms of their work, was often steadfastness as much as skill. Account after account notes the loyalty of the men who worked on the ranches, even on the notorious XIT Ranch, which supposedly was the toughest on its men. XIT cowboys chased down cattle thieves themselves at risk of life and limb. As XIT Ranch foreman's wife Cordelia Sloan Duke noted, "Its men were vigilant and devoted, if not always impregnable."[37] The *San Antonio Light* described the cowboy as "faithful day and night, to the sacrifice of his life, if necessary. . . . and to toil he is so inured he can scarsely appreciate the word fatigue."[38] Teddy Roosevelt described the cowboys he knew as "continually vying with one another in the effort to see which can do the work best."[39]

Such loyalty, however, was not necessarily a reflection of admiration for the owners. As Teddy Abbott recalled: "To tell the truth, it wasn't thinking about the owners' money that made them so anxious to turn out their herd in good shape. What they cared about was the criticism of the other cowpunchers."[40] Eugene Manlove Rhodes reported that "your loyalty was to the job, not to your employer" and that even if you had a disagreement with the boss "you didn't quit unless another man could take your place."[41] Indeed, some cowboys' loyalty to each other could work at cross interests to the ranches. At a roundup between the JC Ranch and Ab Blocker's herd, JC cowboy Joe Johnson silently watched his friend Felix Shaw of Blocker's outfit take an unbranded calf out of the herd that belonged to a JC cow, and even held back the mother so she would not follow her calf. Later, in a bar in Abilene, when Felix professed that "he thought more of him than anybody else" Joe brought up the calf and called him a liar, to which Felix responded, "I thought that if you did not know that was your calf you was the biggest fool I ever saw," thus recognizing Joe's complicity. After this roundup the Blocker outfit never branded another JC calf, but Joe did not report the incident to his bosses either, proving his loyalty was more to the cowboys than the owners.[42]

Nonetheless, the result was often the same: a cowboy who stuck to his job no matter how hard and how many hours he had to work even if it was only to prove himself to the other cowboys. Charles Goodnight reported that "during [m]y ten years on the trail I rarely ever had a man who would shirk his duty; had he been so inclined, he would have been ridiculed out of it."[43] Men who could not follow through with the job or who complained about it were objects of scorn among cowboys and ranchers alike. As Woodson Coffee wrote:

> Eating your breakfast while the stars are still shining
> Complaint from a man was considered just whining
> He did not last long—too soft for the job
> As he could not keep up with the rest of the mob—[44]

James Cook was equally unsympathetic to rich would-be cowboys. He noted that the fanciest looking men were usually the worst workers. "They were often fair-weather sailors, with no pride when it came to doing unpleasant tasks well, how ever much they had of another sort of pride which would make them die game in a saloon brawl."[45] When Teddy Abbott's partner from Massachusetts quit after a week in the hot New Mexico summer, he put it down to just "another case of wanting to be a cowboy; he had stuck it out for four years in Nebraska, but when it came to the Southwest he couldn't take it as well as I could. . . . He had more money than guts, but I don't know as I blamed him."[46] Over the years, many hands had to deal with rich "boys" from the East or England coming out to be cowboys, and their main objection was not their wealth or their origin, but that they never finished their jobs. Some of these men, like Teddy Roosevelt, Abbott noted, turned out to be good cowboys and earned his respect precisely because they *could* do their jobs.[47] Willingness to stick to the job was thus an essential part of a man's worth.

As the work was often dangerous, cowboys also had to have some measure of courage to perform their job on a daily basis. Accounts of electric storms and hailstones are standard fare in any trail narrative. Cowboys repeatedly recall balls of lightning flashing across the horns of the cattle and lacking protection from the large hail while handling stampeding cattle. James Cook recounted a harrowing experience with a herd in one storm with a tornado half a mile wide, six-foot flash floods in the gullies, and hailstones three feet deep.[48] Texas weather is particularly volatile in the spring when most of the herds were first getting on the road, and the Panhandle through which several trails ran is notorious for frequent tornadoes, so it was not surprising that cowboys faced such extremes. John B. Conner experienced his first storm on the trail in 1885 at age nineteen. During the storm "the horses . . . moaned and groaned till I became frightened and decided that the end of time had come . . . I thought I was as brave as any man, but the action of the horses was too much for me, so I got down off my horse and lay flat on the ground and tried to die, but could not."[49] After this baptism by fire, however, in subsequent storms Conner simply went about his work like the other cowboys.

Natural forces were not the only hazards cowboys faced, especially in the 1870s when Indian raids were still common on the frontier. Often short on food, various Indian groups depended on taking cattle from the ranches or under cover of a stampede on the trail. Efforts to recover cattle often led to armed conflict. On the trail in 1873, a storm came through, scattering R. B. Pumphrey's herd. Indians drove some of the lost cattle away and the outfit followed their trail but was not able to overtake them, "which perhaps was a good thing, as we were poorly armed and perhaps would have been three men against ten or fifteen Indians."[50] Some of the fear was exaggerated, but nonetheless it was real for many of the cowboys. When G. H. Mohle's outfit could not get their entire herd across a flooded river, he and two others went ahead with those they got across but were not able to bring many supplies with them. "The next night about twelve o'clock we heard yelling & shouting, but thinking it might be Indians, we remained quiet and did not know until noon the next day that it was some of the boys of our outfit who had brought us some grub."[51]

Even handling the cattle without outside interference could be dangerous in itself. A horse might step in a prairie dog hole and throw the rider at any time, snakes could get into bedrolls, a cowboy risked trampling while trying to stop stampedes, and accidents were common and could lead to permanent injuries or death. In the late 1870s and early 1880s, the *Fort Griffin Echo* reported one shooting accident a month on average on surrounding ranches, and at least one case of a cowboy who was gored by a bull.[52] Gun accidents were always a possibility. Charles Steedman was doing his laundry while another man cleaned his gun nearby and the gun went off, injuring the other man in the chest and missing Steedman by only a hair's breadth.[53]

Other accidents were related to the work itself. Teddy Abbott suffered torn ligaments in his arm at age twenty after trying to help a buddy who was being dragged by his horse. He reached the other horse and got caught on its rigging, resulting in his being stretched between the two horses before dropping to the ground. In addition, while roping and wrestling steer at roundups he got rope burns that injured the cords in the palms of his hands. These injuries took their toll, and in later years, rheumatism set into his arm and he could not open "but the first two fingers of each hand."[54] Cowboy V. H. Whitlock's uncle, George Causey, injured his spine when his horse fell after stepping in a badger hole. He never recovered from his injuries fully and became more despondent after he had to sell his ranch, eventually committing suicide.[55] Bronc busting was probably some of the most dangerous work on a daily basis, and this was one of the reasons why horse wrangling was reserved for black cowboys, who often drew the most onerous or dangerous tasks.[56] Ironically, while they were still slaves most owners had kept blacks from busting broncos or doing dangerous tasks as they were too valuable property to their owners to risk.[57] After Emancipation, however, black and Mexican workers were paid the least and usually considered expendable.

Despite these dangers, cowboys expected all men to take the risks necessary to their jobs as they came along. Abbott told the story of a cowboy who, saying he had lost the herd, disappeared during a frightening stampede, leaving his fellow men at a disadvantage. Cowboys certainly knew the risks of trampling during stampedes "but they didn't quit and didn't hesitate to risk their lives for their outfits. The fellow that quit that night showed lots of sense, but he never got another job with a beef herd."[58] Risk-taking, in fact, was possibly one way in which cowboys were able to gain self-confidence, as their choice of risks they took allowed them to have some level of self-control.

Historian Gunther Peck's study of risk-taking among another all-male society, miners, can provide us with some insights as to similar behavior among the cowboys. As the corporations took control of mines on the frontier, they turned stake owners into wage earners and limited the ability of miners to control their work habits. Mining, like cattle work, involved certain risks, but the risks workers took in the corporate mines were a way of controlling their own lives. Miners evaluated risk based on what they had to win or lose and their individual status, for example whether or not they were single or married. For them, the manly part was not the risk so much as being able to choose to take it and to accept the consequences of their actions. Risk was the great leveler, as with same the basic skills, everyone had an equal chance to succeed or fail.[59]

Mine owners, however, blamed most accidents on the carelessness of the miners, in much the same way ranchers blamed the cowboys in later years for cattle losses. They commented on the seemingly reckless behavior of the miners, and there was perhaps an element of truth to their accusations. Miners were quite nonchalant about having been in explosions, and their actions seemed to risk more of them as they frequently used open flame lights in areas where the presence of gas was a possibility. But in most cases, the risk was calculated. The miners knew there was little chance of explosion as long as the mine operators had installed proper ventilation, and they could work faster with open flame lamps than safety lamps. In many cases, safety regulations imposed far more supervision on the miners than they were used to, and some miners even opposed such regulations as taking away their independence. From being quasi-independent contractors, they now had to follow rules which determined how and when they did their jobs, and they also had to make regular reports to show compliance.[60] Risk-taking, for the miners, was a way of maintaining their independence and showing their manhood.

The parallels with the ranching industry are marked. Cowboys took risks as part of doing their job, but they were often calculated risks. Cattle raising on the scale of the Texas cattle industry was of necessity harsher than in small-scale enterprises. The logistics of range grazing meant that cattle had to travel large distances to reach the market under tight control and sometimes without water. The practice of herding cattle on horseback necessitated the use of the rope to bring cattle down, which is not particularly gentle. But the key factor was the large size of the herds, numbering in the thousands, which the cowboys had to deal with on a regular basis. It was not possible to take time with each animal at branding, nor was it possible to spend much time taming horses. Thus, the cowboys "threw" cattle and "busted" broncs in an abrupt way. They also considered their ability to do so an essential qualification for being cowboys and a measure of their manhood. Like the miners, they saw the ability to handle the danger involved in these activities as part of what made them true men.[61]

Still, seasoned cowboys, no matter their age, did not take foolish risks. While courage was an important part of cowboy masculinity, fear was not necessarily an object of scorn, especially if well founded. Moreover, cowboys had no respect for false bravado. S. A. Wright related the story of a cowboy who stopped in front of an approaching herd, splitting it in two around him and causing a commotion. The other cowboys were not sure why he stopped there, "but he was a silly nut, and it was thought he did it, to show how brave he was. Fools cause a lot of trouble by trying to show their bravery."[62] Displays of nerve were important but not always necessary. Teddy Abbott regretted having lost $17 as a young man, trying to prove his own nerve at a saloon. A man brought in a jar containing a rattlesnake and bet the men a dollar a time that they could not leave their finger on the outside of the jar while the snake struck from the inside. No doubt the other men had a good laugh at Abbott's expense as he tried to show how tough he was. The saloon owners bought the snake and the jar and made quite a fortune from similarly unwise cowboys, until one became so frustrated he shot at the jar and they had to kill the snake.[63] William Lewis gained a reputation while still in his first years as a cowboy for swimming herds across rivers, but on one trail drive he refused to swim a rope across the Canadian as the floodwaters were too high. The foreman threatened to fire him, so he quit rather than take such a risk. After the foreman attempted the swim himself and almost died in the process, however, he promptly rehired Billy without any apology or explanation. For his part, Lewis saw it as "his initiation into manhood, into the tribe, the formal acceptance of him as one of their own by these rough men."[64] The men respected his judgment from then on, and the foreman treated him as an equal. Knowing when a risk was unnecessary was an important part of being a man as it showed good judgment.

Another risk cowboys reported avoiding was mixing drink and work. Teddy Abbott said he only knew of one time that they had broken the "no whisky with the wagon" law as "everybody knew that drinking and cattle didn't mix, and there was never any trouble."[65] Many cowboys were heavy drinkers in town in the off-season but did not bring their habits with them to the ranch. Perhaps with some relief, the editor of the *San Antonio Light* commented, "the brandy season is over for the cowboys and the branding season has commenced."[66] Cowboy work required a clear head, and anyone who was drinking would not be able to do the job properly.[67]

Despite assertions of sobriety on the job in many cowboy narratives, however, it is also true that from the early days of ranching many cattlemen had rules banning alcohol on the ranch, and without a problem there would have been no need for the rule. Rancher Felix Mann told his men they could drink in the houses around the ranch but he would fire them if they brought any whiskey into the cow camp.[68] Drinking on the trail was a constant temptation to the men as they passed towns with their herds going north. Young James Shaw rode with an outfit past Dodge City and all the men but Shaw and a black cowhand abandoned the herd at night to go into town and drink. When the boss realized what had happened, he refused to let any of them go into town at Ogallala except for Shaw because he knew he would not drink.[69] Walter Billingsley, a trail boss for the King Ranch in 1884, had similar problems taking a herd to Wyoming and had to fire some of his trail hands for drunkenness.[70]

Alcoholism seems to have been an issue even for some of the best cowboys. Rancher Bill Paxton once offered one of his top hands one hundred head of beef if he could stay sober for a year, hoping to get him to quit drinking, but to no avail. Eventually whiskey started interfering with his work, and he only survived because a former employer staked him to a small herd and a piece of land.[71] XIT managers worried less about one of their range bosses who was rumored to drink as they were certain he would find no alcohol on their property.[72] XIT ranch manager A. G. Boyce would not even let a British investor bring liquor to the ranch for his own personal use.[73] Spur Ranch manager Spottswood Lomax signed an agreement with Charles Goodnight and H. H. Campbell of the Matador Ranch not to employ men fired for drunkenness.[74] Goodnight may have acted based on experience. In 1880, he had hired one of Hank Cresswell's former employees who was fired after he would not leave town with

Cresswell until he had spent all his money in the saloon. When the employee showed up at the ranch a week later looking sheepish, Cresswell fired him but wrote a recommendation for him to Goodnight, who hired him based on his work record. With Goodnight's general ban on alcohol on his ranch, however, it would have been hard for the man to shirk his duty.[75] Most of the better cowboys seem to have recognized, along with the ranchers, that alcohol interfered with getting the job done, and that good men would leave it in town.

Although swaggering cowboys often figure prominently in the stories of the Wild West, it was the quieter men who gained more respect from their fellows, to whom false bravado was simply a sign of immaturity or even cowardice. Vaqueros on the King Ranch recognized that the best way to handle cattle was with patience, and that younger men did not always have this ability.[76] Risk-taking was an important and necessary part of work, but cowboys practiced restraint when it endangered the livestock, and they were not foolhardy. Nonetheless, the popular image of cowboys among ranchers and the general public was that cowboys were reckless, and needed reining in. As ranching became more corporate in nature and the cattlemen were absent in London or New York, cowboys increasingly came under even tighter regulation. In this situation, risk-taking became a way for cowboys to assert their own authority, but it also became a primary target for restraint.

On the one hand, cattlemen admired the bravery and skill that their men showed. They saw risk-taking as what had helped them conquer and tame the frontier, and early cattlemen in particular recognized something of the same spirit in their own entrepreneurship. As historian Mark Carroll points out, many of the earliest Texas settlers had prized the Jacksonian ideals of "individualism, competitiveness, and a willingness to take risks," and wanted to "live a defiantly unconstrained life" outside of traditional social ties.[77] But the sort of heroic manliness the cowboys embodied was rapidly becoming a thing of the past to many middle-class businessmen, including ranchers, who were quick to respond to market trends and adopt the newest business methods. For the most efficient business, the new self-made man had to practice self-control and restraint as he entered the workplace, and his workers had to do the same.[78] In the age of industrialization, workers were no longer part of a family, but part of the machinery that produced goods.[79] As such, workers had to be as consistent and dependable as possible. Cattlemen planned for long-term development, and they were concerned with the land and the cattle more than the cowboys. Cattleman C. C. Slaughter managed to give a fourteen-page speech entitled "The Passing of the Range" before a group of his peers without once mentioning cowboys.[80]

Early restraints on the cowboys were often couched in paternalistic terms. The relative youth of the men made it easier for the ranchers to think of them as "boys," and since many boys first started to work on ranches in their early teens, in some cases the ranchers had been like sub-stitute fathers to them. Ranchers were tough on their "boys" but looked out for them like their own sons. Gaston Fergensen worked for a boss who used to grumble and complain every payday when he handed out the wages, but who would get really angry if the cook did not make enough food to feed the "fellows" properly.[81] Usually the ranch owners provided basic necessities for their employees. Stores in the cattle country adver-tised to the "stockmen" about food and clothing for their hands, rather than to the cowboys.[82] "Good" bosses generally provided more than the basics, however. A story appeared in the *Amarillo Fat Stock Show Jour-nal* about two bosses in town for supplies for their drivers. One of the partners objected to spending extra money for maple syrup for "the boys" when sorghum would please them just as well. The second boss replied: "them babies have been mighty faithful, they've guarded that herd in the rain and mud" and had not received much in return, and insisted on buy-ing maple syrup. The second boss ultimately bought out the first boss's in-terest in the herd so he could give his "babies" proper care.[83] Such concern was primarily self-interested, as hungry cowboys might be tempted to kill a cow to satisfy their hunger, but the cowboys, especially the younger ones, often saw it in paternal terms.

Beyond providing food and clothing, some cattlemen also took a fa-therly interest in the personal lives of their hands. The *Fort Griffin Echo* reported a wedding on J. B. Carpenter's ranch in 1879 in which the ranch owner gave away the bride, acted as waiter, and loaned the groom half of the money to pay the parson. As the editor described, "it was hard to distinguish which enjoyed the affair most, the young husband or Mr. Carpenter."[84] African American cowboy Daniel Webster Wallace regularly received advice from his boss, a large rancher with holdings in Texas, Oklahoma, and Mexico, about how to build up his own herd. He helped Wallace save up money and then encouraged him to buy his own land. When the rancher died, thanks to his advice, Wallace and his wife were able to build up his own large ranch.[85] These cattlemen took care of their cowboy "families" as they took care of their own children, and provided them with father figures to emulate. Paternalistic concern was genuine in these cases, but even these benevolent relationships set the tone for how bosses were supposed to deal with "the boys." The assertion of paternalism emphasized that the cowboys required both tender care and close supervision.

Bosses were often strict fathers. When future Texas lawman Jim Gober was sixteen or seventeen, for example, he worked for a rancher who always "seemed to be interested in keeping me impressed with the fact that boys should be humble and respectful to older men." Gober bristled at the treatment but was proud to work for a Civil War hero.[86] Zeke Newman, co-founder of the Niobrara Cattle Company, was known as "Uncle Zeke" to his men, and had a reputation as a big spender as well as a big gambler. He always lent money to the cowboys when they needed it, and the men respected him as "one of the greatest men that ever was in the cattle business." In return, however, like a stern father, Newman expected absolute loyalty, "and he sure as hell got it."[87] Charles Goodnight forced all his men to sign contracts before going up the trail, promising to abide by his rules, and enforced his standards even against any men who bothered his own "boys."[88] Even ranch foremen on corporate ranches could adopt paternalistic styles of management. Both Spottswood Lomax and Fred Horsbrugh of the Spur Ranch tried to find jobs on other ranches for the hands they had to lay off, and would often lend them horses to ride to their new jobs or money to tide them over for the winter.[89]

But the use of paternalistic language and concern by the cattlemen and ranch managers was not all altruistic. Paternalism was a way for the middle class to assert authority over workers by putting them in the position of children. Bosses could thus feel justified in providing moral guidance.[90] There were also practical concerns: the ranch was primarily a workplace, and many cattlemen certainly realized that good treatment of their "boys" cemented personal loyalties that ensured they would be working on the same side. Disloyal hands were an economic drain on the ranch, as they could mistreat the cattle, do poor work in general, and perhaps even steal some of the owner's stock for themselves. But whatever the motive for the control, the fact that they did so in paternal terms asserted a gendered hierarchy in which they, as the bosses and father figures, were the men, and the hired hands were, figuratively and literally, boys. In a few cases this relationship did not change over the years. The King and Kenedy ranches maintained their *patrón* system well into the twentieth century, as did the Guerras in Starr County and the Parrs in Duval County.[91] Stephen Justus

Kleberg, manager of the King Ranch from 1977 to 1998, is still known as "Tio" Kleberg to the vaqueros, and in a foreword to a 1997 collection of *kineño* anecdotes, referred to them as "my extended family."[92] As a result, *kineños* believed that they worked *with* the Kleburgs rather than *for* them, and they gained a sense of pride in their work through the continued success of the ranch when most corporations had failed.[93]

The idea that the ranch was an extended family outside South Texas had much to do with the amount of time the owners spent working with their men. Descriptions of early cattlemen often emphasize their willingness to do their share. Charles Goodnight supposedly "never thought of himself as a boss" and always said, "Let's get the cattle to goin'," instead of "You boys get the cattle out." He would swear with the best of his men and stayed by the campfire with them.[94] Cowboy Mose Hayes remembered his former boss, Henry W. "Hank" Cresswell of the Bar CC, as "a good cowman and a good manager. He could go in and cook and go in and cut wood and brand. He had been the [first] man in and the last man out, and kept his own books and run his own outfit."[95] Other testimonials to Cresswell referred to him as "a maker of men," who exhibited all the characteristics of a good cowboy and cattleman, yet never boasted.[96] Yet even these older cattlemen were not entirely integrated with their employees. As Teddy Roosevelt noted, while the cattleman would pitch in and help when necessary, "he no longer has to undergo the monotonous drudgery attendant upon the tasks of the cowboy or of the apprentice in the business."[97] Teddy Abbott noted, "The old man never went up the trail himself—hell no, he left that to his hired hands."[98] Charles Goodnight may have slept in the cow camps, but "He seldom laughed and talked with his men. He heard much but spoke rarely. . . . [He was a] dominant man, fearing nothing." Moreover, Goodnight's partner, banker John Adair, for whom the JA Ranch was named, was never friendly with the cowboys. When he came to the ranch he acted like an aristocrat, giving the men arbitrary orders, referring to them as servants and even irritating Goodnight, who asked him to stop.[99]

It is tempting to blame the rise of corporate ranches for the de-personalization and harsher treatment of the cowboys, but the earlier cattlemen could be just as impersonal in the way they viewed their employees. While most cattlemen were not as imperious as Adair, they were all businessmen first, and the personal approach began to fall out of fashion in business by the mid-1880s. They often saw their employees as property over which they had complete control. For some black cowboys, this attitude was an

obvious holdover from slavery. Many cattlemen were former slave owners, and many black cowboys, especially in the early years of the ranching industry, were former slaves. Harrison McClure, who ran away from
his owners after Emancipation to work for George Littlefield, always referred to him as "Marse George."[100] Cattlemen thus often believed that
their black employees would be loyal in the way their slaves supposedly
had been. They often chose black cowboys to carry out sensitive missions
for them, such as guarding large sums of money while they were on the
trail. Blacks also served as right-hand men and bodyguards to the ranchers.[101] But even Anglo cowboys found that the ranchers expected similar
blind loyalty from them and believed that they "owned" them in the same
way. When Frank Collinson earned $10 for rounding up the horses of two
outlaws passing through the range, the rancher demanded he turn over
the money to him. When Collinson refused, he told him he would charge
it against his account, so he could do little else but give it to his boss.[102]
Charlie Siringo learned a similar lesson when he went to settle up at the
company store after two years of working on a big ranch. The accountant told him that while the ranch owed him $300, he owed the company
$299.25 and gave Siringo a grand total of 75 cents for his work.[103] This
story is so reminiscent of poor black sharecroppers at settling up time
with the furnishing merchant that one cannot help but draw parallels. The
cowboys obviously did not count as equal men.

Another way in which ranchers "handled" their employees was by using them as political pawns. When outside settlers purchased parcels of
school lands in the middle of a larger ranch's range, it often led to conflict
between the "nester" and the ranchers, especially over grazing and ownership of livestock. The owners therefore gave the cowboys money to buy
up school lands and build shacks on them as homesteaders. At the end
of the requisite three years, the cowboys turned over all land rights to the
ranches. In this way ranchers consolidated their holdings, but the cowboys came out of it with nothing of their own.[104]

The ranchers played similar shenanigans at election time. They ran their
men for political office or to be the local lawmen, knowing that their loyalty
would be to the ranch owner and that they could turn out more votes from
the other cowboys on the ranch in close elections.[105] In the Texas panhandle, it
was not the political parties who ran candidates but the XIT and LS ranches.
Either way, cattlemen dominated local politics. XIT ranchers ensured the
Hartley county seat would be in company town Channing rather than Hartley by rounding up illegal votes, presumably from among its workers.[106]

In West Texas the situation was no different. Hart Mussey, general manager and former owner of the Seven D Ranch in Pecos County, would invite all his Hispanic farm workers to a big dance the night before the election and then lock them in and haul them to the polls in wagons to vote for their employer's candidates.[107]

Ranchers also made use of their employees to smooth the wheels of justice. Men from the large ranches served frequently on grand and petit juries which decided on cases of infringement of property rights and thefts of cattle. Not surprisingly, very few juries convicted the ranchers of any charges. Charles Goodnight served on the grand jury of Donely County in its first years, and one of his ranch foremen served as foreman of the petit jury for at least one session of the District Court. In 1886, after a rash of failed convictions in cases of illegal fencing, mostly against ranchers like Goodnight and J. A. Brown, the grand jury decided that it would investigate the situation but would not attempt to bring any more indictments.[108] Ranchers' use of the cowboys as political pawns only furthered their beliefs that they could, and should, control them.

The rise of corporately owned ranches like the XIT or Matador in the mid-1880s certainly furthered the antagonism between cowboys and cattlemen, however. The arrival of the corporations led to increased commodification of the cowboy as just another factor in production costs. The corporate ranches kept track of their costs for feeding their employees to the penny.[109] Ranch managers on the Espuela and Matador ranches began requesting that the wagon bosses in each outfit keep strict accounting of who they gave meals to before they would reimburse them for the supplies. The Swan Ranch managers continued to feed travelers at the ranch headquarters, but insisted that only company employees receive meals at outlying camps. The ranch also instituted a coupon system so that employees who were not directly assigned to these outfits could present them in exchange for meals.[110] It had been common practice to provide a meal for anyone who arrived at the chuck wagon at dinnertime, whether or not they were ranch employees. The recipients of such meals were sometimes riders passing through on their way home or to another ranch. In most cases, those who came to the wagon were employees of neighboring ranches who were there for the annual roundup. As profits in the cattle industry declined in the late 1880s, the cattle syndicates begrudged such extra expenses and saw the cowboys as freeloaders. Such practices as these broke the more paternal bonds between employer and employee that had existed in the open range period while challenging egalitarian social mores that had been present on the frontier, as an ideal, if not in reality.

Many of the investment corporations that ran the large ranches were foreign-owned, which led to a system of absentee owners and professional ranch managers. The companies hired these new managers primarily for their business abilities or their knowledge of cattle breeding, not for their cowboy skills, and in fact most of them had not done cowboy work before. The transition was not always smooth, as exemplified by the changing managers of the Matador Ranch in the Panhandle. Cattleman H. H. Campbell started his career as a trail driver and, like Charles Goodnight, found a financial backer, in this case A. M. Britton, to jointly establish the Panhandle Matador Ranch, which they sold to a British syndicate in 1882. Campbell stayed on as manager but increasingly faced corporate restrictions in his duties. The corporately appointed assistant manager, William Sommerville, ended up bossing Campbell around as it was his duty to pass on the directives from corporate headquarters to the manager. Campbell soon found he no longer had complete freedom to run the business as he had under Britton. He had to write regular reports of all his expenditures and gain approval for any purchase over $500, which significantly hampered his ability to buy cattle. When Campbell became too busy to keep up with his reports, the board of directors severely chastised him. While he ultimately settled into the routine, the board never was entirely happy with him, and in 1890 they asked for his resignation.[111] Campbell's successor as manager, Murdo Mackenzie, came to the Matador Ranch in 1891 after working with the Prairie Cattle Company near Tascosa, but despite his knowledge in running the ranch he "did little work in the saddle" and made a poor cowboy.[112] Nonetheless, Mackenzie thought he knew what was best for the ranch and instated a new set of rules regulating the men and bringing the Matador up to what he considered scientific standards. As a result, he soon reported facing threats on his life from the men, especially from the previous foreman who had worked under Campbell.[113] Hostility against the corporate owners and managers was common, if not always this open.

On the XIT Ranch a similar process of increased bureaucratization occurred. B. H. "Barbecue" Campbell (no relation to H. H.), the ranch's first manager from 1885 to 1888, was a well-known rancher and breeder from Kansas. Unlike his namesake at the Matador, however, B. H. actually came under fire for sending too many long-winded reports to corporate headquarters.[114] But Campbell was far from a corporate bean counter, and in fact ran such a loose ship that rustlers and cowboys alike took advantage of him to steal XIT cattle. An outside investigation showed that Campbell had, knowingly or not, hired outlaws as his employees and that in general his business practices were unsound. In 1888, the XIT board of directors replaced Campbell with A. G. Boyce, whose main concern was maintaining law and order on the ranch and driving off cattle thieves.[115] Boyce, while a former trail boss, came from a strict Methodist background and it was he who instated the infamous set of twenty-three rules governing his employees' behavior. As former XIT cowboy S. A. Bull noted, Boyce "made a good many enemies among the tougher men."[116]

Many of the new managers, like Mackenzie, had difficulty relating to the cowboys. B. B. Groom, the manager of the Diamond F Ranch, "was a pompous Kentucky colonel who treated the cowboys as if they were stableboys."[117] Spottswood Lomax, manager of the Spur Ranch from 1885 to 1889, was a "polished gentleman, well-educated and widely traveled," but had no real ranch experience, and "had a way of unconsciously causing the people around him to feel inferior."[118] His successor, Fred Horsbrugh, while less formal than Lomax, had attended Edinburgh Academy and Saint Andrews University in Scotland. He worked on a stock farm in Iowa, but got his job through friends in London who had helped organize the Espuela Land and Cattle Company, of which the Spur was part. Both Lomax and Horsbrugh had the respect of the men who worked for them, but largely because they took a paternal approach to them, which may have been more a case of *noblesse oblige* in Lomax's case.[119] The investors in the XIT Ranch had little intention of becoming cowboys themselves, although the son of one of them did visit the ranch to get good horses to use as polo ponies back East.[120] The corporate managers were primarily supervisors rather than fellow employees, and the lack of personal relationships between cowboys and cattlemen contributed to the growing antagonism.

Most of the investors who operated ranches in the Panhandle by the mid-1880s, such as the Clarendon Land and Investment Agency or the Francklyn Land and Cattle Company, were more interested in the eventual disposition of the land than the cattle, and so did not concern themselves with the cowboys, who became just another entry in the account books.[121] On the Bar X Ranch, which employed between seventy-five and one hundred cowboys, the manager supervised the ranch from a buggy. He did not know his men personally and on one occasion berated an employee of the Turkey Track Ranch, thinking he worked for the Bar X.[122] In fact, ranch owners increasingly became an annoyance to the hands rather than people they looked up to. In 1889, John McNab, one of the English directors of the Espuela Ranch, visited Texas and wanted to go out with the hands on a roundup. He insisted on walking rather than riding, and wore his business suit, bowler hat, and carried an umbrella to shade him from the sun. When the cattle became skittish as a result, one of the hands took on the responsibility of shepherding him around. The cowboys eventually became fond of McNab, and, in a great role reversal, on subsequent visits it was they who took on the paternal role and looked out for him when he wandered off. Such interactions could only reinforce any anxieties the foreign cattlemen might have had about their masculinity in comparison to that of the cowboys. Most other visitors to the ranch went around in the buggy, however, and avoided any interaction with the working men.[123]

Investors discussed at length the qualities of a good ranch manager, which they saw as vital to the success of the operation. Such men were seemingly hard to find. Isaac Ellwood of the Frying Pan Ranch tried to find a manager "who knows something of land and water problems, can make a good bargain in cattle sales and is able to manage cowhands." His business partner, Henry Sanborn, said that he could not expect to find such a creature and should only ask for an honest man who could get on with the men. A good manager could demand much of his employer. Ellwood chose J. R. Norfleet as his manager for the Spade Ranch but had to concede him the right to run his own cattle along with those of the ranch; he was forever concerned that Norfleet would not maintain the ranch cattle as well as his own.[124]

In the context of the late nineteenth century, the South Texas ranches seemed even more exceptional in maintaining the paternalistic style, but in reality these relationships were never truly static. Even when ranches stayed in the family, the second generation of cattlemen were often much closer to their corporate counterparts than to the cowboys. While Richard King was as rough and ready as some of his men, his successors were of a different kind. His son-in-law, Robert J. Kleberg II, was a lawyer by training and inclination and when he arrived at the ranch was neither a stockman nor a rider. The *kineños* always referred to him as *El Abogao* ("The Lawyer") whether or not they did so fondly, as King Ranch historian Tom Lea implied. Kleberg's nephew Caesar came to help run the ranch in 1900 after serving two years in Washington, D.C. as secretary to his father, Congressman Rudolph Kleberg. As Lea describes it, when Caesar first arrived, his "ignorance of ranching was extensive," although he eventually learned the business.[125] As one of the old time King Ranch hands told Frank Goodwyn's father: "If you want to make a cowboy out of a kid, put him in the *corrida* as soon as he's big enough to sit on a horse. . . . If you wait till he's in his teens, you might make him into a cowman, but never a cowboy."[126] For the Klebergs, ranching was a business like any other—it was just a matter of learning the specifics, rather than having any special affinity for it. The second generation of Kenedys also approached ranching from a modern perspective. John G. Kenedy, Mifflin's son, went to college in Mobile, Alabama and then worked for four years at a banking and commission house in New Orleans, before returning to take charge of his father's ranch using the business methods he had learned.[127] Increasingly the men running the ranch were less likely to work alongside the cowboys, which led to a distancing between them and changing attitudes on both sides.

The view of cowboys as children in the minds of ranch operators became stronger in the 1880s and 1890s. Without the personal connection, moreover, firm control became more important than tender care. Frank Hastings, who grew up in the cattle breeding business and became the manager of the SMS Ranch, viewed the cowboys as common laborers, describing them as "children of nature." He reported that the cowboys followed him around in unfamiliar situations like children. When he took his hands with him to restaurants at fancy hotels, he always ordered for himself what he thought they would like to eat, so they could simply order the same and save themselves any embarrassment. When they teased him about not being a real cowboy, he would challenge them to wrestle by "official rules," believing that no cowboy would take him up for fear of showing his ignorance of them.[128] To Hastings and others like him, the cowboy needed reining in and strict guidance. The model of paternalism that evolved on the SMS Ranch and other large spreads in the 1880s was a stern one, in which cowboys were no longer good sons, but misbehaving ruffians, and rather simple-minded ones at that.

The image of cowboys among the general public also began to deteriorate in this period. Residents of Stephens County complained about the annual roundups, saying that they damaged the livestock and provided too many opportunities for stealing unmarked cattle. Their complaint reflected hostility against the large ranches as much as the cowboys, but they associated the men with the ranches and assumed that dishonesty was a common trait among them.[129] Accusations of theft on the trail were common, especially from farmers whose lands the trails cut through. It was normal practice to round up strays along the trail, and, ideally, return them to their owners at the railhead. However, more often these strays ended up as meals for the trail drivers, as it was common cowboy wisdom that the beef that came from someone else's brand always tasted better. Cattle associations registered trail brands and provided regional inspectors to make sure that the cowboys were not stealing from other ranches. Inspectors who found strays in among trail herds would telegraph ahead to the West Kansas Cattle Association to warn them to look out for more when the herd came into Dodge City.[130] In general, however, the stock associations tended to represent the interests of the large ranchers over the smaller ones. In 1888, in an article on the methods of the "Irrepressible" cowboy, the *San Antonio Daily Light* blamed the early cattle kings for being too lenient on the cowboys while they were building up their fortunes. Without much supervision, the editor argued, cowboys had gained the bad habits of trampling farmland and poaching brands, and in the wake of the blizzards he predicted the ultimate failure of big ranches in favor of farmers and small ranchers.[131] Ironically, the larger ranches and cattlemen actually placed the most constraints on their cowboys.

On the corporate and larger ranches, cowboys became objects of condescension at best and suspicion at worst. One of the early issues of conflict between cowboys and cattlemen was whether or not cowboys could own cattle on the ranch. To the cowboys, the issue was an important one. Without their own herd it was not possible for them to become ranchers themselves or move beyond being hired hands. Cowboys believed they had as much of a right to the mavericks and unbranded calves they found on the range as did the ranchers. But those who owned cattle often could not find jobs on the larger ranches, as the ranchers assumed they would put their own brand on mavericks instead of the ranch's brand. As a result, many cowboys had a friend register their brands for them.[132] Cowboys looked up to early cattlemen T. S. Bugbee, Granville Stuart, and Hank Cresswell, as they encouraged their men to build up their own herds so they would have somewhere to invest their money rather than just spending it in town.[133] These ranchers were exceptions, however. More typical were the actions of cattleman Tom Adair. While chastising one of his hands whom he had caught putting his own brand on a calf, Adair told him to "remember that . . . hereafter . . . you're a cowpuncher 'stid of a cow m[a]n."[134] The implication of the remark is clear: there was a definite distinction between the men and the cow*boys* and a clear presumption that the cattleman was much higher in status. By the 1880s, most

Cattlemen formed stockraisers' associations in large part to prevent cattle rustling. They appointed leading members as well as lawmen to serve as brand inspectors. More often than not they suspected their employees were the main culprits. Veteran brand inspectors of the Texas and Southwestern Cattle Raisers Association and a captain of Texas Rangers. N. H. Sweeney, Lem Chesher, Red Hawkins, Charles Burwell, Captain Tom R. Hickman, Company B, Texas Rangers; W. L. (Lod) Calohan, Fount, 1914–1920s. LC-S6-212, Erwin E. Smith Collection of the Library of Congress on deposit at the Amon Carter Museum, Fort Worth, Texas.

ranchers refused to let the cowboys run their own brands, believing they were stealing from the ranch whenever possible.

When accidents happened, the managers tended to blame the cowboys, in much the same way mine owners blamed the miners for losing them profits. When S. C. Parker was killed when his horse fell, ranch foreman J. R. Norfleet implied it was his own fault. Despite the fact that the horse had also thrown Norfleet in the past, he closed his report of the accident to the ranch manager by commenting "he never was cautious."[135] To add insult to injury, Norfleet paid for Parker's burial expenses but reimbursed himself from the man's wages and then sold his gear to pay for remaining costs.[136] George Tyng, the manager of the Diamond F Ranch, part of the Francklyn Land and Cattle Company holdings, was frequently dismissive of the cowboys who worked on the ranch. He assigned them to put up a windmill but reported "it is ludicrously irritating to put men at mechanical work and to see them trying to do it *with their spurs on*."[137] Tyng could barely hide his scorn for the men, whom he viewed as simple rubes. With seeming paternal concern he encouraged some of them to plant oats on a plot of land that he had been unable to rent, and lent the men the money, tools, and seed to do so. He also showed them how to make the correct farm implements "to their unfeigned admiration." He admitted his true reasons for his generosity to his employer as being both a way to stop weeds from growing on cleared land and "to have them conduct a place at which I could feed and at the same time escape the tax of compulsory hospitality."[138] In other words, he had killed two birds with one stone, making the cowboys think he was helping them and paying lip service to frontier traditions without actually having to do anything himself.

The managers saw the cowboys as opponents as much as employees. Despite his paternal attitude and easygoing reputation, Fred Horsbrugh reported to his employer, "I have found that as a rule one cannot depend on the ordinary cow-hand. This kind of man is peculiar. He will work faithfully and look after his employer's interests in various ways, but his manner of doing this is also peculiar, and he will frequently ride a long way round to prevent seeing what might be inconvenient."[139] Seemingly unsurprised, XIT foreman R. M. Bassett reported that he had found two missing horses that two former XIT cowboys had ridden in to town "in fair condition. Except sore backs."[140] The XIT owners in particular felt the need to closely supervise their men. Colonel Abner Taylor proposed placing "some good men on the Ranch who were not identified with the Cow Boys, . . . and [who] would take our side in any controversy."[141] He also told his manager that the men he sent should just earn board until they were able to do the work, implying that skill was less important than loyalty to the company.[142] When he did not receive regular enough reports on the ranch operations, Taylor even threatened to send a man to keep an eye on his ranch manager.[143]

As worker loyalty became more important than skill, and as unskilled labor was on the rise in the rest of the country, it was inevitable that the ranchers would try to turn cowboy work into unskilled labor. One step in this direction was to install branding chutes, as they did on the XIT Ranch, eliminating the need to rope and throw cattle, taking much of the skill out of the job, and hence, dampening the cowboys' pride in their work. The T-Anchor Ranch manager reported good results from their new branding chutes, which were "a great improvement on last year, be-ing a saving on both men and horses beside being less hard on the cows which do not have to be roped at all as in the old style."[144] Removing the skill from the job meant that it was much easier to replace independent cowboys with more compliant workers. The changing nature of the work did not go unnoticed. Charlie Siringo commented in 1886 that "now-a-days it requires more rough and tumble hard work than skill to command good wages," and the result of breeding shorthorns and tamer cattle was that "it requires but very little skill and knowledge to be a cow boy."[145] Echoing racist attitudes of the day but reinforcing Siringo's comments, B. A. Borroum remarked that outfits in the 1880s were not as skilled as ear-lier outfits, as they only hired "one good white man for a boss, one or two hands, and the rest Negroes and Mexicans," implying that the workers were largely unskilled.[146]

It is little wonder that ranch owners and their friends in England and out East regularly foisted off job seekers on the ranch managers regardless of their skill. In 1883, for example, W. F. Sommerville met two young men who wanted to be cowboys on the train on his way from New York to in-spect the Matador Ranch; he sent them to H. H. Campbell for a job in ex-change for board until they proved themselves. This was not the first nor the last time he would do so.[147] In contrast with earlier parents' fears that cowboy life would prove the ruin of young men, increased regulation now recommended the job to parents seeking discipline for their boys. Hors-brugh took on a young gentleman of a "Bohemian nature" on the urgings of his grandmother "because I think the experience and discipline that he will pass through may prove the best means of developing him into . . . a useful man. . . . While I should be very sorry to believe that he would be content to rise no higher than a cow-boy's position, yet I hope he will do his duty so faithfully and manfully . . . that he will soon [attain] a position more in keeping with his natural ability and birth as a gentleman."[148]

Thus, it was not surprising that the cattlemen began to doubt the skill of their hired hands. As the cattle industry became less profitable, ranch-ers wanted their herds processed quickly, but doing so meant it was not possible to handle the livestock with as much care as they could at a slower pace. As a result, ranchers regularly complained about cowboys' rough handling of the cattle. Teddy Roosevelt reported that professional bronco busters were especially harsh as they got paid for each horse they broke and only had a short time in which to do it. As a result they re-lied on violent measures and many ranchers preferred to have their own hands break the horses rather than bring in the specialist, because he was too rough.[149] The Young County Cattleraisers Association met in 1885 for the sole purpose of addressing the matter. Concluding that the cowboys cared more about display of skills than the actual cattle, they resolved to instruct the cowboys to be more careful and to require their wagon bosses to enforce these instructions.[150] Colorado cattlemen discussed the necessity of "preventing unnecessary cruelty and rough usage to which cattle on the range are subjected by the ordinary cowboy."[151] The *Texas Livestock Journal*, which catered to the cattleman rather than the cowboy, printed regular complaints of rough handling. One experienced trail boss reported seeing cowboys drive their cattle at seven miles an hour for twenty or thirty miles in order to complete their work early. As a result, he said, 75 percent of the trail cattle were lame. His solution was to maintain closer control over the cowboys on the job. He concluded, "There is as much in a boss knowing how to handle men as there is in knowing how to handle cattle."[152]

Many people believed that Mexicans were especially harsh on cattle. Joseph McCoy reported that Mexicans were worse than Indians in that Mexicans "will not drive any other way than in a rush, and have no more feeling for dumb brutes . . . than they have for a store. Their heartless cruelty is proverbial" and unless their bosses watched them very closely they would abuse the animals terribly.[153] Employers charged that South Texas vaqueros were "rough, abusive, and unfeeling in their treatment of stock, and personally untrustworthy."[154] Sam Ragland, who became chief foreman of the King Ranch in 1892, convinced ranch manager Robert Kleberg that the rawhide whips the vaqueros had traditionally used handling cattle harmed the livestock. Kleberg ordered all his men to bring their whips to him and he personally cut up each one with his pocketknife.[155]

Cowboys themselves did not deny they were harsh on cattle. As John Young, a South Texas cowboy, recalled: "That cowhunt was no place for members of the Humane Society." According to this narrative it was common to subdue the cattle by shooting them through the horn or by "tailing" them, a procedure which involved wrapping the cow's tail around their saddle horns and twisting the horse to one side until the cow fell down. Young recalled one time after he had been chased by a steer and needed to prove his mettle to the other cowboys. He tailed the steer, standing it on its head and breaking one of its horns in the process. The horn dangled along the steer's jaw as he walked back to the herd and "the cheers I got were enough to turn the head of any sixteen-year-old boy."[156]

A cowboy might subdue a bronco by "earing it down," or biting his ear; or by roping it around the neck to "choke it down."[157]

But conditions on the ranches often made it difficult to take better care of animals. Ranch managers gave the wilder horses to those cowboys they considered reckless to minimize any damage they might do by riding too fast or hard.[158] It was necessary to take more risks to ride such horses, which could hamper the cowboys' ability to do their jobs properly. In addition, what seemed to many ranch owners to be reckless riding was, in fact, often safer. Former cowboy C. P. Benedict argued that given conditions during stampedes it was better to let the horse have control and to run fast, as it was less likely to fall into prairie dog holes or run into bushes in the cedar brakes.[159] Charlie Siringo wrote a long harangue about inexperienced or foolish would-be cowboys who abused their horses, saying that many real cowboys would quit rather than ride a sore-backed horse.[160] The implication was clear—good cowboys, and good men, protected their horses. Clearly, some of the abuse was avoidable, but much of it was not, as demands for greater efficiency and speed increased at the same time as the ranches started emphasizing loyalty over skill in their hiring practices.

Seeing the cowboys as potentially dangerous employees, the cattlemen felt justified in policing their behavior on the ranch. Like the paternalistic ranchers, corporate ranches like the XIT or Espuela instated rules limiting the men's drinking, gambling, and gunplay. The XIT had the most infamous set of rules, twenty-three of them to be precise, including the usual provisions against gambling and drinking, but also forbidding them from carrying six shooters and bowie knives, keeping private horses in camp, or feeding their own horses with company grain. Cowboys could not own any cattle; kill any cattle for beef without permission; abuse cattle, horses, or mules; hunt game without permission; or tear down a copy of the posted rules. Any violation was grounds for dismissal.[161] Rules like these showed the cattlemen's need to impose appropriate moral behavior in the workplace, but the systematic nature of the rules and the bureaucratic way in which the ranches enforced them was different from the way cattlemen had looked out for their employees in the early ranch days. While Charles Goodnight certainly had material motivations to his attempts to improve his men's lives, and took a paternalistic tone toward them, he still respected their abilities and saw them as individuals. The new impression of the cowboy was that he was an obdurate child who, left uncontrolled, would either steal the livestock or destroy it through his carelessness.

Cowboys who came out West in the 1890s found the work did not meet their expectations. W. H. Thomas grew up on a stock farm and longed to see the "real" West. He envisioned "thousands of cattle grazing on a limitless, fenceless range," but when he first got to Texas, he just found himself on another fenced stock farm.[162] C. M. Crenshaw went to work on a large ranch in Oklahoma Territory around 1890. "I didn't like this way of being a cowpok[e]. seemed to me we were just cogs in a machine because we had a set job to do and nothing else."[163] The nature of cowboy work itself had changed tremendously since the era of the open range. Cowboys were now just as likely to dig fence post holes and bale hay as they were to ride the range. The cattlemen who survived the Great Die Ups and droughts of the 1880s and 1890s had to adjust to industrial society to stay competitive. Indeed, they depended even less on range grazing than before, and grew alfalfa, milo, kaffir corn, and sorghum to feed their livestock. Cowboys thus became part-time farmers.[164] Where it had once required five men for each 800 to 1,000 head of cattle on the larger ranches in the days of the Texas Longhorn and open range, in the era of the tamer shorthorn cattle and wire fences, the ranches only needed one man for the same amount of cattle.[165] Workers now were split into specialized teams for construction, fence mending, and the roundup. Cowboys spent less time overall with the cattle. Moreover, there were fewer chances for cowboys to become ranchers themselves, and the cowboy had become, essentially, a casual wage laborer working for an impersonal business.[166]

But despite their best efforts, cattlemen were never able to completely reduce cowboys to unskilled laborers. They were able to impose a hierarchical management structure, but when it came to actually handling cattle they could not have complete specialization of labor as in a factory, since most cowboys did roping, riding, and branding all at once. Given the cowboys' reticence, they often hired outside labor for the farming jobs. While it was possible to set schedules for cowboys to try to use scientific management techniques pioneered by Frederick Taylor in the factories, it was not possible to make the animals they cared for work on a schedule.[167] Certain traditional skills, such as cattle spaying, were always in demand. Moreover, cowboy skills evolved to include some of the more scientific knowledge the owners wanted. Ironically, control was easier under older paternalistic systems. On the South Texas ranches where the *patrón* system prevailed, the ranches remained total institutions with control over every aspect of their employees' lives from birth to death well into the twentieth century.[168] The work also became the most specialized on these ranches

with different crews to do cow work and fence work. By the early twentieth century on the King Ranch, at branding time an *aventador* roped the
calf, a *tumbadore* threw it to the ground, a *marcador* ran the brand, an
*atolero* rubbed salve on the new brand, and a *capador* castrated the animal.[169] While most ranches never achieved such control, from the 1880s
on, most cattlemen tried to regulate their cowboys' work habits closely.

To the cowboys, who believed control over their own actions and skill
in their craft were the most important aspects of their masculine identity,
such regulation was a direct challenge to their masculinity. Cowboys thus
found a number of ways to resist or deflect the attempts to control them.
A common form of resistance was insubordination. During the roundups,
cowboys frequently shirked their duties to report back to their bosses.[170]
Cowboys refused to work if the risk was too high or there were too few
workers or horses to do the job, and could intimidate their bosses if they
went too far.[171] Jim Gober generally defended his employers' interests, but
if he felt hard done by he was not above re-branding ranch cattle with his
own brand.[172] In truth, many cowboys branded their own cattle when they
thought they could get away with it. One Pecos informant recalled that he
could count on one hand "all the men . . . that never branded anything
but what they knew was theirs and probably have a finger or too left." One
cowboy commented that as long as "the old man did not get his cow book
he would be all wright, but if he gets that I am gone," implying that quite
a few cattle never made it into the official books.[173]

Another option was petty sabotage. In early 1879, a series of maliciously
set prairie fires prompted the *Fort Griffin Echo* to specifically advise the
stockmen to prosecute the perpetrators to the full extent to make an example of responsible parties to "benefit the whole community."[174] Whether
it was cowboys setting these fires or not is uncertain, but vandalism was
not beyond the realm of possibility. Arson was common on the Rocking
Chair Ranch, where co-manager and owner's son Baron Archibald John
Marjoribanks regularly faced intimidation from his men and co-manager,
John Drew. Drew, who had sold the ranch its first herd, allegedly stole it
back bit by bit and encouraged Archie to believe that it was the neighbors who were stealing from the ranch, not him.[175] When Teddy Abbott
worked on the FUF Ranch, the owner forbade them from killing cattle for
beef but only gave them rotten pork to eat. So the men killed a cow and
hid it when the owner came around. Abbott recalled that when the ranch
gave the men bad horses to ride, "there's ways of getting rid of a horse you
don't like," such as when his horse "accidentally" reared up while still tied

to the corral pole, breaking its leg so they had to shoot him.[176] As John Young recalled, "Old time cowhands with a bad temper . . . or a craving for fresh meat, sometimes broke an animal's neck [while roping them] 'accidentally on purpose.'"[177] William Lewis's foreman resented the way the XIT employers refused to participate in roundups, so whenever they saw an XIT calf on the trail, he made a point of killing it for food. "On no other part of the drive did the men enjoy the luxury of so much beef."[178]

Such daily resistance was far from organized, however. Cowboys were known for independent behavior, so the phenomenon of coordinated resistance is somewhat counter to most popular stereotypes, although given the loyalty and friendships cowboys shared, it should not have been surprising. There was no cowboy union and no permanent structure for carrying out strikes, so when they occurred they were most likely on an ad hoc basis and usually unsuccessful. When a cowboy outfit on the Bosque Grande Ranch struck against John Chisum for higher wages, Chisum's response was to pay them all off and let them go. He told the men, "This suits me fine. I need a rest. Just remember that you have struck so you won't get any more grub around here." The only man Chisum kept on was the cook, who had not struck, but the cowboys took offense and tied the latter up and branded him before leaving the ranch.[179] Cowboys struck against rancher John Clay at the roundup in 1884, asking for higher wages and refusing to take the herd to market without them. While the ranch manager wanted Clay to compromise, Clay refused to give in and got his herd to market by using his hay crew as trail drivers along with the few loyal hands who had not quit.[180] In June 1887, a Matador outfit struck for higher wages while still on the trail. The trail boss's solution was to fire two men and give the rest the wages they asked for as "to go through with six men with $5.00 raises will be cheaper than eight men at the rates at start."[181] Of course, the remaining men then had to do the work of the men that he fired in addition to their own, which essentially negated their pay raise. Wildcat strikes such as this one were probably more common than recorded, but usually had similar results.

The most documented strike occurred in the Panhandle in 1883. The official account of the strike in the Federal Bureau of Labor Statistics reported that it involved 325 cowboys, lasted for twelve days from March 23 to April 24, and affected seven ranches. However, these data are likely inaccurate.[182] Most accounts agree the strike involved the men on five ranches: the LIT, T-Anchor, LE, LS, and LX ranches, all of which were controlled by corporate investors or large entrepreneurs. On these ranches there was little contact between the owners and cowboys, so there was little personal loyalty among the men except to each other. A local sheriff cited the superior attitude of the cattlemen, referring to cowboys as "cow servants," as one of the causes of the strike. In February and March 1883, floating outfits from the LIT, LS, and LX ranches under the leadership of Tom Harris met and wrote an ultimatum to the ranches asking for a raise in pay to $50 per month for a regular hand and $75 for range bosses. The twenty-four cowboys who signed the ultimatum were mostly permanent hands, but Harris recruited other cowboys throughout the Panhandle. Estimates of numbers of participants vary from 25 to 325 but numbers fluctuated over the course of the strike. Unfortunately for the cowboys involved, there was a labor surplus in the 1880s, and most ranchers just hired more men to do the job or offered a slight increase in wages, firing those who did not accept it. While there were rumors of violence on both sides, and the ranchers asked the Texas Rangers to come in, the strike simply faded without incident after about two and a half months, although one sheriff reported that the strike still continued in 1884.[183] The Bureau of Labor Statistics reported, however, that the strike resulted in a wage increase of 50 cents a day, the strikers were paid for lost time, and no one was fired for their actions![184]

In the wake of the strike, cattle rustling increased, likely from disgruntled cowboys, and in 1884, the LS Ranch brought in Pat Garrett, the lawman who had captured Billy the Kid, as head of a unit of Texas Rangers, to round up all cattle on the ranch and to identify illegal cowboy brands.[185] Garrett and his men, presumably on the trail of rustlers, also tracked some of the former strikers to a prostitute's house where they were hiding out, and the resulting confrontation ended in a shootout.[186] The men of Charles Goodnight's JA Ranch did not participate in the strike, perhaps in part because he ran such a tight ship. While Goodnight had little respect for the cattlemen who faced the strike, he had no patience for strikers, either. According to his friend and biographer, Laura Hamner, "He felt slight sympathy for the ranchers who laughed at his stringent methods and had let the hoodlum element prevail. All they needed was a little discipline, he declared."[187] At least one observer said the strike failed because the cowboys were idle in town and could not stop spending their money.[188]

Cowboy historian J. Frank Dobie has argued that cowboys did not see themselves as part of any broader "laboring class" but as aristocrats among wage earners.[189] Indeed, Anglo cowboys earned more than the average American male unskilled worker in the 1880s and got room and board as well, so many of them continued working regardless of the treatment they received from their bosses.[190] However, their salaries were still only one-fourth that of most skilled industrial workers, and at least some cowboys had a clear understanding of labor/management relations and unionization.[191] In the years 1884–1887, many cowboys joined the Knights of Labor, the first large-scale union in the United States. Indeed, "Big" Bill Haywood, future leader of the International Workers of the World, a radical labor organization that promoted worker ownership of factories, got his start as a cowboy.[192] John H. Sullivan, a former cowboy turned Wild West show performer, tried to organize cowboys to join the Knights of Labor in 1886 and gave long speeches denouncing capitalists to his audiences.[193] Cowboy songs also reflected resentment of their situation. In "The Old Chisholm Trail" a cowpuncher relates:

> I went to the boss to draw my roll,
> He had it figgered out I was nine dollars in the hole.
> I'll sell my outfit just as soon as I can
> I won't punch cattle for no damned man.[194]

Still, despite awareness and resentment of their situation, cowboys had little power to change it. About the only thing the cowboys could have total control over was when and where they worked, and many clung to this level of independence as job supervision increased. Teddy Abbott said that the best job for a cowboy was one that allowed him the freedom to work on his own, which is why he enjoyed being a representative for the ranch at the roundups. As a "rep," he could go for months without seeing his boss. He admitted that "at worst there never was very much bossing done around a cow outfit," but "any at all was too much to suit the average cowpuncher."[195] Charlie Siringo echoed these sentiments and worked best alone or as a boss. Like many cowboys, he frequently left a ranch when the owners got too bossy.[196] A large portion of the workforce on many ranches was transient. On the Spur Ranch, 64 percent of the hands worked one season or less, and only 20 percent completed a second season of work.[197] The age of the cowboys often contributed to the low retention rate. Many, like Carl Wilson, moved from job to job looking for new experiences: "Like many other young fellows I was restless and I wanted to see what was on the other side of the hill."[198] W. M. Prece preferred trail drives to riding the range, and H. P. Walker kept quitting ranches when he realized they did not offer the romantic life of the cowboy he had envisioned.[199] In just his first eighteen months as a cowboy, Jim Gober worked at two ranches and took his first trail drive to Dodge City.[200]

Wanderlust was a common characteristic among the cowboys. Although Lee Knight generally worked near his family home in Lampasas County, he changed ranches frequently in his first years as a cowboy and took herds up the trail to Dodge City; Cheyenne, Wyoming; and Ogallala, Nebraska. Between 1874 and 1905, E. K. Stuckler, who had joined up with a trail outfit "in a spirit of adventure," worked with the Circle Dot Horse Ranch, John D. Jenkins' cow outfit, the LR Ranch, the Halff Brothers, another outfit at Horsehead Crossing, the 7D outfit, Billy Young's Diamond outfit, the AL Ranch, and finally the U Ranch, where he became manager until 1920.[201] Cowboys could also be capricious in their choice of jobs. Teddy Abbott once hired on with a buddy to take a herd from Oregon to Wyoming, but heard from someone that the weather in Oregon was bad and wet, so he and his buddy quit even before they started the trip and went to New Mexico instead.[202] There were exceptions, of course. Jake Raines worked on the Spur Ranch from 1885 to 1909 as a regular hand, ranch rep, trail boss, fence builder, and odd jobs man. He stayed on the ranch after the Swenson Brothers bought out the Espuela, and was still there in 1931. *Kineños* also stayed on the King Ranch for generations. But these were certainly exceptions. Cowboys valued independence and freedom more than loyalty to any job.

By the late 1880s, cowboys began to lose even what little power they had to move from job to job. Employment was uncertain and there was a surplus of workers. The XIT regularly laid off men who did not meet their standards or who did not behave appropriately. The ranch foreman reported that there were many "cut backs" for the XIT hanging around in town and equal numbers of men "anxious for their positions."[203] Cowboys who had scorned work that was not on horseback were reduced to seeking work of any kind. In 1888, W. Jones sought work on the Matador, writing: "I am now a Cow Boy but claim that I can do as much as any one such as farm work making fence."[204] Jones's wording implies that the general impression of cowboys was that they were useless for any other kind of work, a further indication of their lower status. In 1895, James W. Robison applied for a job on the Spur Ranch, saying that when the new owner took over his old ranch he fired all the hands and started fresh.[205] The uncertainties of employment and the lack of available jobs meant that by the 1890s, cowboys no longer had complete freedom. Even on the King

Ranch, where vaqueros were part of an extended ranch family, they could do little to resist changes. When Kleberg cut up the rawhide whips of his men, one old vaquero refused to stop using one. When the foreman told him he would have to leave, he appealed first to Kleberg and then to the widowed Henrietta King herself. King made sure he did not have to leave the ranch, but Kleberg and Ragland also insisted that the only way he could stay was if he gave up his whip, which he ultimately did.[206]

Historians have suggested that freedom for the cowboys was always a myth. They relieved the boredom of the range by going up the trail and escaped the monotony of the trail by letting loose in the cow towns, but neither action was genuine freedom.[207] They grew up expecting to be taming the frontier like their fathers, but the West they experienced was "a region of narrowing limits, where dwindling resources were pulled beyond their reach or kept firmly in the grasp of others."[208] In the end, cowboys were simply employees and lost what independence they had in the same way workers across America lost theirs in industrial America.

One condescending English observer believed that few cowboys had any aspirations at all beyond being the "boss cowboy, and never to be beaten at anything pertaining to his profession."[209] Whether this observation was true or simply reflected a lack of opportunity, very few cowboys went on to become cattlemen themselves, although quite a few ended up as farmers and ran small herds. Ironically, African American cowboys were most likely to get out quicker and buy their own ranches and herds, perhaps in part as they had fewer opportunities to spend their money in town, but largely because they did not wait around for possible promotion, and realized from the start they would never become bosses except on their own spreads.[210] Many cowboys ended up working in town, hoping to settle down and get married. Convinced he would never get a respectable woman to look at him otherwise, Bruce Sibert's idea of a good job was one where he could wear clean clothes and not smell like cattle all the time.[211] Other cowboys went on to become sheriffs or other types of law enforcement officers, positions which afforded some authority but also freedom to pursue criminals in their own way.[212] Still, even these positions did not always suit them. Ira Kutch applied to work on a ranch in 1898 with the explanation that "while I am A candidate for the office of Sheriff and Tax collector of this county this Business don't suite me as much as working cattle."[213]

If cowboys defined their masculinity in part through their work, it is clear that the cattlemen's attempts to restrain them at work challenged their sense of their own manhood. Cowboys saw competence, self-confidence, and autonomy as signs of a true cowboy and a true man. Competence involved skills as well as dedication to the work. Men who complained or could not stick with the herd through rain and stampedes were not worth knowing and could endanger the other men in some situations. Self-confidence implied a steady nerve in the face of dangerous conditions and a willingness to take risks to do what was necessary, but also to accept the consequences, and the wisdom to know which risks were irresponsible. Autonomy was perhaps most important to these men, especially the ability to decide how, when, and where they would work. If the cowboy could not achieve middle-class respectability through marriage to a good woman, property ownership, or independent wealth, he could at least control his working conditions.

Cattlemen and corporate investors, however, did not see cowboys as independent men, nor was it in their interests to do so. Cowboys were their employees, and whether they treated them as their children or as entries in a ledger, they expected loyalty and obedience from them. As they attempted to bring order to the frontier, they believed that it was more manly to restrain "maverick" behavior, and saw the cowboys as a throwback to an older, more primitive model of manhood. Cattlemen had always regulated the men on their ranches, but the paternalism of the early ranching industry evolved into a more systematic and less personal system of regulations as the owners and employees came into less frequent contact and came from increasingly different backgrounds. Cattlemen saw the cowboys' risk-taking behavior as reckless, and sought to limit it and to more closely supervise their working habits. Worried that the cowboys were antagonistic to their interests (as were workers to factory owners elsewhere in the country), cattlemen sought to replace them with loyal workers and to make the work less dependent on skill. Ultimately, competence mattered less to the owners than obedience. Thus, the regulations they sought to impose and the "improvements" they made to the ranches, such as adding branding chutes, while intended primarily to control an unruly workforce, fundamentally limited their chance to show their manhood. Workers had little power to resist and so more frequently looked to their leisure time to prove their manliness.

# PART II

# Having Fun

# 4

# A Society of Men

Texas ranch life in the late nineteenth century was predominantly an all-male environment that was at the same time both appealing and out of step with modern society. Both cowboys and cattlemen were influenced by this context, but cattlemen looked outside the ranch for affirmation of their manhood, while cowboys looked mainly to each other. Cattlemen spent as much time in town as in the cow camps, and while sharing some of the same beliefs about honor and masculinity with their employees, they valued their interactions with "civilized" society much more. A good cattleman and leader was both physical and intellectual, aggressive and articulate, light-hearted but dedicated to the job, and just as comfortable in the cow camps as in the parlors in town. Ultimately, however, it was in the latter that most cattlemen found their primary social connections.

Cowboys spent most of their time on the ranches with each other, and here, unconstrained by the "civilization" the cattlemen and townspeople seemed to prize, they created their own society. They developed strongly sentimental friendships, and were not ashamed to show emotion. In fact, they viewed displays of true friendship as part of a heroic character, an ideal which was perfectly in tune with standards of manly behavior in the pre-industrial era. As they cemented their friendships, the cowboys also cemented a masculine community among their peers in their outfit, prizing loyalty and camaraderie as well as solidarity against the "civilized" world. Cowardice, false bravado, and a superior attitude earned instant scorn from one's fellows and usually resulted in exclusion from the group. By maintaining a sense of equality within the outfit, the cowboys measured their masculine identity through their acceptance by the others. Indeed, the cow camp and bunkhouse were the only places where they did not have to answer to anyone except each other or pretend to be other than they were. Visitors to ranches frequently commented on the fun and camaraderie around the campfire, and, as we have seen, small boys wanted nothing more than to stay with the men in the bunkhouse and listen to them. In a typical accolade, the *San Antonio Light*, reporting on "The Work Done By Cow Boys During the Branding Season," told its readers that the cowboys were "pleasant companions, and a few hours of our life have been more agreeable than those spent in a cow boy's saddle and cowboys' camp."[1]

But despite their general emphasis on equality, cowboys did create some social hierarchies. They strengthened their self-esteem through jokes about the "dudes" who could not meet their standards, however much wealth or social standing they might have off the ranch. By making fun of the dude, they could turn his alleged social superiority on its head, and increase their own status as men. Anglo cowboys also maintained a sense of self-worth through comparison with and denigration of the many black and Hispanic cowboys. Tied into both Anglo cowboys' and cattlemen's ideals of masculinity was a racial ideology that placed white men, whatever their social status, as being superior to other ethnicities. Thus, the cowboys' sense of masculinity was in part created in defense against social realities. But as society changed around them, cowboys came to seem more like adolescents than true men by middle-class standards.

• • •

Cattlemen held ideals of masculinity that distinguished between working-class ideas of manhood and "gentlemanly" behavior. Not all of the cattlemen cut a fine figure; the *El Paso Herald* described Richard King as "a small swarthy Irishman, with a limping gait" but nonetheless expressed admiration for his 500,000 horses and mules among his other livestock as well as his vast land holdings.[2] Texas trail driver I. P. "Print" Olive never quite found social acceptance in Dodge City due to his somewhat rough past, despite the fact that he was the director of the West Kansas Stockman's Association.[3] But many cattlemen were at pains to show how civilized and restrained they were, contrary to the rowdy reputation of the cowboys. The story that the *San Antonio Evening Light* reprinted from an Arkansas paper in 1883 was typical of these attempts. In "The Cowboy," a man, upon seeing the name of a Texan on the hotel register, was very excited to meet the stereotypical cowboy, but instead found only a gentleman with good taste in clothing and cigars. The fictional William Dillon of "Davis & Dillon cattle dealers," while clearly a cattleman by most standards, nonetheless described himself as a cowboy and told the other man that everyone in Texas was much more refined than people thought.

"The Texas cow boys' life has indeed been a hard one. Deprived of intelligent associations he naturally becomes unsophisticated and seeks his own amusements, but their beats within his manly breast a heart that lawfully realizes right from wrong."[4] Such representations of cowboys and Texas were designed, no doubt, to attract settlers to the region, but when the San Antonio newspaper reprinted the story, it both showcased the refinement of cattlemen and modeled the value of restraint in social situations.

Cattlemen socialized primarily with the people in the towns around them rather than just the men on the ranch and took their definition of masculinity from this wider world. They participated in the social life of their communities and often sponsored social events themselves. As many of their wives came from respected social backgrounds, cattlemen usually built houses in town for their families so they could have access to the institutions of civilized society and could mix with other women of their own social status as they were accustomed. During the off seasons and periods of light work, the cattlemen themselves spent much time in town. As the towns grew, the cattlemen were able to develop associations and entertainments that paralleled those they had known before coming to the frontier, and could socialize more often with men of equal status.[5] R. J. "Jack" Hardesty of the Half Circle Ranch in the Panhandle held regular entertainments and hunting parties for which he had oysters and other delicacies shipped in.[6] Too high standards for social associations could lead to isolation on the frontier, however. Teddy Abbott's educated English father would not socialize with the other English people in the region as they were from a lower social class, and he thought the Americans were the same or worse. As a result, he had few friends and became a bitter man.[7]

Unlike the typical cowboy who was only a temporary resident of the town, to be a real gentleman, the cattleman was supposed to become an integral part of his community and to contribute to it. C. C. Slaughter, in a speech before the Cattle Raisers Association in 1907 looking back on the history of the cattle industry, classified ranchers into two groups: renters and owners. The renters had not improved their stock or sunk new wells as they did not know how long they would be able to keep the land, but the owners were far-sighted and had made the real changes to the land. As a result, the renters had disappeared and the owners had flourished.[8] The *real* cattlemen, in Slaughter's opinion, were clearly the ones who built for keeps. The 1914 *History of the Cattlemen of Texas* recites a litany of ways in which each man profiled has "interested himself in the

Unlike the cowboys, cattlemen had regular social interaction with women and valued the social niceties. Lewis Dinner Party, Spur Ranch, Texas, 1912. P1986-41-105, Erwin E. Smith Collection of the Library of Congress on deposit at the Amon Carter Museum, Fort Worth, Texas.

upbuilding of his community and State," or the "upbuilding of the city," citing numerous examples of productive businesses and institutions the cattlemen helped to found.[9] Civic involvement was an important part of the cattleman's manhood.

The cattlemen's definition of gentlemanly behavior changed somewhat over time but always included a measure of self-reliance and perseverance. Historian Lewis Atherton described the cattlemen as "dedicated and vocal apostles" of the self-made man.[10] In the 1870s, Joseph McCoy praised Charles Goodnight for having succeeded through his energy and "manly determination."[11] In 1899, Teddy Roosevelt opined that the frontier conditions in which they worked necessitated a strong character. "A successful stock-grower must not only be shrewd, thrifty, patient, and enterprising, but he must also possess qualities of personal bravery, hardihood, and self-reliance to a degree not demanded in the least by any mercantile occupation in a community long settled."[12] In 1914, the author of *History of the Cattlemen of Texas* argued that the cattleman "is representative of the very highest of American Manhood. He surmounted every difficulty and achieved success where weaker stock would have failed."[13] Thus, strength of character was also part of the ideals of cattleman masculinity.

How cattlemen defined character, however, may have changed over time. Such characteristics as honesty, thrift, generosity, and business sense were always important parts of the definition. As Rudolph Kleberg, brother of Robert J. Kleberg of the King Ranch, advised his son: "Honesty, industry & perseverance & obedience are the great [factors] to achieve success & without these failure is certain . . . never depart from there and you will come out all right."[14] But as the decades passed, other ideals changed. Joseph McCoy, in his 1874 *Historic Sketches of the Cattle Trade*, elaborated at length on the achievements and character of successful cattlemen. Aside from hard work and a certain dignity, he repeatedly emphasized the nobility of their sentiments toward their fellow man, echoing then current ideas about the ennobling characteristics of feeling and sympathy. While praising Goodnight's manly determination, he also wrote, "he has not lost the higher, nobler, tenderer feelings and sensibilities of an exalted manhood." He described William Peryman as "courteous, kind-hearted and . . . warm and impulsive in temperament." J. M. Choate was "one who suffers in heart when the people of his State are outraged or are made to endure unjust impositions." Robert D. Hunter was somewhat terse in his manner, "But for his friends . . . he has a big heart, throbbing the warmest pulsations of sympathy . . . [and] men freely yield him the palm of manly success." He castigated ungentlemanly men in similar terms as ones "whose heartstrings are but a wisp of base sounding chords, upon which the touch of the higher and purer life have long since ceased to be felt."[15] McCoy's book became a sort of bible in the cattle industry and is still one of its classics, so it is clear that his words did not ring hollow with his audience. His paean to the value of noble sentiment as a marker of masculinity is in clear contrast with his views of cowboys, whom he viewed as incapable of higher feelings.

By the 1880s, however, sentiment was becoming a part of the realm of emotions, associated with femininity, and thus was less important to middle-class manhood. While later accounts still praise the cattleman for his generous spirit, they mostly praise his restraint of passions as his key manly trait. In McCoy's descriptions, the word "impulsive" appears repeatedly as a badge of honor.[16] By 1914, the *History of the Cattlemen of Texas* had a more restrained definition of a true gentleman. Thomas Partain had no formal education but had learned "the great lessons of self-reliance, honesty, and restraint." Men like George W. Saunders and Joseph Henry Nations got ahead because of great thrift and dedication to their business at the sacrifice of other pleasures. A. G. Boyce was "a Christian gentleman; temperate in all his habits."[17] South Texas sheep rancher Walter W. Meek had endorsed a similar view of restraint in his letters to his future wife in the late 1880s. Noting that he constantly tried to watch his temper, he told her "How much better I always feel when able to control myself." Moreover, he noted, "we are so richly repaid when the mastery over self is acquired in ever so small a way."[18] For respectable men like Meek, emotions were things to moderate, not to allow full rein.

Lack of restraint could have serious consequences for middle- and upper-class men, especially when it came to business. George W. Littlefield gave regular sermons to the young men he sponsored about proper behavior for gentlemen, which included being sound with money and avoiding gambling.[19] Jonathan Hamilton Baker experienced failure as a result of lack of restraint firsthand. He met his business partner "Warren" when both were taking their herds up the trail in 1871. Despite the fact that Warren drank a lot and was a poor salesman, Baker formed a mercantile partnership with him, believing him to be essentially a good man. Unfortunately, matters did not improve and within a year, Baker decided to end the partnership, but his partner backed out of their original agreement and demanded an additional $450. Warren believed "he has acted very ungentlemanly," but could do little about it without acting the same way.[20] However, while drinking had led to the partner's downfall, ultimately what Baker considered most ungentlemanly was his reneging on their original agreement.

By the late 1880s, another mark of a man's gentlemanly status was the restraint with which he handled disagreements. In 1886, XIT ranch manager B. H. Campbell explained how gentlemen behaved in a dispute with G. W. Scarborough, a part-time minister who had contracted to build a fence for the ranch. Scarborough had demanded payment for the job, saying he had a group of angry men waiting to get paid, which Campbell took as a threat:

> I positively will pay no man one dollar nor will I make any settlement nor promise to pay while he is holding over me a threat of bodily harm . . . I am ashamed to [have to] write out such a rule and to such a man. I have

had sometimes to explain to a cowboy who never had an opportunity to learn anything better, that it was a crime to demand money of another under threat of harm even tho' the other actually owed him, but I never before had to explain this common-sense proposition to a minister of the Gospel.[21]

Campbell implied that the contract was his word to pay, and should have been sufficient for Scarborough. He also made it clear that violence was not the way to settle matters of honor among gentlemen.[22] Still, not all cattlemen viewed a little youthful aggression as unhealthy. Richard Mifflin Kleberg, grandson of Richard King, was a good student and popular young man, but was at one point suspended from school for fist fighting; an act that only enhanced his manly reputation.[23] Such attitudes mirrored prescriptions for proper boyhood behavior from people such as Teddy Roosevelt, who advised that the American Boy should be able to hold his own in any circumstances.[24]

In praising men who stood up to defend their reputations, cattlemen also drew on Southern traditions of honor. Historian Bertram Wyatt-Brown has described a culture of honor that developed in the South in the nineteenth century that emphasized physical courage, and ritual displays of masculine prowess through fighting, grand displays of wealth, and braggadocio, all of which involved conspicuous lack of control over passions. In this culture, it was important for men to stand up against insults—perceived or real. Wyatt-Brown contrasts this ideal with Northern concepts of conscience which emphasized frugality and restraint and were the motivating force behind many moral reforms such as temperance and anti-dueling laws. In the struggle between the two ideals after the Civil War, he argues, conscience eventually won out, especially with the rise of a more business-oriented middle class who was more concerned with rational behavior.[25] Ironically, as we shall see in the final chapter, as the behaviors associated with this culture faded from middle- and upper-class lives, working-class men adopted them for themselves.[26]

Cattlemen clearly modeled this transition, particularly between generations. While Richard King loved a fistfight, his successors frowned on such behavior as showing a lack of restraint. By the 1880s, rational business ideals had, for the most part, come to dominate the cattleman's mentality. Cattlemen thus based their masculinity on ideals of channeled aggression and ability to maintain appropriate social relations. They identified with a larger community beyond the ranch and saw themselves as having more refined sentiments than their employees. While honor was important, especially to those who had Southern backgrounds, ultimately as they became leaders in the community they saw their role as requiring them to restrain their impulses. Like the cowboys, they identified self-reliance as a key aspect of their manhood. Unlike the cowboys, however, they had greater opportunity for success as a result of their efforts. Their masculine identity was thus reinforced by their business success and social status as gentlemen.

Lacking the economic foundation of a gentleman, cowboys could not show their masculinity through gentlemanly behavior without risking the ridicule of their fellow cowboys who saw them as putting on airs. Unable to get approval of their character from people away from the ranch, they sought approval from each other in the closed society of the cow camps. Whereas cattlemen maintained social hierarchies in their relationships, cowboys prized reciprocity and equality. Like miners, cowboys preferred an all-male society to a heterosocial one as it allowed them to create their own world in which everyone was on equal footing.[27] As one woman who lived near the XIT recalled: "The boys were from every walk of life, the educated and the uneducated, but were equal as cowboys."[28] Equality was important to men who faced efforts to control their lives on a daily basis, and thus giving or receiving friendship was one choice that nobody could control. A cowboy's friend was closer than family and placed fewer restrictions on him, and it was in a spirit of equality that men entered into close friendships. Cowboy friendships, especially those between "pardners" or "buddies," became one way in which cowboys could freely express a masculine identity. Cowboys were sociable at heart, unlike the lone rangers of myth and film.

While all friendships differ according to the individuals involved, it is necessary to attempt an analysis of cowboy friendships since it is clear that they were the most important relationships of these men's lives.[29] Historian Anthony Rotundo's study of boyhood friendships in the late nineteenth century is a good starting place. Based more frequently on availability rather than any deeper connection, these relationships often broke off as quickly as they started. Nonetheless, Rotundo notes that the common basis for the friendship was usually "good companionship and unshakable fidelity." More importantly, these friendships were the first relationships a boy had outside of his family and the first he could choose himself and thus were of great value to him.[30] An example of such friendship appears in the middle of a ranch daybook full of practical remedies and mathematical formulas where two juvenile signatures appear:

Joseph Sanders the best man to his size

Allen Mc[F]addin the best man to his size[31]

In this case, the son of the ranch owner and his young friend attested to their friendship by putting it in writing. In these boy friendships, we see the root of cowboy friendships, which grew out of childhood relationships but became deeper.

In urban areas, as society became more industrialized, close, intimate male friendships became less common among working-class men. One reason was the increasing intimacy between men and women as the ideal of marriage became one of partnership more than submission of the wife to the husband. Men and women also mixed more in public in commercial leisure venues such as movie theaters and amusement parks.[32] At the same time, men began competing more directly with each other for wages, which could raise barriers to close friendships. Urban men still socialized with each other in taverns and pool halls, but these friendships were not emotionally intimate in the way women's friendships remained. In predominantly isolated, all-male environments like the ranches, however, the barriers to close male friendships were less apparent. While cattlemen may have been able to choose a companionate marriage, cowboys did not have this option, and they did not compete with each other for wages, which were fairly standard between ranches. Cowboys thus followed an older ideal of friendship among men.

According to this ideal, men had a unique capacity for loyalty, devotion, and self-sacrifice which women were not capable of. Men placed their friendships on a higher moral/spiritual plane and saw them as elevating their masculinity. Women supposedly fought against each other, but men "were most manly when they [were] fighting side by side in a world without women."[33] This idealized "heroic" friendship in literature of the period was one in which friends were young and brave, shared dangers and adventures, were devoted and generous to each other throughout their lives, and valued their friendship over all other relationships. The death of one friend was always the worst tragedy the other could endure, and the men were not afraid to express their open admiration and affection for one another.[34] This idyllic friendship was largely not feasible in most situations where men had real responsibilities to their wives and families, but it was ideally suited to cowboy life, which existed in its own world away from such social responsibilities.

Tejano vaqueros drew on another tradition of friendships, the *compadre de benedicción*. Boys formed bosom friendships with each other and would often go before a priest to ask for a ritual blessing of their connection. Such bonds were considered lifelong pledges of brotherhood, and compadres became part of the extended family, at times even closer than blood relatives. Compadres would make great sacrifices to help one another in times of hardship.[35] It is possible that Anglo cowboys who worked on South Texas ranches with Tejanos were both aware of this tradition of friendships and adapted it to their own situations. Frank Goodwyn, the son of a ranch foreman on the King Ranch, grew up close friends with several Mexican workers whom he called compadre.[36] Certainly the term "compadre" became part of the standard cowboy repertoire.

Friendships allowed cowboys to escape their troubles. Their friends were the only people who made no demands on them and they provided support when times were hard. Ironically, the men associated these attachments with freedom rather than ties that bound them to society, like wives and children.[37] As historian J. Evetts Haley described it, they relished "the freedom of the frontier, and the breaking of the bonds of propriety that cramped some men in a settled land."[38] Pinkney Joel Webb worked on a number of ranches for low pay "but there is no work that carries with it the pleasure, freedom, and comradeship which we found when we worked on the ranches."[39] While cowboys frequently moved from ranch to ranch when they became dissatisfied with conditions or got an urge to move on, they did not necessarily break all ties, and it was quite common for two buddies to leave together and seek work elsewhere. Willie Hugh sought work for himself and his friend at the Matador Ranch in 1887, for example, and African American cowboy Dick Sparks sought work for himself and a cook's position for his buddy at the same ranch the following year.[40] In at least one case, friendship appears to have trumped marriage. Robert Hodgkins and E. F. Springford applied to the Spur Ranch in 1890, despite the fact that Springford had a wife in Massachusetts. The two men had worked in Florida together breaking horses and wanted to come to Texas. Hodgkins told Fred Horsbrugh, the ranch manager, that Springford's marriage would present no difficulties as he had saved enough money for a cottage for his wife and could leave her well provided for. "Our reason for wishing to leave this country is a natural one, I think—We want a change—, and being able to make a living here we think that we can do it there and get out of the old ruts at the same time."[41]

Cowboys depended on their buddies for both hard work and good fun. Despite
the proscription on gambling, many cowboys found time for cards on the ranch.
Charley Thompson (left) and Ed Bomar (right) Having a Game of Seven-up,
Turkey Track Ranch, Texas, 1906. LC-S59-217, Erwin E. Smith Collection of the
Library of Congress on deposit at the Amon Carter Museum, Fort Worth, Texas.

Cowboys were not ashamed of expressing affection or admiration for
their friends and would often go to extremes to help the men they admired. In a brief, five-paragraph narrative of his experiences as a cowboy,
the only story Joseph Cruze Sr. chose to elaborate on beyond the basic
facts was the death of his friend, Pete Owen, who was killed in a fight.
Cruze noted, "He was a good friend to me, we had been soldier com-
rades for nearly three years, worked cattle together, and I loved him as
a brother. . . . The Owens boys were good soldiers, upright, honest and
brave men."[42] In the wake of the shootings in Tascosa surrounding the
cowboy strike of 1883, Jim Gober swam a flooded river and rode all over
the Panhandle ranches collecting nearly $600 for his buddies who had led
the strike and had been involved in the shootout.[43] V. H. Whitlock and
his buddy Sutty were inseparable and worked together on day herd, night

guard, and branding; and "we would fight each other like two bobcats but if anyone butted in, he had us both to whip."[44] When Benjamin S. Miller heard his former partner was sick, he rode forty-five miles and eight hours in one day to see him, only to return the next day.[45] Bill Arp Oden and his buddy, Henry Cummins, were the only hands on a small ranch together and when word reached Oden on a visit home that Cummins was sick, he rode 180 miles in three days to reach him and make sure he was all right, in the process suffering a fall and smashing his thumb between the saddle horn and a rock. Henry returned the favor, however. While pulling Oden out of a well he was cleaning, the rope slipped and Henry suffered terrible rope burns, and the handle of the windlass smacked him in the lip as he tried to stop his buddy from falling. Oden sewed him up with a needle and thread. Even after Cummins left the ranch following a dispute with the boss, Oden still described them as "best friends."[46]

To modern sensibilities, some of these friendships appear to have been more than just platonic. Cummins and Oden's relationship seemed much like a marriage at times: "Henry and I for six years did most of the ranch work. Henry being the old man and I the old woman, he doing the milking, horse rustling, etc., while I would do most of the cooking, churning, and attending to the chickens, and in the six years, we never had a cross word."[47] Jimmie Donnelly and Ed Fletcher owned the Washita Ranch in the Panhandle in the late 1870s, although neither were especially promising ranchers and did not try to increase their herd or land holdings. But "Jimmie would come in and say hello to Fletcher just like a sweetheart," and the two men fought "like sweethearts" if Jimmie got drunk. They were also each other's sole heirs.[48] When Frank Wright's bunkie, John Hollicott, came down with smallpox, Wright refused to leave, saying, "I would not desert an old pard for anything like that, and blankets are scarce anyhow."[49] Hollicott, range boss on the LX Ranch and a "highbred" gentleman Scot, was known as "a lover of boys, a maker of men," who reportedly befriended many young men and stopped them from going astray. On one occasion when he caught a seventeen-year-old boy branding an LX cow with another brand, he took the boy under his wing, believing he had come under a bad influence. "From now on you'r goin' to be my boy; you're not Blank's boy or Doe's boy any longer. . . . Come with me. I'll help you to make a man of yourself." The boy became his shadow and eventually became a respected man in the Panhandle.[50] When a young boy in Teddy Abbott's outfit who had come West to help cure his tuberculosis got sick, the ranch boss asked Teddy to stay in town and nurse him. Unfortunately, the boy grew worse and died after a week. But Teddy's recounting of the death scene is fraught with sentiment, as the boy would not sleep "unless he could lay his head on my arm," and when he was dying he asked Teddy to lie down next to him on the bed and let him rest his head on his shoulder. When the boy died, calling his sister's name, Teddy was clearly deeply affected by the experience.[51] Such descriptions make modern readers curious as to the "true" nature of these friendships.

But we must be sure to understand the context in which these events occurred, rather than just judging them by twenty-first century standards or assuming that the men must have been hiding something.[52] In a post-Freud age in which we are aware that many seemingly innocent objects have sexual meanings to our subconscious, and in an environment where the majority of men have defined their masculinity as purely heterosexual, we often read subtexts into nineteenth-century sources that may or may not be there. Historians now generally agree that what we currently define as "homosexual" or "heterosexual" behavior, like masculinity itself, is specific to our own historical context and that some behaviors that fall within the category of "homosexual" today have not always done so. In addition, attitudes toward different aspects of contemporary homosexual behavior have changed over time.[53] Men have freely admitted their love for each other through the centuries without shame or embarrassment and without erotic feelings. Certainly, there have always been men whose primary sexual attraction was to other men rather than women, the example most often cited being an idealized sexual relationship between an older man and younger pupil in Classical Greece. But it was not until the late nineteenth century that social scientists classified this behavior as homosexual, labeling these men a "third sex" or "inverts." Men from all social backgrounds historically engaged in a variety of behaviors we would today consider at the very least effeminate, without anyone doubting their masculinity.[54]

One of the issues that makes many modern readers unnecessarily curious is the matter of bunkies. It was normal for men to share a bunk or bedroll on the ranch or trail, just as it was common for unrelated men, women, or children to share a bed anywhere in the United States during this period. Jim Gober "spliced beds with my old chum Jim Stroope and got along fine until the fall work was finished."[55] V. H. Whitlock and his buddy Sutty also slept together: "Neither of us had much bedding, so we threw our suggans into one roll and slept together"[56] Many cowboy narratives report the hijinks that could result from such an arrangement. Dick Withers recalled a sticky incident when he shared a bedroll with the boss who spent the night in camp. "We slept on a pallet together. Mr. Ellison undressed, but I did not, as I always slept with my entire outfit on . . . so as to be ready for any emergency. During the night the cattle made a run, and when I started to get up one of my spurs caught in Mr. Ellison's drawers and he was rather painfully spurred."⁵⁷ Charlie Walker and his buddy shared a bedroll one night, with Charlie facing east and his buddy facing west. When strong winds blew up from the east, his buddy said, "You're light[,] I can turn you around. Just lay in bed. I'll get hold of the feet and turn it around." So he turned Charlie to face west but in the process, Charlie's hat blew away as the bedroll was no longer on top of it.⁵⁸ Charlie told the story with no embarrassment, the main point being to show how he had lost his hat, but the story also shows how prosaic the relationship between bunkies could be.⁵⁹ Charlie and his bunkie were simply keeping warm and sharing company. There is no record of sexual relationships between bunkies, although the situation may have created opportunities for them.

In addition to these accounts, there are a number of stories of cowboys acting in a seemingly less than manly fashion. Former cowboy W. B. Foster described a seventeen-year-old boy in his outfit who was beaten up by a "bad man" in Cleburne while they were on the trail. "Wilder never carried arms of any kind; he was more like a girl than a boy and everyone in the outfit loved him."⁶⁰ Jack Meyers Potter and his buddy Jim Oliphant were sent out forty miles from the Pecos River to ride the line and watch for drifting cattle. Having first had the luxury of sleeping in an old fort, they were disappointed with their new environment and so built a dugout with a window and even a separate kitchen. Jim, who was born in the city, called the kitchen "the tea room." The two set up house together but Jim said his "soul was starving for beauty," so they built a mantle over the fireplace and used a lid from a shirt box to make a "God Bless our Home" sign complete with fancy lettering and pictures of leaves and flowers in colored pencil. When Jim later tried to toss the sign in the fire, Jack stopped him and fiercely defended it any time he tried to take it down.⁶¹

One factor that makes it difficult to interpret the meaning of these friendships is the persistent use of sentimental language in period accounts. The most often cited homoerotic poem is a 1914 verse by Badger Clark entitled "The Lost Pardner" which includes the following lines:

We loved each other in the way men do
And never spoke about it, Al and me,
But we both *knowed*, and knowin' it so true
Was more than any woman's kiss could be.

. . .

I wait to hear him ridin' up behind
And feel his knee rub mine in the good old way[62]

On the surface, the poem seems to describe a same-sex affectionate and intimate relationship, yet this poem was in a published book of cowboy poetry that received almost universal praise from former cowboys and no one suggested removing it. The poems in the volume concerning women and the author's desire to marry a nice girl are equally sentimental. Furthermore, in the tradition of heroic friendships, sentimental language about the death of a friend follows a clear model. Consider the following lines from the classical epic *Gilgamesh*:

Enkidu, whom I love dearly
Whoever went through hazards with me
The fate of man has overtaken him.
All day and night have I wept for him,
And would not have him buried.

. . .

Since he is gone I can no longer comfort find
Keep roaming like a hunter in the plains.[63]

In other words, Clark's poem might be following a poetic model, and his use of sentimental language is part of the formula.

In nineteenth-century literature, such language was the norm. Writers viewed appeals to sentiment as uplifting, bringing one closer to God through the heart rather than the mind.[64] Popular novels of the day like the Leatherstocking Tales of James Fenimore Cooper frequently described manly sentimental friendships, in an era before any "homosexual panic" had set in.[65] In the 1870 Street and Smith weekly pulp magazine story, "Buffalo Bill, The King of the Border Men," Wild Bill Hickok kills the bad guy for Buffalo Bill, who gushes gratefully: "Mate, I loved you before better than I loved my own life—I don't know how I can love you more. But if I ever have a chance to *die* for you, I'll laugh while I am going."[66] Moreover, such language can be taken out of context. The informant who described Ed Fletcher and Jimmie Donelly as being like sweethearts also called them old bachelors and "fine men."[67] Bill Oden and Henry Cummins experience was part of a tradition of "batchin'" camps, in which two older bachelors often divided chores while living out on the fence line.[68] The truth is, it is often difficult to distinguish between sentimental convention and true affection in the sources and very easy to import significance to language that does not merit it.

While some have hastily concluded that all sentimental language and displays of emotion between men imply an erotic relationship, other scholarship suggests additional explanations for romantic and sentimental language among men.[69] Feminist scholar Eve Sedgewick has argued that the intense male homosocial bonding that was essential to maintaining a patriarchal society was only possible if there was assurance that there was no homosexuality involved.[70] In other words, the cowboys would not have felt free to openly express their emotions unless they were certain they would not be misconstrued. Other scholars have focused on the fact that many writers saw intimate male friendships as elevated to heroic because they were *distanced* from the erotic. In his 1580 essay, *On Friendship*, for example, French Renaissance writer Michel Montaigne openly boasts about his close friendships with men because they are of a higher nature than just sexual love. Historian Richard Halperin has posited that male friendships tend to be erotically charged when there is a power differential between the men either through age, class, or race, and that scholars should distinguish between these erotic relationships and the tradition of egalitarian heroic friendships that rise above physical attraction.[71] By this definition, cowboy friendships, which placed a premium on equality and reciprocity, would be less likely to be erotic in nature. Historian Jonathan Katz notes that nineteenth-century men saw their friendships as being on a higher spiritual plane than the physical so that no one would have even thought of asking about sex.[72] However, it is not always possible to make such a clear distinction, as we cannot simply define same-sex relationships only in sexual terms, nor can we pretend that homosexual relationships do not occur between equals.[73] Nonetheless, no matter how much historians would like to make a definitive statement based on the historical evidence, it simply is not possible to do so as there is a decided lack of it, a fact which, in itself, tells us that such behavior was not open for discussion.[74]

Film scholar Hubert Cohen has noted that in early Western films lots of cowboys shed tears and talked about their feelings, but revisionist

Westerns robbed the cowboy of these emotions, preferring an unsentimental John Wayne or Clint Eastwood.[75] In fact, the historical cowboy was renowned for his sentimentality: "he could shed tears as easily as a woman when his friends were bowed in grief."[76] Mild-mannered cowboy Burt Phelps, who was killed by a villain, was buried "by a bunch of cowboys, who, with hats in hand, tried to say a prayer, and failing, their eyes dimmed with tears, one member on his knees, with eyes raised to heaven, said, 'Oh God, look down on this Thy child.'"[77] Will D. Howsley, a teamster on the Reynolds Ranch, kept a small notebook which he filled with brands and a slew of sentimental poetry he copied in there.[78] Professional entertainers doing shows in the cow towns sang mostly sentimental ballads like "Sweet Genevieve," "Oh Promise Me," or "Home Sweet Home" and attracted large audiences from among the cowboys.[79] But most accounts of the old-time cowboy (and some modern cowboy poets) seem to take pride in his sentimentality; indeed, it is an integral part of the mythic cowboy persona: tough when it counts but gentle on the inside.

Unfortunately for the cowboy, by the turn of the century, sentimentality was under attack in terms of proper masculine behavior. Concerned that society had become over-feminized, middle-class men scorned any sign of gentleness or emotions that might leave them vulnerable, and created boyhood activities designed to teach boys to suppress those emotions.[80] Women's sentimentality moreover both elevated their own status as sensitive beings and, in the words of historian Robert Haywood, "reassured men that their own composed demeanor was a sign of strength."[81] Increasingly these men relegated sentiment to the women's sphere and mocked it as affected and frivolous. Male authors turned away from sentimental writing, and critics lambasted those who did not. If the new model for middle-class masculinity praised passion and aggression, it derided sentiment and tender feeling.[82] People came to see sentiment in men as a thing of childhood, when boys were still under the care of their mothers. Literary scholar Jane Tompkins argued that sentimentality seemed to offer a way to avoid responsibility and the world of the adult. Men perhaps believed they could prolong their boyhoods in this sentimental world.[83] Some scholars have also argued that sentimentality became a way to keep the working classes mollified, showing that reformers were sympathetic to their plight ("I Feel Your Pain") without pushing for legislation to change matters.[84]

Indeed, many of the cowboys saw women's sentimentality as part of the trappings of civilization they wished to escape. Nonetheless, it was an important part of their all-male culture, perhaps because they were separated from home so entirely, or because many of them had left home at a young age. But it is also clear that they did not see expressions of manly sentiment as anything to be ashamed of. Strong emotions were part and parcel of being a man. Cowboys lived fully and without restraint when they were by themselves and saw no reason to rein in emotions to fit society's standards. Expressing love for a friend was an affirmation of the ability to choose friends and the manliness to stay loyal to them. Nonetheless, to the outside world the cowboys increasingly seemed more childlike as a result of their sentimentality, reinforcing ideas that middle-class men who had mastered these emotions were manlier.

But cowboys defined their masculinity in contrast to civilized society and created their own standards of manly behavior. One of the most important of these was loyalty to one's outfit. Men in each outfit looked out for each other as they would protect a family. William Lewis's cowboy foreman was strict, but when Lewis was the last to appear after a storm and stampede took him far from camp, the foreman was worried: "Cattle may be our business, but on a night like this, I want to be damn sure all my men are accounted for."[85] Charles Goodnight remembered the men in his outfit always staying a little longer than their shift on night guard so as to be sure they did not call the next man too soon. As a result, the last shift was significantly shorter than the rest.[86] When Woodson Coffee got sick and was out of work for several months, he ran up large debts and doctors' bills. Two of the cowboys in the outfit he had worked with for a long time heard about his predicament and offered to loan him their savings, asking for no security or contract. One of the men actually loaned him $200, a sizeable amount considering the average hand earned only $30 a month. Coffee remembered the incident with the comment, "Talk about men who are men."[87] As a substitute for a traditional family to provide for, the outfit allowed the men, while on equal footing, to provide for one another in the way a man was supposed to provide for his own family.

Camaraderie was another trait cowboys valued most among the men they worked with. They did their best to entertain each other to avoid the boredom and isolation of the work season. The key characteristic necessary to a good companion was one who did not take himself too seriously. The most common form of entertainment was storytelling, particularly tall tales or stories in which they made fun of themselves or tenderfeet.[88] A favorite type of story to tell tenderfeet was a "circular" story, which was a long, strung out, and impossibly detailed narrative of chasing a steer or hunting wolves that made its final sentence the same as the first. If told properly, the cowboy might be halfway through a second recitation before the tenderfoot realized he was telling the same story again.[89] Vaqueros on the Rincón Ranch would tell each other ghost stories around the campfire to pass the time, particularly one about "El Muerto," a former outlaw who had terrorized settlers in South Texas. According to the story, the people caught and beheaded him, then tied him to a wild mustang and let him loose as a warning to rustlers. Many reported seeing the headless horseman in years that followed.[90] Irvin Bell rode back with his outfit to Texas after wintering a herd in New Mexico. The men hunted along the way and each night prepared a formal debate on a predetermined question.[91] Card playing or dominoes were also popular, particularly poker, monte, seven-up, or hearts. Since gambling was not technically allowed on the ranches, however, they would often use stakes such as fetching water or chopping firewood.[92]

The prohibition on gambling seems to have been circumvented quite frequently nonetheless. Cowboys especially liked leisure time activities that had an element of competition to them. They would stage fights between tarantulas or snakes and bet on the outcome.[93] They also put on horse races or foot races when they could. It was rare, however, for cowboys in the same outfit to race each other, preferring to test their horses against visiting cowboys or professional horse racers who went from ranch to ranch. They also raced local Indians. They relied as much on knowledge of the terrain in these contests as skill, as they had the home advantage and knew the location of all the prairie dog holes. Lacking stopwatches, in 100-yard foot races they always estimated the winning time at ten seconds, since that was the American record set on the East Coast and they reasoned that since Eastern dudes rode horses so poorly it would be no trouble at all for a Westerner to equal their fastest time on foot. Such reasoning was also a way to tweak the image of cowboys as somehow lacking in comparison to the middle-class dudes, who thought themselves superior.

The men pitched horseshoes, held shooting contests, and hunted or roped anything that moved on the prairie—all activities that allowed them to show off their skills. However, they did not play any of the organized sports that middle-class men were advocating for boys as a way to let loose and still channel aggression. One historian has said that the men would rather fight with their gun than their fists, but however true, the men certainly did not box with gloves and all the proper rules. They also did not play baseball or other team sports.[94] What is interesting about the types of sport the men enjoyed is that they involved individual contests of skill, with few rules and little structure. As such, they reinforced the cowboys' self-esteem if they did well and also met the ideal of freedom. If cowboys had to obey rules in the rest of their lives, when they were with each other, beyond a basic code of ethics, they did not have to worry about following anyone's orders. Such individualism was tempered however by limiting aggressive competition within the outfit, where harmony and loyalty were as important to the cowboys as they were to the cattlemen.

Aside from these more formal types of leisure, cowboys found what time they could to have a little fun and let loose some of the tension that came from long work hours and dangerous jobs. In the winter, especially, it was hard to schedule much outdoor activity and so the men sought other forms of amusement than sport. Jim Gober and his fence-riding partner Charlie Hall were responsible for maintaining sixteen miles of fence, and every day they each rode eight miles in the opposite direction before returning home at night. The men "spent the evenings playing cards and talking of home folks, our escapades with the girls, and we built air castles about the things we would do when we went back home."[95] Another outfit adopted a rooster that had been injured in a storm as their mascot. The men and the cook nursed it back to health and "it was a source of pleasure and amusement to the whole camp."[96] In 1896, a group of cowboys in their twenties and thirties experienced two feet of snow while working to build a levee for a rice marsh. None of them had seen snow before "and we were a lot of kids. We played in [i]t very near all the time it was snowing. We would shake it off of saplings on each other and lie down and wallow in it, and rake up big piles and crawl through them."[97] Cowboys also used to memorize the labels of the canned goods they ate on the ranch and would often challenge each other to recite them verbatim with a fee for the person who skipped a word or punctuation mark. Such activity was also a way to keep tenderfeet somewhat bewildered in the first nights in camp as cowboys would interrupt stories and conversations when someone yelled out a brand name and everyone began reciting, only to resume their previous activities when they had finished. The point was to keep the tenderfoot slightly confused.[98] Such activities forged a sense of belonging among the men as they emphasized special knowledge that outsiders did not have.

Another form of knowledge the cowboys shared and which forged bonds of camaraderie was their use of song. Singing was not entirely a leisure time activity, as cowboys used it to get the cattle moving in the daytime and to keep the cattle from becoming startled at night. Indeed, it was not possible for a cowboy to get a job in some outfits unless he could sing. The tune was not as important as the lyrics, however. Cowboys first sang songs they knew from home, including hymns and minstrel songs, but by the 1870s, they had developed their own lyrics to many of them. "Bury Me Not on the Lone Prairie," for example, was sung to the tune of the sentimental parlor ballad "The Ocean Burial." The important thing for the men was to invent new lyrics and verses to keep themselves both entertained and awake while night herding.[99] Cowboys preferred sentimental songs as a rule, particularly ones about dying mothers or partners and lonely cowboys. These songs were generally reserved for the nighttime campfire, however, and they sang livelier songs in the day while herding the cattle or going up the trail. The songs would vary from outfit to outfit and would grow progressively longer as the men attempted to add a new verse each day.[100] The songs spread from ranch to ranch as the cowboys moved between jobs, and a newly arrived hand or rep for a roundup was usually called upon to share new songs within a short time of his arrival.[101] Not all of the songs were fit for public consumption, however, and cowboys had traditions of songs they could not sing in polite company, once again marking out a separate territory for themselves outside of "civilization."[102]

While the reading materials the cowboys enjoyed were as varied as the men themselves, they also influenced their ideas of masculine behavior. Although a number of cowboys were functionally illiterate, there were others who read Shakespeare or the Bible for pleasure. On one ranch in the Panhandle, the Midland newspapers were a welcome diversion. Everyone in the ranch house and bunkhouse would read every word of every article including the advertisements. Even if they were a few weeks old, they still provided news and entertainment.[103] Often those who could not read as well were somewhat contemptuous of well-educated people, negating a characteristic which might lower their self-esteem.[104] The preferred reading materials for the bunkhouse were thus often heavily illustrated. Mail-order catalogs were a source of endless enjoyment, as the men dreamed of what their lives might be when they settled down with their sweethearts. The Montgomery Ward's catalog and Sears and Roebuck "wishbook" were so popular that men made jokes about ordering mail-order brides from Montgomery Ward's.[105] Many ranches set aside money for the men to choose one monthly subscription paper, and the one most of them chose was the *National Police Gazette*.[106] Originally a professional aid for policemen searching for criminals, beginning in 1845 under a new editor, the paper began to publish more true crime type stories, ultimately by the 1870s printing on cheaper pink paper with smaller pages and many illustrations.[107] Most of the content was lurid or racy and the targeted audience was men and boys. There were many pictures of scantily dressed women (at least for the time), showing ankles and legs almost to the knee. What made the paper even more desirable was the fact that respectable people condemned it.[108]

The imagery and editorial content and perspective of the *Police Gazette* reflected and shaped many of the cowboys' views about what made an ideal man. In some ways the standard was not much different than that of the middle-class male. The stories emphasized physical rather than mental prowess, covered manly sports such as boxing, and reflected many of middle-class men's concerns with challenges they were facing from women in the public sphere. They reinforced the idea that a woman's role should be submissive and encouraged readers to practice physical and mental self-control.[109] But the view of the working class the paper projected was by no means an inferior one. The *Gazette* solicited and printed stories of everyday working-class heroes and their lives and focused on individual acts of bravery and heroic physical strength. The paper also participated in the cult of the cowboy hero, painting the men of the Wild West as manly heroes and perfect gentlemen.[110] It depicted native-born strikers as heroic and the factory owners as effete. Yet the paper was not radical. It opposed immigrant workers and strikers, and its description of factory owners as less than manly was more in a spirit of fun than one of rebellion.[111] In general, the paper made fun of authority figures—something the cowboys and other working men no doubt enjoyed immensely. It targeted ministers as hypocrites and snobs; reformers, especially temperance advocates, as meddlers; the rich as exploiters of the working class; and college students as foppish and intellectual.[112] Here was an East Coast paper confirming the suspicions of the cowboys that the dude was less manly than themselves, whatever his control over them on the job. That confirmation, plus the half-naked women, was a guaranteed formula for sales to the cowboys, who eagerly passed the latest copy among themselves in the bunkhouse.

Cowboy humor was another way in which the men were able to turn social hierarchies upside down. Cowboys often played pranks on each other and on tenderfeet, but most pranks were reciprocated at some point or at least the cowboy caught on to the joke. They teased the tenderfeet and "lints," or boys from the cotton fields who came to work on the ranch for a season.[113] They teased each other about girls and played tricks on their friends. When John Bratt met his old buddy Guy Barton in Chicago, Barton followed him into a barbershop and paid the bootblack twice his fee to polish only one of Bratt's boots. Bratt went around town with Barton in tow trying to get the other boot shined, only to have Barton pay off the other bootblacks as well.[114] The joke appealed to a mischievous sense of humor but also showcased Barton's willingness to spend money on frivolous items, an important part of a cowboy's public persona. The jokes the men played on each other were generally harmless and designed simply to entertain and keep the others on their toes. As we have seen, they were also a way to weed out any tenderfoot who was not likely to make it on the job, and were done in a spirit of equality.

When cowboys played tricks on the dude or told jokes about him, however, there was a different subtext. By definition a dude was a fish out of water and incapable of either recognizing a prank or reciprocating it. A dude was usually a tourist or sojourner in the West from out East or abroad and did not plan to settle permanently. He did not bring his family and he did not try to adapt to Western ways, assuming his own to be superior (just as Westerners considered their ways superior). Westerners in general tended to have a hostile attitude toward foreigners and Easterners, who they lumped together. They disliked that the "dudes" seemed to get all the profit from Western products, and that they only visited to inspect crops or livestock or to play at being cowboys. Westerners believed that if such "effete weaklings" dared to come out West with the real men, they deserved whatever they got. Indeed, in transactions with dudes, it was less important whether or not the cowboy or cattleman made financial profit than if they were able to outwit or make him look ridiculous.[115] It was great fun to fool a dude, and whether true or not, the men had many stories of doing just that. Moreover, as the dude was sometimes the boss, it was a way of making fun of social hierarchies.

Dudes were generally useless on the ranch. When one Texan told the *El Paso Lone Star* that many cowboys were East coast college graduates, the editor opined, "This is much the worst charge that has yet been brought against them."[116] When Wirt White's dude cousin came to Texas after being orphaned, White thought him "the sissiest looking boy that ever came to live on a farm." Although the cousin learned some basic riding techniques, "he was the regular laughing stock among the cowboys."

After six months, the cousin was homesick and returned home and White imagined he "was just anxious to get home and tell his associates of his wide experience as a Texas cowboy."[117] William Lewis came to Texas at age fourteen wearing knickerbockers, long black stockings, and a sailor hat with ribbons and was the object of much laughter among the other boys of his age. When he went to work on his uncle's ranch, the foreman was especially tough on him, boasting that he would "punish him so hard he'll have to give up and go back to town where he belongs."[118]

More than just a nuisance, the dude could be bad for business or even dangerous. While Lewis eventually overcame his "dude" identity, his cousin's husband did not. Lewis's cousin married a gambling man who liked to live the life of a dandy. When it became clear he was going to ruin the family, they moved out to Texas so he would lead a more responsible life as co-owner of a ranch with Lewis's father. There was no curing this dude, however, and he soon slipped back into his dissolute ways and was never at the ranch, leaving it to falter.[119] The owner and manager of the FUF Ranch was from Vermont and knew little about Western-style cattle ranching and cowboys. He proceeded to hire an outfit of dudes which included the nephew of the company president, a Frenchman from Louisiana, and the son of an English aristocrat, none of whom had any experience with cattle either. Desiring to cut costs, he used straw rather than sand in the train cars he was shipping horses in, and when a spark from the engine ignited the straw, the horses burned to death. As Teddy Abbott said, "A man like that had no business trying to run a cow outfit. He didn't know nothing and he couldn't get along with cowpunchers."[120]

Given the dude's level of incompetence, cowboys loved to tell stories that made the dude look the fool. When a New York businessman came to visit the XIT Ranch to experience the Wild West, the cowboys saw a chance to get the best of him. He professed great admiration for Sam Houston and the cowboys sold him a grubby old cowboy hat at a high price, saying it had belonged to Houston. When he expressed a desire to own a Comanche weapon or artifact, the cowboys gave him the broken pointed end of a crowbar, saying it was genuine Comanche. The man went back to New York none the wiser, and the cowboys proved their superiority to the dude.[121] When a rich boy from Kentucky came up the trail and repeatedly told his outfit that they would have no idea how to behave in high society, the cowboys decided to show him "high cow camp society" by playing a number of pranks on him, none of which he caught on to. Ultimately the boy packed up and went back home and the cowboys congratulated themselves for having bested him.[122] When Bones Hooks picked up a fancy cattle buyer to bring to the ranch near Clarendon, he let the horses run full speed all the way so that the man was thrown around but unable to jump out.[123]

Teasing could turn violent at times. When German immigrant John Weyert first arrived in Alpine from San Antonio in 1886, the cowboys surrounded him, pointing pistols at his head, or more precisely, his derby hat. Weyert took the hat off and put it on a post and the "boys" shot it full of holes.[124] Another unfortunate tourist got off the train while it was briefly stopped at Alpine, wearing slippers, a smoking jacket, monocle, and Derby hat. The cowboys roped him, shouting, "I roped it first, now I get to brand it!" and the man's fellow passengers had to get the conductor to rescue him.[125] Cowboys in the Panhandle had a field day with Archibald John Marjoribanks, the British baron and owner of the Rocking Chair Ranch. They shot at his feet and continuously made fun of his formal clothes, English horses, and use of fox and hounds to hunt deer. Their main complaint, however, seemed to be that he held himself aloof from the men, refusing to discuss his personal life with them.[126]

Cowboys always appreciated a good laugh at the boss's expense. Black cowboy Bones Hooks was out on the range with his boss Bill Ross, when he spied a maverick bull, which Ross insisted on catching for his son. When Ross was not able to take the bull down by himself, he yelled to Bones for help and ran off to the brush once he had taken hold of the horns. Realizing his boss expected him to do all the hard work, Bones let the bull go, which subsequently charged Ross and knocked him to the ground, pawing and slobbering over him. Bones took his time coming to the rescue, in part because he was enjoying the spectacle too much. Ross was so embarrassed he paid Bones a dollar not to tell anyone. Needless to say, the story made the rounds among the cowboys anyway.[127] The social gap was ever present between cattlemen and cowboys, however, and some tricks could backfire. In 1882, H. H. Campbell of the Matador Ranch charged cowboy D. D. Singleterry $1 to stay in camp for the night, so when Campbell, who rode around in a nice buggy and smoked fine cigars, came to stay at the ranch Singleterry worked on, he charged him $2.50 in retaliation. Campbell laughed and paid the amount but when he met Singleterry's boss in town, he told him to fire the cowboy as he was a thief.[128] Cowboys thus saw humor and tricks as a way to challenge their so-called "betters," but more overt stunts were risky, particularly when the boss knew what he was doing.

Bones Hooks' actions were unusual among black cowboys in part because he saw himself as a cowboy more than as a black man. As such,
he shared the same values with his fellow cowboys. But he was certainly
aware of the handicaps his race brought him. Unfortunately, there are so
few other firsthand accounts from black or Hispanic cowboys or cattlemen that it is nearly impossible to make generalizations, but we can get a
few peeks into what life was like for them both through an examination
of what others said about them and through an understanding of race
relations and attitudes in this period. Black and Hispanic men were as
concerned as Anglo men about maintaining a sense of manhood and self-
respect. However, in an environment in which racism was an accepted
social practice and in which white Americans frequently based their own
concept of manhood on being white, and therefore superior in their own
eyes, it was difficult for nonwhites to express masculinity in an Anglo-
dominated world.[129]

Ironically, white cowboys were themselves social outcasts, which in
some circumstances could work to blur racial barriers. Certainly many
white cowboys had no difficulty courting Mexican or Indian women and
were willing to acknowledge talented cowboys when they saw them, regardless of ethnicity. In the 1850s, Mexican vaqueros and mesteños had
been the mentors to Anglo cowboys as well as African American slaves,
teaching them methods of roping and breaking horses.[130] In addition, many
young white boys or tenderfeet were often placed in the care of the black
cook or horse wrangler to teach them the ropes before they were let loose
on the cattle, and they formed close relationships with these men.[131] William Lewis was a double outcast in his own cowboy outfit as he was both
a greenhorn from out East and the boss's son, and as a result "formed a
defensive comradeship" with a thirteen-year-old black boy. He also greatly
admired the riding and roping skills of black cowboy Billy Freeman and
envied the Mexican cowboys' equipment so much he adopted the Mexican-
style stirrup covers known as *tapaderos*, which were designed to keep the
foot from slipping through rather than wear uncomfortable high-heeled
cowboy boots that were supposed to do the same. While Lewis eventually
entered the inner circle of his outfit, however, presumably his young play-
mate never did.[132] Another outsider, immigrant Frank Collinson, likewise
became close friends with black cowboys and admired their skills, despite
the vast distance between them in education and social status.[133]

Often men were loyal to their outfit regardless of race. When authorities jailed a black cook in Abilene in the new town jail, his trail outfit

staged the first jailbreak there to free him.[134] When two cowboys, one black, one white, went into town at the end of the trail, a white drunk harassed the black cowboy and his buddy jumped in and defended him. When a white cattleman berated the cowboy for defending a black man, the white cowboy picked a fight with him as well. In a criminal court case resulting from a shooting incident on the JA Ranch, a black ranch employee was among those testifying in court against the white outsider accused of doing the shooting, something that would have been unheard of in the rest of the South.[135] In a San Angelo saloon, when Bill Oden refused to serve a black cowboy named "Golden," he came behind the bar and tried to serve himself, precipitating a fight in which several whites, possibly from his outfit, came to Golden's defense.[136] When Bones Hooks was refused service at a restaurant in town at the end of the trail, his buddy Bob Donald reached for his gun, saying, "I came a thousand miles to kill a so-and-so like you. Bring the boy his meal." Bones ate but did not enjoy it.[137]

Despite several friendships and generally easygoing relations between whites and nonwhites on the ranch or trail, racism pervaded most interactions. Even while praising black cowboys, most whites referred to them in derogatory terms as "boys" and "niggers." Teddy Abbott explained that the Olive Brothers hired blacks and Mexicans because they were cheap labor but that they were "mostly hard on Mexicans and niggers because being from Texas they was born and raised with that intense hatred of a Mexican, and being Southerners, free niggers was poison to them."[138] Ironically, the word "boy" was both a term of endearment and an insult, and its regular use to describe men of color during this period inevitably raises comparisons with its use to describe cowboys. Anglos frequently used the word "nigger" as an adjective to describe something bad or inferior. An example was the term "nigger brand" which referred to a sore on a horse's back that came from careless treatment.[139] The cowboys got lessons in racism from the magazines they read like the *National Police Gazette*, which regularly printed sensational accounts of lynchings of black men accused of raping white women, and reported the alleged crimes in lurid detail.[140] Cowboys accepted many racist stereotypes without question. Even Charlie Siringo, who acknowledged that black cowboys had saved his life on several occasions, nonetheless joked that he had tried to write a "nigger love story" but all the characters got arrested for theft and ran off with carpetbaggers, so he did not like them and gave up.[141] Even the black cowboys accepted the term. Bones Hooks reported that almost all black cowboys' names were prefaced with "Nigger" but insisted that it was a term of the times and not necessarily intended as an insult.[142]

Hispanics fared little better when it came to racism. James Cook reported that Mexican cowboys who were expert ropers and riders earned $2 less a month than he did with little experience.[143] By the 1870s and 1880s, Anglos believed that Mexicans liked to live primitively and had no need for more money, and since they thought they would just spend it on idle pleasures like gambling, it was not necessary to pay them very much. Anglos saw Mexicans as culturally inclined to indolence, and morally lax. Early discussions of Mexicans had dwelt on their mixed blood heritage, which many saw as mongrelization. Threatened by the idea of miscegenation, Anglos painted people of mixed blood as degenerate, and attributed all sorts of negative behavior to mestizos and mulattoes. Since Mexicans could be a mix of white, black, and Indian ancestry, they seemed less than human to most Anglos. While many light-skinned "Spanish" *criollos* still mixed freely with whites in urban areas, whites began to see Mexicans as dirty and barbaric, drawing on the cruelest traditions of both Spanish and Indian heritage. They even believed Mexican bodies were made of nonhuman flesh and that scavengers would not eat dead Mexicans on the battlefields. Little surprise that during the Mexican American War many Anglos reported they could kill Mexicans as easily as they killed turkey or deer.[144] Walter W. Meek painted a degraded picture of a neighboring South Texas ranch by claiming that the owners were very dirty, and that "every Mexican on the place is free to go in and out of the house at will."[145]

Given prevailing racial attitudes, most cowboys of color kept their heads down rather than risk a problem. There was a standard racial etiquette for dealing with whites. Black cowboy Joe McFarland remembered, "I was the only cullud fellow on de place an' was there 'cause McClish knew I could hold my place as a nigger an' warnt so uppity as some of de niggers."[146] Indeed, one white cowboy, upon meeting the famous black bulldogger Bill Pickett, reported liking him because he "always like[d] a good nigger that don't get smart."[147] Speaking out could be dangerous. When tenderfoot James Shaw and a black cowboy named Albert were the only men to stay with the herd while the rest of the outfit ran away to drink in Dodge City, they were not pleased. Albert rebuked the ringleader of the other cowboys, saying pointedly, "Where do you suppose dem cattle would abin if Mr. Shaw and me had went to town," but his complaint backfired. The man drew his pistol on Albert, saying, "It's all right, ain't it, Albert?" leaving Albert only able to reply "Yes, sah cos it [is]."[148]

A study of Mexican workers in South Texas showed much the same pattern. Mexicans had to be deferential to whites at all times, although whites could talk to them on familiar terms. They could laugh *with* the Anglos but never *at* them, although Anglos could make fun of Mexicans whenever they liked.[149] Visiting journalists to the King Ranch praised the vaqueros, who they said would never play tricks on dudes such as giving them broncos to ride or shooting at their feet. Instead, these men stood up and took off their hats whenever a visitor entered the camp.[150] While these journalists no doubt intended to correct stereotypes about cowboys or even show up Anglo cowboys' rude behavior with their accounts of Tejano workers, the likely reality is that the *kineños* showed deference to Anglos out of habit, rather than respect. Vaqueros on the Kenedy Ranch valued propriety in social relations, especially with the owners, whom they considered to be living in a different world with different rules.[151]

Segregation between whites and nonwhites was not always consistent on different ranches. In the 1890s, on one ranch near San Antonio, the Anglo cowboys slept and ate in the ranch house with the owner, but the Mexicans camped out with the herds and got weekly rations because the Anglos objected to eating with them.[152] However, black cowboy George McJunkin found that mess time on the Panhandle ranches was first come first serve regardless of race. Black cowboys also found they had ways of deflecting racists. Bones Hooks camped out one winter night with a racist from his outfit who had not brought enough bedding and Bones had extra. The white man refused to ask to share until he was too cold, at which time Bones let him stew a little before the man finally moved over to share with him. "We slept warm and neither of us was hurt."[153] Bones was somewhat unusual, however. He was born after slavery and never adopted the subservient tone that some former slaves did. He earned a reputation as a top bronco buster and acted as an independent contractor. He used humor to break down many racial barriers and took any practical jokes the white men played on him in stride, returning them when he had the opportunity. He also knew how to deal with racists and used what power he had to deflect them. In one case, he was a little over-sensitive, however. Bones was illiterate and so asked one of the white cowboys to read a letter for him, and when the cowboy refused, Bones assumed he was a racist. He used his position as wrangler to make sure that every horse the white cowboy got from the remuda was a bad one, only later realizing that the other cowboy was illiterate, too.[154] Bones had a strong sense of his manhood, nonetheless, and refused to allow racists to stop him from doing his job. He saw himself as a cowboy, rather than a black cowboy, and thus used the same measures of manliness the other cowboys used.

In addition to racism from whites, there was also the problem of intraracial prejudices, especially between "Spanish" and Mexican people. In cities like San Antonio and Corpus Christi, Mexican Americans distinguished between permanent landed residents and landless Mexicans who worked on the ranches. Those Mexicans who were "good citizens," or permanent, often ate next to whites in restaurants and drew strong distinctions between their "Castilian" background and the mixed background of others.[155] In 1874, Kansas City cattle trader Joseph McCoy recognized similar distinctions among the sheepmen of New Mexico when he described Pedro C. Armejo as "one of the mostly pure Castillians" who dominated the region as having a "vivacious intellect" and strong education in contrast to other Mexicans whom he generally distrusted.[156]

Joseph Mora, a son of a Catalonian father and French mother, came across a supposedly Basque Spanish cook while traveling with an outfit in Arizona. Although Mora was fluent in Spanish, he only spoke to him in English, but when the cook let out a string of Catalan curses, Mora told the boss he was no Basque. He then translated for the boss and the cook revealed that he was traveling with some canned Spanish delicacies which he did not trust to leave with the Mexican cook back at the ranch, but planned to travel down to Mexico as "he was just plain lonesome for his kind."[157] Mora's decision not to speak Spanish initially reveals reluctance on his part to be identified with poorer Spanish speakers (Basque descendants were often sheepherders). But the story also suggests that either there were fewer Mexican cowboys in Arizona than Texas, or they were just not of the caliber that the cook and Mora would consider worth talking to. The fact that the cook did not trust the Mexican cook at the ranch suggests the latter. Certainly Mora chose to try to blend in. Discussing a later visit to Mexico, Mora, a native of Uruguay, described it as any Anglo tourist might, and commented on the excessive drinking of the men he encountered as well as "the customary embrace and patting of backs so characteristic of those races."[158] His attitudes were not uncommon among lighter-skinned elite Hispanics who claimed pure descent from Europeans and who tried to adapt to Anglo culture when possible. In later years, however, as racism deepened against both blacks and Mexicans, Anglos stopped making these sorts of distinctions and placed all Hispanics in the same category.[159]

Given the racism most faced, however, it was also common for non-whites to cooperate in a sense of racial solidarity. Blacks were known to fight alongside Indians in raids against whites, although many blacks were captured by Indians themselves.[160] When a white foreman abused a black boy by tying him onto a bucking bronco until he was bleeding, it was a Mexican cowboy who roped the horse and released the boy, swearing at the foreman in Spanish, and it was the black cook who took care of his injuries.[161] And despite restricted circumstances, many found ways to reinforce their sense of manhood. Vaqueros on ranches like the Kenedy and King ranches did not believe that their dependent situation made them less manly. In fact, they felt that their displays of manhood through their work and control of the cattle and their families more than made up for their second-class status. After all, the ranchers were dependent on them to do the work properly and they were largely left alone to do their work on the range.[162] *Kineños* passed on that sense of manhood through their sons as they trained them to work in the roundups and measured their own masculinity in part by how well their sons performed. A modern description of a roundup on the King Ranch illustrates practices that extended back to the nineteenth century. After closely watching teenage sons "audition" for jobs during the spring roundup, the older vaqueros did not "hesitate to take a father aside and speak to him about his son's mistakes, offering criticism and encouragement. They fully expect that the father will do his duty and that the son will listen and obey his father."[163] Thus, vaqueros were able to find masculinity through their role as fathers and in their public role of training sons to become productive members of the community. Ironically they found comfort in a pre-industrial concept of masculinity that had become less relevant, as in industrial society a man was judged on his personal achievements more than those of his family.

However varied the degree of racism they faced, nonwhites ultimately found themselves on the wrong side of the color line. Anglos often used the supposed superiority of whites as not only justification for taking land and economic exploitation of workers, but also to reinforce their own social status. This was particularly important for Anglos who were at the bottom of the economic scale and had little chance of rising beyond manual labor. This category included cowboys, and while there were many individual cases of reaching across the color line in friendship, the reality was that it was in their interest to have a group of men lower on the social scale than they were, as it gave them some self-esteem in comparison. Being white was also intimately tied into middle-class ideals of masculinity in the late nineteenth century, as manifested in the many calls to build up white manhood. Only by building up the manly white American race could the United States reach its full potential, and miscegenation would only weaken it. Victorian Era white Americans also believed that the "primitive" nonwhite races had not evolved sufficiently to achieve true manhood. By their understanding of evolutionary standards, the most advanced races had to have the most perfect manliness and thus white supremacy and masculinity were linked.[164] By either standard, middle- or working-class, whites were manlier in part because they *were* white.

In an all-male environment of the cow camp, cowboys were free to express themselves and to show their manhood without fear of reprisal. They could demonstrate their mastery of specialized knowledge through practical jokes and their dealings with "dudes," thus gaining a feeling of superiority. They could test their manhood against other men through contests of skill, but they did not challenge the men within their own outfit, so they shared any failure with the group rather than having it reflect on their personal sense of manhood. Cowboys defined their masculinity against that of the dudes who controlled their lives or came to visit them and play cowboys. Anglo cowboys and cattlemen also defined their masculinity in racial terms, creating a hierarchy of masculinity based on ethnicity. Most importantly, cowboys performed their ideals of masculinity through the rituals of friendship and through their loyalty to their outfit and to their buddies. These friendships were equal relationships in which both men could choose to provide for the other, simulating familial relations without interfering with the personal freedom they valued. They made any cowboy see himself as "the best man to his size."

# 5

# Men and Women

The relationships that cowboys and cattlemen established with women affected their concept of their own masculinity but also reflected class differences. Although cattlemen spent much time in the company of their wives and daughters, most cowboys had only episodic contact with women. But both shared prevailing Victorian attitudes about respectable women as innocent and in need of protection. The degree to which men could protect women, moreover, was a traditional marker of manhood. To the cattlemen, women could only enhance their masculine image. As a prominent member of society, the cattleman could add to the community with his choice of a wife. He sought first of all a helpmeet who could serve as hostess and survive among the cowboys. He proved his role as provider by ensuring that he met her every need, including frequently building a second house for her in town so that she might find more feminine pleasures and a social life such as she was accustomed to. The production of children, especially sons, also reinforced the cattleman's masculinity and could ensure his business legacy. Women thus gave his business success a larger purpose, and in his role as head of the household he took on all the trappings of respectable masculinity.

In contrast, outside of the South Texas ranches where vaqueros generally lived with their wives and families on the ranch, the cowboy had few opportunities to play family protector and provider. In addition, the women he could associate with were not the sort that society deemed worthy of protection. Not surprisingly, cowboys' attitudes toward women reflected a sense of ambivalence. They rejected the moral world in which good women lived but placed the women in it on a pedestal. They reveled in the freedom they felt in the company of prostitutes but also did not really value these relationships. Thus, the cowboy played at chivalry with the "bad" women he had access to and idolized the "good" women he could not possess. Associating respectable women with family and childhood, they created sentimental attachments in the off-seasons, and performed prescribed courtship rituals they read about in magazine stories or heard of from other men. But few felt comfortable in this role, which they perhaps saw as robbing them of some of their masculinity, especially when young women ridiculed them. Indeed, many were happy to get back to the ranch with their buddies where they could be themselves. In town, the men saw disreputable women as equals and freely competed to capture their affections, earning the respect of their peers in the process. However, in general, their interactions with "good" women only emphasized the cowboys' inability to achieve respectable manhood, even if they could still demonstrate manliness through their sexual prowess with prostitutes. For cowboys, women could just as easily detract from their masculine image as enhance it. Cowboys thus both feared and pursued affairs with women, but given the complications surrounding these relationships they often preferred the company of men.

• • •

Like men everywhere, much of both cowboys' and cattlemen's ideas of how to relate to women came from their images of their mothers. Finding that life was brutal enough in an industrial world, writers at this time idealized the pretty and the tender, and men absorbed these images of women.[1] Sentimental novels and short stories, serialized in local newspapers and magazines around the country, elevated the status of motherhood, hearth, and home to idyllic proportions. Stories depicted women in their iconic roles as mothers, with their "selfless maternity" evoking the highest moral values in those around them. Newspapers took on melodramatic tones in reporting on female victims of crime, perpetuating the idealized image of pure womanhood.[2] Motherhood was a sacred task, one which no man could duplicate. In 1840, for example, the Pennsylvania Supreme Court granted custody of the children to the mother in a divorce case, declaring that "no substitute can supply the place of *her*, whose watchfulness over the sleeping cradle or waking moments of offspring is prompted by deeper and holier feelings than the most liberal allowance of a nurse's wages could possibly stimulate."[3]

For many boys who left home, the hardest part was leaving their mothers. Black future cowboy Will Crittenden left his schoolteacher father and mother's home to ride up the trail with a herd and never forgot his mother's tears: "I kept telling her dat I wasn't goin' to stay, but she didn't feel none so good anyway."[4] When William Lewis left home at age sixteen to go to his first roundup, he saw his mother watching with a worried look on her face and "only [my] fear of appearing unmanly kept [me] from riding back to reassure her one more time."[5] T. E. Hines recalled his mother crying a great deal when he left home, but after his father took her aside and spoke with her she became resigned to his departure. The fact that Hines was twenty-one at the time he left home seemed to make little difference.[6] Mothers were clearly angelic figures in the both public and private imagination.

Such ideals soon became accepted truths, in part because women themselves promoted an image that emphasized their superior morality and sensitivity. Women embraced sentimentalism as a way to make their lives relevant. Bound to the private sphere of home, they elevated its significance, arguing that sentiment and feeling were truly powerful weapons allowing them to transform society.[7] Women often gladly took on caretaker roles. Amanda Burks, who went up the trail in a buggy, played a strong mothering role to the cowboys in the outfit. Branch Isbell trailed with the Burks at age twenty as a tenderfoot and was tremendously grateful that she took him under her wing. Over forty years later he still held her in high sentimental regard. "My prayer for her is that she never grow less, and may she 'live to eat the hen that scratches above her grave.'"[8] For her part, Burks remembered that "[b]eing the only woman in camp, the men rivaled each other in attentiveness to me. They were always on the lookout for something to please me, a surprise of some delicacy of wild fruit, or prairie chicken, or antelope tongue."[9] Mrs. Charles Goodnight was alone with the cowhands on her husband's ranch for six months without another woman around for at least eighty miles, during which time she kept home, raised chickens, and patched the cowboys' clothing.[10] Black cowboy Matthew "Bones" Hooks held her and the other white women of the Panhandle he encountered in great esteem, as they often protected him from the white cowboys who tormented him by shooting blank cartridges at his feet among other cruel actions.[11] Luther A. Lawhon reported that there was an unwritten law that any time a cowboy outfit rode up to a ranch they could ask the woman to bake bread for them and she would cheerfully comply, not because she was afraid of them but "from an accommodating spirit and a kindness of heart which was universally characteristic in those days."[12]

Women also recognized the power of sentimental femininity. When Mary Taylor Bunton's husband refused to let her go up the trail with him, saying it was "neither a safe or a sane thing to do," she was "on the verge of hysteria when I thought of a woman's weapon—tears." Seeing his wife cry for the first time, her husband would have agreed to anything and Mary got her wish. On her trip up the trail, she liked to decorate her hair and her horses' bridles with wildflowers, and the men humored her. "If any of them chanced to pass anywhere near and see me arrayed in flowers . . . they would stop their horses, take off their hats, and make a sweeping bow, and as they bent low over their saddle horns would exclaim 'Hail to the cowboys' beautiful queen of the flowers.'"[13]

Western author Larry McMurtry proclaimed in his introduction to a reprint of *The Trail Drivers of Texas* that "cowboys are romantics, extreme romantics and ninety-nine out of a hundred of them are sentimental to the core. They are oriented to the past and face the present only under duress."[14] While McMurtry himself was a purveyor of cowboy stereotypes, his image of cowboys as sentimental was undoubtedly true of them when it came to "respectable" women. A woman's life on the frontier was difficult, and men who grew up there often sentimentalized their mothers in tune with popular images of womanhood.[15] Cowboys on the trail talked longingly about going to "God's Country," meaning back home to their mothers, when the season was over.[16] Teddy Blue Abbott felt sorry for his mother, a lady used to servants who moved to a cabin where they had no beds and slept on the dirt floor. "Poor Mother. She did the best she could, but times were hard . . . she did all the cooking and all the housework for that great big family, thirteen children before she got through, and I never heard her complain."[17] Teddy, like many cowboys, sentimentalized his mother as an angel, and no doubt listened fondly to the many syrupy songs about mothers that were popular in the mid- to late nineteenth century.[18]

Accounts of both cowboys and cattlemen abound with evidence that Victorian ideals of innocent womanhood came with them to the frontier and the men modified their behavior accordingly. When Jim Gober moved a herd to the Frying Pan Ranch, his ranch boss brought along his wife, their two small boys, and her sister. The cowboys had never experienced having women in camp before, and so they all agreed they would have to watch their language and behavior.[19] When Mrs. Gregor Lang arrived at her husband's ranch in South Dakota, the ranch hands began observing the Sabbath and cursed less. One Texas cowboy, asked to escort a woman around the ranch he worked on, could not bring himself to tell her that the horse she rode was called 'Old Guts,' for its constant stomach rumbling, and instead told her it was called 'Old Bowels.' Historian Lewis Atherton observed that "such niceties of language were reserved for one's mother and other good women."[20]

Ironically, cowboys filled their memoirs with impossible images of women as flowers of purity on the rough frontier, despite all evidence to the contrary. "And, of course, the girls all rode side saddles," wrote S. A. Wright, reminiscing in 1937. "If a girl had rode a stride then, she wouldn't have been invited to dances."[21] Teddy Abbott reported that "If the cowpunchers of them days had ever seen a woman wearing pants, they'd have stampeded to the brush."[22] Yet Mary Taylor Bunton recalled the first time she rode astride in the mid-1880s, wearing the new riding breeches her mother had sent her. One of the locals was astonished and her own husband "viewed me with surprise but had no time to comment."[23] Such images from both men and women distort the fact that many women were as good hands as their male counterparts, having grown up with them on the ranches and farms.

Frontier women's lives often necessitated that they take on extra hardships that their Eastern counterparts avoided, which led frontier children to see their mothers as somewhat heroic figures themselves. Women rarely had the opportunity to avoid ranch work, especially as the trails ended and work became more sedentary.[24] The women on the Kenedy Ranch were primarily in charge of their son's religious educations, but when the vaqueros were off at the roundups they were in charge of everything.[25] Annie Hightower of Bell County worked with the boys on her family ranch from age ten until she was married. She did leave some of the most strenuous work for the men, but had her share of spills and accidents. Luckily, her brother taught her how to handle her body during a fall, which saved her from some broken bones.[26] A. G. Anderson was certainly familiar with working cowgirls and reported seeing a girl on the Nueces who was able to rope a calf better than him. His wife, Mattie, came with her sister and brother-in-law from Uvalde to Edwards County with a herd and proclaimed she was "the biggest cowboy they had."[27] Troy Cowan remembered Ethel and Bess Andres, who were good riders and ropers, doing fancy riding and expertly cutting head from the herd. "They were what I'd call boys in girl's clothing, because they sure took the place of a boy on the range."[28] However, as Dee Garceau argues, the explanation for this seeming contradiction in images is that the cow camp was such a strictly masculine world that women who entered it ceased to be perceived as real women.[29]

It was rare for women to go up the trail with their husbands, although some, like Amanda Burks and Mary Taylor Bunton, obviously did. Most of the women who did were wives and daughters of cattlemen. Mrs.

George T. Reynolds went up the trail to Colorado in 1868 with her husband and brother-in-law and his wife. They faced harassment from Indians and tough conditions, but she only remembered it as thrilling. She later went on other trails to Cheyenne and Salt Lake City, riding in the hack and sleeping by campfires.[30] In 1874, Bell Vanderver, the daughter of a Texas ranchman, married D. M. Barton from a ranch in a neighboring county, and a year later helped him to deliver 500 head of cattle to West Kansas for their delayed honeymoon. The *Kansas Weekly Star* reported that she brought their infant daughter with them and the cook looked after the baby in the mess wagon while she worked alongside the cowboys.[31] Mina Holmsley, wife of Captain James Holmsley of Comanche, made two trips up the trail with her husband, the first in a $1,700 buggy the captain had bought for her. On the trip, she created a remedy to treat the effects of poison oak and later published the formula in a medical journal.[32] Such cases were rare and worthy of special newspaper reports, nonetheless. When the women did go, they usually traveled in relative comfort like Burks, Bunton, and Barton. Louis Atherton has theorized that cattlemen were attracted to women with an independent spirit, but it is also true that these women had the freedom to be able to leave their homes and travel, and the servants to take care of their families.[33] And while, like Bunton, these women certainly enjoyed the opportunity for some sightseeing, they also had an economic stake in the venture.[34]

Many cattlemen's wives were competent ranchers in their own right, often running the ranches when their husbands were absent or when they became widows. Laws in Mexico, and later Texas, allowed widows to own property, and the tradition of women ranchers started even before Texas independence with a number of Tejano *doñas* who took over ranches after their husbands died.[35] Widows often hired foremen to run day-to-day affairs and only took control of the business side. A few exceptional women took control of ranches for their husbands. Mrs. W. A. Miskimon grew up with cattle but married a man who "wasn't no cowman" no matter how much she tried to teach him. When they went up the trail she took control of the men and the herd, and later she opened a millinery shop on the side to supplement the family income. Commenting on the birth of her child, she exclaimed, "At last God gave me a boy."[36] After her husband died in 1887, Lizzie Crossen switched from sheep to cattle and was one of the first in the Big Bend to bring in Herefords. She was quite successful, with as much as 144,000 acres under her control. She ran her ranch from a buggy, making her sons managers when they were old enough to do the work. Even then, she still told them what to do.[37] Rachel Ann Northington Hudgins bought nearly 11,000 acres of land in Wharton County in 1882, nine years after her husband had died, and started her own brand.[38] Mabel Day, nicknamed "The Cattle Queen of Coleman County," kept her husband's ranch intact after he died and just managed to pull it out from under perpetual debt. Hers was the first completely fenced ranch in Texas.[39] Frontier conditions on the ranches both attracted and created independent women, and fragile flowers were not likely to thrive in the environment.[40]

In truth, most daily work on a ranch was gendered. As many cows as there were around them, few men would actually milk a cow unless they had no other choice, as they considered milking to be women's work. In 1885, when James W. Mathis and his family came to his grandfather's ranch from Arkansas, they were shocked to find there was no milk or butter on the ranch. James's grandfather explained to his mother that "it was disrespectful for a cowhand to milk a cow and none of his men would lower their dignity to such an extent."[41] Cowboys preferred to drink canned, condensed milk in their coffee and even wrote songs in praise of Carnation brand milk:

> Carnation milk, best in the land,
> Comes to the table in a little red can,
> No teats to pull, no hay to pitch,
> Just punch a hole in the son of a bitch.[42]

Women were also in charge of churning butter and collecting eggs, and many men went without these items when there was not a woman around to produce them. While women often did men's work out of necessity, they mostly did so in addition to their regular work and without permanently threatening gender boundaries. It seems that fewer men performed women's tasks, although since women's work in general had less prestige, it is likely that men were reluctant to report when they did have to take it on.[43] In a situation where both boys and women crossed gender lines, Lizzie Crossen's sons helped their mother with the laundry regularly while their mother was running the ranch.[44] Among some immigrant groups it is likely that gender distinctions were less firm, as German dairy farmers, for example, did not have problems milking cows. Nonetheless, on most ranches there were clear divisions of labor. Most women who performed "male" tasks saw their work as being for the sake of the ranch rather than as independent achievements. As historian Dee Garceau has argued, when women did men's work they did so in the name of helping the family, and thus did not challenge any gender ideals. In addition, by the early 1900s, as cowboys lost many other outlets for showing their masculinity, cattle work increasingly became off limits to women, who were relegated to training horses or tending sheep.[45]

Despite the obvious fact that women on the ranches and farms worked alongside men rather than sitting in their parlors embroidering doilies, men still perpetuated sentimental imagery of women as the "tamers" of the frontier. Susan Lee Johnson's study of California miners during the Gold Rush explains why another frontier all-male society idealized women. In any community, life revolves around interconnectedness, and the miners perceived women as the glue that held it all together. Johnson suggests that the miners felt incapable of making society cohere without women, but the few women who came to mining camps in the Gold Rush did not act in the "normal" Victorian middle-class way. In addition, the men felt challenges to their social traditions from the Mexican and Indian people around them who had different standards of feminine behavior. With this perspective, the men soon became nostalgic for an ideal "women's society," in much the same way cowboys sentimentalized their mothers and families.[46]

Like the miners, cowboys created their own bonds to replace those of traditional communities, but they nonetheless recognized that their own frontier community did not mirror what the rest of society deemed normal. Sentimental conventions might have helped to restore that normality they craved. Middle-class Americans in the late nineteenth century talked a great deal about achieving a harmony of interests. This harmony meant cooperation rather than class strife in the public sphere, and maintaining proper gender roles in the private sphere. The popular literature of the day also focused on harmony as the ideal.[47] Women could be the facilitators of this harmony in both private and public spheres by using sentiment to stir society to act in a more virtuous manner. However accurate the image, the Cult of True Womanhood was alive and well on the frontier. No wonder George W. Saunders defended cowboy honor by saying that "woman's virtue was their highest ideal, and their respect for womanhood was unbounded."[48]

During the work season cowboys had few regular dealings with any women other than the rancher's wife and felt ill at ease around respectable women they encountered.[49] In reality, many men were intimidated by the ideals they set up, and women often took advantage of their seeming superiority. Teddy Abbott asserted that "there were only two things the old-time cowpuncher was afraid of, a decent woman and being set afoot."[50] Tom McNelly was bashful around girls when he was growing up, especially those on a neighboring ranch when he went there for a meal. The girls came out on the porch and had great sport talking baby talk to him, calling him "honey" and teasing him for being so scared. "Taking a man's place at the ranch didn't help me in the girls' presence."[51] At age eleven, Tom Boone discovered that he could thwart the teasing kisses of three girls in town only by offering to pay them for the kisses. The girls left him alone very quickly.[52] When Branch Isbell was rejected by a girl at a dance he was embarrassed and so tried to return the favor, only to have her sass him right back. "Since then I have known that the 'Yellow Rose of Texas' grows on a thorny bush."[53] A ledger from the records of the Matador Ranch clearly shows the fun two young girls had teasing the hands. The 1898 ranch diary records the arrival of "Miss Robertson" and "Miss Houston" with the following commentary: "Have growled almost consistently to-day. Drove all over the ditches and stumps I could to hear them yell. Girls are peculiar. Hope I can hold out while they are here—."[54] The fact that the entry is in ink when the rest of the entries are in pencil, and not clearly in the same hand, suggests that the young ladies might have been having some sport at the expense of the ranch manager. A later entry, this time in pencil, reads, "Misses Houston and Robertson leave to-morrow & strange to say I am alive to tell the tale.—Oh for a peaceful smoke once more!"[55] Whether the manager wrote the entries or the girls, it is clear that the female presence on the ranch disrupted normal routines and that they delighted in it.

It was not always the women tormenting the men. Sometimes the men played tricks to embarrass each other in front of them. One hot Sunday afternoon on the trail, the cowboys stripped down to their underwear to keep cool. Their trail boss, who could not resist the opportunity, came across a group of girls headed to a camp meeting and instructed them to pass the herd on either side for a better view, precipitating a "stampede" as the men rushed to hide themselves. "Some of the boys went off at a tangent east to see how the range looked, others went west in search of water to fill their canteens, a few thoughtfuls dropped to the rear to push up the drags, while others held their ground trying to hide their embarrassment by trying to put the words 'I would not live away, I ask not to stay' to music."[56] Jim Gober's boss left him in charge of his wife and sister-in-law while he was gone and when he returned he teased Gober about being too familiar with them. In the presence of the other men, his jokes turned more ribald, but he later embarrassed him in front of both the men and women by saying that the women had spoiled him so much that he "[wasn't] any account for anything except a ladies' man," and so needed to work further away from the ranch house.[57] The cowboys on the Panhandle ranches where black cowboy Matthew "Bones" Hooks worked swore constantly and gave their horses vulgar names. When a woman came to visit the ranch, Bones liked to tease the other men by asking, "What did you say your horse's name was?" The cowboy in question's face would inevitably turn bright red.[58] Given the multiple opportunities for embarrassment and loss of confidence around respectable women, however, it was not surprising that many men preferred to avoid them when possible. Luckily for them it was not always that difficult, as few such women came into their circles. In 1887, Walter Meeks, who had lived near San Diego, Texas for over a decade, reported that the arrival of a Mexican woman in the area caused "a ripple of pardonable excitement," as in the time he had lived in the region, with the exception of the neighbor's wife and daughter, he had only once before seen another woman on his or the neighboring ranches.[59]

While there might have been few women nearby who were available to them, the men could always turn to the somewhat safer form of written correspondence for romance. C. F. Doan, who ran Doan's Store along the Western Trail, recalled that "many a sweetheart down the trail received her letter bearing the postmark of Doan's and many a cowboy asked self-consciously if there was any mail for him while his face turned beet red when a dainty missive was handed him."[60] Teddy Roosevelt related meeting up with two Texas cowboys and possible outlaws riding line in the Dakotas who asked him to mail letters "evidently the product of severe manual labor" to their girlfriends. When Roosevelt stopped to talk with them, they regaled him for over an hour with the women's' respective charms and virtues.[61] Montana-born cowboy George Flanders remembered long winter months in the Badlands of South Dakota isolated with his fellow cowboys with little to do. At night in the bunkhouse, the men answered personal ads in the *Heart and Hand* paper whose main purpose seems to have been matchmaking. "The boys [answered] all such adds and had a heck of a time reading each other's answer. In fact, once in a while a cowhand would get himself a mailorder wife that way."[62] John J. Baker reported that the men would pick the best writer among them to "fix up" their letters and got some "heart breaking replies."[63]

The correspondents were not always honest, however, and the cowboys often played tricks on each other. Henry Price asked his buddy Bill to write a letter in response to an ad, and when the "lady" sent him an elegant response and a beautiful photograph, Henry sent her a picture of the boss rather than himself and lied that he owned a ranch in Montana. At this time, the other cowboys perhaps decided he had gone too far and when he proposed to her in his next letter, he got a rather illiterate response that came too quickly for the woman to have sent it. As the response also implied that the lady was black, Henry realized he was the victim of a practical joke and claimed to be so embarrassed by the incident that he left the ranch.[64]

When the men did encounter respectable women in person, they often did not know how to act. After flirting with two girls from New York who had moved to town, Charlie Siringo proposed to one of them in Texas slang, asking her to "jump into a double harness and trot through life with me." The girl misunderstood and threw hot corn ears at him, giving him a black eye. "You can imagine the boys giving it to me about monkeying with civilized girls, etc."[65] On the train on the way back from a trip up the trail, Jack Potter met up with some emigrant girls and was nonplussed when one of them asked him for an autograph. He first wrote down all the road brands he knew and then when she insisted on a poem, wrote a children's verse he remembered from school.[66] Bill Arp looked after his boss's wife and sister-in-law while he was away from the ranch, and seems to have made a favorable impression on the women. The sister-in-law left him a note asking him to take care of her cat and chickens and to remember him but "she was a sweet girl whom I felt so far above me that I never could muster courage to write to her."[67] Cowboys would do almost anything to please "good" women, and one early 1890s observer noted a large number of cowboys who went to camp meetings and loudly confessed their sins and avowed their religion in order to gain their favor.[68] The awkwardness they felt around these women reflected a clear awareness that the cowboy was not a respectable person himself. However, this realization did not stop the men from aspiring to claim such a woman for their own.

Cowboys who were close to town, especially those who came from respectable families, had many more opportunities to meet respectable women. Jim Gober, who lived in town as a young man, at age sixteen had a sweetheart and two more girls reportedly seeking his favor.[69] Growing up, Will Hale, the son of a rancher and businessman, had ample opportunity to meet girls while away in New York or St. Louis for school. In New York, he and a friend bought candy for their girls, which they delivered with a note "From your lovers." In St. Louis, he and another friend visited their girlfriends every Sunday, playing games with them or going for walks. In fact, Hale was such a ladies' man that one summer he even decided to forgo the pleasures of the ranch to stay in town courting.[70] At home, he also spent a lot of time in town on errands for his father. The men who went up the trail regularly also had an opportunity to meet more women. George Saunders had a reputation as "a lover of fine clothes and pretty girls," and on one stint as trail boss stopped the herd just six miles short of a stock pen and made camp so he could visit one of his girlfriends.[71]

But most men were isolated from town and other people for long periods and could not pursue courtships. Sam Wootan of Llano County had to settle for bunkhouse stories of "beautiful senoritas" from old Mexico when he was a young boy on the ranch. He was so enthralled by these tales that he moved to Mexico himself at age twenty-three.[72] Ed Bell reported moving with a herd to Frio Canyon in October, and although there were twelve men in the outfit, "there wasn't one of us saw a woman we knew until Christmas." When they did get out on Christmas Eve, they were thwarted in their attempts to meet some boarding school girls by a vigilant housemother and were only able to finally meet them at a dance.[73] In 1883, Teddy Abbott went up north to work the range near Forsyth, Montana. The town had only two women: the storekeeper's wife, and "a fat old hay bag who had been scalped by Indians . . . a few years before, and was laying up with the barber."[74] Ultimately, most cowboys had to limit their serious courtship to the off-season when they traveled home to see their families. When cowboy Will Carpenter returned to the Texas Panhandle from Missouri, the *Fort Griffin Echo* reported he had spent "the past three months eating apples and sparking the girls and was now "bound for the ranche and hard work."[75] The clear implication was that work and romance did not mix.

One of the few places cowboys were likely to have contact with women was at a dance. The gender imbalance on the frontier was most visible at these events, which drew men from miles around. One account of dances in the northwest claimed that there were often over one hundred men and only two to twelve women, many of whom were married or young girls. In such circumstances, the common practice was to give the men numbers and call them up when it was their turn to dance with the women.[76] At one dance Rollie Burns attended in 1881, there were thirty cowboys

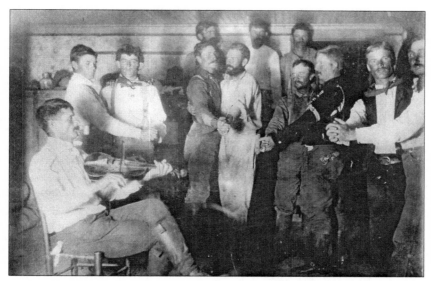

The relative scarcity of women on the ranches meant that most dances were "stag" affairs and men had to partner with each other, a source of much cowboy humor. Men Dancing. Photo courtesy of Southwest Collection/Special Collections Library, Texas Tech University, Lubbock, Texas, SWCPC E332-E1 #59.

and only nine women, three of whom were married.[77] The imbalance was worse in the early years of the frontier but persisted until the twentieth century. British observer Helen Jaques attended a dance in the early 1890s at which men still far outnumbered women and had to buy the numbers to be able to dance with them, the proceeds going to the musicians.[78]

The obvious solution that many decided on was for men to dance with each other when there were no women available. By all accounts, this practice was not uncommon, and there was a suitably cowboy term to describe it: taking the heifer brand.[79] Despite the implications, such behavior was more a source of humor than true gender bending. As Charles Holden remembered, "to give all a chance at dancing, some of the stags would take the part of does, which caused a heap of fun."[80] The normal practice was for men to wear some kind of indication that they were taking the woman's role, whether a white handkerchief around their arm, a ribbon, or in some cases a long apron.[81] Once marked they "were thenceforth accepted as 'ladies fair'" and the men would sometimes refer to these male partners as "she" during the evening.[82]

Such gender play fit into a larger context of cross-dressing for entertainment or humor. Much of the transvestite humor in cowboy poems and stories usually involves mistaken identity of girls rather than boys, but there are also a number of stories involving prostitutes persuading cowboys to dress as women to fool their buddies. Dee Garceau and literary scholar Blake Allmendinger both note that cross-dressing humor has always been a way to parody "respectable" society associated with women, and could have provided an enjoyable release from Victorian morality that fit well with cowboys' desires to escape civilization.[83] One of the more celebrated cases occurred when Jake De Puyster saw there were not enough women to go around at a dance in Ogallala, Nebraska and told his buddy he would go find him a "she-partner." He came back a few minutes later wearing a red hat with flowers and a green feather, a pink sash tied around his waist with a bow and a pair of bloomers which hung down over his chaps, gun belt, and spurs. Although his buddy was not amused, Jake, by all accounts, became the belle of the ball.[84] Teddy Abbott related with great relish his own experience in drag. Having heard about Jake's exploits, Abbott, at the teasing of one of his favorite prostitutes, decided to do the same. She had already wound her scarf around his hat and put her gold necklace on him, and now she gave him her underwear, which he put on and proceeded to parade around the streets. The story traveled all over the ranch country via the reps at the roundups and Teddy kept the underwear as a trophy of the event, pinning it on the bunkhouse wall like a flag.[85] Allmendinger sees such play as a way to mock the "preciousness" of women and their sentimental worlds. In addition, it also served the purpose of humorously defusing any same-sex attraction in isolated all-male groups.[86] While there may have been a few men who preferred playing the women's role, the only recorded cases seem to have been in the service of humor rather than any serious attempts to challenge gender roles.

The object for most cowboys at a dance was thus to meet women rather than to take on their role. When preparing for a dance, the men did what they could to look respectable but often just wore their work clothes, minus the guns.[87] Ben Mayes and Rollie Burns both recalled cowboys taking turns sharing good clothes in order to appear acceptable to the women at the dance.[88] Accounts of cowboy dances are full of similar stories. In one incident, the boys attempted to starch and iron their white shirts, only to end up with yellow spots and rust marks from the iron.[89] When they finally got to dance with the women, it was hardly surprising that the men were unclear as to how to behave. As Mayes described it, unaccustomed to female company, the cowboy "felt out of place and bashful around the girls. He would look first at the ceiling and then at the floor and put his hands behind him and in front of him and when he'd finally think of something to say the girl would look at him like she thought he was out of his head or something. He would be so plagued, he just wanted to tell her to go to Helena, Montana."[90]

Of course, not all the cowboys were as shy, and many carried out a series of courtship rituals with the women they encountered at the dances. Since before the Civil War, commercial valentines had been available for purchase, as well as chap books with standardized verses of sentimental poetry to write in them.[91] Cowboys used these items to carry out their courtships. They exchanged gifts of chewing gum and candy and took advantage of the rather sentimental advertising cards that came with the candy to express their feelings. An example of such a card that Helen Jaques obtained on her visit to a Texas ranch clearly shows the romantic conventions of the day:

ADORABLE ONE!—

Where is the light of my eyes this dreary night? Darning papa's socks? Ah me! The weary, weary injustice of cruel fate! Tell me dearest, tell me that as soon as your tiresome task is finished you will hasten to me. Remember the old meeting place. *** I shall be there, with my heart beating in a wild double-shuffle. *** I will bring whatever change I can raise *to buy more of Heisel's delicious love-letter juice.*

*Yours till we meet, EVER THINE*[92]

While clearly encouraging the purchase of the product, the text also incorporates sentimental imagery of selfless womanhood that Western men would expect of respectable women. It would seem that a commercial valentine such as this one would defeat the purpose of showing true sentiment and feeling that women were taught to value in Victorian America, but by 1860 hand-made valentines were rare.[93] Moreover, the exchange of these items actually marked a link between commercialism and romanticism. Women believed that material objects carried with them the emotions of the people they came in contact with. Thus, they could treasure even mass produced items as a sign of pure feeling.[94] That cowboys would take part in the exchange of such items, however ritualized, showed that their ideal of manhood, in common with nineteenth-century ideals of masculine be-havior, did not preclude sentimental displays toward women.

But while cowboys followed the rules of sentimental courtships with respectable women, most of the women they interacted with on a regular basis were not respectable. Cattlemen had the respectability and wealth to attract women from their own social backgrounds, but the reality for most cowboys was that the women they were able to have relationships with likely did not come from that category. For each good woman they placed on a pedestal they most likely knew two or three society consid-ered unworthy of respect or protection. As a result, their ideals of wom-anhood affected these relationships negatively. If the women were not re-spectable, then the cowboys had no obligation to treat them with respect or even kindness. Indeed, their involvement with the women both sym-bolized their masculinity and left it lacking in comparison with that of the cattlemen. That they could publicly possess a woman was a marker of their virility.[95] That they could not protect her from others, or possess her exclusively, suggested impotence.

Nonetheless, cowboys developed strong relationships with the prosti-tutes and referred to them as their "girlfriends." They were far more at ease with women of lower social status than they were with the ranchers' wives and daughters. As a boy, Bill Walker was free and easy with the prostitutes and working women he met, reporting their willingness to engage in sex, although not necessarily with him as he was too young. When one woman told him she preferred a man with a mustache "that hacked me so bad I'd have give a thousand dollars for just a few hairs up there."[96] Prostitutes were common features of frontier towns. Deputy Sheriff Henry Heron of Fort Worth estimated that between 1876 and 1879, one-half of the women in town were prostitutes. Settler Jessica Young said that the Panhandle town of Mobeetie was full of prostitutes who were quite open about their profes-sion.[97] Prostitutes also followed trail herds to Wyoming and Colorado as they moved north for the season. Cowboys often engaged in quasi-rela-tionships with the prostitutes with weeklong "marriages" when they were in town, and it was quite possible that when a cowboy said he had a girl in town she was a prostitute.[98] Teddy Abbott's interactions with prostitutes constituted his primary relationships with women while he was a cowboy, even preferring to stay with a prostitute when he had the offer of staying at a parsonage with the preacher's daughter who had shown an interest. When he talked about cutting a swathe in town with a girl, he added, "I do not mean that she was a decent girl: we knew very few of those."[99]

Early newspaper reports about prostitutes were common, but not entirely negative. The *Jacksboro Frontier Echo* archly referred to Mollie Mc-Cabe's brothel as "palace of beautiful sin" for "damsels of spotted virtue," and the editor often sided with the women when they were accused of disorderly behavior, blaming the cowboys more than them.[100] Even in later years when there were efforts to eliminate the prostitutes, many newspapers had sympathy for them, characterizing some women as innocent victims of the madams who had lured them into bad behavior.[101] Cowboys may have relished their interactions with prostitutes as one more way to challenge Victorian morality and "civilized" behavior, or they may simply have felt more comfortable with women who, like themselves, were on the margins of respectable society.[102] As Teddy Abbott said, "I suppose those things would shock a lot of respectable people. But we wasn't respectable and we didn't pretend to be."[103]

Prostitutes were thus a common part of cowboys' lives. Cow towns at railheads especially catered to the sexual needs of cowboys as well as cattlemen coming off the trail, and there were a wide range of women available, from those who worked at the relatively prosperous saloon/brothels to the "snake charmers" who called to men out of cribs in back alleys.[104] The prostitutes came from all racial backgrounds; in San Antonio, there were white, black, and Mexican women involved in the sex trade. Farther north in Austin, there were fewer Hispanic women, perhaps reflecting a smaller population of single Hispanic males in the city, geographic distance from Mexico, or increased availability of white women. However, Austin authorities made their primary distinction not on race, but between discreet high-class prostitutes who catered to the politicians and those, whatever ethnicity, who carried out their business in the streets. Some women came West as professionals, others saw prostitution as an economic opportunity, and some were victims of poverty or abuse.[105] Some, known as "snowbirds," were addicted to drugs.[106] Few lived the glamorous life depicted in Westerns, but there were certainly some who had a better situation than others. Not surprisingly, the incidence of sexually transmitted diseases was high among cowboys and the prostitutes. One informant recalled that all of the eleven men in his trail outfit suffered from gonorrhea and many cowboys carried around medicinal remedies with them. One of the men in the group assured his fellow cowboys of the efficacy of his remedy, saying that he got gonorrhea about every two years and would not be without the recipe.[107]

Cowboys were fully aware that their relationships with prostitutes were mainly financial ones. The Waco Tap was a notorious "queen parlor," saloon, and gambling house that Bud Brown remembered in some detail. Not surprisingly, the main business was to use the women to sell the customers expensive drinks, and allegedly, the women received a percentage of what they sold. The women drank with the men but the bartenders mixed their drinks with little alcohol so that they could stay sober. The second floor of the Waco Tap had twenty rooms where the women took the men for sex, but the main profits were clearly in the alcohol and the men knew it, making a conscious trade of money for female company.[108] Teddy Abbott flirted with many prostitutes in his youth, spending most of his salary on equipment, clothes, and women. Of one of his paramours he commented: "Of course she loved me. They always do as long as you've got money. I was just one more sucker on a string."[109] The cowboys took it easily for the most part. Their normal practice was to spend money when they had it and go back to the ranch or camp when they were broke. S. B. Brite recalled that "like most of the boys of the early days, I had to sow my wild oats, and I regret to say that I also sowed all of the money I made right along with the oats."[110] These experiences with prostitutes no doubt gave birth to such colorful gems of cowboy wisdom as "Y'u never can trust women, fleas, nor tenderfoots."[111]

Despite their generally friendly relations with prostitutes, cowboys (and other frontier denizens) still did not see them as ideal women, as testified to by the number of incidences of violence these women endured.[112] As the ideal women lived in the private sphere of home and the prostitutes operated in the public sphere, they had no protection from insult and violence.[113] For women without protection, the line between respectable and disreputable was easily crossed. When Jim Gober became sheriff in 1887, he warned men not to bring their girlfriends and wives into gambling houses and saloons because the cowboys and railroad workers viewed women in those places as public property.[114] D. D. Singleterry and his buddies crashed a dance in the Panhandle that was supposed to be for cattlemen only. He swore when a girl they knew refused to dance with him, and when she said he should not swear in front of the ladies, he replied, "Ladies, hell: they're nothing but a bunch of sports." The women ran out of the room and the cowboys ran to their boss, George Littlefield, to get their pay and leave town.[115] While recalling that many cowboys in the 1880s were willing to marry prostitutes, Abbott "never would have married that kind. I always secretly had in my heart the hopes of meeting a nice girl."[116]

While respectable women who had been lured into prostitution due to tragic circumstances deserved the full sympathy that sentimental reporting could provide, newspapers made distinctions for hardened prostitutes and madams, who deserved not maternal redemption, but paternal punishment in the courts.[117] Some cowboys also believed it was their role to keep these women in line. Pat Bullis, a line rider from the East Panhandle in the 1880s and 1890s, recalled a number of horrific incidents involving cowboys and prostitutes. He and a friend visited two prostitutes at their place on the Canadian River, one of whom had a pair of mockingbirds in a cage. The friend was so annoyed with the birds that "Finally he jumped up, pulled the birds' heads out between the bars of the cage, and cut their heads off." He threw the birds' heads into the kitchen and one fell on the plate of the prostitute to whom they belonged. When the women threatened to call the sheriff and tied the men's saddle ropes to the door so they could not escape, the men got the horses to pull the doors off their hinges to get away. In this case, the women were spared from further violence, as the men were too scared to come back for two or three months, but that they would expect to come back at all following such an incident shows both the women's vulnerability to and dependence on the cowboys.[118]

Another story Bullis told privately illustrates both the dynamics of cowboy relationships with prostitutes and, ironically, the esteem in which they held respectable women. Bullis and his outfit visited a dance hall in Oklahoma Territory to let loose. A prostitute newly arrived from the East Coast immediately tried to get friendly with the cowboys, but they were not ready for company and one of them told her not to bother them. Rebuffed, the prostitute called him a "son of a bitch." Bullis explained that this particular term was

> dangerous language to use to a cowboy or any Westerner. . . . and in those days it was a "fightin'" word. We couldn't hit a woman, so a couple of the boys grabbed her by the legs, and stood her on her head. Another puncher picked up the spittoon and dumped all it's filthy contents between her legs. The others held her until all that nasty stuff had saturated her clothes and completely covered her body. She took the next train back East.[119]

The hypocrisy of degrading a woman in defense of the purity of womanhood clearly did not touch these men, who thought their actions entirely appropriate. Undoubtedly, the "boys" thought it was their prerogative to police disreputable women, and the story has the tone of any of the many cowboy caper tales in other narratives. Our shock at such actions today only highlights the difference in perception. The further irony that "we couldn't hit a woman" shows that prostitutes occupied a middle ground: they were women but did not merit respect they gave other women. Nonetheless, prostitutes were still women, and many cowboys acted with great chivalry toward them, trying to protect them. Teddy Abbott claimed that cowboys would never cheat a prostitute and would beat up pimps and other men who abused them. He even defended one prostitute's honor, almost killing a man simply for calling her a whore. Abbott himself recognized the irony of the situation: "Knight of the plains. Had to protect all females. Lord!"[120]

But ideals of chivalry were simply ideals, and in reality many men did not adhere to them in their personal lives. While prostitutes were certainly more vulnerable to violence, even respectable women were not free from it. Just as some fathers were abusive parents, some husbands abused their spouses, and there were often few people around to restrain them.[121] Texas women had made frequent complaints against their husbands for brutal violence in the 1840s and 1850s, and many Anglo Texan men intimidated their wives with their rough treatment.[122] The frequency of assaults against women in the court records of the late nineteenth century suggests times had not changed much.[123] Although such stories are rare in memoirs, it is quite likely that the narrators censored their writings and that there was far more of this behavior than they saw fit to report to decent society.[124]

Patriarchal authority often justified such violence under the guise of controlling the household, and such concepts of masculine power existed across ethnicities. In African American society, patriarchal behavior was common in private relationships, as black men experienced emasculation in the public sphere.[125] On the Kenedy Ranch, male authority was supreme among vaquero families to the point that the oldest son had more authority than his mother.[126] Patriarchal identity within Mexican homes often meant strict control over their daughters, and many cowboys who attempted to date Mexican girls had their hope squashed by their fathers. Will Hale and a fellow cowboy began courting some Mexican girls who lived near his ranch but faced heavy opposition from the family. "We came very near to killing a whole bunch of them, but they got us stopped just the same." When two cowboys Hale knew became friendly with a Mexican family, they assumed that their attentions to the daughters of the household were welcome. When they eloped with the girls to Corpus Christi, however, the father swore to kill both the cowboys and his daughters as he "believed his girls had disgraced themselves and his family."[127]

There were clearly different rules at work for how men treated women on the frontier. On the one hand, the cult of true womanhood led the men to sentimentalize respectable women as pure and moral beings, on a pedestal they could not hope to approach unless they had something to offer the women in terms of property or respectability. The cowboys, having neither, were in awe of these women and preferred to avoid them if possible. The majority of their daily interactions with women, however, were with women who did not meet the standards of respectability and with whom they could feel more comfortable, provided of course that the women were not trying to cheat them or challenge their masculine authority. If manhood involved the possession of women, the cowboys were at a disadvantage. They were lower on the social scale than cattlemen and could not compete as easily for women. But at least they could feel assured of their manhood in their relations with prostitutes, where the little money they had could ensure their possession of a woman, if only for a short time. They sometimes tried to create imitations of refined sentimental relationships with these women, but the prostitutes who lived in frontier towns did not fit in with the mythology and could not use sentimentalism as a cloak to give them legitimacy or protection. The cowboys could play the role of protector, but however torn between this fantasized normality and the reality of the situation, they neither believed these women unworthy of protection, nor could they protect them.

A late nineteenth-century observer of life in on a Texas ranch noted that "all unmarried men are 'boys,' regardless of age; but let even a youth of eighteen marry, and he is immediately designated 'old man' so and so."[128] By most standards of the day, even those of the cowboys, marriage was a definite sign of reaching adulthood. Nevertheless, it was not one that many were anxious to rush into. Indeed, judging by many of their narratives, cowboys resisted marriage as one of the signs of "civilization" that they hoped to escape, along with regular baths, fancy clothes, and proper manners. Ike Pryor told the story that when a phrenologist had examined his head and told him that women would always have influence over him, he decided to go off and become a cowboy to avoid his fate.[129] When the daughter of a Tascosa hotel owner started to coquettishly harass D. D. Singleterry and his friends for playing poker with her naïve brother, he told her, "Lady, I didn't come up here to get married, I came up here for work."[130] But few cowboys had the chance to marry anyway. Aside from prostitutes, the cowboys met very few single women in the course of their normal activities. Those they met might have parents who objected to them marrying a rough cowhand with few prospects. Cowboys were not known for their thrift, but even at their best, it was hard for them to save money beyond their living expenses in the off-season, which meant that many delayed marriage until their thirties or forties, by which time a large number had become confirmed bachelors.

In the long run, however, many cowboys decided that they needed more than just temporary relationships with women and decided to settle down and marry. Marriage often meant the end of a cowboy's career. Most ranchers did not like to employ married men as they earned a higher salary and required separate housing, and so the couple usually settled down to farming. Ironically, in so doing, the cowboy crossed the last threshold of manhood by respectable society's standards. He took on responsibility for a family and so had finally grown up. On the other hand, adjusting to a sedentary life was not easy for cowboys, whatever they gained in social respectability through marriage.

The estimate in the *Trail Drivers of Texas* was that about 50 percent of cowboys eventually married and quit droving, but a surprising 20 percent both married and continued working on the ranch.[131] These figures might include Hispanic cowboys who often married and lived on the ranches with their families, but it more likely reflects a number of cowboys who simply left their wives when it did not work out. One such case was that of William Bush, who left his wife and three small children in Silver City, New Mexico and came to Texas where he took up work on a ranch. His wife, Laura, wrote to the XIT ranch manager to gain his help and sympathy, explaining that she had received no help from her parents, had obtained a divorce, and was about to adopt the children out to other families. Appealing to sentiment, she wrote: "I hope I live long enough to see B. drowned in his own tears to see the finger of scorn pointed at him until he becomes a raving maniac and surely God will send no less punishment to a man who would leave such darling little babies helpless & alone in this cold world."[132]

Such cases were not uncommon, but it was more likely a married cowboy would leave his family on a temporary basis during the work season. In March 1883, Charlie Siringo married a woman he had met in Caldwell, Kansas. He went back to the Panhandle to work the roundups and drive a herd but did not get back to Caldwell until September, and within a few days was supposed to go back and get another herd. "But what then could I do? I hated to give up a good job, with no prospects of making a living by remaining in town." At the last minute, Siringo decided it was time to change careers after all and quit his cowboy job to become a merchant.[133] Most settler women did not want to let their husbands stay on the range all season or go up the trail, leaving them alone to take care of the house. Instead, they expected their husbands, as responsible men, to take up farming or a business and stay with their families. Cowboys thus looked at marriage as taking on responsibility, which made them more of a man in the eyes of society; but also taking away their freedom and independence, which they had come to define as part of their own masculinity. As Teddy Abbott stated, "In 1889 a good woman got her rope on me, and I have stood hitched ever since."[134]

For most cowboys, the decision to marry was in part a financial calculation. With low wages the men could not expect to save up to buy a farm or start a business, and cowboy culture encouraged them to spend their money as they got it. In the years following the Civil War, it was easier. In 1865, when he returned from the war, George Hindes worried that his girlfriend would not accept his proposal when he told her that he was broke, but luckily "she merely laughed and said 'everybody was broke' and that she would help me and so we were married."[135] But for most cowboys in later years, an increase in wages was necessary to make marriage possible. Charlie Weldon reported getting a raise from $25 to $35 a month "so in the fall of '88 I married Sally Chamberlain."[136] For some cowboys better finances did not help. Black cowboy Bones Hooks stayed single while breaking horses on ranches around West Texas because "when I was in all of those places, it'd be two or three years before I'd see another colored person."[137]

There were competing ideas about whether ranchers should let their cowboys marry. Cattleman Frank Hastings believed that a working outfit should be unmarried; otherwise, the wives could call the boys home all the time for legitimate reasons and they would not get any work done.[138] Allowing cowboys to marry had its drawbacks from a business perspective. Building separate accommodations was more expensive than housing the men in one bunkhouse, and the demands on the men's time could interfere with work. If a worker married, there was also the question of whether or not to raise his salary. When Spur ranch boss W. Dawson married in 1901, it took almost five months of letters to the board of directors of the Espuela Land and Cattle Company before they agreed to give him a raise in light of the marriage and to allow him to become an understudy to the bookkeeper.[139] But often the larger ranches preferred married cowhands. Richard King found that having the vaqueros live with their families on the King Ranch led to a more stable workforce as the men were not constantly leaving for work elsewhere.[140] The managers at the Spur Ranch also believed that married men were more stable workers and so encouraged their most dependable hands to marry by keeping on married cowboys all year and laying off the rest for the winter. They let married couples live in line camps or even built separate houses for them.[141] The XIT Ranch also allowed some of its married cowboys to live in permanent camps with their wives.[142]

Married couples sometimes applied for work jointly, as did R. W. Hester to the Matador Ranch in 1889, asking for "such work that would be suitable for a man with a wife, a farm or fence line." But there were just not enough suitable jobs for both a man and his wife on smaller ranches where there were no permanent line camps. Most couples applied as cooks, one of the few jobs open to women on the ranches. Eva Spann and her husband Ernest worked together on a ranch for four years, she as a cook and he as a hand. She got a lot of praise for her work and affection, as well as presents from "her boys," but after four years insisted that they quit and start a farm of their own.[143] Like the Spanns, many married couples who started off working on a ranch ended up quitting after a few years.

Most cowboy wives lived off the ranches. S. A. Wright recalled that all but two of the cowboys in one of his outfits were married, so before they left for the trail they went home to spend the night with their families.[144] If the cowboy continued working while his wife stayed on the farm, the arrangement did not always work out for long. When A. G. Anderson married his cowgirl wife in 1893, his honeymoon was the twenty-mile ride to his new job at another ranch. He worked in the day and came home to his wife at night, and she worked for other people for a while as well but settled into the life of a respectable woman. Within a few years, the couple leased and then bought a ranch of their own. At this juncture, Anderson had to stop his cowboy hijinks, since his wife told him he could not ride his pitching horse again. He obviously saw this ban as an affront to his manhood, as he tried to bet the men in the cow camp that he could ride the horse, but none would take his bet.[145] Once again, becoming respectable meant giving up the usual ways in which the cowboy measured his masculinity in order to gain another. In 1885, at age twenty-six, Edward E. Jones "got the idea I wanted to travel double, and the woman insisted that I anchor at some spot close to her so she could get a peep at me when she was so inclined." Jones soon quit cowboying, moved to Fort Worth, and became a carpenter.[146] In later years, when cowboying became less excit-ing, many men found it an easier choice to quit. James E. Schultz did not have a hard time settling into farming in 1900 because there had been so many changes in the job. Longhorns had all become Herefords, fenced ranches replaced the open range, and rustlers and outlaws were few and far between. "At the time I quit, I was married and living in a house on the range, which was a lot different from living behind a chuck wagon."[147]

Like the cowboys, cattlemen also delayed marriage until they could afford it, and they usually married women from their own social strata. Their marriages were the final step on the road to manhood, as their abil-ity to provide for their families was a key marker of middle-class mas-culinity. They could also be advantageous in other ways. When Mifflin Kenedy married Petra Vela, he married into a prominent Mexican ranch-ing family and his wife gave him the connections he needed to do business in the region.[148] Cattlemen were also in a position to cater to the Cult of True Womanhood. They lavished their wives with gifts and bought them houses in town so that they would have other women to visit and easy ac-cess to doctors and schools for the children.[149] Some also built expensive homes on the ranch which served as showplaces for the family wealth. In the early 1870s, George W. Fulton built a four-story mansion for his wife and family on the water's edge between Fulton and Rockport. The house had indoor plumbing—a luxury in those days—electric lights, marble mantles, black walnut trim, and a host of luxurious furnishings shipped in from New Orleans, Philadelphia, Baltimore, and New York City. One newspaper editor estimated the cost of the house to be near $100,000 and so impressed the wife of Fulton's partner, Thomas Coleman, that she insisted her husband build her a similar one on their ranch so that she could entertain in equal style. Built at an estimated cost of $150,000, the Coleman house was completed in 1880.[150] Such displays reinforced the cattlemen's position as provider for his family and community leader.

A large number of men who worked on the Texas ranches never mar-ried, though how much of that was choice rather than a lack of opportu-nity is hard to say. Some could not settle down at all. Ed Bell took several trips up the trail as a hand after his marriage, and then later went back to a ranch as foreman for three years.[151] John H. Fuller's father tried to settle down with his family in Kansas, but in 1896, after eight years farm-ing, decided to go back to work as a ranch hand, taking his wife and son with him. John, for his part, soaked up life on the ranch and ended up becoming a cowboy himself.[152] Many cowboys simply left their wives at home and went back to work. But others saw leaving the cowboy life for marriage as inevitable. At age twenty-seven, after working as a cowboy for seven years, F. M. Polk concluded that "about all I had gained was experience, and I could not turn that into cash, so I decided I had enough of it, and made up my mind to go home, get married, and settle down to farming."[153] Polk's reflections were not unique, but most men hung on to their independence as long as possible, and, like Teddy Abbott, referred to getting married in less than flattering terms.

Cowboys' and cattlemen's relationships with women and attitudes toward marriage were complex. In the abstract, they placed women on a pedestal and appropriated sentimental ideals of pure womanhood. Yet they also recognized that most women on the frontier did not meet these ideals. Cattlemen had the luxury of being able to interact with respectable women and provide them with means to meet their ideals. Yet many of the women they married were not exactly the delicate flowers they were supposed to be and took on equal partnerships in the ranch, often in the guise of sentimental maternalism. Marriage for the cattlemen only solidified their manhood, as society valued men's ability to protect and provide for their families and to contribute to the community.

Self-conscious of their lower status, cowboys were uncomfortable around "good" women, while they easily formed relationships with women on the margins of society. But they clearly did not value these women very highly, and ironically, they were not even able to protect those women they could possess. On the one hand, they would fight to protect any woman they considered worthy of their protection, on the other they were just as capable of violence toward those they deemed unworthy. Their sole hope for achieving respectable manhood themselves was to marry and settle down, and that was what they wished for in the bunkhouse. Yet marriage implied giving up independence and freedom and conforming to social rules they had flaunted as part of their masculine identity. The fact that cowboys did not want to conform was a sign of extended adolescence to the respectable people around them. Like Huck Finn on the river, they were in a no-win situation. By refusing to give up their independence, they remained imprisoned in boyhood, yet if they gave it up, they lost part of their identity.[154]

Ultimately most chose to settle down, but often it was later in life rather than sooner. Women and work did not mix, and for cowboys, work was a paramount part of their identity. Women were complicated at best and at worst could rob a man of his self-respect. It was better to look to other men for reliable companionship and postpone the issue of marriage until they could afford it. While frontier conditions prevailed, moreover, it was easy enough to compartmentalize women into leisure time activities rather than as central aspects of their lives. If a man could win a woman's affections or pay for them, it certainly added to his reputation among the other men, but given the low wages and scarcity of women, public possession of women was not a necessary adjunct to cowboy masculinity.

# 6

# In Town

As cowboys faced increasing restrictions at work, they relied more on their leisure activities to provide them with a sense of manhood. They relished their freedom when they were done working, but in letting off steam they also publicly showcased their own standards of masculine behavior while mocking civilized society. Many of the early frontier towns owed their existence to working men and their needs, so economics usually triumphed over morality. However, as more settlers moved into the region and as the cattlemen built houses in town for their families, the towns developed other economic interests as well as social values. The cowboys' sprees were less welcome, and the townspeople soon found ways to restrain them.

They began with moral legislation, so-called blue laws, but also gave regular lectures to the cowboys in the newspapers about proper behavior. When these lectures did not work, they tried to ridicule the cowboys in a variety of ways, suggesting that their unrestrained behavior was less than manly. As the cowboys became marginal to the lives of the town, they became subjects of humor and were relegated to the status of oddity or criminal. Their ideas of masculinity discredited in a modern world, and mocked by the society they had themselves scorned, cowboys seemed out of step—throwbacks to an older time.

• • •

If the ranchers had stopped with just work regulations, one could make an argument that they were simply protecting their property against wayward workers, but it is clear that the ranchers intended more. Cattlemen and other prominent local citizens did not just want to control the cowboys on the range and trails; they also felt threatened by them in their leisure time in town. Texas frontier newspapers in the 1860s and 1870s were full of accounts of cowboys coming in to town on a spree, and indeed, such stories were part of the masculine image of the cowboy. "Fighting rustlers and attending a herd was a he man's job, so when the cow hand played, he played as a he man" recalled former cowboy Earnest Cook.[1] Like working-class men elsewhere, cowboys asserted their masculinity in the strongest terms possible in the places they were still free to do so. Young men in particular proved themselves through fighting, drinking, and sexual conquest.[2] Andre Jorgenson Anderson, who opened a gun store in Fort Worth in 1877, said that it was natural for the cowboys to love gambling in town because they gambled with their lives every day. "The cowboy is not interested [in] pink teas, ping pong or any other entertainment of that nature. He desired he-man stuff."[3] Much of the cowboys' town spree was a public performance, for each other as much as for the townspeople. The spree involved a number of rituals associated with male bonding and masculinity, such as drunken fights, gambling, and visits to brothels. These rituals allowed the cowboy to show his friends and the locals that whatever else, he was a man.[4]

The first thing men did when they came to town was to get cleaned up and properly dressed. Some of this was simply necessity. Spending several months on the trail could be rough on clothes. One group on the trail to California arrived "so ragged and torn up that not one had a decent pair of pants to ride into town in." One of the men stitched together a pair of pants out of a wagon sheet and went into town to buy clothes for the rest of the group.[5] H. D. Gruene remembered having to stop in Salt Lake City on the trail out West for new clothes and a cleanup, "for we were pretty well inhabited by body lice, the greatest pest encountered on the trail."[6] The men were also in need of haircuts and a shave as there were few razors on the ranch and fewer barbers. William Walter Brady was in camp all winter and his hair was two or three inches below his shoulders when he heard of a woman at a nearby ranch who had a pair of scissors and rode ten miles there and back to borrow them. His buddy cut half of his hair and then as a prank threw the scissors into a frozen creek, forcing Brady to ride twenty miles into town to buy a new pair.[7] Given their infrequent contact with women, cowboys were also anxious to look their best for their "sweethearts," and many narrators proudly give detailed reports of the clothing they bought at the end of the trail to impress the women.[8]

Yet there was also something of a show about the clothes the men bought that went beyond simple necessity or desire to impress. Clothing was the second largest consumer industry in the cattle towns as a result of its cowboy customers, and boot making made up a sizeable portion of the market as well.[9] Charlie Siringo spent most of his paycheck in town on fancy clothes and boots with stars around the top.[10] Teddy Abbott came off the trail with his paycheck and like so many other cowboys bought new clothes and got his picture taken. Among the clothes he bought were a $10 Stetson hat and $12 pair of pants, a good shirt, and fancy boots with red and blue tops emblazoned with a half moon and star. These were the first clothes he owned that his mother had not bought or made for him and "Lord I was proud of those clothes! They were the kind of clothes top hands wore, and I thought I was dressed right for the first time in my life." When Abbott went to show his sister his new clothes, she yelled at him to take his pants out of his boots and told him he looked like an outlaw.[11] These clothes were obviously not "respectable" to townspeople but they were important to the men who bought them, both as signs of independence from parents and as a statement that they thought little of civilized standards. The fact that many of them had their pictures taken in these clothes—often in pairs with their buddies—as well as the poses they struck, suggest that this was the image they wanted most to project and that they were most proud of.[12]

The fact that the cowboys spent so much of their wages on clothes and leisure pursuits was also part of the performance of reckless spending. In part it was a function of idleness. Both cattlemen and cowboys spent a great deal of time in town waiting for a herd to sell and to make final transportation arrangements. While they were waiting, they had money to burn, and merchants targeted them with sidewalk displays and by serving liquor in merchandise stores.[13] But it was more than just boredom for cowboys. Charlie Siringo spent his paychecks as quickly as he got them on clothes, a fancy pistol, and an expensive saddle. He was like that for most of his life. After years of struggling for money, when he finally hit upon a successful scheme of shipping melons to factory hands up the river, he instantly spent all his profits in a game of monte. Recognizing his weakness, he objected to having to go to Chicago to settle up accounts, as he knew he would end up spending all his money there.[14] At age twenty-one, Teddy Abbott received an inheritance of $3,000 which he hoped to use to buy a herd and some land, but within four years he had spent it all. Most of it went when he was sick and forced to rest in town, during which time he started drinking and spent all his money on his "girlfriend."[15] This reckless spending was part of a larger attitude toward money and risk that was most evident in the men's gambling.

Gambling, for working-class men, allowed the men to strengthen bonds of reciprocity between them, as each shared the risks and often ended up both winning against and losing to the same people. It was also a way to escape the workplace and its regulation.[16] In gambling, risk was theoretically homogenized, and anyone could get rich, assuming the game was an honest one. The risks men took were dependent on luck and shared equally by all, unlike the workplace where they had little hope of succeeding financially. Businessmen might gamble on the stock market or an investment, but their risk was always calculated and rational, or at least they thought so. The type of gambling the cowboys did was spontaneous and took nerve as it was by no means guaranteed to succeed.[17] Gambling thus became a public show of manhood for cowboys, even if it seemed profoundly irrational to the people around them. When former cowboy Jim Gober was at rock bottom emotionally and financially after his daughter died and he was ill, he tried to rebuild his fortune by gambling on cards. He lost his last dollar in a rigged poker game, but when a man whose life he had saved in the past offered to give him money he refused, asking for a loan of $50 instead. Gober took the $50 and went right back to another poker game to win his money back. Although he ended up winning $590, the fact that he had a job waiting for him but preferred to gamble is indicative of something beyond a gambling addiction.[18] His risk-taking was his choice and he won the money on his own terms, which made him feel more like a man than if he had taken charity his friend offered him.

If gambling allowed men to choose their own risks, public drinking rituals defied efforts to control them further. Drinking in public was associated with manhood, since taverns and saloons were off limits to respectable women, and generally men went there to be with each other and relax.[19] Drinking was thus a "badge of masculinity" which also allowed workers to thumb their noses at respectable society, which disapproved of it.[20] As a result, drinking was big business and saloons proliferated in frontier towns (as did brothels). The Kansas railhead towns were perhaps the most notorious for their nightlife. Abilene had eleven saloons in 1871; Ellsworth had ten, and Wichita fifteen. Dodge City had between eight and fourteen saloons, and Caldwell had eleven in 1880. The saloons in the Kansas cattle towns ranged from the hole-in-the-wall dive to spectacular venues like the Alamo in Abilene, which had glass entry doors, mirrors, and felt-topped gaming tables.[21]

Texas towns experienced similar development. Texas Ranger George W. Arrington, sent in to maintain order in the towns in the Texas Panhandle in 1880, reported on the profusion of saloons and gambling halls in even the smallest towns.[22] One of the most notorious of these towns was Fort

Griffin, founded in 1867 to cater to the soldiers, then until 1879 to buffalo hunters, and lastly, after the fort was abandoned in 1881, to cowboys on the Western Trail. Described as a "gambler's paradise and the outlaw's rendezvous," half of all the businesses in town were saloons, and prostitutes were common.[23] In the 1870s, Sheriff John Selman allegedly robbed and killed buffalo hunters at will until they ran him out of town to El Paso.[24] The town fell prey to the railroad, however, first from competition from Fort Worth and then from Albany, the county seat, when the railroads came to the Panhandle and bypassed Fort Griffin.[25] Fort Elliott, another Panhandle fort, gave rise to the town of Mobeetie, which in its early days also had a "wild and woolly" reputation. Charles Goodnight recalled that the town was surrounded by "outlaws, thieves, cut-throats and buffalo hunters, with a large percentage of prostitutes."[26] Tascosa, another Panhandle cow town, had a similar reputation. Originally a settlement of New Mexican sheepherders, it became a cow town after cattlemen began moving into the region in the 1870s, displacing the sheepherders and making Oldham County center for cattle production. The town had many saloons and a shady business section known as Hogtown.[27] Tascosa was also famous for playing host to Billy the Kid in 1878, and a surprising number of cowboys from Texas claim to have encountered him there during his brief stay.[28] According to XIT cowboy S. A. Bull, after the big roundups everyone would come to Tascosa, and "drink and gambling . . . were the main sports."[29] Reportedly, there were few prostitutes and no dance halls at first, so dances were only held at the hotels.[30]

In other parts of Texas, cow towns took on similar characters. San Angelo in West Texas boasted fourteen saloons in 1883, including the First and Last Chance Saloon and The Blue Ribbon. San Angelo was a gambler's town with monte as the game of choice.[31] Alpine, Texas, in the Big Bend region was also a rowdy cow town. The first man buried in the town cemetery was the loser of a gunfight over a poker game. On hot summer days gambling would move from inside the saloons to outside on the porches, further disturbing the peace for more respectable citizens. One of the town's most famous saloons was named for the notorious Buckhorn in San Antonio, as many of the area's residents came from around there.[32] Pecos, in West Texas, was another famed cattle town and was home to five saloons in 1883.[33]

Although many townspeople objected to saloons, they could do little to stop them in the early years. Most of the more respectable permanent town citizens in Kansas railhead towns like Dodge City were actually dependent on the transient Texas cowboy population to make a living.[34] The same was true within Texas itself. Shopkeeper Andre Anderson stated that the citizens of Fort Worth had to choose either rough entertainment or no trade at all in the early days of the city, and so they chose to provide what the cowboys wanted.[35] Herman Koeler, who ran the store and saloon at Fort Stockton just north of the Davis Mountains/Big Bend region, obviously knew where he made his money. He marked all his items clearly for the cowboys to see and kept track of the drinks men bought for themselves and their friends on a black slate. At the end of each night he wrote the amounts down in his account books and erased the slate. Then he put down all his blankets and quilts and let the men, up to twenty-five or thirty, sleep in the store and saloon. Those who stayed would play poker until 1 or 2 a.m., with one man acting as banker, and in the morning Koeler would apply those debts and credits to his account books too. In that way the men never had to worry about being cheated, and were likely to give all their business to Koeler's saloon. Not surprisingly, one cowboy recalled: "he was one of the best men I ever saw."[36] The owner of one saloon in Montana gave free Mulligan stew to any man who wanted it and, like Koeler, allowed the men to sleep on the floor in their blankets, even giving them a free drink in the morning. As Teddy Abbott said: "He figured that when they got a hundred dollars they would blow it right over his bar, and they did."[37]

Most frontier towns gained reputations as "wild and woolly" places to live. Part of the drinking ritual involved buying rounds of drinks for friends and not leaving until everyone in the group had bought drinks for the rest. The larger the group, the more drinks the saloons sold, and saloon owners were not above herding men into larger groups. But the act of buying a drink for a friend was a bonding one for the men and was part of the public performance of masculinity, as it gave them a sense of honor.[38] Drunkenness often led to wild behavior, although most of it was simple high spirits. In 1875, a group of cowboys got rowdy in a saloon in Jacksboro, and when a marshal threatened to put them in jail, "one of the aforesaid cow boys bumped the ceiling of the house with the upper storey of his hat, cracked his heals together, jingled his spurs and cut up various antics." The incident ended with the marshal wounding one of the cowboys with buckshot and one arrest.[39] Celebrations could also lead to excessive spirits. When the XIT opened a new large store in Channing in 1897, they organized a dance and people came from all over the area to celebrate. The cowboys joined in all the dances, alcohol ran freely, and a number of fights broke out over poker games among them.[40]

"Anything goes, boys, but me and the mirror." This Panhandle saloon was typical of those in cow towns in the 1880s, with the mirror often being the most conspicuous ornament. Man behind bar in saloon. Photo courtesy of Southwest Collection/Special Collections Library, Texas Tech University, Lubbock, Texas, SWCPC 334-E2 #11.

Many town marshals were on the payroll of the local saloons and let cowboys get away with drunken stunts. Still, arrests for being drunk and disorderly were common. In Fort Griffin in 1879, several cowboys were arrested for yelling, shooting, and disturbing the peace, prompting the editor to lecture the cowboys on proper behavior in town.[41] In 1884, a cowboy was arrested in El Paso for riding into town on a binge and causing a commotion when he rode his horse into the saloon and the bartender refused to serve him.[42] Tales of rowdy cowboys were common in the *San Antonio Light* in the mid-1880s. In 1885, cowboys rode through town in the middle of the night "yelling like demons" and shooting their rifles in the air, and a cowboy was arrested in a brothel for threatening to kill one of the prostitutes who had abandoned him after he bought her drinks.[43] In 1886, cowboys managed to escape the police who were trying to arrest them for causing trouble in another brothel, but "two cowboys who attempted to paint the town of Ballinger a Cardinal color" were not so lucky and ended in jail "meditating on the effects of a blue rain."[44]

Some descriptions recognized the behavior for what it was or even defended the cowboys. The *Texas Livestock Journal* reported in its "Panhandle Notes" section simply that the cowboys were in town after the roundup "hearty and happy," and "after a little spurt of a day or two" they had gone back to the ranches.[45] The *Fort Griffin Echo* even blamed the shooting at a brothel on a town resident, defending the cowboys and asking them to protect their reputation by giving up the name of the man responsible.[46] Even the saloon owners preferred the cowboys' rowdy behavior to no business, and one savvy owner told the cowboys "Anything goes, boys, but me and the mirror," and then bet them their drinks that they could not shoot a wine glass at the end of the bar. "Of course that took all the fun out of it, and there was never much shooting in his place."[47]

Former cowboy W. E. Oglesby defended the cowboys' actions in later years, saying the shooting in the town was all in fun, usually no one was hurt, and the boys would always go back later and settle for damages.[48] The latter assertion was likely an exaggeration, but there were cases in which a trail boss paid for the damages his men caused, and at their local saloons men tended to be a bit more circumspect in their actions. In at least one case the town wrongly blamed the Texas cowboys for the trouble. As teenagers, Teddy Abbott and his brother earned money herding for their Nebraska neighbor and went into Lincoln, where they got drunk, shot out the lights, and whooped and yelled through the night. They escaped arrest because a Texas herd was coming through and "they got the blame, as everything was laid to the Texas men," but there were no arrests since the herd left the following day.[49]

Despite Oglesby's assertion that no one was usually hurt, in fact numerous violent incidents resulted from drunken sprees. In the early 1870s, many Texas cowboys resented the lawmen in the northern states because most of them were ex-Union soldiers and the cowboys were ex-Confederates. As a result, the cowboys often picked fights with them when they were arrested and ended up getting killed.[50] A group of Texas cowboys in town in Wyoming got drunk and rowdy, and when one cowboy tried to get his buddy to go sleep it off, the buddy shot him, and in the uproar another drunk shot the sheriff. The sheriff arrested both men and the buddy was seriously hurt.[51] When a group of cowboys tried to "take" the town of Marionfield, a battle ensued between the cowboys and the sheriff and his posse, ending with one cowboy dead and another mortally wounded.[52]

Drunken violence usually backfired on the cowboy when it came to confrontations with the law, but it was part of the ritual of public drinking and could also enhance a cowboy's manly reputation.

Drunkenness often exacerbated racist attacks. Ethnic minorities were always "safe targets" in that they were less likely to fight back and usually fewer people would defend them. African Americans were frequent victims of racist violence at the hands of inebriated white men. In 1874, a white cowboy started a fight with a black hod carrier in town and both were arrested, but upon release the cowboy killed the hod carrier and escaped prosecution. In 1879, when a group of drunken white cowboys came through Ogallala, Nebraska on their way from Texas, they decided it would be fun to shoot at a black man's feet. No one stopped them until one shot went astray and nearly hit the wife of the stationmaster, at which point the sheriff got a posse together and drove the cowboys out of town.[53] In Dodge City, a group of rowdy Texas cowboys saw a black man dressed in a fancy hat and bet they could shoot a hole through it and proceeded to shoot it from his head. When the man ran off, the boys kept the hat as a souvenir and hung it up in the saloon like a trophy.[54] Bones Hooks never stayed long in Mobeetie, as it had a reputation of being rowdy and unfriendly to blacks, despite the fact that before 1890, the majority of African Americans in the Panhandle lived there.[55] Hispanics also faced violence in town. In 1895, Monroe Clayton was indicted for aggravated assault in Pecos County for assaulting Cesario Martinez, a Mexican sheepherder, by roping him and dragging him from his horse as well as striking and bruising him. The case was dismissed for lack of evidence.[56]

Racial hierarchies persisted on the frontier, especially sexual ones. Dodge City had two main brothels, one with white prostitutes which was segregated, and the second which had black prostitutes but was open to both black and white men.[57] One historian has reported that vaqueros adapted poorly to trail drives in part because, with the exception of gambling venues, the cow town residents would not let them in many of the saloons or brothels, even those that admitted blacks.[58] The white sheriff of San Angelo had a black mistress, which, to the respectable townspeople, added to his disreputable image. Blacks could mix freely with whites in the streets and enter saloons, but in truth the bar itself was often segregated, with blacks relegated to one end and whites to the other. Even then there might be conversations between blacks and whites from the same outfit in the middle, and in a few black-owned businesses, segregation was not enforced. The Blue Ribbon, a saloon in San Angelo, was owned by two black veterans and served both blacks and whites.[59]

In 1881, one drunken Anglo cowboy found his racist attack backfired. He rode into Camp Rice (later Fort Hancock) near El Paso "with blood in his eye," saying he was going to drive out all the Chinese from the country, went into the Chinese-owned restaurant and began shooting at them. The cowboy drove the owners out of the restaurant and continued shooting in the street, endangering bystanders, until local citizens returned fire and killed him.[60] But whites were not the only ones to engage in drunken violence; "Old Dick," a black cowboy, came into Fort Griffin, got drunk and threatened trouble, so the sheriff and his posse chased him into a nearby thicket, where a shootout started. Although Dick suffered many hits, he survived the incident after several weeks of nursing.[61] Whether the sheriff would have called out a posse for similar talk from a white cowboy is uncertain, but Dick nonetheless stood up for himself by firing back when most black cowboys would not have done so, proving his manly demeanor, even if few whites would acknowledge it.[62]

Physical violence was very much a part of masculinity in the nineteenth century, especially in the South, where many of the cowboys and cattlemen originated. Anthropologists have noted that herding societies tend to have high levels of aggression and violence because their livestock are always vulnerable to loss. In addition, frontier areas where law enforcement is spotty tend to operate more on the rule of retaliation rather than the rule of law. The colonial South met both of these conditions, as did Texas in the nineteenth century, and migrants to Texas came from the South as well as from Scots-Irish backgrounds associated with similar cultures. In such an environment, a "culture of honor" is likely to develop, in which honor equates with the strength and power of a man to enforce his will on others, in other words, his status in society. In this culture, a man has to be ready to strike back at all times and must strike back at any insult, no matter how slight, or risk losing credibility.[63] Honor was thus tied very strongly to concepts of masculinity; and honor necessitated violence.

Fighting was therefore often as much about performance as the opponent or reason. For working-class men, fighting was also often the end result of excessive drinking bouts which just made it more exciting, as there was always the risk of violence.[64] Moreover, violence was not always a sign of hostility, as aggressive exchanges such as charlie horses had always been a masculine way for boys to express friendship.[65] There are a number of parallels between cowboys' behavior (indeed, that of many working men in the late nineteenth century) and that of Virginia gentry in the colonial era associated with Southern honor culture. These men sought to prove their prowess by grand boasts at the gambling table as well as extravagant bets, like half a year's earnings on a single cockfight. Their attitude turned risk and irrational and reckless spending into a virtue. They also were willing to fight for what they considered the slightest insult. Self-assertion and manly pride were marks of status in this society.[66] According to historian Ramón Gutiérrez, a similar culture of honor existed in colonial New Mexico. The Spanish elite felt the need for an exaggerated moral code based on honor since there were few legal or social institutions to maintain social order.[67] By the late eighteenth century, most Southern aristocrats had given up the coarsest forms of violence and channeled their aggression into duels and mental domination, whereas poorer men in the backcountry and on the frontier continued rough and tumble fighting in which the goal was to best the other with a show of physical strength. But whether through duels or street fighting, violence was essential to proving one's manhood.[68]

In the effort to rehabilitate the cowboy image, it was the concept of honor that most former cowboys stressed, while downplaying the violence itself. Former cowboy William A. Preist explained violence within an honorable context, reporting that few "tough" men killed for money or did so in a dishonorable way. "They calculated that if you [were] not willing to match shooting ability with them . . . they had no business taking part in a difference with them. However, they would not intentionally take undue [advantage] of anyone."[69] Brook Campbell, trying to argue that movie cowboy shootouts were not accurate, stressed that while cowboys carried guns "sometimes," they did it mostly to kill deer.[70] Most sources, however, suggest that violence between men was a common aspect of life on the ranch and in town and tend to discredit such defenses of cowboy honor.

Cattleman Hilory G. Bedford believed that men became "more and more depraved" when separated from women, and noted that soldiers, buffalo hunters, freighters, and cowboys all drank and swore more as a result.[71] Much cowboy violence occurred between men from different outfits. Proximity was not always conducive to friendship, especially when it involved the honor of an outfit. When two men from neighboring ranches shared a winter camp in 1880, they got in a fight about the correct version of a song, which led to both pulling their guns and shooting each other. The incident led to unpleasant feelings between the men of the ranches they represented, and while the men had all got on well before, the two ranches could not camp together again.[72] Even men in the same outfit could tire of each other's company, however. Woodson Coffee recalled that cowboys who stayed on the ranch all winter were always anxious for the spring work to start, and likened the men to insects emerging from their winter chrysalises. "Naturally the change would prompt the new creature to flit about for new scenery and companionship."[73] Another observer put it more bluntly: "It is strange how two men who are thrown together daily for months, without seeing anyone else, will get to hate the sight of each other and yet remain the best of friends at heart."[74] Will Hale reported that the men on his father's ranch got along well as a rule but when there was not enough work to do, or his father was away from the ranch, they began to fight among themselves and it was all the ranch manager could do to prevent them killing each other.[75]

The violence usually seemed out of proportion to the reason for it, and deaths often came as a result of small insults. But in working-class tradition the emphasis had always been to do as much damage to one's opponent as possible, and the "best" man in a community was often the best and most vicious fighter.[76] Fights often arose suddenly and for trivial reasons, but could end just as quickly. Two cowboys stayed alone for three months in the winter of 1887 without speaking a word, each cooking his own meals, even throwing out the scraps so the other would have to cook from scratch. When one forgot to wash a pan, the men ended up chasing each other with axe and six-shooter. One of the cowboys transferred to another ranch, but despite the incident, when they saw each other again it was as if nothing had ever happened and they were friends.[77] This story tallies with working-class concepts of the role of violence as restoring order. Violence was supposed to solve the dispute, and when it was over, the two sides were not supposed to hold a grudge.[78] In a fight, the winner proved his manhood and dominance, but as long as the loser stood up and fought as well, he maintained his own honor; thus there was no reason to continue the argument. Unfortunately, as what had been fighting with fists in the eighteenth century turned into fighting with guns in the nineteenth, the results of such fights were often lethal for the loser.[79]

Cowboys themselves did not think the violence excessive, however. In 1880, a cowboy from the Millett Ranch, in Baylor County, wrote to the *Fort Griffin Echo* to defend the reputation of the cowboys against charges of undue violence. He reported that in the past five years there had only been two men killed, and that considering the ranch employed between sixty-five and seventy men each spring, all of whom came armed, the fatality rate was fairly low.[80] Charlie Siringo advised the tenderfoot that above all else he needed to have a pistol, even at the expense of other equipment, as if he did not have one the cooks and other men would not respect him in camp.[81] With so many guns, violence seemed to be a normal part of cowboy existence.

While violence was common on the ranches, it was more so in town. John Weaver was arrested in Pecos for aggravated assault after he hit a gambler at his establishment with a chair. With only fellow gamblers as potential witnesses, however, the case was dismissed for insufficient testimony.[82] The homicide rate in Dodge City, Kansas, in the 1870s was ten times that of New York City. Most of these deaths were from gunshots, and two-thirds of those killed were unarmed at the time of their deaths.[83] George Claiborne Harris, who moved to Abilene, Texas, to open a store in 1881, reported that cowboys fought with guns all the time and two men were killed each week on average.[84] In the 1880s, the newspapers made regular reports of cowboys killing each other, usually as the result of a trivial dispute.[85] Jewish cowboy Morris Wilds, a herd boss for the King Ranch and an ace billiards player, refused to pay a man who had beaten him in Corpus Christi and so the man shot and killed him.[86]

Revenge killings were not unusual. According to his autobiography, when white outlaws killed his buddy, Will Hale swore he would kill the men who had done it. Hale and another friend split up to find the men responsible. His friend found one of them in Kiowa lands and killed and scalped him, and Hale finally tracked down the other man in Caldwell, Kansas, and killed him in a fight at the roundup.[87] Hale's autobiography is an interesting document, as many of his stories stretch credulity and seem designed for the most excitement rather than accuracy. However, the stories he chose to tell, true or not, are almost unrelentingly violent ones in which he was the aggressor or the avenger, interspliced with many tales of courtship. If his purpose was to show what a great man he was, Hale did so by showcasing his fighting and killing abilities, as well as his sexual prowess.

In the 1870s and 1880s, most violent incidents went unpunished. Hale shot a Mexican gambler who had cheated him at cards, and when his victim's brother showed up to avenge him, Hale shot him as well. However, although Hale was arrested, he was released, and the case never came to trial.[88] When C. B. Burnett killed a man who had stolen some of his cattle and who, upon discovery, "approached B[u]rnett in a threatening manner," the jury ruled the death a justifiable homicide.[89] Similarly, few cases in the early years of Donely County ever made it to trial despite the many charges of murder.[90] Crimes against property such as cattle rustling, however, often faced very steep fines. This fact conforms to Southern honor-based culture in which it was more honorable to kill than to steal in some circumstances, particularly if it involved theft of livestock. Moreover, few people took disputes over personal insults into courts, preferring to settle it between themselves, perhaps believing *real* men fought it out rather than complaining to a judge.[91] In 1876, W. E. Race and Henry Gadberry were indicted for challenging each other to a duel in Uvalde County, but charges were dropped as there had been no clear legal violation.[92] In 1878, even the *National Police Gazette* carried out a campaign in charging that "the murderer is a hero with the people, press and clergy of Texas."[93] In the mid-1880s, when Walter W. Meek, a Pennsylvania native, served on the grand jury in San Diego, Duval County, however, he was astonished at the prevailing values among his fellow citizens. He reported that horse stealing received the harshest punishment, with some even advocating the death penalty for rustling, whereas murderers received far more lenient treatment. Meek personally believed the death penalty should be reserved for murder and that murder was by far the worst crime.[94] But Meek was somewhat in the minority at the time.

Indeed, if leading men carried out violence in the name of social order, then it too could be an assertion of superior manly morals. Charles Goodnight complained of the lack of social order in the Panhandle, particularly in Mobeetie and surrounding Wheeler County, which, he claimed, had been organized in secret by gamblers and "dance hall people." According to Goodnight, every county officer except one judge was living with a prostitute and thus the officials' concern was to prevent law and order rather than maintain it. Moreover, even when the officials were honest men, it was common for cattle thieves and criminals to escape conviction because of the testimony of perjurers, who testified in return for free whiskey and prostitutes provided by the defendant's compatriots. Given this environment, the cattlemen eventually began to threaten taking extralegal action in the form of lynchings to punish cattle rustlers. Faced with the threat of violence, the thieves agreed to leave the area.[95] In Goodnight's eyes such violence would have been more than justified as it represented the interests of the respectable men in the county.

Cattlemen did not always oppose violence if done for a "just cause." Will Hale, who was the son of a rancher and eventually a ranch owner himself, seemed to identify more with a Southern ideal of honor that many of the older cattlemen embraced. While not all cattlemen came from Southern backgrounds, and in fact after 1880 most ranch owners came from outside the South, a number of them adhered to the older form of masculinity that centered on honor. As such, these men were not above violence themselves. Moreover, some of the early cattlemen came from less than genteel backgrounds. Historian Tom Lea reports that Richard King was fond of a little fisticuffs on occasion and relates the story of how Richard King got into a fight with an employee. When King strongly berated the cowhand, the man told him he would never get away with being so harsh if he was not rich or a captain. King replied that they should forget his title and just fight, which they proceeded to do for a half hour, emerging bloody in "mutual admiration."[96] Still, King was not a typical cattleman in any way, and his actions reflected as much his working-class New York Irish background as any Southern sense of honor. As historian Lewis Atherton reports, violence and shows of force were rare among cattlemen. But cattlemen were also used to enforcing the law—at least their law—on the frontier in the absence of other authorities. Charles Goodnight claimed that south of Mobeetie, before 1882 when Donely County was officially organized, the cattlemen enforced the law including a ban on whiskey, and there were no murders as a result.[97]

In later years, when the frontier had become more settled, violence seemed counterproductive to both cattlemen and townspeople. Moreover, it was increasingly clear that not all violence was as honorable as either cowboys or cattlemen would have liked to have claimed. Despite the twentieth-century stereotype that only a bad man or coward would shoot someone in the back, it happened enough for people to excuse it. One such incident reported as a true story of the Wild West stemmed from a minor dispute over an insult to a prostitute. Big Bill Thompson shot at Jim Tucker from the door of the saloon, and Tucker fell. Thompson started to leave, believing he had killed him, but, Tucker, who was only wounded, rose and shot Thompson in the back with his shotgun, killing him.[98] Tucker was clearly the hero of the story and maintained his honor despite shooting a man in the back, and was presumably acquitted of all charges, if charged at all. The events surrounding a murder of an unnamed victim in El Paso in 1890 highlight both the volatile nature of drunken gambling and the willingness of people to see even random violence as a matter of honor. Around 3 or 4 a.m., a number of men were standing around outside the Gem Saloon after an evening of gambling, clearly drunk. W.

G. Caldwell got in a dispute with another man after asking about his winnings, and when Caldwell pulled his pistol, the man ran so Caldwell shot him in the back. After that, it seems the victim ran into the saloon and fell face down, Caldwell followed him in, and then shot him twice in the back again as he lay on the floor. The case was removed to neighboring Reeves County to secure an impartial jury, but the first trial still resulted in a hung jury and the second jury found Caldwell not guilty.[99] Given the witness statements, including one from a private security man ("merchant sheriff"), the failure to convict is startling. But it is clear that the bar for proving murder was high. In a more typical case, near Canyon, in the Panhandle, R. M. Moore turned himself in after claiming he killed Jess McMahon in self-defense in a dispute over stolen cattle, and eventually the death was ruled as self-defense in Armstrong County.[100]

Other forms of violence also went unpunished or earned lighter sentences than expected. In 1886, Ike Duggan was arrested in Guadalupe County for unlawfully carrying a pistol and assault with intent to rape, but he did not appear for his first hearing. When he was finally brought in, he was found guilty only of aggravated assault and then sentenced to just two months in the city jail, a sentence he appealed. Even when convicted, the defendant could often escape the charges through legal appeals. Ezekiel Morgan was also found guilty of assault with intent to rape in 1887 but managed to get the decision overturned and the charges dismissed.[101]

But by the 1890s, most violence did get a hearing in the courts. W. D. Browning was arrested and brought to trial for assault with intent to kill after attacking J. B. Atkinson, who had called him a lying son of a bitch in the course of a debt dispute, an affair of honor that perhaps would not have reached the court in earlier years.[102] Convictions were most likely if the death involved an employee of one of the large ranches and the killer was from elsewhere. In these cases, the ranch owners would marshal the whole outfit to go to court to testify against the killer. An example of such a case was the trial of George Jowell for assault with intent to murder John Lindley, who died of his wounds in late September 1902. The Spur's lawyer reported to the ranch manager that although the grand jury had indicted Jowell, the "best men" had all excused themselves from the petit jury, leaving a less than law-abiding panel to decide the case. The result was a hung jury, so the lawyer got a change of venue to Armstrong County and told Fred Horsbrugh to make sure all the Spur "boys" who had witnessed the attack would show up to the new trial. The tactic seems to have been effective, as the new jury convicted Jowell, who was sentenced to two years in the state penitentiary.[103] The increasing involvement of the courts and ranch managers in these disputes reinforced a changing attitude between ranchers and cowboys. For cowboys, violence was necessary to restore order and honor; for the modern cattlemen, violence destroyed order and was itself generally dishonorable.[104]

One of the reasons for the changing view of violence was the decline in the traditional basis for patriarchy. In an industrial world, property loss was impersonal and far more common, thus the concept of male honor was less relevant. Since it was easier to lose property, it was no longer feasible or rational for gentlemen to resort to violence against an impersonal market force. Thus, violence among the middle and upper classes no longer had a purpose, at least when aimed at each other.[105] Middle-class men in the late nineteenth century expected to be aggressive in the marketplace, but tried to control and channel their aggression into activities such as sport, or bodybuilding, in their leisure time. Physical strength was part of the new ideal of manhood, but brute force was not.[106] Untamed aggression was limited to boyhood. Novels like *Huckleberry Finn* celebrated boys as harmless savages with only a crude sense of morality such as respecting women and being loyal to a buddy. Novelist Charles Dudley Warner, in his 1877 book *Being A Boy*, argued that a good boy was a natural savage who inhabited an ideal world that was a refuge from sentimental women and too much civilization.[107]

To middle-class men, the distinction between a boy and a man increasingly became the ability to restrain aggression and impulses, as well as a sense of responsibility to family and the larger society.[108] George Littlefield, who was decidedly restrained as a rule, voiced his indignance when his nephew was nearly cut to death in a fight. "I am sorry you did not have a Pistol and Shoot the Cowardly Devill down at [the] time." But despite his outrage, he deferred to legal punishment. He warned his nephew to wait before responding. "It would be a good thing to get the Drop on him as He did you and give it to him. But the Law would be against you." Instead, Littlefield advised, he should wait until the man was arrested and pursue a lawsuit once he was in jail.[109] Matador Ranch manager Murdo Mackenzie credited the fact that he did not carry a gun as the reason he avoided further violence. When he first took over the ranch, the former ranch foreman threatened his life but Mackenzie simply confronted him man-to-man without weapons and won him over by calling his bluff.[110] Manhood became equated with self-discipline, and those who did not practice it were stigmatized as less manly.[111] Not surprisingly, judged by these standards, the cowboys looked more like boys than men, and accordingly were in need of restraint.

Cattlemen and townspeople thus tried to impress upon the cowboys that truly masculine behavior was nonviolent. Newspapers praised peaceful resolutions of disputes. In 1877, the *Lampasas Dispatch* printed letters of apology ending a feud between two ranches which had resulted in several shootings. The editor commented: "This is manly, and exhibits more true courage than to shoot down an enemy."[112] Descriptions of cattlemen often emphasized the restraint they showed in the face of violence. Author Victor White saw William Lewis, who became the owner of the RO Ranch, as a taming force against the violence of the Panhandle. "The polite young man from Maryland apposed his own brand of strength to the violence of the Panhandle—a stubborn Sunday-school kind of nonviolence, backed by courage instead of guns." Lewis neither swore nor wore a gun, and thus made the ideal model of manly behavior by middle-class standards.[113] Even cowboys recognized the difference between themselves and the cattlemen. Joe Meador worked as the straw boss on the Stripe Ranch in the mid-1890s, where he described the owner, "Captain Morriss," as "one of the finest men I ever knew to keep out of trouble." When Morriss expected a group of outlaw cowboys at the roundup, he told his men to leave their guns at home and then talked to the outlaws, telling them that his men were all unarmed. "He told them we were all law abiding citizens and the only way they could take any of the cattle would be by force of arms, and if they did that we would appeal to the law."[114] Such an approach might not have been effective in the 1870s, when law enforcement officers and courts were few and far between, but evidently it worked well in this case, proving the value of restraint over force and showing Morriss to be the better man as a result.

Those who owned the ranches and the businesses in town essentially wanted to recreate the society many of them had known in more settled areas. The wealthier pioneers came not just for economic profit, but to establish proper social order with the main focus on family, home, and well-behaved children. They encouraged their children to be outspoken and independent, but also taught them to accept traditional morals and channeled them into more restrained behavior.[115] Ranchers interpreted their masculine role to be taming the land, but did so in order to create a space for domestic life.[116] They may have resisted settlers encroaching on, or next to, their land, but that did not mean they did not want settlers in the region at all, or that they did not want to extend "civilization" to the frontier.[117] Many prominent cattlemen helped to establish the towns near their ranches, and all the cattle syndicates were also land companies, so both were interested in attracting settlers to the region. In most cases, the syndicates only planned to raise cattle on their land until such time as settler demand for it increased enough to sell at a profit. Ranchers and prominent citizens sponsored newspapers that extolled the virtues of settling in their town and promoted the local businesses as much as possible. Dime novels may have celebrated the "he men" who shot up the town after a long stint on the trail, and movies later turned gunslingers into manly heroes, but the cattlemen's vision of civilization did not include wild cowboys firing their guns in the air. Ultimately, they saw cowboys, with their "savage" behavior, as a problem off the ranch as well as on it.

As the towns became more settled, the richer families built their homes away from the business district so that the saloons, brothels, and gambling houses that were so prevalent in the frontier town would not contaminate their families.[118] The towns also began to develop trade and industry that was not dependent on the cowboys' patronage. While most of the moral objection to gambling, drinking, and prostitution came from the women and clergy; the farmers, ranchers, and merchants also had an economic argument against these businesses. The middle-class economic order was one based on hard work and self-restraint, and these three vices were far from either.[119] Furthermore, they produced nothing of any value to the community and often led to violence which could damage business interests. Late nineteenth-century middle-class men, in defining their own masculinity, moreover, became determined to decide which forms of risk were acceptable and manly for themselves and the working class.[120] When the cowboys and other working men showed no sign of restraint in their activities despite the increased presence of women, churches, and schools, they began to restrain the men themselves.

Cattlemen and merchants once again came into conflict with cowboys about the necessity for restraint. Cowboys saw no reason to practice rational economic restraint as they had little hope of rising financially, and they paid little heed to moral standards of respectable women, who were largely unavailable to them or irrelevant to their existence.[121] Denied the middle-class masculine privileges of property and family, cowboys clung to their working-class male privileges of drink, cards, and prostitutes, thus reinforcing their status as morally suspect.[122] As attitudes toward the cowboys worsened on the job, many attacked their moral character as well. In a speech in San Antonio in 1882, General Winfield Scott

Hancock contrasted the rough cowboys unfavorably with the steady sons of farmers who were raised in "the ways of sobriety and honesty" to become "useful members of society."[123] By 1914, the image of cowboys had so deteriorated that John Clay, who managed the Wyoming cattle interests of a Chicago corporation, could say in a speech before the Feeders Convention that "the chief obstacle of the range at that time . . . was the cowboys, who were mostly illiterate, uncivilized; who drank and thieved and misbranded cattle, and with a kind of rough loyalty, never told on one another in their crimes."[124] As historian William Savage has noted, by the 1890s, journalists routinely castigated the cowboy for his appearance, his violence, and his seeming lack of morals. "He was not the sort of person one would take one's children to see; he was, rather, a pernicious influence best avoided by responsible persons."[125] The very behavior that cowboys believed was manly, the people around them saw as childish or savage, and thus, one by one, the towns began to restrain this particular form of unbridled masculinity.

Early efforts to regulate cowboy behavior were not successful as the courts were not zealous in their prosecution of the law. In 1869, men were arrested in Gonzales County for horse racing on Sunday, and retailing liquor without a license, only to have the charges dismissed when they got to court, as happened frequently elsewhere.[126] But as the towns' populations of "respectable" people increased, they insisted on law and order. One of the first targets was the cowboys' weapons. All cattle towns had wanted to regulate violence from the beginning because it was bad for business, so disarming the cowboys was the most logical first step. The usual process was to incorporate the town and then hire police officers and pass concealed weapon laws.[127] Even the notorious town of Fort Griffin, in Shackelford County, started to regulate use of guns within town limits. Beginning in the late 1870s, the citizens of Fort Griffin repeatedly petitioned the governor to declare that Shackelford County was no longer a frontier county so that they could enforce the state laws against side arms. The governor finally did so in 1881.[128] In that year the *Fort Griffin Echo* admonished the boys for a disturbance at one of the local brothels. "This shooting does no good but may unintentionally cost a life; it is not an indication of bravery or manly spirit, but evidence of a depraved nature."[129]

In 1883, the *El Paso Lone Star* reported that the movement to disarm cowboys in that city, once derided, was gaining strength and that many ranchers refused to hire men who carried weapons.[130] The paper printed regular reports on the impact of gun violence that year. In January, for example, it told the story of five cowboys on the train from Colorado City to Toyah who were drinking heavily and brandishing their revolvers. The men ended up in a shootout with Texas Rangers, and two of the cowboys were wounded, although the cowboys who escaped planned to come back with reinforcements.[131] In July, the paper reported the arrest of several cowboys for firing their weapons in town and that the justice of the peace had fined each of them $50. The message in these reports was twofold: first, rowdy cowboys with guns promoted further violence; second, cowboys could expect to face arrest or run-ins with the law for flaunting the regulations. Few towns wishing to attract settlers wanted any gun violence in town, so most passed laws restricting weapons as soon as they had a large enough population to do so. While there was some profit in tourism catering to those who wanted to see real cowboy life firsthand, even the tourists wanted a more sanitized version.

Having got the guns under control (or at least subject to fine), the towns next turned to what they considered the cowboys' immoral behavior. Townspeople recognized that much of the violence stemmed from the cowboys' presence at dancehalls, saloons, and gambling houses, and so had additional reasons to want to pass so-called blue laws or morals legislation. But some cattlemen were truly appalled by the immorality they saw in some towns. Robert J. Kleberg, II, manager and later owner by marriage of the King Ranch, complained that Laredo was a "dirty demor[a]lized hole" at which drinking and gambling "carried on openly both day and night."[132] The "Variety Show" that played in San Angelo was one of the bawdiest, as the owners knew that they could attract more customers the more vulgar they were.[133] Jonathan Hamilton Baker took his herd up the trail to St. Louis in 1870 and was invited to attend the Olympic Theater with another rancher. This was his first visit to a theater and he was shocked: "There must be so much evil in the taste and inclinations of this generation of society, showing a very low standard of moral excellence. [T]hat talent and energy should be turned into such ridiculous channels. It is a deplorable comment upon the depraved condition of our degenerate race."[134] Despite his shock, three days later he attended another theater "in order to learn something more of what is going on in the world." Not surprisingly, this performance (most likely a burlesque) was no better. "No person with any pretensions to chastity and decency should ever visit such a place."[135] It takes little imagination to see Baker leading the campaigns against cowboy vice in the nearby town of Graham.

Brothels frequently came under attack from local authorities, as did prostitutes conducting their business in the streets. In Austin in the mid-1870s, arrests of poor prostitutes were fairly constant, with some women arrested as many as nine times in one year, and on average each woman arrested three or four times, regardless of race. Beginning in the mid-1880s, as formal racial segregation set in to the South, a new pattern emerged with about twice as many black prostitutes arrested as white. In San Antonio there was less of a distinction based on race, and while there was a large military presence in the city, authorities were more tolerant of prostitutes in general.[136] In the Panhandle, where brothels proliferated in the towns around the ranches, there were regular arrests and fines for keeping "a disorderly house" from the mid-1880s on.[137] However, after 1889, such charges were classified as misdemeanors and dealt with by the newly established county courts. The Kansas cattle towns were unable to eliminate prostitution, but instead, under the leadership of Joseph McCoy, established a semi-official "licensing" program whereby each woman would come to court once a year and pay the maximum fine for prostitution and would thus avoid prosecution for the rest of the year. On the basis of this process, historian Robert Dykstra has claimed that cowboy chroniclers have exaggerated the number of prostitutes in these towns, as only between thirteen and twenty-five women are listed in the Kansas towns' official criminal records as "licensed." He does admit, however, that many of the women who worked at the dance halls in town were also prostitutes but were less subject to fines.[138]

Efforts to eliminate the prostitutes were less than successful, although many towns were able to remove them from visibility in the main streets. Wyoming cattleman John Clay complained about prostitute Ella Watson, nicknamed "Cattle Kate," who was "the common property of the cowboys for miles around" and accepted payment in mavericks, which the boys branded for her presumably from their bosses' herds. Thus, she not only practiced prostitution but encouraged cattle rustling, but could not be arrested for it. In the end, after several warnings to Watson and the man who ran the saloon where she worked to clean up their acts, the townspeople lynched them.[139] Obviously attacks on prostitution could be about more than just unregulated sex.

Nonetheless, accompanying the effort to regulate prostitution was an increasing belief among middle-class men that excessive ejaculation could sap a man of his manhood permanently and incapacitate him for marriage and business alike. Doctors claimed that one drop of semen was the equivalent of forty drops of blood. Men should thus try to practice "spermatic economy"; moreover, the exertion of willpower in reserving sexual energy would empower their manliness.[140] One sign of the fear of the weakening effects of frequent sex was the appearance of a growing number of advertisements for "Manhood Remedies" in both the *Texas Livestock Journal*, which catered mostly to cattlemen, and the cowboys' favorite *National Police Gazette*. These advertisements were cautionary tales in themselves, as they promised to cure impotence caused by "self-abuse," "youthful imprudence," "early vice," or "sexual excess in maturer years." Often promising to cure syphilis and gonorrhea as well as restore virility, the remedies involved a number of patent medicines as well as electric belts and even sarsaparilla.[141] While it is unlikely that any of these remedies actually worked, it is also clear that there was a common belief that promiscuous sexual prowess had its downside, a belief strengthened, no doubt, by the prevalence of venereal diseases among cowboys.

The effort to regulate drinking was far from new in America, and temperance efforts among factory workers had been especially common with the advent of the factory and the need for greater worker efficiency. Similarly, cattlemen often enforced sobriety on their ranches, and many avoided excessive drinking themselves, whether under the influence of wives, trying to set an example for the men, or by choice.[142] Former slave Harrison McClure's description of George Littlefield could apply to most of the cattlemen: "He never was no man for drinking whiskey, running around, and gambling."[143] Indeed, self-discipline and middle-class manhood depended on being able to control behavior like drinking. The added fact that excess alcohol could lead to a loss of restraint in other areas made it an easy target. As the editor of the *History of Cattlemen of Texas* opined in 1914 in his discussion of the reining in of the cow towns and cowboys: "The business world will no longer tolerate a worker who drinks to excess and in fact a 'drinking man' is looked upon with suspicion in every industry. The livestock industry took the same trend and with its gradual transformation into a systematic and business-conducted institution, the demands upon its workers became more exacting."[144] Increasingly, middle-class men saw drinking as a sign of weakness and a barrier to success, and as success defined middle-class masculinity, it was a barrier to manhood as well.

Prohibition was an attack on working-class male culture as much as an attack on sin. When towns had few settlers there was little effort to stop the saloons, but as more people moved into town, they witnessed drunkenness firsthand, and in many ways it was the public nature of drinking—the basis of working-class leisure, and masculine performance—that they objected to as much as alcohol.[145] The temperance movement was strong in Texas. Carrie Nation, the "battleaxe" of the Women's Christian Temperance Union, lived in Richmond, Texas from 1879 to 1889 and viewed drunken violence firsthand when her husband was beaten by drunken saloon patrons.[146] Most towns passed licensing laws and laws prohibiting the sale of alcohol on Sundays. After 1876, all Texas counties had to pass local option laws, and by 1895, fifty-three counties were completely dry.[147]

Beginning in the 1880s, the townspeople had help in their fight against drunken cowboys in unlicensed drinking establishments in the form of the Texas Rangers. In 1880, Ranger George W. Arrington was assigned to the Panhandle for the purpose of maintaining order. He toured the local towns and shut down a number of unlicensed whiskey sellers which seemed to be the root of the problem. Nonetheless, he and his men encountered resistance. In Teepe City, he reported a rumor that the men "intend giving us a fight Christmas night, that they intend to shoot as much as they please, and I was told that the gang intend to charge the place Christmas night firing at everything they see." Arrington blamed the illicit whiskey vendor for encouraging them and also reported that the men usually came in fifteen to twenty at a time, leaving only four to stand with the herd.[148] "Respectable" citizens increasingly relied on the Rangers and the courts to deal with rowdy cowboy behavior, but very few convictions of the sellers ever resulted, only fines for individual cowboys, which had little long-term impact.[149] Moreover, the process took hold slowly in less settled areas. The Big Bend region held out longer than the rest of the state. In the 1886 referendum on prohibition there were only two votes cast in favor of the measure in all of Presidio County.[150] Alpine citizens did not vote their town dry until 1909.[151]

Not all leading men objected to drinking themselves. Richard King and Mifflin Kenedy sponsored a celebratory trip for the business and civic leaders of Corpus Christi when they finished the railroad to Laredo. The passengers drank forty cases of champagne and other liquors and smoked an astonishing 2,000 cigars. As Robert J. Kleberg Jr. described it, in consequence "quite a number of our leading citizens & Pillars of the church were perfectly exhausted with pleasure by the time they reached Laredo."[152] He apparently did not find it ironic to describe Laredo in the same letter as demoralized due to drinking and gambling. Many businessmen did not object to drinking in moderation and even some temperance advocates opposed prohibition by law. When a state constitutional amendment for prohibition failed in 1887, prominent South Texas sheepman Walter W. Meek told his fiancée, "I am, in great measure, down on liquor myself, and believe it causes much evil and tends to blunt and dull the moral faculties and causes a large increase in crime. Yet I rather favor letting a man, or rather a person, be their own judge, even in such dangerous matters." Meeks believed that strict licensing laws were a more efficient solution since few really supported the enforcement of prohibition. He also confessed that he believed a little beer on the ranch might be beneficial in hot weather, but agreed to a total temperance pledge to please his future wife.[153] For Meeks, perhaps, he wanted not only the ability to choose for himself, but also the chance to show he could resist temptation.

Cattlemen were not always immune to temptation, however. Joseph Heneage Finch, the 7th earl of Aylesbury, came to Big Springs, Texas in 1883 with the nickname "Sporting Joe," a name he had earned for his raucous entertainments for the Prince of Wales. In social exile because of his wife's scandalous affair and subsequent divorce, Finch bought a 2,500-acre ranch and began running cattle with his two brothers. He also continued drinking heavily and was a great favorite with the hands for sharing both his whiskey and his stories of travel around the world, but died of cirrhosis of the liver only two years later.[154] In Finch's case, his lack of restraint endeared him to the cowboys as they saw in him a fellow sinner, equally scorned by "society" despite his noble background. To the townspeople around, however, he was more likely viewed as another decadent European aristocrat in contrast to decent Americans.

In the late nineteenth century, it was common for young men from respectable families to experiment with drinking and sex, the sorts of leisure activities they associated with the working class. This activity was also part of a rebellion against their fathers that they went through in the process of establishing independent identities. But they knew that if they wanted to succeed in the business world they would have to give up this freedom, and most eventually returned to the values of success and morality they had grown up with.[155] Similarly, many middle-class and upper-class men came out West to become cowboys, often in this same spirit of rebellion. However, those who wanted to succeed in the cowboy world did so by adopting the working-class cultural style of their fellow cowboys rather than imposing their own standards of masculinity on the men in their outfit.[156]

The attempts to restrict gambling also focused on passing local ordinances limiting the practice on Sundays and arrests of people for violation

of these laws. By the late nineteenth century, to many middle-class townspeople and most cattlemen, gambling seemed like a throwback to the pre-
industrial era. In the popular imagination, gambling was tied to the frontier, and when the frontier moved farther west, it seemed to have no place
in settled areas. Since gamblers did not work for their earnings, they could
not be trusted to work hard on the job, or to keep sober. The ties between
gambling and the saloon made it a reason to advocate prohibition, and by
banning both gambling and drink, reformers hoped to eliminate "tavern
fellowship" of working men in exchange for more "enlightened" and respectable leisure.[157] While there were a few exceptions, most cattlemen did
not gamble, once again marking a distance between themselves and their
men. J. S. Wynne reported only rarely seeing any ranch owners gamble
in Mobeetie, a heavy gambling town.[158] Cattleman George W. Littlefield
despised gambling and tried to teach his nephews and the boys he sponsored the error of their ways when they visited gambling halls or billiard
parlors. He told one of them: "Business men do not like for their employees to go to such places—They do not improve the business relations or
knowledge of young men."[159] By the end of the nineteenth century, gambling in business was no longer manly. A 1914 description of cattleman
Benjamin Johnston Tillar painted him as "of the new generation of stockmen, a generation that has placed the livestock industry on a firm and
businesslike basis, and has relegated to oblivion the 'trust to luck' spirit of
an earlier day."[160] Thus, for middle-class men, gambling was irrational and
the sure road to disreputability.

Much of the effort to restrict gambling painted it simply as an unnecessary risk. Many of the new fraternal orders middle-class men joined reinforced this aversion to risk. Moving up in the ranks was dependent only
on paying dues, the men earned health benefits only in accordance with
what they had paid in, and one of the key reasons to be excluded was
being a financial risk. To these men, gambling seemed "potentially sub-
versive and unmanly." Working-class fraternal groups, in contrast, tended
to share benefits equally and thus members shared the risk equally that
funds would be available. In addition, these orders often depended on
fundraisers that involved gambling, lotteries, or prizefighting.[161]

The initial response to the new regulation of "vice" was not promising. Cowboys thought the laws were ridiculous. In Amarillo, many cowboys just laughed at the constables who had to enforce the laws, saying
they could not possibly afford to pay the fines. However, over time, the
cowboys became convinced that the townspeople were serious, especially

when they ended up in the courts multiple times resulting in repeated fines.[162] Bastrop County court records reveal the typical efforts to crack down on gamblers. From the late 1860s well into the late 1880s, by far the most common offense was aggravated assault, with a few gambling cases each month.[163] Beginning in July 1890, however, the authorities made a concerted effort to wipe out gambling in the county. On July 28, fourteen men were indicted on charges of betting or exhibiting monte, the favorite card game among gamblers. Between September 22 and September 30, the courts recorded thirty-three arrests for either playing cards, betting, or exhibiting monte. Most pled guilty and were fined $10 or $25. In late October, there were nine indictments for playing cards in a public house, of which only three were fined; twenty-five counts of betting at monte (twelve of whom were fined); and four indictments for exhibiting monte (resulting in two fines). The courts also heard an additional ten cases of gaming, betting at, or exhibiting monte that month. After a winter respite, in January 1891 there were ten more charges, and by this time several repeat offenders. After another nine cases in March, Bastrop seems to have either quieted down or the authorities decided that prosecutions were not worth the effort, as there seemed to be no mass arrests for the rest of the year. It is most likely that they gave up on prosecutions for a while, as gambling did not disappear from the town. In January 1895, prosecutions resumed, with ten arrests, and on July 3 of that year, fifty-seven men were arrested on a total of ninety-four charges ranging from disturbing a religious worship to aggravated assault, including thirty-two charges of betting at monte, eighteen of betting at craps, and fourteen of gaming. On October 1, an additional fifty-two gambling-related charges were brought. The mass arrests continued periodically for the next few years: thirty-four arrests in January 1896, thirteen in June 1896, twenty-eight in January 1897, and thirty-five in January 1898, but gradually they became fewer in number, though assaults and other crimes still persisted. The repetition of names in the court records suggests, however, that most of the men did not alter their behavior or attitudes toward gambling.[164]

Bastrop County had both ranches and lumber mills, which increased the number of single men who came to the towns to let off steam, making it hard to keep order. In smaller cow towns, however, the townspeople were no less concerned with gambling. Uvalde County started prosecuting gamblers early. In March 1872, the records showed forty-seven charges of betting or exhibiting monte, with an additional twenty indictments in the same session. Eventually almost all these cases ended in fines, although a fairly large number of them took over a year to arrive at that point, and some even extended into 1876. The town seems to have settled down for a year as the cases went through the courts, but again, in January 1876, there were forty-three gambling indictments, including repeat offenders. Gambling eventually came under county court jurisdiction and as in Bastrop County, a decade later there were still mass arrests, with a relentless attack on gambling between 1883 and 1886 in particular. These attacks again appear to have been effective, as in 1890 there was no indictment for gambling in the county.[165]

Atascosa County started a brief crackdown on gambling in 1873 with the arrest of seventeen men on gambling charges, but carried it out only intermittently in the 1870s. In 1883, Atascosa officials began again in earnest with arrests on fifty-four counts of betting or exhibiting monte; while arrests continued in the years that followed, the numbers generally diminished.[166] Although there are no records for Reeves County in West Texas before 1885, it is clear that starting in the 1890s, there was a massive attack on gambling in the county, which was home to the cow towns of Toyah and Pecos. There had been almost no charges in the county court before 1890, but between 1891 and 1894, there were ninety-four indictments for gambling, more than any other charge and approached most closely only by thirty-three counts of unlawfully carrying a pistol. Despite the number of arrests, however, the situation did not abate much; there were an additional sixty-four indictments in the three years that followed, and regular arrests for gambling continued into the early twentieth century.[167] By the 1880s, licensing laws and other peacekeeping measures had come to be accepted as normal in most settled areas. In addition, most town leaders supported informal "licensing" measures such as regular fines for gamblers and prostitutes as a good source of income to pay for a police force they necessitated.[168] Cowboys perceived these new restrictions as part of a general effort to control them, but, fines notwithstanding, few changed their behavior much.

In tandem with their legalistic approach, the towns' leading men tried to couch their efforts to restrain the cowboys in terms of paternalistic advice, further asserting a greater claim to masculinity. Many newspapers regularly lectured the cowboys on what was proper "manly" behavior. *Jacksboro/Fort Griffin Echo* editor G. W. Robson made a career of writing on behalf of the stock raisers, and from the late 1870s on, often tutored the cowboys on appropriate behavior.[169] He printed boilerplate material which included poems and columns on "Advice to the Boys," or "What to Teach the Boys." This included advice to be brave, pure, unselfish, and polite, self-reliant but "gentle in mien, words and temper."[170] The editor also directly addressed the cowboys when there had been incidents of violence. "Go slow on the racket, our citizens do not want to see you punished but you are almost certain to be [cala]boosed or fined—maybe both—if you do not chop on the noise."[171] The *Texas Livestock Journal* printed a long story giving advice to cowboys on how to spend their leisure time between seasons. A good cowboy should beware of liquor, go straight home, talk with his parents, tease his little sister, and then go visit his sweetheart and talk about settling down eventually. The author also advised him to save money for the next year so he did not have to borrow more from the boss.[172] Such advice, while cloaked in the language of paternal interest, showed the ranchers' desire to keep the cowboys away from the towns where they might cause too many problems for the regular citizens. It also showed how they emphasized restraint as the proper manly model for leisure.

Often, as a way of modeling good behavior, the papers would praise men who showed restraint. The *Texas Livestock Journal* highlighted the restrained example that cattlemen set in public in comparison to the stereotypical rowdy cowboy. From the National Convention of Cattle Growers in St. Louis, the editor reported that "the only disappointment to the average St. Louisian was the absence of the wild man of the West. The wild and wooly man remained at home or disguised himself as a gentleman."[173] The *Texas Panhandle* tried to shame the cowboys into good behavior by defining proper cowboy behavior in restrained terms. When an outfit came through town swaggering and swearing "in a futile attempt to appear wild and woolly," and roughly handling their horses, the paper asserted that they were not real cowboys, but "silly boys just emancipated from the cotton patch." In contrast, "The old, sure enough cowboy, worthy the name of gentleman, is the sort we are used to here, and the invasion of weaklings with assured coarseness shows the contrast vividly."[174]

A few cattlemen tried to regulate the cowboys' morals with a direct paternal appeal. Some ranchers sent their own sons out to work alongside the men to try to set an example of moral behavior. Hilory Bedford even brought a circuit preacher to the ranch to try to bring the cowboys under religious influence. But many of these efforts backfired. Some of the sons ended up being more like the cowboys, and while the cowboys showed up to listen to the preacher, they just did so to be polite.[175] Most cowboys were not especially religious, believing more in their own skills than divine providence in daily life. Teddy Abbott estimated that about 90 percent were "infidels," as their experiences out on the range had shown them that "You could pray all you damn pleased, but it wouldn't get you water where there wasn't water."[176]

When cowboys did not respond well to paternal lectures on manly restraint, the townspeople denigrated their manhood in racial terms. In 1873, the Ellsworth, Kansas newspaper compared Texas cowboys to Indians. "The Lipan and Comanche are not more unlike civilized white man than is the nomadic herdsman to the Texan who dwells in the city or cultivates the plains."[177] In 1883, the *San Antonio Light* compared a group of rowdy cowboys who had stolen apples from some local Mexicans to Indians on the warpath, calling them bullies and praising the "brave" police who "taught" them to obey the law.[178] In the late nineteenth century, society automatically relegated all nonwhites to a less manly category than whites, both in the sense that people considered them "childlike" races, and in the Rooseveltian sense that the white race was the manliest of all because it had conquered the rest. By putting cowboys both below Mexicans and in the same category as Indians, the editorial robbed them of any claim to manliness.[179] *Fort Griffin Echo* editor Robson used racial comparisons to put the cowboys in their place. In an 1879 editorial entitled "To the Cowboys," he chastised the men for coming into town and disturbing the peace. "You damn the Mexican and ape him by running your horses and firing your guns and pistols, just to hear them roar; you despise the half-naked lousy Indian and then try to m[i]mic his unearthly yell: . . . Many of the stock raisers come to town, get tight, and have what they think is fun and lots of it, too, but seldom do you see one of them down, or hear him yell or fire his pistol."[180] The *El Paso Lone Star* wondered why the cowboys who were so anxious to shoot up the town were always missing when hostile Apaches were around.[181] Ironically, the cowboys often referred to themselves as "white Indians" for their wild behavior, but meant it more as a celebration of their lack of civilization than a real racial equation, as the qualifying "white" showed.[182]

Joseph McCoy described the cowboys in Abilene, Kansas as having lives that bordered "nearly upon that of an Indian," and humor "wherein abounds much vulgarity and an animal propensity." He did excuse their behavior, however, as in part a result of drinking alkali water on the trail. "No wonder the cowboy gets sallow and unhealthy and deteriorates in manhood until often he becomes capable of any contemptible thing; no wonder he should become half-civilized only, and take to whisky with a love excelled scarcely by the barbarous Indian."[183] Sheepman Walter W. Meek described the cowboys on a neighboring ranch in equally conde-scending terms as he watched them scramble to be first to get to the cof-fee can at the ranch house. "Poor wretches," he told his fiancée, "as I stood looking at them I thought of thy query about the heathens: 'why should we try to give them more light', and I applied the words not to their reli-gion, but to their way of living—civilizing these people would take away much of their happiness."[184]

While these comments were not intended for the cowboys themselves, the papers also used public ridicule as another, perhaps more effective, method of restraining "the boys," and one of the best ways to ridicule a cowboy was to challenge his masculinity. In one such report, a wild cow-boy came into San Antonio on a spree, only to face charges for being drunk and disorderly. At his court appearance he "hung his head in a vain endeavor to choke down his sobs," and "left amid the audible smiles of the spectators."[185] The wording of an 1880 appeals court decision in Navarro County shows similar patronizing tones. Alonzo Matthews had been sen-tenced to five years in the penitentiary for stealing a horse he had lost in a card game. Matthews and Tobe Green had played cards, and Matthews first lost his money, then his coat, his saddle, and finally his horse (or pos-sibly $25 with his horse as security). Green took everything and left "proud and happy, whilst the appellant followed on foot, sad and dejected." Green locked up the horse at his brother's blacksmith shop, and Matthews left "a sadder but not a wiser man" only to return that night to steal back his horse. The court affirmed the original judgment, and it was clear that the defendant was an object of condescension to the members of the court.[186] In a poem entitled "That Awful Cowboy," published in the *San Antonio Light* in 1883, a poorly dressed cowboy comes to town on a spree with a big pistol with which he shoots the Mayor's hat, with lots of outrageous boasts, and no money or respect for the town officials or law enforcement:

> But a fellow met this cowboy
> And caught him by the ear
> And said quite coolly, "Now, boy,
> T'is time you get from here!"
> Then shook up his digestion
> In a way that raised a laugh,
> And proved beyond a question
> That the cowboy was a calf.[187]

These depictions of cowboys challenged their masculinity directly by ridiculing the behavior they considered manly, even suggesting it was all simply false bravado.

Newspaper editors played on cowboys' insecurities and plied stereotypes of them as rubes as ways to keep them from becoming too assertive. Such anecdotes became staples for the readers. A typical example would be the story of a cowboy who offered a woman two carloads of mules as an added incentive to marry him after she rejected his first offer.[188] Other stories ridiculed the cowboys' clothes, their lack of sophistication, and their language. The *Austin Statesman* made fun of a cowboy's angora goatskin chaps in which he was "parading about town."[189] The *San Antonio Light* printed the recollections of an opera singer who had once performed in Marshall to an audience of twelve cowboys. When the cowboys realized there were no women in the show, they shot out the footlights and invited the performers to come across the street with them to the saloon.[190] The *El Paso Herald* caricatured cowboy ritual boasting in a story that appeared to be an advertisement for a variety of businesses in town. In "A Hero of the Plains," A "Texican" comes to town wearing boots with a picture of Sam Houston and lone stars on them and a sombrero with a snake coiled around it. After shopping at the various establishments and having fifteen drinks in the saloon, the cowboy rides out of town with a whoop, declaring, "I am a prairie wolf with steel horns on my side. I was raised on mesquite beans baled in mustang blood and my first shirt was a rawhide. My father was born on a sand bar, sucked a cow whale, and my mother was an Apache squaw; I can outride a monkey, outswim a fish, out jump a kangaroo, out curse a bee bitten parson and I can shoot out the eye of a flea."[191] Such caricatures minimized the cowboy's masculinity by making him a humorous figure rather than a manly threat to society.

Stories of naïve cowboys who did not know how to work simple technology when they came to town were legion. Cattleman George W. Saunders told the story of a cowboy on a Pullman car, who, unable to understand the explanation of lower and upper berths, simply slept in the aisle.[192] The *San Antonio Light* reported the story of a cowboy staying in a hotel in Denver who did not know what a folding bed was, and so slept in a drawer of the bureau when he misunderstood the bellboy's explanation.[193] Cowboys themselves recalled many similar incidents in their memoirs. Jack Potter's first trip to the city in 1882 after bringing a herd up the trail terrified him. He did not understand train tickets or checked luggage, and when the train stopped and another train went by, one of his fellow cowboys, Old "Dogface" Smith, aged thirty, panicked. He and the other cowboys later "tried" the engineer in absentia for startling them.[194] The storytellers all painted the cowboys as superstitious, almost primitive, men whose fear of technology made them objects of pity and humor.[195] These stories created a very different image from the manly hero of the dime novels.

In the new model, cowboys were easily subdued or manipulated. Cattlemen with access to northern ranges congratulated themselves that the winter was so cold in Montana that the frostbite had subdued the cowboys. "A new crop of cowboys will have to grow in Montana before you hear anything about their capturing a town or stampeding a court in that region."[196] In another story in this genre, a conductor on a train going through North Dakota subdued a rowdy group of cowboys headed for Fort Worth who were drinking and brandishing their guns, by slipping some opium in their whiskey. The trick was so successful that when they changed trains in Minnesota, the conductor passed along the drug to his counterpart on the southbound train in case he needed it.[197]

A unique genre of humorous anecdotes at the cowboys' expense appeared in the mid-1880s. These stories downplayed the cowboys' masculinity in the face of better and wiser "dudes" who had previously been the object of ridicule for the cowboys. In one such story, three cowboys attempted to intimidate a well-dressed salesman on a train platform by stepping on his feet, but the salesman sent them away "completely cowed," after shooting three apples in mid-air. The punch line was that the salesman was a rapid shot medal winner.[198] In another story, "the doodest dood" who dressed in ridiculous clothes, drank only lemonade, and had come to Texas to fight consumption, bested in a fight one of the toughest men in the local bar who had made fun of him and tried to get him to drink gin. The dude was so impressive that when he asked the other men to drink lemonade with him, they quickly agreed to do so.[199] This tale had the added benefit of proving the value of temperance. These stories were ways of asserting superiority over the cowboys by showing that they were less manly than the "civilized men" who bested them. The Dude, long the object of derision among cowboys, now owned the ranch where the cowboys worked, and was determined to put them in their proper place.

While cowboys resisted complying with many of the regulations in town, when the ranchers made good behavior a prerequisite to keeping their jobs, they had little choice. Many ranchers had rules banning drinking and gambling on the ranch, but some ranches like the XIT Ranch took the regulations a step further. In addition to the twenty-three rules they had to follow while working, XIT men knew that if they got a bad reputation in town for drinking, fighting, or gambling, the ranch would not re-hire them the following year.[200] One account credited the XIT Ranch rules with improving the region around the ranch by gradually doing away "with Xmas Hell variety, this and gambling dens and anything that are compatible with them which led many good boys to destruction."[201] Teddy Abbott experienced similar supervision on the FUF Ranch in Montana, when the New Englander owner banned the *National Police Gazette* from the ranch and followed the men in town to make sure they did not drink. Unfortunately for the cowboys, "We couldn't do nothing but to give in to him, more or less. We were strangers up north and winter was coming on. We were getting big wages. We had to take a tumble."[202] On many ranches, the owners scrutinized the private lives of their hands as much as their work credentials. In 1889, J. E. Farrington, ranch manager of the J. A. Ranch, told his range bosses that he would not dock a good hand's pay if he was sick "unless he's brought it on by unnecessarily exposing himself around town."[203]

Faced with fines and arrests in town, and punishment on the job, cowboys had little choice but to comply with the regulation of their public leisure. While the saloons and brothels never completely disappeared, and cowboys did not stop gambling or drinking, they did so out of the public eye in the more settled towns. As in urban areas in the South and East, by the end of the century, working-class male recreation had become restricted and sanitized in public.[204] By the 1890s in more settled regions, and by the early 1900s in the Panhandle, stories of cowboy sprees all but disappeared in the newspapers, where they had been a regular feature in the 1870s and 1880s.

Discredited at work and in leisure, cowboys seemed more and more marginalized and out of step with the rest of American society. Their sentimentalism similarly became a target of derision. If sentiment in the early to mid-nineteenth century had emphasized sincerity of feelings and elevated morals, by the end of the century it had come to be more ritual than reality. Sentiment could be a marker of gentility but need not be genuine.[205] As a result, its value declined to middle-class men. Nonetheless, women continued to see sentiment as a way to bring about reform, as well as a way to ensure social order. Giving children an inner sentimental compass, for example, was a way to replace corporal punishment.[206] For women who lived in the West, social order implied taming masculine behavior and promoting a new masculinity that was opposed to gambling, violence, drinking, and prostitution.[207] But masculine sentiment increasingly came into disrepute by the early twentieth century. With the rise of sexuality studies and Freudian ideas, social scientists interpreted the heart, which received such prominent mention in sentimental literature, to simply be a substitute for sexual organs, thus, sentimental language of the sort men had used with each other seemed to lose its innocence.[208] Emotion and gentleness became signs of weakness and were associated almost exclusively with women, and sentiment in men was therefore effeminate.[209] Literary critics increasingly argued that sentimental writing was simply women's prattle and not deserving of the label of serious literature, and male authors adopted a less flowery, more unsentimental tone in their books and chose subjects that reflected the modern world.

Sentiment belonged in the world of women and children, and its presence was infantilizing. Descriptions of Christian conversions of Indians discussed how the conversion experience reduced them from barbaric savages to sentimental penitents on bended knee before the missionaries. The association of subjugation and sentiment served to emasculate them and make them less of a threat.[210] Thus, descriptions of sentimental cowboys now also seemed to tame them and make them less of a threat to the town. In 1887, the *San Antonio Daily Light* printed an editorial entitled "A Cowboy Sheds Tears," which both mocked snobbery and made the cowboy in question seem ridiculous. Two cowboys attended the theater fresh off the trail and ready to get rowdy, but when one of the performers sang "Nearer My God to Thee," one of the cowboys started crying because it reminded him of his family at home. While some people condemned the theater as vile, it nonetheless was good for something, wrote the editor, tongue firmly in cheek.[211] Presumably sentiment had once again tamed the savage beast.

Gradually, cowboys and their revelries were pushed into back streets and out of town. The Fourth of July celebrations in most towns were an excuse for a rowdy celebration. Many annual rodeos and contests of skills took place on the Fourth, and the cowboys looked forward to the break in the work and the chance to visit town. But these celebrations began to become more sedate, as Western towns mimicked their counterparts in the East by adopting Memorial Day as their main holiday, and toning down the celebrations on the Fourth. In 1884, the Dodge City Driving Park and Fair Association put on a Spanish Bullfight for the Fourth of July. The cowboys and cattlemen saw the event as a last hurrah for the old Wild

West, but reformers protested the fight as brutal. As the event gained national attention as well as the potential for huge profits, the townspeople decided to ignore the reformers and hold the fight. Nonetheless, they conformed to respectable society's standards at the last minute by getting the town deputies to segregate the cowboys and prostitutes from the rest of the citizenry, including the cattlemen.[212] It was also the last celebration of its kind and the last hurrah for cowboys in Dodge City after all.

• • •

The effort of cattlemen and townspeople to restrain cowboy masculinity reflects a number of intertwined issues of class and gender that many Americans faced in the late nineteenth century. The frontier was no more egalitarian than the "settled" regions of the United States; and in frontier Texas, as elsewhere, power rested with those who could afford it. Racial hierarchies also determined social position, and appeals to white manhood gave all white men some measure of status. But there were also clear gender hierarchies that reinforced the class structure. Cowboys tried to demonstrate their masculinity through their independence on the job and through working-class masculine rituals in town. But cattlemen defined their masculinity in middle-class terms of restraint, which they expressed in part through their ability to restrain other men at work and in leisure. Cattlemen and townspeople viewed the cowboys not as men, but as naïve or recalcitrant boys who needed tight control. The image of masculinity they promulgated was not dependent on physical strength but manly restraint, which by definition the cowboys, however strong or skilled, could never hope to achieve. In this way, the cowboys remained permanent adolescents, and seemed no real threat to social order.

Cowboys, whether they perceived these attacks consciously or not, resisted control at all levels and looked to each other to maintain their masculine self-images rather than to society. They did not change their behavior to adapt to middle-class ideals, but, after the mid-1880s they found themselves increasingly restricted both at work and in town. Depicted as both children and hooligans by the respectable citizens around them, they created a separate society for themselves in which being respectable was not important and where they felt at ease with other men (and some women) who were social outcasts. They clung to older heroic and artisanal ideals of manhood and increasingly seemed out of place in modern society. That they did not fade away, however, had more to do with mythic ideals of them than social reality.

# Epilogue

## The Cowboy Becomes Myth

By 1900, many people had come to see cowboy skills such as riding and roping as simply decorative. As one former cowboy noted, "the expert roper and rider, is admired only for his skill, and not for his usefulness."[1] As the frontier became more settled, the cowboy of old had become more of a public spectacle than ideal worker. Denison, Texas, near the Red River and the Shawnee Trail, had been as wild, if not more so, than Fort Griffin in its early years; but even by 1876, genuine cowboys were a rare sight in that town. At the age of nineteen, cowboy Rollie Burns worked for a Denison butcher in the off-season, who attracted customers by getting Burns to ride a wild steer on Main Street.[2] By the mid- to late 1890s, large trail herds were rare enough in Abilene to cause a teen-aged Wirt W. White to describe the cowboys that came past town with 3,500 head of cattle almost as exotic beings.[3] The people who came out to see Burns ride a steer or the cattle herd in Abilene were already nostalgic for an imagined past that they had read about in novels or seen in Wild West shows. Ironically, the heroes of the Western, at the very time Owen Wister's *The Virginian* was published in 1902, were in reality discredited to the cattlemen and townspeople of the West.[4] As historian Dee Garceau argues: "In the late Victorian mind, cowboys were drifters, morally suspect and socially crude." But cowboys were also avid readers of dime novels and participants in Wild West shows, and by the 1920s, when most cowboys began writing their memoirs, their defense was to embrace the myth of the dime novel heroic and genteel cowboy and claim it as reality, ironically glorifying middle-class ideals of masculinity in the process.[5]

Why Westerns had such appeal at the end of the century and how the cowboy became the knightly hero and aristocrat of the plains is a somewhat complicated question. Most historians see the popularity of the Western as a reflection of nostalgia in the face of an increasingly industrialized and urbanized society. With the 1890 census declaring that America no longer had a frontier, and with historian Frederick Jackson Turner theorizing that the frontier had made America strong and given it democratic values, many Americans speculated that the country would grow weak.[6] Teddy Roosevelt, among others, saw the frontier as capable of making men and held up cattlemen and cowboys as the sort of virile specimens of masculinity Easterners would do well to emulate. "They have shown the qualities of daring, endurance, and far-sightedness of eager desire for victory and stubborn refusal to accept defeat, which go to make up the essential manliness of the American character."[7]

Young boys who grew up reading dime novels with Western heroes also credited men in the West with a kind of supermasculinity. Owen Wister believed that the changes that took place in the 1880s and 1890s in America marked a decline in the nation's morals, and idealized the cowboy as a "wellspring of national regeneration."[8] Literary scholar Jane Tompkins has argued that the emphasis on masculinity in the Western itself is what made them so popular, as they reflected a backlash to the rise of the New Era woman, active in public affairs and the workplace and dominating reform activities. The late nineteenth century seemed over-feminized to many, and the Western was the perfect antidote.[9] In truth, all of these factors combined to make the Western immensely popular in the late nineteenth century, and in the process elevated the cowboy from scoundrel to hero.

More than anyone, William "Buffalo Bill" Cody was responsible for rehabilitating the image of the cowboy. Having been a frontiersman and scout, if at least briefly, and earning fame for a colorful fight with an Indian in the wake of Little Bighorn, Cody began a career on the stage telling larger-than-life stories about his alleged exploits, eventually moving on to a more elaborate format that was similar to the traveling circuses that were popular at this time. He staged the first of his Wild West shows in North Platte, Nebraska on the Fourth of July in 1882. The show involved approximately a thousand cowboys competing in riding and roping events, and from that Cody went on to create one of the most successful traveling shows in the world. One of the reasons for his success was that he tapped into white middle-class anxieties about the influx of immigrants, the end of the frontier, and the decline of masculinity by presenting an image of unique American white male virility existing in the West. While black and Hispanic cowboys were featured equally in his show in early years, Cody eventually reduced them to weak stereotypes in contrast to the manly Anglo cowboys, who always saved the day.[10]

Moreover, Cody's publicity machine very carefully promoted a masculine image for the show that middle-class men could partake of by attending it. When they came to town, Cody and his promoter hosted a series of all-male get-togethers for local dignitaries which featured crude dining and copious amounts of whiskey, the preferred drink of rugged frontiersmen.[11] Yet clearly this manly presentation was a performance. Cody realized that in order to achieve financial success, he would have to domesticate his show so that middle-class women would feel comfortable attending. As traveling shows often had reputations for low morality and disreputable personnel, he always referred to the show as an "exhibition." After 1884, one of the main scenes of the show was an Indian attack on a settler's cabin in which Cody and the white cowboys defended hearth, home, women, and children by driving off the attackers. To make gunplay seem more respectable, Cody featured father and son shooting acts as well as the virginal and feminine Annie Oakley, who shot at cards, cigarettes, and money, thus symbolically targeting vices. Lastly, he had men and women perform folk dances like the Virginia Reel on horseback, tying his show into the tradition of wholesome country entertainments. Buffalo Bill's success inspired a host of imitators such as Pawnee Bill, who later became Cody's business partner. Cowboys thus became spectacles, even if the show presented them as "upwardly mobile white men." When the show traveled to London the spectacle became more pronounced, as visitors to the shows' camp gaped at the cowboys as much as the Indians and taunted them as they might animals in a zoo.[12]

A similar form of entertainment that evolved in part from cowboy recreation and in part from the Wild West show was the rodeo. Whereas the Wild West shows were pure entertainment and generally performed in larger cities, rodeos were at first local events that used working cowboys. Wild West show cowboys were salaried performers, rodeo cowboys were competitors who paid entry fees. Rodeos evolved from informal contests cowboys held on ranches at roundups, and had their counterparts in the Mexican *charreadas*, in which the *charro* would compete to pick things up from the ground on horseback and rope and ride bulls and horses. Vaqueros performed in such contests and undoubtedly influenced Anglo cowboys. Thus, the first recorded rodeos were in the 1820s in Mexico, Texas, and California, with the first Anglo contests coming after the Civil War. The town of Pecos, Texas held the first competition in 1883, but Prescott, Arizona claimed to have the first professional rodeo, and in its rodeos of 1886–1888 charged admission and awarded prizes to

Cowboys play cowboys and Indians play Indians in a Wild West Show. Note the entrepreneur, Pawnee Bill, in regular clothes in comparison to the others' flamboyant costumes. Performers with stage coach in Pawnee Bill's Wild West Show, Jun-08. LC-S6-338, Erwin E. Smith Collection of the Library of Congress on deposit at the Amon Carter Museum, Fort Worth, Texas.

competitors. Cowboys often performed exhibitions in local Fourth of July celebrations as they were readily available, and eventually, by the 1920s, many small towns began to see the commercial possibilities of rodeo as a spectator sport and built rodeo grounds.[13]

Commercial rodeos, while claiming to come from the traditional cowboy pastimes, nonetheless represented a hybrid of tradition and entertainment. In traditional rodeo, the races and stunts the cowboys enacted were largely for each other and were part of social interaction. Commercial rodeos made rodeo more of a ritual performance. Elements such as the Grand Entry and the rodeo clown were borrowed directly from the Wild West show, eventually becoming part of "rodeo tradition." Moreover, the performances were now tied into a larger association with heritage, patriotism, and community. The spectacle was local and community-based, but it was still, nonetheless, spectacle.[14]

Wild West shows and rodeos were as popular in Texas as they were in the East. As early as 1884, a Wild West show featuring ten cowboys, two "lady riders," eighteen horses, and a six shooter sham battle played in San Antonio and Fort Worth to appreciative crowds.[15] A group of cowboys entertained San Antonio residents at the racetrack that fall with "exhibitions in throwing the lasso."[16] The following year, promoters organized a "wild west cow-boy troupe" in the city to tour the Northeast United States.[17] The unintended message of these shows was that the work skills the cowboys used to prove their manhood were entertainment, rather than real work, thus further marginalizing cowboy masculinity. By the 1890s, the cowboys had become exotic spectacles in the minds of most people, and the citizens of Texas were as much believers in the myths about them as were the people on the East Coast. Their masculine feats had been contained in an acceptable form as entertainment and were increasingly irrelevant on the job, as were the cowboys themselves.

There is some evidence to suggest that cowboys were willing partners in the spectacle. B. R. Pearson went on a visit to Europe fully rigged out in cowboy gear, but seemed to enjoy the attention. Banned from wearing his pistol, he commented, "I guess the Frenchies was scared I'd get a wild hair in the butter and drop one of them. Maybe even thought I'd scalp one of them. Who knows? I didn't care though because I got plenty of attention." In the course of his trip he met a number of promoters who asked him to perform exhibitions all over Europe and North Africa, and then he toured Germany with a circus before homesickness brought him back home.[18] Rodeo was the one form of recreation left to cowboys, and the cowboys' choice to give up the supervision and humdrum work of the ranches for rodeo work was a way of thumbing their noses at society and keeping the fun going.[19] In addition, in a time when ranch jobs were scarce and salaries averaged around $40–$75 a month, performers in Buffalo Bill's Wild West Exhibition earned up to $120 a month and traveled the world, which was certainly worth a little discomfort in front of an audience.[20] But even in the glamorous world of entertainment there was a clear hierarchy of men. Cowboys served as waiters alongside the Indians at Cody's manly get-togethers, and Cody himself treated them with great condescension.[21] In addition, when rodeo cowboys became professionals, they were more like employees again and, in the early years, could not count on the rodeo organizers to give out the prizes they promised. Rodeo professionals did not form a union until 1936 and were so slow to do so, they initially called themselves the Cowboy Turtles Association.[22]

While cowboys themselves became marginalized, their fictional reputation grew. A main source of the Western myth was the dime novel. Born in the publishing house of Beadle & Adams and continued by Munro's Ten Cent Novels, Frank Tousey, and Street & Smith, dime novels reached the peak of their popularity between 1865 and 1900. Aimed largely at working-class readers, and particularly young boys, the cheap, formulaic, adventure novels commonly sold over 600,000 copies each, more than any books before in the history of publishing. On average, 1,000 of these books were published each year ensuring that they had a wide readership. Three-quarters of the novels dealt with adventures on the frontier, often featuring woodsmen and Indian scouts in the first years.[23]

Dime novels gained their inspiration from the popular James Fenimore Cooper Leatherstocking Tales, which featured woodsman and friend to Indians, Natty Bumppo, on a series of adventures. These novels helped create an image of the frontier as a metaphor for the conflict between the savage and the civilized. They emphasized both the allure and freedom of the savage in that the main characters operated outside the rules of proper society, but ultimately reinforced the superiority of civilization.[24] The first heroes were old trappers and hunters, but, realizing they needed a romantic interest, authors began to introduce the character of the young tenderfoot accompanying them on their travels in the wilderness. By the 1860s, the young man had become the hero, and the plainsman himself became more refined rather than colorful. Historian Daryl Jones traces the evolution of Davy Crockett to show this process. Originally portrayed as an uncouth braggart who avoided women in the late 1860s novels, a decade later, Crockett spoke perfect English with only a few colloquialisms, had several girlfriends, and even married one of them. The new hero could both have adventures *and* get the girl. He was also at home in both parlor and woodlands. Crockett's gentrification was followed by that of scout and Indian fighter Kit Carson, as well as Buffalo Bill himself, who, thanks to writer Ned Buntline, became the hero of many dime novels in the 1880s. Buffalo Bill's transformation was due to the efforts of writer and press agent Prentiss Ingraham, who changed him from Buntline's rough backwoodsman to a well-spoken and courtly hero whose sidekick, Wild Bill Hickok, took on the dirty work.[25] These literary transitions paralleled a change in values from the older heroic masculinity to the more refined, society-oriented middle-class masculinity of the late nineteenth century.

Cowboys themselves were only minor figures when they first appeared in dime novels in the 1870s, and when they first became the main hero, they differed little from the earlier plainsmen except for wearing boots rather than moccasins and using a lariat instead of a bowie knife. The first actual cowboy hero was *Parson Jim, King of the Cowboys* (1882), but the one that most people first knew was Buck Taylor, who appeared in a series of novels starting in 1887. Ironically, Buck Taylor was a cowboy from Buffalo Bill's Wild West, and his exploits downplayed ranch work in favor of fighting Indians and other adventures. A few early novels tried to picture the cowboy as the defender of the little guy against the evil corporate cattlemen, but in these 1890s novels, cowboys were mostly just plainsmen in fancier clothing, as they rarely came close to cattle.[26]

Still, as a fictional character, the cowboy was getting a new positive image, and nowhere more so than in the first serious Western novel to appear, Owen Wister's *The Virginian* (1902). Wister's hero is a defender of women and civilization, and above all a gentleman, embodying decidedly middle-class values of masculinity especially in contrast to Trampas, the villain of the piece who is more in tune with working-class ideals.[27] The Virginian is the model of restraint. When he celebrates winning a bet he refuses excess liquor as he "has got to stay responsible." In true Rooseveltian form he tells the narrator after an uncharacteristic outburst of anger that "any full-sized man, ought to own a big lot of temper. And like all his valuable possessions, he'd ought to keep it and not lose any." Moreover, the hero is never fully in charge in the face of his betters. The Judge is wiser than he and tests him for his fitness to become foreman. The narrator starts as a tenderfoot but ends as an equal, perhaps even a superior, as a sentimental Virginian sobs about the loss of his friend Steve, whom he has just lynched, lost in a whirlwind of emotion. "Thus we had come to change places."[28] Nonetheless, *The Virginian* placed the cowboy squarely as the central figure of the Western, and was followed by a number of "serious" Western novels which reinforced Wister's image, such as Zane Grey's *Riders of the Purple Sage* (1912) and Max Brand's *The Untamed* (1917).[29]

While the novels created an image of heroic struggle against the elements and introduced the idea of the frontier as a metaphor, artists created visual images of the West that perpetuated some of these ideas. In illustrations for the novels and in national magazines, these artists created set pieces that focused especially on the cowboy, and for the first time included scenes of him at work. But whereas authors like Wister and Teddy Roosevelt believed in the regenerative power of the West, the artists furthered the idea of the passing of the West. Cowboy artist Charlie Russell grew up in St. Louis obsessed with wanting to become a Western hero like those he read about in the dime novels. In 1880, when he was sixteen, his parents finally arranged for him to go to a ranch in Montana, where he worked as a horse wrangler and eventually learned the skills to become a cowboy. An artist from a young age, Russell began painting pictures of what he saw around him but increasingly came to see his subject as a vanishing way of life. Imbued with a romantic image of the West before he got there, Russell, while an authentic cowboy, also contributed to the nostalgia surrounding the West.

Russell's pictures were filled with a romantic sense of a passing age. His first painting to gain recognition, in fact, was one of a starving cow entitled, "Last of the 5000, Waiting for the Chinook," which in some versions is surrounded by wolves. Other nostalgic titles include "When Wagon Trails Were Dim," and "The Last of His Race." Russell's paintings commonly have themes of conflict, be it man versus beast, as in "Cowpunching Sometimes Spells Trouble"; man and/or beast versus nature as in "Waiting for the Chinook"; or man versus man as in "The Ambush." Nature is clearly the most powerful of the forces at play: when a cowboy's horse falls on him, Russell includes a cow skeleton as a memento mori. These images are in tune with those of Romanticist artists in Europe in showing the greatness of the land and the heroes of the age, as he often focused on imaginary or historical scenes. Nonetheless, Russell also painted some of the more realistic depictions of cowboy daily life, such as "Cattle Drive," in which a cowboy stops to light a cigarette while trailing a herd. Russell established a log cabin studio in Montana in 1903 and began a full-time career as an artist and illustrator as his work became widely known. His wife became his business manager, organizing gallery shows and sales and marketing his brand. When asked about the arrangement, Russell supposedly replied, "She lives for tomorrow, an' I live for yesterday." His biographer, Ramon Adams, saw him as "driven by an urge to picture the frontier in its glory before it became engulfed by the ruthless march of the white man's civilization," with a belief that it was his mission to "rescue from oblivion . . . the glories of the Old West that was passing."[30]

The other most famous Western artist, Frederick Remington, illustrator for Teddy Roosevelt's *Ranch Life and the Hunting Trail*, similarly painted a nostalgic West. Unlike Russell, Remington was never a cowboy himself, although he visited the region. His paintings were not life studies, however, but mostly done in his studio on an island in the St. Lawrence River on his return. As a result, most of them were stylized representations of his images of the West and more manipulated to create a message than Russell's work. Like fellow Easterner Teddy Roosevelt, Remington saw the West as "the last enclave of sincerity, independence, and virility," but believed it was being destroyed by the encroachment of civilization. According to Remington in 1907, "my West passed utterly out of existence so long ago as to make it merely a dream."[31] Remington's paintings were thus symbolic in their imagery and, as he progressed, increasingly concerned with form and geometry as much as content. The backgrounds of his paintings were usually blank, with only a hint of landscape, so that viewers would focus on the figures themselves. His cowboys defended water holes against Indian attacks, fought Indians for stolen cattle, and sometimes were only recognizable as cowboys by their dress, with chaps and a gun belt signifying their identity.[32] Most of Remington's pictures focus on Indians and scouts, and when cowboys do appear, such as in "The Puncher," the horse is often more carefully painted than the man himself, or, as in "Turn Him Loose, Bill," and "His First Lesson," the men are suspiciously clean. Remington's cowboy was an imagined one, as were Russell's buffalo herds and Indians.[33]

The rise of the Western film also contributed to the evolution of the cowboy image. The Western was a uniquely American genre of film that allowed the American film industry to compete with the European studios which were turning out better-quality features. The visual imagery of artists such as Russell and Remington provided inspiration for the new medium, and Western adventure stories provided a chance to showcase best what film could do in contrast to still photography and art: continuous action. It is not surprising that some of the first films ever made featured Western subjects. From 1894 on, Thomas Edison filmed Western scenes as documentary footage, some of which featured Buffalo Bill as well as cowboys at work. The first feature-length Western, *The Great Train Robbery* (1903), was a groundbreaking film, and one of the first films of any kind to achieve widespread popularity. As were many of the earliest films, *The Great Train Robbery* was filmed in New Jersey; however, as the film industry moved to California, neighboring Arizona provided both easily accessible and spectacular backgrounds that European film producers could not hope to rival. Within a few years, people expected to see the cowboy "in his natural habitat," and it was these Westerns that helped place the American film industry on a steady footing. By 1910, 21 percent of all American movies made were Westerns, a percentage that would not decrease until the 1940s. Moreover, when the B-movie, the short feature that accompanied the main film, appeared in the late 1920s and 1930s, the dime novel Westerns provided simple good versus evil plots that were ideally suited for the form. The cowboy himself, as a rolling stone, moving from ranch to ranch, was perfect for a serial adventure: he could save the ranch and get the girl at the end of each reel, but then move on the next week to another ranch to do it all over again.[34]

The image of cowboys that evolved in Western film both drew on dime novel and art conventions and built on them. Broncho Billy, the first named "cowboy" hero who was the subject of films in the 1910s, dressed in an elaborate cowboy costume, but was in reality an outlaw. Nonetheless, his characteristics such as being rough but gallant toward women, good-natured, and free and easy, became shorthand for cowboy characteristics as well. Actor and filmmaker William S. Hart, desiring to make Western films more "authentic," refined this image further. The films in which he starred between 1913 and 1917 featured a cowboy hero who was a loner, aloof from other people. Hart's supposedly more authentic cowboy thus actually strayed further from the historical tradition of strong cowboy friendships and cow camp camaraderie, but loner status later became a prerequisite for most movie cowboy heroes. In the 1920s, however, it was Tom Mix who set the tone for cowboy persona as "footloose knight of the plains." For Mix, entertainment was far more important than reality, and it was in his era that stunt action sequences and glamorous clothing took center stage. Mix also did much to clean up the image of the cowboy. His serials were aimed at children, and so he did not drink, kill, or smoke in any of his films. In the 1920s, a number of imitators followed, each reinforcing these trends, culminating in the 1930s with Gene Autry, the singing cowboy who codified the cowboy's alleged restraint in his Ten Cowboy Commandments. Autry's cowboys are always gentle to old people, children, and animals; never smoke or drink; are never racially or religiously intolerant; are always clean in thought, deed, and personal grooming; respect women and the law; and above all are patriots.[35] Ironically, many of his commandments would have been equally at home as a list of rules on the bunkhouse wall of a corporate ranch in the 1890s.

Cowboys themselves were complicit in the creation of the movie myth. Raoul Walsh, a former cowhand in California, was first hired by a film company to round up stray cowboys from the saloons near filming locations and bring them to the set in the San Fernando Valley to be extras. Walsh later became a Western director himself. Los Angeles had real cowboys roaming the streets in its early days who also inspired filmmakers. Early movie cowboys Art Acord and Jack Holt were originally working cowboys, although their film characters did not differ greatly from those of other performers. The ties were greater, however, between the films and the Wild West shows. Tom Mix got his start in the Miller Brothers 101 Ranch Real Wild West Show, Ken Maynard was in Pawnee Bill's show in 1920, and both men went back and forth between the two genres. Art Acord, Buck Jones, Tim McCoy, and William Boyd had also appeared in Wild West shows at one time or another. Perhaps the clearest link was when early Western movie company Bison Films contracted with the Miller Brothers to provide them with cowboys and Indians from their 101 Ranch Show to act in films. The company renamed itself Bison 101. Other film companies saw the advantage and followed suit. Universal Studios took over the old Taylor Ranch where many of the earliest Westerns were filmed, and Buffalo Bill himself was there for the opening of Universal City in 1915.[36]

Westerns remained an important part of the film industry, and the mythic cowboy one of its most successful characters. While the cowboys who appeared in feature-length Westerns were not quite as spotless as Autry might have liked, the heroes nonetheless always practiced restraint or learned the value of it through the course of the story. John Wayne in *Stagecoach* (1939), Alan Ladd in *Shane* (1953), and Jimmy Stewart in *Destry Rides Again* (1939) all turn down whiskey or order soda or milk in contrast to those who show no such restraint around them and thus, by implication, are lesser men. Indeed, as film scholar Lee Clark Mitchell points out, the whole nature of a Western hero's manliness is tied to his ability to maintain his composure when provoked, to resist his desires, and to restrain his emotions when badly injured or in pain.[37] While the real cowboys may have practiced the last type of restraint, it is clear that practicing the first two might have lessened their reputation as men amongst themselves, rather than increased it.

In Western movies, those who cannot restrain themselves are destined to ride into the hills like the heroes of *Shane* or *Will Penny* (1968). And while the latter two men gain heroic status through their refusal of civilization, the reality is that they never feel quite complete by middle-class standards. Both characters long to be a part of a real family. Unconsciously echoing the middle-class perspective of the townspeople in the late nineteenth century, Jane Tompkins argues that the Western hero is liberated from "stuffy interiors and bad family scenes," but is too isolated to be a real human and participate in the benefits of civilization.[38] According to this perspective, manliness without civilization is empty, and the cowboy's job is to defend civilization and then get out of the way.

Ultimately cowboys chose to see themselves through the mythic lens. Debates in the 1920s about "the real cowboy" usually involved former cowboys (or cowboy admirers) objecting to overly rough or crude depictions of them as scoundrels. These defenses of the cowboy stressed his chivalry and code of honor and, often, his education and refinement.[39] Old-time cowboys complained that rodeo cowboys were not "real" cowboys because they drank and caroused with women too much, and had bad work habits such as quitting the ranch on a whim to follow the rodeos. Similarly, rodeo cowboys claimed they were real cowboys because, aside from the roping and riding skills, they dressed and spoke like cowboys and followed a "cowboy code" which included all the mythical ideals of chivalry.[40] Ironically, such debates reflected the acceptance of middle-class concepts of masculinity, involving the restraint and gentlemanly behavior that cattlemen had promulgated on the frontier, not the cowboys themselves.

But as the public image of the cowboy was rehabilitated as being "respectable," cattlemen could also claim it for themselves, creating a marriage of the cowboy and cattleman persona. Rancher Joe Miller of the 101 Ranch even managed to get himself elected as president for life of the Cherokee Strip Cow Punchers' Association.[41] Formed in 1939, the National Old Time Cowboys' Association admitted both cowboys and ranchers to "promote that old Western spirit of friendliness, loyalty and fair-play that was so characteristic of the old time cattle fraternity."[42] By acting (and dressing) like the heroic cowboy, middle-class men could thus claim the masculine identities of both middle and working classes. Some ranchers even tried to make the cattleman a hero in his own right. By 1907, Buffalo Bill Cody had added a drama to his show in which he played the rancher. He based the story on his own ranch in Wyoming, but only loosely. The Miller Brothers, who owned the 101 Ranch in Oklahoma, also tried to feature the ranchers as heroes in their Real Wild West Show, as they believed it was the cattlemen who deserved more credit for taming the West than the cowboys, who were simply hired hands.[43] But these efforts were not successful for a number of reasons. By all accounts, Cody himself was a poor cowboy. When he showed up at the roundups, the other men let him drive a few steers and old heifers around but kept him away from the cows that had calves, as his fancy riding style made them nervous.[44] Moreover, unfortunately for the Miller Brothers, most people thought of cattlemen as old and stodgy or exploitative businessmen, and few people at the turn of the century considered businessmen to be heroes.[45] Commercial rodeos such as the Texas Cowboy Reunion in Stamford thus tended to evolve with the cowboys featured up front, and the businessmen/cattlemen, who played no symbolic role in the new Western myth, behind the scenes.[46]

While cowboys have occupied a unique position in the American historical myth and mystique, in truth they were little different from other workers who used physical skill to perform their tasks. White middle- and upper-class men made similar attempts at this time to control railroad men, miners, and other industrial workers by downgrading their masculinity. But in the case of the cowboys, the myth took on a life of its own, albeit in slightly modified form, as former cowboys began to write their memoirs. As a result, while Americans succeeded in marginalizing factory workers by imagining them as dumb brutes, the cowboy maintained his masculine image, whether or not he actually remained in control of his life. Ironically, the myth still plays into the hands of those who would use the cowboy personae to maintain gender hierarchies and power structures. Thus, modern cattlemen, oilmen, and politicians now appropriate the cowboy image to denote masculine authority, ensuring their social and political status, and providing sanction for missions of civilization and profit on new frontiers.

# Notes

INTRODUCTION

1. This phrase occurs repeatedly in many narratives, and refers to the governorship of Miriam "Ma" Ferguson from 1924 to 1926. See Sam J. Rogers Narrative, 1 and H. P. Walker Narrative, 1, WPA Life Histories.

2. "Manuscript on Texas Ranches," [1940s], Wallet 1, Ranching In Texas Collection, Southwest Collection, Texas Tech University, Lubbock, TX (hereafter SC-TTU).

3. Michael Kimmel, *Manhood in America: A Cultural History* (New York: Free Press, 1996), 150. For discussions of masculine anxiety at the turn of the century, the major sources are ibid., 43–78; E. Anthony Rotundo, *American Manhood: Transformations in Masculinity from the Revolution to the Modern Era* (New York: Basic Books, 1993), 178–93; Gail Bederman, *Manliness and Civilization: A Cultural History of Gender and Race in the United States, 1880–1917* (Chicago and London: University of Chicago Press, 1995), 10–15, 77–120; Peter N. Stearns, *Be a Man!: Males in Modern Society*, 2nd ed. (New York and London: Holmes & Meier, 1990), 48–79; and Peter G. Filene, *Him/Her/Self: Sex Roles in Modern America*, 2nd ed. (Baltimore and London: Johns Hopkins University Press, 1986), 72–93.

4. For examples of sentimental cowboys, see the narratives of George L. Flanders and John J. Baker, from Texas, WPA Federal Writers' Project Collection, Manuscript Division, Library of Congress, pages 16 and 19 respectively. Found at http://memory.loc.gov/ammem/wpaintro/txcat.html on 10 October 2005. (Hereafter cited as "WPA Life Histories.") Note on sources: The Library of Congress has digitized most of the WPA Life Histories and posted them online as part of their American Memory Project. The web address is the introductory page for the Texas narratives, of which there are 445 total. It is not possible to give a more specific URL for individual narratives as they can only be called up by a search from this page or the main page, so any attempt to duplicate the address without doing the search would result in an error. Anyone wishing to access these accounts should go to the Texas page and then link to the list of all Texas narratives. They are listed in alphabetical order, not by last name but by first letter of the entry (Jim Smith is therefore alphabetized under "J" not "S").

5. Karen R. Merrill, "Domesticated Bliss: Ranchers and their Animals," in Matthew Basso, Laura McCall, and Dee Garceau, eds., *Across the Great Divide: Cultures of Manhood in the American West* (New York: Routledge, 2001), 171; J. Marvin Hunter, ed., *The Trail Drivers of Texas*, 2nd ed. (1925; reprint, Austin: University of Texas Press, 1985), 25.

6. Richard Slotkin, *The Fatal Environment: The Myth of the Frontier in the Age of Industrialization* (Norman: University of Oklahoma Press, 1985, 1994), 45–47; Richard Slatta, *Comparing Cowboys and Frontiers* (Norman and London: University of Oklahoma Press,

1997), 33. Some historians, such as Susan Johnson, Linda Gordon, and Mack Faragher, have argued that before the arrival of middle-class settlers, there was a period of relative equality. I would argue, however, that such a situation did not exist in the cattle industry, where there were middle-class employers and working-class employees from the very beginning.

7. Gail Bederman offers an excellent analysis of the term in *Manliness and Civilization*, 3–10.

8. Jeff M. White," A Trip to California," in Hunter, ed., *Trail Drivers*, 52. Similarly, Samuel Dunn Houston recalled, "I had a boy with me by the name of Gus Votaw. He was about twenty years old." "When a Girl Masqueraded as a Cowboy and spent Four Months on the Trail," in ibid., 73.

9. Walter Smith, "Raised on the Frontier," in ibid., 52.

10. James H. Cook, *Fifty Years on the Old Frontier as Cowboy, Hunter, Guide, Scout, and Ranchman* (1923; reprint, Norman: University of Oklahoma Press, 1957), 95.

11. Quoted in Philip Durham and Everett L. Jones, *The Negro Cowboys* (1965, reprint, Lincoln and London: University of Nebraska Press, 1983), 30–31. Teddy Blue Abbott also reports hearing a similar phrase in E. C. "Teddy Blue" Abbott, *We Pointed Them North: Recollections of a Cowpuncher*. With Helena Huntington Smith (1939; reprint, Norman: University of Oklahoma Press, 1955), 36.

12. Craig Heron, "The Boys and their Booze: Masculinities and Public Drinking in Working-class Hamilton, 1890–1946," *Canadian Historical Review* 86, no. 3 (September 2005): 411.

13. Abbott, *We Pointed Them North*, 5.

14. J.G.K. McClure, "Among the Cowboys of Texas April 23–May 7 1896," Manuscript Interview. Panhandle Plains Historical Museum, Canyon, TX (hereafter PPHM).

15. Hubert E. Collins, *Storm and Stampede on the Chisholm* (1928, 1958; reprint, Lincoln and London: University of Nebraska Press, 1998), 35.

16. I am indebted to Dr. David Doyle and Dr. Louis Warren for their comments and suggestions on the idea of the cowboy as a passing figure.

17. Theodore Roosevelt, *Ranch Life and the Hunting-Trail* (New York: Century, 1899), 6.

18. Quoted in Gene M. Gressley, *Bankers and Cattlemen* (New York: Alfred A. Knopf, 1966), 59.

19. John T. Schlebecker, *Cattle Raising on the Plains: 1900–1961* (Lincoln: University of Nebraska Press, 1963), 1–2.

20. For a discussion of middle-class ideals of restraint, see Filene, *Him/Her/Self*, 70–71. For working-class men, see Elliott J. Gorn, *The Manly Art: Bare-Knuckle Prize Fighting in America* (Ithaca, NY: Cornell University Press, 1986), 131–36, 141.

21. Stearns, *Be A Man!* 81–82.

22. Charles A. Siringo, *A Texas Cowboy: Or Fifteen Years on the Hurricane Deck of a Spanish Pony* (1886; reprint, New York: Penguin Books, 2000); Abbott, *We Pointed Them North*.

23. Hunter, ed., *Trail Drivers*, xv.

24. Richard Slatta has a basic discussion of the problems of sources relating to cowboys in his book, *Comparing Cowboys and Frontiers*.

25. The main secondary sources on black cowboys include Sara R. Massey, ed., *Black Cowboys of Texas* (College Station: Texas A & M University Press, 2000); Durham and

Jones, *The Negro Cowboys*; and Kenneth W. Porter, "Negro Labor in the Western Cattle Industry, 1866–1900," *Labor History* 10, no. 3 (Summer 1969): 346–73.

26. Peter Iverson, *When Indians Became Cowboys: Native Peoples and Cattle Ranching in the American West* (Norman and London: University of Oklahoma Press, 1994).

27. George S. Stiers Narrative, WPA Life Histories.

28. Quentin Colville, "Masculinities and Categories of Class: A Case Study of the Royal Navy, 1900–1960," paper given at "What Is Masculinity? How Useful Is It as a Historical Construct?" 15–16 May 2008, Birkbeck College, University of London; Dan Herman, *Under the Tonto Rim: Honor, Conscience, and Culture in the West, 1880–1930* (New Haven, CT: Yale University Press, forthcoming); David C. Beyreis, "'What Is All the Gold in the Klondike Since I'm Love's Millionaire?' Virtuous Masculinity and the Klondike Gold Rush," paper given at the Mid-America Conference on History, 25–27 September 2008, Springfield, Mo.

29. Quoted in Elliott J. Gorn, "'Gouge and Bite, Pull Hair and Scratch': The Social Significance of Fighting in the Southern Backcountry," *American Historical Review* 90, no. 1 (February 1985): 35.

30. Beverly June Smith Stoeltje, "Rodeo As Symbolic Performance" (PhD diss., University of Texas at Austin, 1979), 75.

31. Roosevelt, *Ranch Life*, 56.

32. Hunter, ed., *Trail Drivers*, xix–xx.

33. George W. Saunders, "Origin and Close of the Old-Time Northern Trail," in Hunter, ed., *Trail Drivers*, 25.

34. Branch Isbell, "Days that Were Full of Thrills," in Hunter, ed., *Trail Drivers*, 582–83.

35. William W. Savage, Jr., *The Cowboy Hero: His Image in American History and Culture* (Norman: University of Oklahoma Press, 1979), 24.

36. "Cowboy Life in West Texas," from a speech by John A. Lomax (listed as John "J." Lomax) in Hunter, ed., *Trail Drivers*, 334.

37. Bulah Rust Kirkland, "The Real Cowboy," in Hunter, ed., *Trail Drivers*, 548.

38. Savage, *Cowboy Hero*, 100.

39. Siringo, *Texas Cowboy*, xviii. Thanks to Dan Herman for pointing out the origins of this quote. Lee D. Leverett Narrative, 6, WPA Life Histories.

40. Bruce Siberts, *Nothing But Prairie and Sky: Life on the Dakota Range in the Early Days*, Walker D. Wyman, ed. (Norman and London: University of Oklahoma Press, 1954), 90, viii. Dee Garceau first used this great quote in Dee Garceau, "Nomads, Bunkies, Cross-Dressers and Family Men: Cowboy Identity and the Gendering of Ranch Work," in Matthew Basso, Laura McCall, and Dee Garceau, eds., *Across the Great Divide: Cultures of Manhood in the American West* (New York and London: Routledge, 2001), 150. However, in the interest of full disclosure, Walker D. Wyman, who edited and polished Siberts' memoirs, confesses in the preface, "I have put words in his mouth hundreds of times"; thus, Siberts may not actually have spoken them.

42. "The Passing of the Cowboy," *San Antonio Daily Express*, 3 December 1892, found in "History of Grazing in Texas: Excerpts from Newspapers, 1890–1894 Vol. 5, "Historical Records Survey, Works Progress Administration, 1935, Box 2R 333, Grazing Industry Papers, 1537–1940, 1973, The Center for American History, University of Texas, Austin, TX (hereafter CAH–UTA).

CHAPTER 1

1. Stearns, *Be A Man!* 81–82.

2. Thomas Winter, *Making Men, Making Class: The YMCA and Workingmen, 1877–1920* (Chicago and London: University of Chicago Press, 2002), 47, 65; Judy Hilkey, *Character Is Capital: Success Manuals and Manhood in Gilded Age America* (Chapel Hill and London: University of North Carolina Press, 1997), 143.

3. This and the following paragraphs incorporate a broad summary of the works of Peter G. Filene, Gail Bederman, E. Anthony Rotundo, and Michael Kimmel among other scholars of masculinity in the late nineteenth century, and will be developed in more detail throughout the book.

4. Theodore Roosevelt, *The Strenuous Life: Essays and Addresses* (New York: Century, 1911), 257.

5. Stearns, *Be A Man!* 139.

6. Winter, *Making Men*, 6–7.

7. Hilkey, *Character Is Capital*, 142–44.

8. Stearns, *Be A Man!* 129.

9. See Robert R. Dykstra, *The Cattle Towns* (New York: Atheneum, 1979), and Robert C. Haywood, *Victorian West: Class and Culture in Kansas Cattle Towns* (Lawrence: University of Kansas Press, 1991).

10. Lewis Atherton, *The Cattle Kings* (Bloomington: Indiana University Press, 1961), 111.

11. Clara M. Love, "History of the Cattle Industry in the Southwest, I," *Southwestern Historical Quarterly* 19, no. 4 (April 1916): 397.

12. Paul I. Wellman, *The Trampling Herd: The Story of the Cattle Range in America* (London: W. Foulsham & Co., Ltd., for The Fireside Press, [1958]): 11–23; Jerald Underwood, "The Vaquero," in Lawrence Clayton, Jim Hay, and Jerald Underwood, eds., *Vaqueros, Cowboys, and Buckaroos* (Austin: University of Texas Press, 2001), 2, 12–14; Tom Lea, *The King Ranch* (Boston: Little, Brown, 1957), 1: 112–14; Jack Jackson, *Los Mesteños: Spanish Ranching In Texas, 1721–1821* (College Station: Texas A & M University Press, 1986), 593–95; Andrés Tijerina, *Tejano Empire: Life on the South Texas Ranchos* (College Station: Texas A & M University Press, 1998), xxx.

13. Love, "History of the Cattle Industry, I," 372.

14. J. Frank Dobie, *The Longhorns* (New York: Bramhall House, 1941), 30–34.

15. Forrest McDonald and Grady McWhiney, "Celtic Origins of Southern Herding," *Journal of Southern History* 51, no. 2 (May 1985): 166–72; Grady McWhiney, *Cracker Culture: Celtic Ways In the Old South* (Tuscaloosa and London: University of Alabama Press, 1988) 53–54; Terry G. Jordan, *Trails to Texas: Southern Roots of Western Cattle Ranching* (Lincoln: University of Nebraska Press, 1981), 3–24; Rowland Berthoff, "Celtic Mist Over the South," *Journal of Southern History* 52, no. 3 (August 1986): 523–46; Jackson, *Los Mesteños*, 593–95.

16. See for example Lea, *King Ranch*, 1: 107–8.

17. Jackson, *Los Mesteños*, 596–601; Arnoldo De León, *They Called them Greasers: Anglo Attitudes Toward Mexicans in Texas, 1821–1900* (1983; reprint, Austin: University of Texas Press, 1992), 59–60; David Montejano, *Anglos and Mexicans in the Making of Texas, 1836–1986* (Austin: University of Texas Press, 1987), 52–53.

18. Montejano, *Anglos and Mexicans*, 50–63; Jackson, *Los Mesteños*, 601–2, 607–10, 613–15.

19. Jackson, *Los Mesteños*, 606–7.

20. Alwyn Barr, *Black Texans: A History of African Americans in Texas, 1528–1995*, 2nd ed. (Norman and London: University of Oklahoma Press, 1996), 91, 149; Lawrence D. Rice, *The Negro in Texas: 1874–1900* (Baton Rouge: Louisiana State University Press, 1971), 196.

21. Jackson, *Los Mesteños*, 587–88, 606.

22. Underwood, "Vaquero," 14; Lea, *King Ranch*, 1: 114; Montejano, *Anglos and Mexicans*, 80–81.

23. Robert V. Hine and John Mack Faragher, *The American West: A New Interpretive History* (New Haven, CT and London: Yale University Press, 2000), 304.

24. Edward Everett Dale, *The Range Cattle Industry: Ranching on the Great Plains from 1865 to 1925* (1930. Reprint. Norman: University of Oklahoma Press, 1960), 33–38; John T. Schlebecker, *Cattle Raising on the Plains*, 6.

25. July 5–7, 1870, September 1870, December 16, 1871, "Diary of Jonathan Hamilton Baker (1832–1918) of Palo Pinto County Texas 1858–1919, pt. II," 420–21, 440–41, 492, Box 2Q418, Jonathan Hamilton Baker Diaries, CAH–UTA.

26. Hine and Faragher, *American West*, 304; Hunter, ed., *Trail Drivers*, 20–22.

27. Dale, *The Range Cattle Industry*, 43; Hine and Faragher, *American West*, 305. See also Gressley, *Bankers and Cattlemen*, 111.

28. Frank S. Hastings, *A Ranchman's Recollections: An Autobiography* (Chicago: The Breeder's Gazette, 1921), 11, 17–18; *San Antonio Express*, 9 August 1876, found in "History of Grazing in Texas: Excerpts from Newspapers, 1837–1879 Vol. I" Historical Records Survey, Works Progress Administration, 1935, Box 2R 333, Grazing Industry Papers, 1537–1940, 1973, CAH–UTA.

29. Walter Nugent, *Into the West: The Story of Its People* (1999; reprint, New York: Vintage Books, 2001), 74; Hastings, *A Ranchman's Recollections*, 148–49; *Fort Griffin Echo*, 9 September 1879.

30. F. H. Earnest to J. Evetts Haley, 26 May 1932, manuscript interview, JEH II J–I, J. Evetts Haley Memorial Library and Historical Center, Midland, TX (hereafter JEH–MLHC).

31. Roberto M. Villareal, *Vaqueros de Sarita* (Riviera, TX: Vamos, 2006), 73–74.

32. A. Ray Stephens, *The Taft Ranch: A Texas Principality* (Austin: University of Texas Press, 1964), 16–17.

33. Douglas, *Cattle Kings of Texas*, 278–80.

34. Lloyd Wendt and Herman Kogan, *Bet-A-Million! The Story of John W. Gates* (Indianapolis, IN: Bobbs-Merrill, 1948), 34–51.

35. Montejano, *Anglos and Mexicans*, 53, 56–57, 61, 63–72; Jackson, *Los Mesteños*, 606.

36. Hastings, *A Ranchman's Recollections*, 150; W. M. Pearce, *The Matador Land and Cattle Company* (Norman: University of Oklahoma Press, 1964), 25; V. H. Whitlock, *Cowboy Life on the Llano Estacado* ( Norman: University of Oklahoma Press, 1970), 151.

37. Andrew R. Graybill, *Policing the Great Plains: Rangers, Mounties and the North American Frontier, 1875–1910* (Lincoln: University of Nebraska Press, 2007), 126–30.

38. Jim B. Wilson to J. Evetts Haley, 1 January 1982, 22, JEH II J–I, JEH–MLHC.

39. Dale, *Range Cattle Industry*, 52, 54, 55.

40. *Fort Griffin Echo*, 17 April 1880.

41. Dale, *Range Cattle Industry*, 108.

42. For cattle prices, see *San Antonio Light*, 5 March 1885, found in "History of Grazing in Texas: Excerpts from Newspapers, Vol. III, 1885–1886," Historical Records Survey, Works Progress Administration, 1935, Box 2R 333, Grazing Industry Papers, 1537–1940, 1973, CAH–UTA; *San Antonio Daily Light*, 21 March 1888, in ibid. Vol. IV; *San Antonio Daily Light*, 28 August 1898, in ibid. Vol. VI. On the plans to create a new slaughterhouse, see "Closing the Cattle Trail," *San Antonio Express*, 23 July 188[4], found in ibid. Vol. II.

43. Siringo, *Texas Cowboy*, 174.

44. David L. Wheeler, "The Blizzard of 1886 and Its Effect on the Range Cattle Industry in the Southern Plains," *Southwestern Historical Quarterly* 94, no. 3 (January 1991): 418–19, 426–27.

45. Maude T. Gilliland, *Rincon (Remote Dwelling Place): A Story of Life on a South Texas Ranch at the Turn of the Century* (Brownsville, TX: Springman-King Lithograph, 1964), 5.

46. Stephens, *Taft Ranch*, 54–57.

47. Jordan, *Trails to Texas*, 59–75.

48. Douglas, *Cattle Kings of Texas*, 33–52.

49. Jackson, *Los Mesteños*, 606–7.

50. For a comprehensive and highly informative study of the Kenedy Ranch, and especially the role of Mifflin Kenedy's wife, Petra Vela, in creating schools and churches for the workers, see Jane Clements Monday and Frances Brannen Vick, *Petra's Legacy: The South Texas Ranching Empire of Petra Vela and Mifflin Kenedy* (College Station: Texas A & M University Press, 2007).

51. Montejano, *Anglos and Mexicans*, 79, 80–81.

52. Ibid., 88–89.

53. George A. Wallis, *Cattle Kings of the Staked Plains* (Dallas: American Guild Press, 1957), 7.

54. Frederick W. Rathjen, *The Texas Panhandle Frontier* (Austin and London: University of Texas Press, 1973), 101–2, 230, 232–33, 238.

55. Ruth Allen, *Chapters in the History of Organized Labor in Texas* (1941; facsimile edition. Dallas, TX: William P. Clements Center for Southwest Studies, Southern Methodist University, 2006), 34–35.

56. Rathjen, *Panhandle Frontier*, 245–46.

57. Louis Trujillo to J. Evetts Haley, 9 November 1927, 127, JEH II J-I, JEH–MLHC.

58. Rathjen, *Panhandle Frontier*, 103.

59. Elliott West, *Growing Up With the Country: Childhood on the Far Western Frontier* (Albuquerque: University of New Mexico Press, 1989), 6, 17; Dale, *Range Cattle Industry*, 110.

60. Rathjen, *Panhandle Frontier*, 234–35, 244.

61. *Fort Griffin Echo*, 21 June 1879.

62. *Austin Statesman*, 29 January 1884, found in "History of Grazing in Texas: Excerpts from Newspapers, 1880–1884 Vol. II, " Historical Records Survey, Works Progress Administration, 1935, Box 2R 333, Grazing Industry Papers, 1537–1940, 1973, CAH–UTA.

63. William C. Holden, *The Espuela Land and Cattle Company: A Study of a Foreign-Owned Ranch in Texas* (Austin: Texas State Historical Association, 1970), 35–43.

64. Cordia Sloan Duke and Joe B. Frantz, *6,000 Miles of Fence: Life on the XIT Ranch of Texas* (Austin: University of Texas Press, 1961), 4–6; J. Evetts Haley, *The XIT Ranch of*

*Texas and the Early Days of the Llano Estacado* (1929; reprint, Norman: University of Oklahoma Press, 1967), 73, 77.

65. Duke and Frantz, *6,000 Miles*, 6.

66. "Don Milton: Milton Faver, The Big Bend's First American Cattle King," from *Voices of the American Border* (Sept. 1933), 23, found in "Favor, Milton," Vertical Files, ABB–SRSU; W. B. Mitchell, "Biographical Notes Copied From Hancock Hall Materials on Brewster County residents," 1, in Collection Summary, W. B. Mitchell Collection 1896–1969 Guide, The Archives of the Big Bend, Bryan Wildenthal Memorial Library, Sul Ross State University, Alpine, TX (hereafter ABB–SRSU).

67. Walter Roberts, "Early Developments Leading to the Establishment of the A. S. Gage Ranches of the Big Bend-Davis Mountain Area of Texas 1883–1917" (Undergraduate thesis, Trinity University, San Antonio, 1957), 9, 21. Found in Folder 24, Box 1, Gage Family Papers 1860–1928, ABB–SRSU. For biographical details see also Collection Summary, Gage Family Papers Guide, ibid.

68. Jim B. Wilson to J. Evetts Haley, 1 January 1982, 22, JEH II J–I, JEH–MLHC; "H. L. Kokernaut Arrived as Cowboy in 1883," *Alpine Avalanche*, 28 June 1962, found at ABB–SRSU.

69. "Gene Parr Pioneer Brewster Rancher," *Alpine Avalanche*, 28 June 1962, found at ABB–SRSU.

70. W. B. Mitchell, "Biographical Notes Copied From Hancock Hall Materials on Brewster County residents," 1, in Collection Summary, W. B. Mitchell Collection 1896–1969 Guide, ABB–SRSU.

71. Holden, *The Espuela*, 46; Duke and Frantz, *6,000 Miles*, 6.

72. "Manuscript on Texas Ranches," 142 [1940s] Wallet 1, Ranching in Texas Collection, SC–TTU.

73. *History of the Cattlemen of Texas: A Brief Resumé of the Livestock Industry of the Southwest and a Biographical Sketch of Many of the Important Characters Whose Lives Are Interwoven Therein*, Introduction by Harwood P. Hinton. (1914; reprint, Austin: Texas State Historical Association, 1991).

74. Wallis, *Cattle Kings of the Staked Plains*, 84–90; J. Evetts Haley, *George W. Littlefield, Texan* (Norman: University of Oklahoma Press, 1943), 7–8, 33–48, 78, 87.

75. *History of the Cattlemen of Texas*, 172, 205.

76. Joseph G. McCoy, *Historic Sketches of the Cattle Trade of the West and Southwest* (Kansas City, MO: Ramsey, Millett & Hudson, 1874), 11–13.

77. Wallis, *Cattle Kings of the Staked Plains*, 14–16.

78. Montejano, *Anglos and Mexicans*, 62.

79. Pearce, *Matador*, 7.

80. Douglas, *Cattle Kings of Texas*, 114.

81. Gressley, *Bankers*, 81, 88.

82. *History of the Cattlemen of Texas*, xiv, xi, 93, 103, 185.

83. Haley, *Littlefield*, 4.

84. Lea, *King Ranch*, 1: 2–9, 45, 99–100, 136–37, 260.

85. Douglas, *Cattle Kings of Texas*, 91.

86. Hunter, ed., *Trail Drivers*, xi.

87. Savage, *Cowboy Hero*, 6–9.

88. Hunter, ed., *Trail Drivers*, x.

89. David Hamilton Murdoch, *The American West: The Invention of a Myth* (Reno and Las Vegas: University of Nevada Press, 2001), 47.

90. Holden, *The Espuela*, 116–17.

91. Frank Collinson, *Life in the Saddle*, Mary Whatley Clarke, ed. (Norman: University of Oklahoma Press, 1963, 1997), 31.

92. Siringo, *Texas Cowboy*, 187–88.

93. Vaqueros on the Kenedy Ranch in 1894 received an average of 33 cents per day. Display, Kenedy Ranch Museum, Sarita, TX.

94. Stephens, *Taft Ranch*, 117. In 1897, ranch owners proposed further money-saving measures including firing all the white cowboys and employing Mexicans in their place as they could pay them less. Ibid., 130.

95. These numbers are extremely difficult to arrive at, given the lack of clear data. For a discussion of the number of black cowboys, see Massey, ed., *Black Cowboys of Texas*, xiii–xiv; and Savage, *Cowboy Hero*, 6–9. Savage argues that most estimates are not based in fact as we cannot know the total number of cowboys with any certainty.

96. Porter, "Negro Labor," 347–48; William C. Holden, *Rollie Burns: Or An Account of the Ranching Industry on the South Plains* (College Station: Texas A & M University Press, 1932, 1986), 218.

97. Will Crittenden Narrative, 1, WPA Life Histories.

98. Tom Garrett Narrative, 2, WPA Life Histories.

99. Will Hale, *Twenty-Four Years a Cowboy and Ranchman in Southern Texas and Old Mexico: Or, Desperate Fights with the Indians and the Mexicans* (Santa Barbara, CA: Narrative Press, 200), 75.

100. Cook, *Fifty Years*, 7.

101. Laura V. Hamner, *The No-Gun Man of Texas: A Century of Achievement, 1835–1929* (Amarillo, TX: privately printed, 1935), 102.

102. Arnoldo De León, *Racial Frontiers: Africans, Chinese, and Mexicans in Western America, 1848–1890* (Albuquerque: University of New Mexico Press, 2002), 100–101.

103. Ibid., 53–54.

104. De León, *They Called Them Greasers*, 87–88, 90–92, 96–97.

105. See William D. Carrigan, *The Making of a Lynching Culture: Violence and Vigilantism in Central Texas, 1836–1916* (Urbana and Chicago: University of Illinois Press, 2004), 112–61.

106. Durham and Jones, *The Negro Cowboys*, 11–12.

CHAPTER 2

1. E. Anthony Rotundo, "Boy Culture: Middle-Class Boyhood in Nineteenth Century America," in Mark C. Carnes and Clyde Griffen, eds., *Meanings for Manhood: Constructions of Masculinity in Victorian America* (Chicago: University of Chicago Press, 1990), 18–19.

2. Rotundo, "Boy Culture," 16.

3. C. H. Rust, "What Has Become of the Old–Fashioned Boy?" in J. Marvin Hunter, ed., *Trail Drivers of Texas*, 2nd ed. (1925; reprint, Austin: University of Texas Press, 1985), 41.

4. George W. Littlefield to "Lizie" H. Dowell, 23 September 1893, Reel 1, George W. Littlefield Personal Papers, SC–TTU.

5. Hiram G. Craig, "Days Gone By," in Hunter, ed., *Trail Drivers*, 355–57.

6. Stearns, *Be A Man!* 132, 141.

7. T. E. Hines Narrative, 3, WPA Life Histories.

8. George W. Littlefield to "Lizie" H. Dowell, 15 July, 1897, Reel 1, George W. Littlefield Personal Papers.

9. Joanne Bailey, "'The Convergence of the Twain': Analysing the Twin Categories of Masculinity and Fatherhood," paper presented at What Is Masculinity: How Useful Is It as a Historical Construct" conference held at Birkbeck College, University of London, 14–16 May 2008.

10. Lea, *King Ranch*, 321–22.

11. West, *Growing Up*, 110–12, 126–27, 131–33.

12. Ibid., 115–16.

13. Troy B. Cowan Narrative, 4, WPA Life Histories.

14. Linda Peavy and Ursula Smith, *Frontier Children* (Norman: University of Oklahoma Press, 1999), 104–5.

15. Shawn Johansen, *Family Men: Middle-Class Fatherhood in Early Industrializing America* (New York and London: Routledge, 2001), 120–21, 125.

16. John James Haynes, "His Father Made Fine 'Bowie' Knives," in Hunter, ed., *Trail Drivers*, 243.

17. Walter R. Morrison, WPA Life Histories, 1–2.

18. Peavy and Smith, *Frontier Children*, 92.

19. S. A. Wright, "Adventures of a Texas Cowpuncher, Hunter and a Rambling Hobo," 27, typescript MSS, 1937, Box 2R312, CAH–UTA.

20. Auberry A. Aikin Narrative, WPA Life Histories, 1.

21. George W. Saunders, "Reflections of the Trail," in Hunter, ed., *Trail Drivers*, 426.

22. James E. Schultz Narrative, WPA Life Histories, 4.

23. Siringo, *Texas Cowboy*, 7, 17–22.

24. Jim Gober, *Cowboy Justice: Tale of a Texas Lawman*, James R. Gober and B. Byron Price, eds. (Lubbock: Texas Tech University Press, 1997), 8–9.

25. Abbott, *We Pointed Them North*, 12–13.

26. Sam J. Rogers Narrative, WPA Life Histories, 2.

27. Tijerina, *Tejano Empire*, 54.

28. Peavy and Smith, *Frontier Children*, 79.

29. Wirt W. White, MS Reminiscences # 1, 44. Reel 1, Wirt W. White Papers, SC–TTU.

30. Albert K. Erwin Narrative, 1–2, WPA Life Histories.

31. Harry Buffington Cody Narrative, 2–3, WPA Life Histories.

32. Willie Newbury Lewis, *Tapadero: The Making of a Cowboy* (Austin and London: University of Texas Press, 1972), 55–56; see also Marilyn Irvin Holt, *Children of the Western Plains: The Nineteenth Century Experience* (Chicago: Ivan R. Dee, 2003), 62; Bruce G. Todd, *Bones Hooks: Pioneer Negro Cowboy* (Gretna, LA: Pelican Publishing, 2005), 33–34; Willie Newbury Lewis, *Between Sun and Sod* (Clarendon, TX: Clarendon Press, 1938), 145–51.

33. Gaston Fergensen Narrative, WPA Life Histories, 2–3.

34. Henry Young Narrative, WPA Life Histories, 1–6, 9.

35. Gober, *Cowboy Justice*, 16.

36. For a discussion of the sentimental attitudes toward children that were common at the end of the nineteenth century, see West, *Growing Up*, 74.

37. Ibid., 165–66.
38. Abbott, *We Pointed Them North*, 10, 19.
39. J. P. Benard Narrative, WPA Life Histories, 4–5.
40. *Amarillo Daily News*, 22 May 193[7] found in "Doshier, Mrs. FB Newspaper Excerpts Armstrong County," Box 2H485, Vandale (Earl) Collection, CAH–UTA.
41. Richard Murphy Narrative, WPA Life Histories, 4.
42. Holden, *Rollie Burns*, 50–51.
43. Alberto "Lolo" Trevino, Speech at Kingsville High School, 21 March 2000, South Texas Archives, Texas A & M University, Kingsville, TX.
44. Abbott, *We Pointed Them North*, 22, 25.
45. Whitlock, *Cowboy Life*, 27, 29, 34–35.
46. F. J. "Sam" Wootan Narrative, WPA Life Histories, 3; Whitlock, *Cowboy Life*, 28.
47. West, *Growing Up*, 162.
48. Branch Isbell, "Days that Were Full of Thrills," in Hunter, ed., *Trail Drivers*, 571.
49. Reminiscence of C. P. Benedict, 1936, 10. Typescript 2–23/750, Archives and Information Services Division, Texas State Library and Archives Commission, Austin, TX.
50. Lea, *King Ranch*, 2: 522–23.
51. Villareal, *Vaqueros of Sarita*, 86.
52. Ramon F. Adams, *Charles M. Russell, The Cowboy Artist: A Biography* (Pasadena, CA: Trail's End Publishing, 1948), 70.
53. Frank March Narrative, WPA Life Histories, 5, 8.
54. B. R. Pearson Narrative, WPA Life Histories, 4–5.
55. Brook Campbell Narrative, WPA Life Histories, 1–3.
56. Abbott, *We Pointed Them North*, 20–21.
57. "Department Notes. Executive Department," *Austin Statesman*, 3 January 1884, found in bound typescript, "History of Grazing in Texas: Excerpts from Newspapers, 1880–1884, Vol. II," Historical Records survey, WPA, 1935, Box 2R333 Grazing Industry Papers, 1537–1940, 1973, CAH–UTA.
58. William Owens Narrative, WPA Life Histories, 10.
59. Irvin Bell to J. Evetts Haley, 18 March 1927, 20, JEH II J–1, JEH, MLHC.
60. Claude Hudspeth, "Now a Member of Congress," in Hunter, ed., *Trail Drivers*, 953.
61. Auberry A. Aikin Narrative, WPA Life Histories, 1–2.
62. Tom Boone Narrative, WPA Life Histories, 4–5.
63. West, *Growing Up*, 196.
64. Edward E. Jones Narrative, WPA Life Histories, 1–2.
65. Villareal, *Vaqueros de Sarita*, 84–85.
66. Alberto Trevino, Speech at Kingsville High School.
67. Alf Matthews to Rollie C. Burns, 23 March 1886, Folder 8, Box 1, Rollie C. Burns Collection, SC–TTU. Since most letters of this sort to ranch managers and owners are nearly illegible and exhibit poor spelling and grammar, this letter stands out. Nonetheless, it is also possible that someone wrote the letter for him (a schoolteacher, perhaps?)!
68. Hudspeth, "Now a Member of Congress," 953.
69. Spence Hardie Narrative, WPA Life Histories, 8.
70. Hillard J. Hay Narrative, WPA Life Histories, 15.
71. West, *Growing Up*, 196.
72. Hale, *Twenty-Four Years*, 16, 36, 41–42.

73. "Don Milton: Milton Faver, the Big Bend's First American Cattle King," *Voice of the Mexican Border* (September 1933), 23. Found in "Favor, Milton" Vertical Files, ABB–SRSU.

74. "H. L. Kokernaut Arrived as Cowboy in 1883," *Alpine Avalanche*, 28 June 1962.

75. Lea, *King Ranch*, 325, 523, 560–64.

76. Ben Kinchlow Narrative, WPA Life Histories, 1.

77. Hilory G. Bedford, "Memoirs of H.G. Bedford," typescript, 1926, 20, Box 2Q435 Hilory Bedford Reminiscences, CAH–UTA.

78. W. B. Mitchell, "History Notes," 4, undated typescript, Folder 3, Box 1, W. B. Mitchell Collection, ABB–SRSU.

79. Ernest Marshall Narrative, WPA Life Histories, 1.

80. Sr. M. Berchmans to Lizzie Crossen, 1 June 1905, Folder 32b, Box 1, Crossen Ranch Collection, ABB–SRSU.

81. Hamner, *No-Gun Man*, 93.

82. Charles Goodnight, "Autobiography," 127–28, Literary Productions: Charles Goodnight's Autobiography [1927?], Box 2Q74, Charles Goodnight Papers, CAH–UTA; Hamner, *No-Gun Man*, 217–19.

83. Abbott, *We Pointed them North*, 40.

84. Leslie A. Fiedler, *Love and Death in the American Novel* (New York: Criterion Books, 1960), 580.

85. Tijerina, *Tejano Empire*, 49.

86. Peavy and Smith, *Frontier Children*, 97.

87. Hine and Faragher, *American West*, 316.

88. Wirt W. White, MS Reminiscences #1, Wirt W. White Papers, SC-TTU. Many other cowboys recall riding calves and practicing roping skills on them. See for example Holden, *Rollie Burns*, 8; J. W. Jackson, "The Platte Was Like a River in the Sunshine," in Hunter, ed., *Trail Drivers*, 374.

89. West, *Growing Up*, 83–84, 105.

90. Elliott West, "Children of the Plains Frontier," in Elliott West and Paula Petrik, eds., *Small Worlds: Children and Adolescents in America, 1850–1950* (Lawrence: University Press of Kansas, 1992), 36.

91. W. H. Childers Narrative, 4, 5, WPA Life Histories.

92. West, *Growing Up*, 74, 89–90.

93. Elario L. Cardova Narrative, 1, 7–9, WPA Life Histories.

94. William Owens Narrative, WPA Life Histories, 2.

95. See for example Neal S. Watts Narrative, 6, WPA Life Histories; W. M. Prece Narrative, 3, WPA Life Histories.

96. Todd, *Bones Hooks*, 24–25.

97. A. P. Townsen Narrative, WPA Life Histories, 2.

98. W. A. Tinney Narrative, WPA Life Histories, 2.

99. West, *Growing Up*, 87.

100. Peavy and Smith, *Frontier Children*, 108.

101. Tom McLure Narrative, WPA Life Histories, 1.

102. Lila Baugh, "King Kenedy and Company," 53, undated typescript, Box 2Q431, CAH–UTA; Tijerina, *Tejano Empire*, 53; Lea, *King Ranch*, 2: 515; Tijerina, *Tejano Empire*, 53.

103. Joe Chapman, "An Old Frontiersman Tells His Experiences," in Hunter, ed., *Trail Drivers*, 416.

104. Fred S. Millard, "For the Trail Drivers," typescript, 20 August 1923, "Scrapbook Material, 1849–1967 General 1849–1929," Wallet 3 A 19.3 D, W. R. Bearce Collection, SC–TTU.

105. A. M. Garrett Narrative, WPA Life Histories, 4.

106. H. P. Cook Narrative, WPA Life Histories, 3.

107. See discussion of boys taking on men's workloads in Peavy and Smith, *Frontier Children*, 145–46.

108. Sam J. Rogers Narrative, WPA Life Histories, 2.

109. Frank March Narrative, WPA Life Histories, 5.

110. West, *Growing Up*, 185.

111. G. W. Mills, "Experiences 'Tenderfeet' Could Not Survive," in Hunter, ed., *Trail Drivers*, 236.

112. Charlie Bargsley, "Dream Was Realized," in Hunter, ed., *Trail Drivers*, 682–83.

113. George W. Saunders, "Reflections of the Trail," in ibid., 430.

114. H. P. Walker Narrative, WPA Life Histories, 7

115. William F. Dayton Narrative, WPA Life Histories, 2.

116. J. M. Brown Narrative, WPA Life Histories, 2–3.

117. Ellis Petty Narrative, WPA Life Histories, 1.

118. Buster "Dad" DeGraffenreid Narrative, WPA Life Histories, 1–2.

119. Sam J. Rogers Narrative, WPA Life Histories, 7.

120. "George W. Saunders, "Reflections of the Trail," in Hunter, ed., *Trail Drivers*, 430–31.

121. Typescript, Kate Longfield, "The Cowboy as I Knew Him," *Lampasas Record*, 14 May 1936, Texas, Western or Cowboy Lore, Folklore Project, Box A685, LCUSWPA, Works Progress Administration Records, Manuscript Division, Library of Congress.

122. E. A. (Berry) Robuck, "Dodging Indians Near Saddle Pack Mountain," in Hunter, ed., *Trail Drivers*, 32.

123. F. M. Polk, "My Experiences on the Cow Trail," in Hunter, ed., *Trail Drivers*, 142.

124. C. M. Crenshaw Narrative, WPA Life Histories, 1, 3–4.

125. C. W. Ackermann, "Exciting Experiences on the Frontier and on the Trail," in Hunter, ed., *Trail Drivers*, 155.

126. Abbott, *We Pointed Them North*, 60, 91, 221.

127. "When a Boy Bossed a Herd," in Hunter, ed., *Trail Drivers*, 466.

128. Savage, *Cowboy Hero*, 141.

129. Frank March Narrative, WPA Life Histories, 8.

130. Fred W. Whetaker Narrative, WPA Life Histories, 4.

131. Abbott, *We Pointed Them North*, 22.

132. For a discussion of treating, see Kathy Peiss, *Cheap Amusements: Working Women and Leisure in Turn of the Century New York* (Philadelphia: Temple University Press, 1986), 4, 20–21.

133. Holden, *Rollie Burns*, 11–12.

134. Abbott, *We Pointed Them North*, 26.

135. T. E. Hines Narrative, WPA Life Histories, 1–3.

136. W. Dawson to Fred Horsbrugh, 21 November 1902, Folder 15, Box 2, Espuela Lands and Cattle Company Records, SC–TTU.

137. A. M. Hocart, "Initiation and Manhood," *Man* 35 (February 1935): 20–22.

138. West, *Growing Up*, 108–10.

139. Holden, *Rollie Burns*, 216.

140. Pat Bullis, "Ranging the East Panhandle," 6, undated typescript, Bullis (Pat), Box 2H468, Earl Vandale Collection.

141. Lea, *King Ranch*, 2: 514–15; Villareal, *Vaqueros de Sarita*, 107.

142. Avery N. Barrow Narrative, WPA Life Histories, 3, 5.

143. For another example of a Kangaroo Court, see Don Biggers, "The Old-Time Round-Up," in Ramon F. Adams, ed., *The Best of the American Cowboy* (Norman: University of Oklahoma Press, 1957), 104–6. Light T. Cummins has chronicled the hazing activities of the unauthorized, student-run Kangaroo Court at Austin College in Sherman, Texas in this period. Like the cowboys, the students used the activity to initiate newcomers, in this case freshmen, to their social group. Light Townsend Cummins, *Austin College: A Sesquicentennial History, 1849–1999* (Austin, TX: Eakin Press, 1999), 181–85.

144. F. M. Polk, "My Experience on the Cow Trail," in Hunter, ed., *Trail Drivers*, 143–44.

145. John J. Cullison, "The Cowboy's Winding Sheet," in Adams, ed., *Best of the Cowboy*, 268.

146. Henry D. Steele, "Played Pranks on the Tenderfoot," in Hunter, ed., *Trail Drivers*, 137–38.

147. See David Dary, *Cowboy Culture: A Saga of Five Centuries* (Lawrence: University of Kansas Press, 1981, 1989), 278–79, 281, on the unwritten rules of cowboys and the consequences of breaking them.

148. Lea, *King Ranch*, 1: 358. Dick Kleberg became the manager of the Laureles Ranch upon his marriage as well.

149. Rotundo, "Boy Culture," 31.

150. Gober, *Cowboy Justice*, 13–15.

151. Will Crittenden Narrative, WPA Life Histories, 2.

CHAPTER 3

1. David Leverenz, *Manhood and the American Renaissance* (Ithaca, NY and London: Cornell University Press, 1989), 85–88.

2. Quoted in Hilkey, *Character Is Capital*, 145.

3. Quoted in Hine and Faragher, *American West*, 314.

4. Collins, *Storm and Stampede*, 36.

5. R. F. Stevenson Jr. Narrative, WPA Life Stories, 1.

6. James R. Wagner, "*Cowboy*: Origin and Early Use of the Term," in Paul H. Carlson, ed., *The Cowboy Way: An Exploration of History and Culture* (Lubbock: Texas Tech University Press, 2000), 17–18.

7. Holden, *Rollie Burns*, 14–20, 24, 38–39.

8. George W. Saunders, "Reflections of the Trail," in Hunter, ed., *Trail Drivers*, 433–34.

9. Lewis, *Tapadero*, 78, 87–88.

10. Siringo, *Texas Cowboy*, 103–4.

11. Mark Withers to J. Evetts Haley, 8 October 1932, 31, 34–35, JEH II J-I, JEH–MLHC.

12. Todd, *Bones Hooks*, 13, 37, 65–66, 76–77.

13. Durham and Jones, *Negro Cowboys*, 41, 96–98, 197.

14. *Texas Livestock Journal*, 5 July 1884, 7. It is possible that this praise was actually intended to be an insult to Anglo cowboys, whom many cattlemen believed were becoming careless with the cattle. See chapters 5 and 6 on cattleman distrust and newspaper discrediting of cowboys in racial terms.

15. Porter, "Negro Labor," 348–49, 354–57, 359.

16. Whitlock, *Cowboy Life*, 136–17.

17. Mark Withers, for example, took a herd up the trail to Chicago of Joseph McCoy with two Mexican cowboys and commented that "The Mexicans were fine ropers, as fine as I ever saw." However, he did not name them, although he named his Anglo buddy who went with them. Mark Withers to J. Evetts Haley, 8 October 1932, 14 JEH II J–I, JEH–MLHC.

18. J. Frank Dobie, *A Vaquero of the Brush Country* (New York: Grosset & Dunlap, 1929), 13.

19. Theodore Roosevelt, *Ranch Life and the Hunting-Trail* (New York: Century, 1899), 8, 11.

20. Villareal, *Vaqueros de Sarita*, 46, 103.

21. Lea, *King Ranch*, 2: 482; Don Graham, *Kings of Texas: The 150-Year Saga of an American Ranching Empire* (Hoboken, NJ: John Wiley & Sons, 2003), 66. When Lauro Cavazos served as the foreman of the King Ranch's Norias Division he was only boss over Mexican workers, and if whites worked in his outfit there would always be a white straw boss they could answer to. Montejano, *Anglos and Mexicans*, 83–84.

22. Lila Baugh, "King Kenedy and Company," undated typescript, Box 2Q431, CAH–UTA; Lea, *King Ranch*, 1: 307; Graham, *Kings of Texas*, 173.

23. Villareal, *Vaqueros de Sarita*, 74.

24. Lea, *King Ranch*, 2: 514.

25. Graham, *Kings of Texas*, 5.

26. Gilliland, *Rincón*, 24.

27. Lea, *King Ranch*, 2: 514.

28. Quoted in Bederman, *Manliness and Civilization*, 182. See also ibid., 16, 95–99, 178–82, 185–86, 190–92; John Donald Gustav-Wrathall, *Take the Young Stranger By the Hand: Same Sex Relations and the YMCA* (Chicago and London: University of Chicago Press, 1998), 24–30; Harvey Green, *Fit for America: Health, Fitness, Sport and American Society* (Baltimore, MD: Johns Hopkins University Press, 1986), 182–215; Kimmel, *Manhood in America*, 135–41. Ramón A. Gutiérrez argues that dominating the land by plowing it was also an indicator of manhood for Spanish colonials in New Mexico. Ramón A. Gutiérrez, "'Tell Me With Whom You Walk and I Will Tell You Who You Are': Honor and Virtue in Eighteenth Century Colonial New Mexico," in Basso, McCall, and Garceau, eds., *Across the Great Divide*, 30.

29. Abbott, *We Pointed Them North*, 7–8.

30. Allmendinger's analysis on this point is especially problematic as it relies almost entirely on psychoanalytical supposition and literary criticism. He cites sources ranging from Freud's *Civilization and Its Discontents* to 1960s Elizabeth Taylor movies and 1980s cowgirl poetry, but has very little from nineteenth-century cowboy sources to support his argument. That the author grew up in the mid-twentieth century on a ranch in Colorado lends only slight credence to his suppositions. Blake Allmendinger, *The Cowboy: Representations of Labor in and American Work Culture* (New York: Oxford University Press, 1992), 50, 55.

31. Unidentified fragment, found in typescript "History of Grazing in Texas: Cattle Brands," Historical Records Survey, WPA, 1935, Box 2R232, Grazing Industry Papers, 1537–1940, 1973, CAH–UTA.

32. G. F. Boone Narrative, WPA Life Histories, 14.

33. "Qualifications for a Cowboy," *San Antonio Light*, 13 August 1889, found in bound typescript, "History of Grazing in Texas: Excerpts from Newspapers, 1887–1889 Vol. IV," Historical Records Survey, WPA, 1935, Box 2R334, Grazing Industry Papers, CAH–UTA. Interestingly this article seems to have been first published in the *Philadelphia Times*.

34. Lewis, *Tapadero*, 11–12.

35. Jo[seph Jacinto] Mora, *Trail Dust and Saddle Leather* (New York: Charles Scribner's Sons, 1950), 32.

36. Hastings, *A Ranchman's Recollections*, 116–17.

37. Duke and Frantz, *6,000 Miles*, 116.

38. *San Antonio Light*, 17 March 1884, found in bound typescript, "History of Grazing in Texas: Excerpts from Newspapers, 1880–1884, Vol. II," Box 2R333 Grazing Industry Papers, 1537–1940, 1973, CAH–UTA.

39. Roosevelt, *Ranch Life*, 71.

40. Abbott, *We Pointed Them North*, 212–13.

41. Jack Weston, *The Real American Cowboy* (New York: Schocken Books, 1985), 29.

42. "Frontier Times–Pecos County," 11–12, undated typescript, Folder 1, Mrs. O.L. (Alice Jack) Shipman Collection 1855–1956, ABB–SRSU.

43. Charles Goodnight, "Managing a Trail Herd," 4, Miscellaneous written by Charles Goodnight, undated, Box 2Q74, Charles Goodnight Papers, CAH–UTA.

44. Woodson Coffee, "Reminiscences of the Open Range," in "Memories, Incidents and Tales," 18, bound typescript Papers of Woodson Coffee (1862–1953), Woodson Coffee Collection, Panhandle Plains Historical Museum, Canyon, TX (hereafter PPHM).

45. Cook, *Fifty Years*, 101.

46. Abbott, *We Pointed Them North*, 42.

47. Ibid., 191–94.

48. Cook, *Fifty Years*, 64–68.

49. John B. Conner, "Some Interesting Things Seen on the Cattle Trail," in Hunter, ed., *Trail Drivers*, 378.

50. "R. B. Pumphrey, "The Pumphrey Bros' Experience on the Trail," in Hunter, ed., *Trail Drivers*, 30.

51. G. H. Mohle, "Cyclones, Blizzards, High Water, Stampedes and Indians on the Trail," in Hunter, ed., *Trail Drivers*, 42–43.

52. See for example *Fort Griffin Echo*, 15 January 1879 for a typical accidental shooting, as well as 1 November 1879 and 17 January 1880. For the bull goring accident, see ibid., 16 October 1880.

53. Charles J. Steedman, "A Wild Night," in Adams, ed., *Best of the Cowboy*, 262–63.

54. Abbott, *We Pointed Them North*, 44–45, 99.

55. Whitlock, *Cowboy Life*, 129–30.

56. Massey, ed., *Black Cowboys of Texas*, xvi.

57. Durham and Jones, *Negro Cowboys*, 16–17; G. F. Boone Narrative, WPA Life Histories, 9.

58. Abbott, *We Pointed Them North*, 200–201.

59. Gunther Peck, "Manly Gambles: Politics of Risk on the Comstock Lode, 1860–1880," in Basso, McCall, and Garceau, eds., *Across the Great Divide*, 74, 75, 89.

60. Ibid., 89; Anthony F. C. Wallace, *St. Clair: A Nineteenth Century Experience with a Disaster-Prone Industry* (New York: Alfred A. Knopf, 1981, 1985, 1987), 265–70, 296.

61. There are many accounts and firsthand narratives that stress such heroics. "Brave and fearless" almost inevitably appear in any description of the cowboy. For a few good examples of this connection with manhood, however, see G. F. Boone Narrative, 14, WPA Life Histories; Earnest Cook Narrative, 8, ibid.; Pat Bullis, "Ranging the East Panhandle," 6, 8, Bullis (Pat) Box 2H 468, Vandale (Earl) Collection, CAH–UTA.

62. S. A. Wright, "Adventures of a Texas Cowpuncher, Hunter, and Rambling Hobo," 53, typescript, 1937, Box 2R312, CAH–UTA.

63. Abbott, *We Pointed Them North*, 45–46. This stunt also appears in the 1968 film *Will Penny*, whose screenwriter seems to have paid close attention to Abbott's narrative!

64. Lewis, *Tapadero*, 96–97.

65. Abbott, *We Pointed Them North*, 97.

66. *San Antonio Daily Light*, 3 April 1886, found in "History of Grazing in Texas: Excerpts from Newspapers, 1885–1886, Vol. II," Historical Records survey, WPA, 1935, Box 2R333 Grazing Industry Papers, 1537–1940, 1973, CAH–UTA.

67. Cook, *Fifty Years*, xiii.

68. A. H. Murchison to J. Evetts Haley, 23 September 1946, 5, JEH II J–I, JEH–MLHC.

69. James Shaw, "From Texas to Warbonnet," in Adams, ed., *Best of the Cowboy*, 221–24.

70. Graham, *Kings of Texas*, 173. It is likely that most of these hands were not regular vaqueros on the ranch as King contracted outside for trail drivers.

71. Abbott, *We Pointed Them North*, 52, 53, 55.

72. Abner Taylor to B. H. Campbell, 1 November 1885, Letters Received by B. H. Campbell 1885–1887, E.1, D.3, XIT Ranch Records, PPHM.

73. J.G.K. McClure, "Among the Cowboys of Texas April 23–May 7, 1896," Manuscript Interview, PPHM.

74. Holden, *The Espuela*, 48.

75. Mose Hayes to J. Evetts Haley, 8 November 1931, 2, JEH II J–I, JEH–MLHC.

76. Frank Goodwyn, *Life on the King Ranch* (College Station: Texas A & M University Press, 1951, 1993), 182–83.

77. Mark Carroll, *Homesteads Ungovernable: Families, Sex, Race and the Law in Frontier Texas, 1823–1860* (Austin: University of Texas Press, 2001), 85.

78. Cecilia Morgan, "'Better Than Diamonds': Sentimental Strategies and Middle Class Culture in Canada West," *Journal of Canadian Studies* 32, no.4 (Winter 1998): 135.

79. Peck, "Manly Gambles," in Basso, McCall, and Garceau, eds., *Across the Great Divide*, 73–74.

80. C. C. Slaughter, "The Passing of the Range," speech given before the Cattle Raisers' Association, 1907, typescript, Folder 26, Box 1, C. C. Slaughter Papers, SC–TTU.

81. Gaston Fergensen Narrative, 9, WPA Life Histories.

82. *Fort Griffin Echo*, 24 January 1880.

83. Typescript, *Amarillo Fat Stock Show Journal* (September 1926), Texas, Western or Cowboy Lore, Folklore Project, Box A685, LCUSWPA, Manuscript Division, Library of Congress.

84. *Fort Griffin Echo*, 16 August 1879.

85. Douglas Hales, "Black Cowboy: Daniel Webster '80 John' Wallace," in Carlson, ed., *The Cowboy Way*, 38; John Hendrix, *If I Can Do It Horseback: A Cow-Country Sketchbook* (Austin: University of Texas Press, 1964), 163–65.

86. Gober, *Cowboy Justice*, 22.

87. Abbott, *We Pointed Them North*, 85.
88. Durham and Jones, *Negro Cowboys*, 99.
89. Holden, *The Espuela*, 123.
90. Stearns, *Be A Man!* 129–31.
91. De León, *Racial Frontiers*, 64.
92. Graham, *Kings of Texas*, 215, 219.
93. Lea, *King Ranch*, 2: 483.
94. Hamner, *No-Gun Man*, 91.
95. Mose Hayes to J. Evetts Haley, 3 March 1935, 39–40, JEH II J–I, JEH–MLHC.
96. Paul E. Patterson and Joy Poole, *Great Plains Cattle Empire: Thatcher Brothers and Associates (1875–1945)* (Lubbock: Texas Tech University Press, 2000), 166–67.
97. Roosevelt, *Ranch Life*, 26.
98. Abbott, *We Pointed Them North*, 8. In this case the old man was Abbott's father.
99. Hamner, *No-Gun Man*, 91, 126–28.
100. Harrison McClure to J. Evetts Haley, 22 September 1935, JEH II J–I, JEH–MLHC.
101. Porter, "Negro Labor," 361–62. See for example Frank Collinson's discussion of former slaves William and Tobe Chandler in Collinson, *Life in the Saddle*, 140.
102. Collinson, *Life in the Saddle*, 29–30.
103. Siringo, *Texas Cowboy*, 46–47.
104. Holden, *The Espuela*, 98–99.
105. Allen G. Hatley, *Texas Constables: A Frontier Heritage* (Lubbock: Texas Tech University Press, 1999), 115. In at least one case this backfired, however. In King County, the cowboys voted to make the county seat in Guthrie rather than in Ashville, the preferred location of the Louisville Land and Cattle Company. Historical Marker "King County," State Route 82, Guthrie, Texas; see also "Guthrie, Texas," Texas State Historical Society, Handbook of Texas Online, http://www.tshaonline.org/handbook/online/articles/GG/hlg41.html. Accessed 19 April 2009.
106. Duke and Frantz, *6,000 Miles*, 40; S. A. Bull to J. Evetts Haley, 6 July 1927, 64, JEH II J–I, JEH–MLHC.
107. "Frontier Times–Pecos County," 10, undated typescript, Folder 1, Mrs. O. L. (Alice Jack) Shipman Collection 1855–1956, ABB–SRSU. The author identifies Mussey as head of the Mule Shoe Ranch but he was in fact head of the Seven D Ranch. See *Handbook of Texas Online*, "Seven D. Ranch," http://www.tshaonline.org/handbook/online/articles/SS/aps3.html (accessed 23 August 2008).
108. See Civil Record, No. 1 District Court, Donely County, especially pages 138, 140–42, 143–67, 196, Donely County Courthouse, Clarendon, Texas. Even in 1896, when convictions for cattle theft brought sentences of two to five years in the state penitentiary, juries seldom convicted. Minutes of the District Court Vol. 2, 352, 442, Donely County Courthouse, Clarendon, Texas. In fact, in the early years of the District court it was very rare to have a conviction of any kind.
109. For example, the Espuela Ranch records disclose that J. A. Stokes' outfit of 12 men cost $594.71 to feed in 1889, not including the beef they killed. Holden, *The Espuela*, 55.
110. [J.] P. Drace to H. H. Campbell, undated, Folder 3, Box 13, Matador Land and Cattle Company Records, Headquarters Division, Southwest Collection, Texas Tech University, Lubbock, TX; J. Earle Hodges to Fred Horsbrugh, 17 September 1902, 1 October 1902, Folder 16, Box 2, Espuela Land and Cattle Company Records.

111. Pearce, *Matador*, 18–23.

112. Nellie Snyder Yost, ed., *Boss Cowman: The Recollections of Ed Lemmon, 1857–1946* (Lincoln and London: University of Nebraska Press, 1969), 260–61.

113. Pearce, *Matador*, 39–41; Murdo Mackenzie to J. Evetts Haley, 22 August 1932, 1–2 ,JEH II J–I, JEH–MLHC.

114. Gressley, *Bankers*, 120–21.

115. Haley, *XIT Ranch*, 98–104.

116. S. A. Bull to J. Evetts Haley, 6 July 1927, 65, JEH II J–I, JEH–MLHC.

117. Lewis, *Tapadero*, 118.

118. Holden, *The Espuela*, 47.

119. Ibid., 48–51.

120. Duke and Frantz, *6,000 Miles*, 176, 179.

121. Lewis, *Tapadero*, 117.

122. Typescript on Bar X and Diamond F Brands, undated, Cattle Brands, Box 1, Vernona Buie Collection, CAH–UTA. Buie recounts, perhaps apocryphally, that the Turkey Track man then beat up the manager, who insisted thereafter that all Bar X employees cut off their saddle horses' ears so that he would know them. The story is typical of the tall tales cowboys told around the campfire about dudes from out East, but in this case it is likely that the manager did not know his men by sight, even if the rest of the story was embellished.

123. Holden, *The Espuela*, 50–51.

124. Gressley, *Bankers*, 70, 118, 136, 139.

125. Lea, *King Ranch*, 2: 482–83, 510.

126. Goodwyn, *Life on the King Ranch*, 101–2.

127. "John G. Kenedy," in Hunter, ed., *Trail Drivers*, 957–58.

128. Typescript, 190, Testimony and Articles by Frank S. Hastings, Box 2G 466, Swenson Land and Cattle Company Papers, CAH–UTA.

129. *Fort Griffin Echo*, 26 April 1879. See also *Comanche Chief*, 1 May 1879.

130. Minutes of the Stockraisers' Association of Northwestern Texas, 14–16 March, 1881, Wallet 1, Stockraisers' Association of Northwestern Texas, SC–TTU. See, for example, several articles in *Texas Livestock Journal*, 2 August 1884, 1 on a group of swaggering cowboys from the Espuela Ranch who had thirty-seven strays in with their herd as they came through town.

131. "The Cattle Industry Past and Present: Methods of the Irrepressible Cow-Boy," *San Antonio Daily Light*, 2 May 1888, found in "History of Grazing in Texas: Excerpts from Newspapers, 1887–1889, Vol. IV," Historical Records Survey, WPA, 1935, Box 2R334 Grazing Industry Papers, 1537–1940, 1973, CAH–UTA.

132. Gober, *Cowboy Justice*, 49.

133. Woodson Coffee, "Wild Game were Plentiful," in "Memories, Incidents and Tales," 32, bound typescript, Papers of Woodson Coffee (1862–1953), Woodson Coffee Collection, PPHM; Abbott, *We Pointed Them North*, 86.

134. Typescript, 98, "Letters & Stories 1940," Box 2Q 502, Earnest, Dave C. Collection, CAH–UTA. The cowboy in question may well have been stealing from his employer given that it was easy to alter the CA Bar brand to match his own. It is not possible to know the exact words Adair used to chastise the offender. Since the story is a cowboy recollection, nonetheless, the language he remembers is still instructive, and the intent is clear.

135. J. R. Norfleet to D. N. Arnett, 29 July 1893, Folder 6, Box 1, D. N. Arnett Papers, SC–TTU.

136. J. R. Norfleet to D. N. Arnett, 1 August 1893, Folder 6, Box 1, D. N. Arnett Papers, SC–TTU.

137. George Tyng to Frederic De P. Foster, 1 April 1887, George Tyng Letter Files May 29 1886 to April 25, 1887, Box 4, Francklyn Land and Cattle Company Records, PPHM.

138. Ibid.

139. Fred Horsbrugh to [J. Earle Hodges] 4 January 1901, quoted in Holden, *The Espuela*, 215.

140. R. M. Bassett to B. H. Campbell, 2 August 1886, Letters B. H. Campbell from various persons 1886, E.3, D.3, XIT Ranch Records, PPHM.

141. Abner Taylor to B. H. Campbell, 4 February 1886, Letters to B. H. Campbell from Abner Taylor, 1886, E.2, D.3, XIT Ranch Records, PPHM.

142. Abner Taylor to B. H. Campbell, 19 March 1886, Letters to B. H. Campbell from Abner Taylor, 1886, E.2, D.3, XIT Ranch Records, PPHM.

143. Abner Taylor to A. G. Boyce, 31 October [1888], in Margaret C. Josserand, ed., "XIT Letters, Abner Taylor Letters 1888–1889" (Master's thesis, West Texas State Teachers' College, 1946), 38.

144. T-Anchor Ranch weekly report, 19 May [1888], T-Anchor Ranch Letterpress Copy Book 1888–1890, T-Anchor Ranch Records, PPHM.

145. Siringo, *Texas Cowboy*, 186.

146. B. A. Borroum to J. Evetts Haley, 7 October 1926, Manuscript Interview, PPHM.

147. W. F. Sommerville to H. H. Campbell, 14 August 1883, Folder 8, Box 13, Matador Land and Cattle Company Records–Headquarters Division, SC–TTU.

148. Annie J. W. Hobson to Fred Horsbrugh, 22 September 1997, Folder 16, Box 2, Espuela Land and Cattle Company Records, SC–TTU.

149. Roosevelt, *Ranch Life*, 33.

150. *Texas Livestock Journal*, 25 July 1885, 4.

151. Las Vegas (NM) *Daily Optic*, August 1885, quoted in Gressley, *Bankers*, 125.

152. *Texas Livestock Journal*, 8 August 1885, 1.

153. McCoy, *Historic Sketches*, 86.

154. "A Man Suited to His Times," in Adams, *Best of the Cowboy*, 13.

155. Lea, *King Ranch*, 2: 488, 513.

156. Dobie, *Vaquero*, 15–16, 19.

157. Patrick Dearen, *A Cowboy of the Pecos* (Plano: Republic of Texas Press, 1997), 136.

158. Rollie C. Burns, "Reminiscence of 56 Years," 67, Folder 18, Box 1, Rollie C. Burns Collection, SC–TTU.

159. Carl Peters Benedict, *A Tenderfoot Kid on Gyp Water* (1943; reprint, Lincoln and London: University of Nebraska Press, 1986), 23, 24.

160. Siringo, *Texas Cowboy*, 181–85.

161. "General Rules of the XIT Ranch, January, 1888," in Haley, *XIT Ranch*, 241–45.

162. W. H. Thomas Narrative, WPA Life Histories, 1.

163. C. M. Crenshaw Narrative, WPA Life Histories, 4.

164. Schlebecker, *Cattle Raising on the Plains*, 7–12; *History of the Cattlemen of Texas*, 29.

165. *History of the Cattlemen of Texas*, 29.

166. Montejano, *Anglos and Mexicans*, 87.

167. Weston, *Real Cowboy*, 56–60.

168. Montejano, *Anglos and Mexicans*, 300–301.

169. Goodwyn, *Life on the King Ranch*, 99–101, 117–21. The glossary to this book lists ten different specializations in addition to *caporal* and *caudillo* (foreman and second-in-command). Ibid., 287–89.

170. In August 1898, for example, Spur Ranch boss W. Dawson could only report that "none of the Camp boys have been in . . . so I can give you no news as to the branding." W. Dawson to Fred Horsbrugh, 11 August 1898. See also letters from same to same between 1898 and 1902 in Folder 15, Box 2, Espuela Land and Cattle Company Records, SC–TTU.

171. Weston, *Real Cowboy*, 86, 88–89.

172. Gober, *Cowboy Justice*, 67–69, 74–76.

173. "Frontier Times–Pecos County," 11, undated typescript, Folder 1, Mrs. O. L. (Alice Jack) Shipman Collection 1855–1956, ABB–SRSU.

174. *Fort Griffin Echo*, 25 January 1879, 22 February 1879.

175. Lawrence M. Woods, *British Gentlemen in the Wild West: The Era of the Intensely English Cowboy* (New York and London: Free Press, 1989), 155–56.

176. Abbott, *We Pointed Them North*, 83–84.

177. Dobie, *Vaquero*, 16.

178. Lewis, *Tapadero*, 100.

179. Collinson, *Life in the Saddle*, 142.

180. Atherton, *Cattle Kings*, 182.

181. Pearce, *Matador*, 30–31.

182. Due to a smallpox epidemic in Mobeetie, there was no accurate reporting of numbers. Ruth Allen, *Chapters in the History of Organized Labor in Texas* (1941; facsimile edition. Dallas, TX: William P. Clements Center for Southwest Studies, Southern Methodist University, 2006), 36.

183. Robert E. Zeigler, "The Cowboy Strike of 1883," in Carlson, ed., *The Cowboy Way* 78, 81, 83–84. For newspaper coverage see also *Fort Worth Gazette*, 29 March 1883, found in Folder 5, Box 2E309, Labor Movement in Texas Collection, CAH–UTA, and *El Paso Lone Star*, 7 April 1883; Allen, *Chapters*, 37–38.

184. Allen, *Chapters*, 36.

185. Gober, *Cowboy Justice*, 51.

186. James R. Gober, "A contention between capitol and labor," undated typescript, James R. Gober personal accounts, Box 2H469, Earl Vandale Collection, CAH–UTA; for a slightly different account, see Gober, *Cowboy Justice*, 52–57.

187. Hamner, *No-Gun Man*, 185.

188. John Arnot, "My Recollections," *Panhandle Plains Historical Review* 6 (1935): 58–79.

189. Dobie, *Vaquero*, xiii.

190. Weston, *Real Cowboy*, 60.

191. Murdoch, *American West*, 47.

192. Allen, *Chapters*, 34.

193. Weston, *Real Cowboy*, 92–95.

194. Quoted in Weston, *Real Cowboy*, 74–80.

195. Abbott, *We Pointed Them North*, 87.

196. Siringo, *Texas Cowboy*, xix.

197. Holden, *The Espuela*, 120.

198. Carl Wilson Narrative, WPA Life Histories, 1.

199. W. M. Prece Narrative, 14, and H. P. Walker Narrative, 3, 5, WPA Life Histories.

200. Gober, *Cowboy Justice*, 41.

201. "Manuscript on Texas Ranches," 104–5, 70–71, undated [1940s?] unidentified typescript, Wallet 1, Ranching in Texas Collection, SC–TTU.

202. Abbott, *We Pointed Them North*, 41.

203. R. M. Bassett to B. H. Campbell, 2 August 1886, Letters to B. H. Campbell from various persons 1886, E.3, D.3, XIT Ranch Records, PPHM.

204. W. Jones to H. H. Campbell, 22 February 1888, Folder 2, Box 13, Matador Land and Cattle Company Records–Headquarters Division, SC–TTU.

205. James W. Robison to Fred Horsbrugh, 15 January 1895, Folder 3, Box 3, Espuela Land and Cattle Company Records, SC–TTU.

206. Lea, *King Ranch*, 2: 513–14.

207. Don D. Walker, *Clio's Cowboys: Studies in the Historiography of the Cattle Trade* (Lincoln and London: University of Nebraska Press, 1981), 85–87.

208. West, *Growing Up*, 259.

209. Bunny, "Dog On Cowboy," in Adams, *Best of the Cowboy*, 86.

210. Porter, "Negro Labor," 360–61, 363.

211. Siberts, *Nothing But Prairie and Sky*, 90.

212. Duke and Frantz, *6,000 Miles*, 216.

213. Ira Kutch to Fred Horsbrugh, 6 January 1898, Folder 2, Box 2, Espuela Land and Cattle Company Records, SC–TTU.


CHAPTER 4

1. *San Antonio Light*, 6 July 1883, found in bound typescript, "History of Grazing in Texas: Excerpts from Newspapers, 1880–1884, Vol. II," Box 2R333 Grazing Industry Papers, 1537–1940, 1973, CAH–UTA.

2. *El Paso Herald*, 7 June 1882.

3. Robert C. Haywood, *Victorian West: Class and Culture in Kansas Cattle Towns* (Lawrence: University of Kansas Press, 1991), 43.

4. *San Antonio Evening Light*, 4 August 1883, found in bound typescript, "History of Grazing in Texas: Excerpts from Newspapers, 1880–1884, Vol. II," Box 2R333 Grazing Industry Papers, 1537–1940, 1973, CAH–UTA.

5. Atherton, *Cattle Kings*, 94–95.

6. Haywood, *Victorian West*, 42.

7. Abbott, *We Pointed Them North*, 14.

8. C. C. Slaughter, "Passing of the Range," speech before the Cattle Raisers Association, 1907, Folder 26, Box 1, C. C. Slaughter Papers, SC–TTU.

9. See for example *History of the Cattlemen of Texas*, 116, 120, 127, 135.

10. Atherton, *Cattle Kings*, 102.

11. McCoy, *Historic Sketches*, 386.

12. Roosevelt, *Ranch Life*, 7.

13. *History of the Cattlemen of Texas*, 30.

14. Rudolph Kleberg to August Kleberg 19 May 1896, Letters by Writer: Rudolph and Mathilde Kleberg, 1866–1914, Box 2J49, Rudolph Kleberg Family Papers, CAH–UTA.

15. McCoy, *Historic Sketches*, 13, 17, 36, 138–39, 386.

16. H. M. Childress was "Generous, scrupulously honorable and honest, chivalric and impulsive." J. W. Tucker was "a young man of generous impulse and manly aspirations." William Peryman was "a fine type of Southern gentleman . . .warm and impulsive in temperament." McCoy, *Historic Sketches*, 13, 62, 87–88,

17. *History of the Cattlemen of Texas*, 70, 153, 163, 221.

18. Walter W. Meek to Eliza Duis, 7 August 1887, "Meek Letters," 76, bound typescript, Box 516A, A1989–021.002, South Texas Archives, Texas A & M University, Kingsville, TX.

19. See for example George W. Littlefield to John W. Dowell, 25 June 1869, typescript of letters Sept. 15 1860 to Dec. 12, 1868, Reel 1, George W. Littlefield Personal Papers, SC-TTU.

20. "Diary of Jonathan Hamilton Baker (1832–1918) of Palo Pinto County Texas 1858–1918," Part II "1861–1872," 478, 494, 509, Part III "1873–1918," 235, Box 2Q418, Jonathan Hamilton Baker Diaries, CAH–UTA.

21. G. W. Scarborough to B. H. Campbell, 13 November 1886, Letter B. H. Campbell from various persons 1886, E.2B, D.3, XIT Ranch Records, PPHM.

22. See chapter 6 for a further discussion of changing views on violence and social order.

23. Lea, *King Ranch*, 2: 560–61.

24. Theodore Roosevelt, "The American Boy," in Roosevelt, *Strenuous Life*, 155.

25. Bertram Wyatt-Brown, *The Shaping of Southern Culture: Honor, Grace, and War, 1760s–1890s* (Chapel Hill and London: University of North Carolina Press, 2001). See also Herman, *Under the Tonto Rim*, Introduction.

26. Gorn, "Gouge and Bite," 21–23.

27. Susan Lee Johnson, "Bulls, Bears, and Dancing Boys: Race Gender and Leisure in the California Gold Rush," in Basso, McCall, and Garceau, eds., *Across the Great Divide*, 45, 47–48; Susan Lee Johnson, *Roaring Camp: The Social World of the California Gold Rush* (New York and London: W.W. Norton, 2000), 59.

28. Duke and Frantz, *6,000 Miles*, 187.

29. Dorothy Hammond and Alta Jablow, "Gilgamesh and the Sundance Kid: The Myth of Male Friendship," in Harry Brod, ed., *The Making of Masculinities: The New Men's Studies* (Boston: Allen & Unwin, 1987), 243.

30. Rotundo, "Boy Culture," 19–20.

31. 1877 Arithmetical Rule Book, Ranch Records, Box 2E430, McFaddin Collection, CAH–UTA.

32. See Kathy Peiss, *Cheap Amusements*, for a discussion of the rise of heterosocial leisure.

33. Hammond and Jablow, "Gilgamesh," 241–42.

34. Ibid., 247, 248, 257.

35. Tijerina, *Tejano Empire*, 55.

36. Goodwyn, *Life on the King Ranch*, 35.

37. Literary scholar Chris Packard proposes that intimate friendships between men did not hamper their spontaneity because they had no domestic or reproductive consequences. Chris Packard, *Queer Cowboys and Other Erotic Friendships in Nineteenth-Century American Literature* (New York: Palgrave Macmillan, 2005, 2006), 7.

38. Haley, *Littlefield*, 91.

39. Pinkney Joel Webb Narrative, WPA Life Histories, 1.

40. Willie Hugh to H. H. Campbell, 25 March 1887, Folder #2, Box 13, Matador Land and Cattle Company Records, Headquarters Division, SC–TTU; Dick Sparks to "Foreman of Matador Ranch," 29 March 1888, Folder 9, Box 13, ibid.

41. Robert E. Hodgkins to Fred Horsbrugh, 20 November 1890, Folder 1, Box 3, Espuela Land and Cattle Company Records, SC–TTU.

42. Joseph Cruze Sr., "Parents Settled in the Republic of Texas," in Hunter, ed., *Trail Drivers*, 57–58.

43. Gober, *Cowboy Justice*, 57–60.

44. Whitlock, *Cowboy Life*, 159.

45. Benjamin S. Miller, "Fire on the Range," in Adams, ed., *Best of the Cowboy*, 114–15.

46. Typescript reminiscences, [13], [14], [19], Oden, Bill Arp, Box 2H479, Earl Vandale Collection, CAH–UTA.

47. Typescript reminiscences, [13], Oden, Bill Arp, Box 2H479, Earl Vandale Collection, CAH–UTA.

48. Mose Hayes to J. Evetts Haley, 3 March 1935, 15, JEH II J–I, JEH–MLHC.

49. J. Evetts Haley, "Life of Jim East," typescript, 30, Box 2H480, Earl Vandale Collection.

50. Laura V. Hamner, "History of the Early Panhandle Ranches: The LX Ranch," typescript, 23, Box 2H480, Earl Vandale Collection, CAH–UTA.

51. Abbott, *We Pointed Them North*, 81–82.

52. C. L. Sonnischen bemoans the modern trend of assuming that when an account discusses sex in graphic terms, it is more accurate and that therefore everyone was having sex with each other and animals. C. L. Sonnichsen, *From Hopalong to Hud: Thoughts on Western Fiction* (College Station and London: Texas A & M University Press, 1978), 159–60.

53. David Halperin, "How to Do the History of Male Homosexuality," *GLQ* 6, no. 1 (2000): 88, 99–100.

54. Even sexual relations between men have not always been the defining feature of homosexuality. In the early twentieth century, as in certain all-male contexts today, if a man had sex with another man he was not necessarily an invert, or homosexual in orientation, or even emasculated by the act, as long as he took the dominant role. George Chauncey, *Gay New York: Gender, Urban Culture and the Making of the Gay Male World, 1890–1940* (New York: Basic Books, 1994), 24–25, 65–86, 95–97; Peter Boag, *Same-Sex Affairs: Constructing and Controlling Homosexuality in the Pacific Northwest* (Berkeley: University of California Press, 2003), 23–24.

55. Gober, *Cowboy Justice*, 79.

56. Whitlock, *Cowboy Life*, 159.

57. Richard (Dick) Withers, "The Experience of an Old Trail Driver," in Hunter, ed., *Trail Drivers*, 313–14.

58. J. Evetts Haley interview with C. W. (Charlie) Walker, W. W. (Walter) Walker and W. D. (Bill) Walker, 7 August 1937, 69–70, Box 2H483, Earl Vandale Collection, CAH–UTA.

59. Dee Garceau also argues that bunkies were probably asexual for the most part, and were not even heroic friends but more like an old couple or family. Dee Garceau, "Nomads, Bunkies, Cross-Dressers, and Family Men: Cowboy Identity and the Gendering of Ranch Work," in Basso, McCall, and Garceau, eds., *Across the Great Divide*, 154–55. Popular

Western writer Larry McMurtry has suggested that cowboys were not repressed homo-sexuals but repressed heterosexuals "complicated by a heroic concept of life that simply takes little account of women." Quoted in Clifford P. Westermeier, "Cowboy Sexuality: A Historical No-No?" *Red River Valley Historical Review* 2, no. 1 (Spring 1975): 105.

60. W. B. Foster, "No Room in the Tent for Polecats," in Hunter, ed., *Trail Drivers*, 657–58.

61. Cora Melton Cross, "Col. Jack Meyers Potter Tells about Life on Cattle Range in Early Days," *Dallas SemiWeekly Farm News* [1934], found in Folder 2, Box 3D204, John A. Lomax Family Papers, CAH–UTA.

62. Badger Clark, *Sun and Saddle Leather* (1915; reprint, Stockton, CA: Westerners Foundation, 1962), 84–85.

63. Quoted in Hammond and Jablow, "Gilgamesh," 247.

64. Gregg Camfield, "The Moral Aesthetics of Sentimentality: A Missing Key to Uncle Tom's Cabin," *Nineteenth Century Literature* 43, no. 3 (Dec. 1988): 321, 339.

65. Martin, "Knights-Errant," 182.

66. Christine Bold, *Selling the Wild West: Popular Fiction, 1860 to 1960* (Bloomington and Indianapolis: Indiana University Press, 1987), 12.

67. Mose Hayes to J. Evetts Haley, 3 March 1935, 15, JEH II J–I, JEH–MLHC.

68. Hendrix, *If I Can Do It Horseback*, 140–41.

69. A recent example of a work that makes broad and anachronistic assumptions is the above-cited Chris Packard's *Queer Cowboys*, which assumes that any mention of affection between men in pre-1900 literature that is homoerotic by today's standards meant the same thing in the nineteenth century. Packard, *Queer Cowboys*, 3, 4–5.

70. Discussed in Roger Horrocks, *Male Myths and Icons: Masculinity in Popular Culture* (New York: St. Martin's Press, 1995), 11. Sedgewick's work predated much of the scholar-ship on homosexuality that suggested it was a changing concept over time so may be more relevant for twentieth-century relationships than nineteenth, but her basic premise is still valid. See also Robert K. Martin, "Knights-Errant and Gothic Seducers: The Representa-tion of Male Friendship in Mid-Nineteenth Century America," in Martin Duberman, Mar-tha Vicinus, and George Chauncey Jr., eds., *Hidden From History: Reclaiming the Gay and Lesbian Past* (New York: Meridian Books, 1989), 180.

71. Halperin, "How to Do the History," 98.

72. Jonathan Katz, *Love Stories: Sex Between Men Before Homosexuality* (Chicago: Uni-versity of Chicago Press, 2001), 6.

73. George E. Haggerty, "Male Love and Friendship in the Eighteenth Century," in Katherine O'Donnell and Michael O'Rourke, eds., *Love, Sex, Intimacy, and Friendship Be-tween Men, 1550–1800* (New York: Palgrave Macmillan, 2003), 71–74.

74. The lack of clear evidence either way makes the question of same-sex relation-ships among cowboys harder to address. Whether or not cowboys had sexual relations or fell in love with each other, there are almost no firsthand accounts that talk about it. It was likely that some men were attracted to cowboying precisely because it was an all-male environment with erotic possibilities. There was no widely publicized homosexual scandal among the cowboys such as those in Portland in 1912 and 1913, which could re-ceive widespread publicity. Boag, *Same-Sex Affairs*, 1–3. There are no love letters between cowboys, or gay cowboy memoirs from this period that any historian has uncovered. It is difficult to analyze court records in part because there are so few, and in part because

the legal definition of sodomy in Texas involved more than just same-sex relationships. The Texas Appeals reports list only eight appeals of sodomy cases between 1869 and 1896, and of those that list the facts in the case, at least two involved sex with an animal, another involved a woman, and one was oral sex with a child. See *Frazier v. State*, 39 Tex. 390; *Fennel v. State*, 32 Tex. 378; *Lewis v. State*, 35 S.W. 372; *Prindle v. State*, 21 S.W. 360; *State v. Campbell*, 29 Tex. 44; *Cross v. State*, 17 Tex. App. 476; *Ex parte Bergen*, 14 Tex. App. 52; *Medis v. State*, 11, S.W. 112. Jonathan Katz lists only 24 cases from Texas from 1800 to 1899. Katz, *Love Stories*, 62–63, 70, 358n. In one of only two misdemeanor cases of sodomy listed in representative county courthouse records for this period, the target was a cow. The second case was seemingly never brought to court, nor were the charges explicitly defined. Minutes, District Court B Atascosa County, 300, 6 May 1880 case #135 had not been brought for judgment as of 27 October 1886 Atascosa District Clerk's Office, Atascosa County Courthouse, Jourdanton, TX. *State v. Marselino Ramires*, 1896, involved sodomy of a cow. Final # 3071. County Clerk's Office, Gonzales County Courthouse, Gonzales, TX. Having searched the criminal dockets of representative courthouses in ranch country between 1865 and 1900, these are the only two cases I have found listed in extant records. Even scholars who focus on the history of homosexuality and are used to examining a wide variety of documents admit there is a "dearth of historical evidence," and base their conclusions about cowboys on assumptions more than documentation. Neil Miller, *Out of the Past: Gay and Lesbian History from 1869 to the Present* (New York: Vintage Books, 1995), 41–42; Packard, *Queer Cowboys*, 16. Walter L. Williams, whose work on the *berdache* Indian tradition is otherwise well-researched, writes the following preface to his chapter on same-sex relationships among sailors cowboys and other all-male societies: "Those who insist on documentation may want to skip over this chapter . . . My approach to this chapter is based on the reasoning that all-male fringe societies are not asexual, and that individual men who had less need for women would be precisely the type of men who would gravitate to male fringe groups." Walter L. Williams, *The Spirit and the Flesh: Sexual Diversity in American Indian Culture* (Boston: Beacon Press, 1986), 153. Given that in private cowboys could make up the bawdiest of songs about sex with women or tell stories about bestiality, this is a singular omission. See Guy Logsdon, "The Cowboy's Music: Not Always 'G' Rated," *Red River Valley Historical Review* 2, no. 1 (Spring 1975): 135–46 for a discussion of bawdy songs, as well as *"The Whorehouse Bells Were Ringing" and Other Songs Cowboys Sing*, ed. Guy Logsdon (Urbana: University of Illinois Press, 1989). One of the randier unexpurgated cowboy narratives tells the story about a cowboy who came upon the cook having sex with a mule. Instead of being embarrassed, the cook offered the cowboy a turn, which he just passed off as a joke and walked away. J. Evetts Haley interview with C. W. (Charlie) Walker, W. W. (Walter) Walker and W. D. (Bill) Walker, 7 August 1937, 13–14, Box 2H483, Earl Vandale Collection, CAH–UTA. Another firsthand account implies that men might have had sex with sheep but says only "I could write more but I wont, for the Ladies might want to read it." "Frontier Times Pecos County," undated typescript, 12, Folder 1, Mrs. O. L. (Alice Jack) Shipman Collection 1855–1956, ABB–SRSU. The scholarly discussions usually revolve around analysis of photos of men dancing with each other, stories about cross-dressing soldiers on the frontier, the Kinsey report which stated that in the 1950s there was "a fair amount of sexual contact among older males in Western rural areas," and a few lines of homoerotic poetry. This evidence was perhaps first presented in Clifford P. Westermeier, "Cowboy Sexuality: A Historical No-No?" *Red River Valley Historical Review* 2, no. 1 (Spring 1975): 93–114. See also Jonathan Katz, *Gay American History: Lesbians and Gay Men in the U.S.A.: A Documentary* [1978] (New York: Crowell, 2001), 508–12; Williams, *The Spirit and the Flesh*, 160; Packard, *Queer Cowboys*, 17. Williams does cite one seemingly legitimate document that discusses how men often paired off on trail drives and that sex was common between them; however, he gives no dates or context for the document.

75. Hubert Cohen, "'Men Have Tears in Them': The Other Cowboy Hero," *Journal of American Culture* 21, no. 4 (Winter 1998): 57–78.

76. "Courage and Hardihood on the Old Texas Cattle Trail," in Hunter, ed., *Trail Drivers*, 128.

77. Fred Sutton, "The Chisholm Trail," in Hunter, ed., *Trail Drivers*, 292.

78. Notebook, Reel 1, Will D. Howsley Collection, SC–TTU. The sentimental Howsley later went on to join the KKK!

79. Haywood, *Victorian West*, 207. Cowboys also liked rougher entertainments such as minstrel shows and burlesque that appealed to working classes elsewhere. Ibid., 174. For discussion of white working-class patronage of minstrel shows, see David R. Roediger, *The Wages of Whiteness: Race and the Making of the American Working Class* (Rev. ed. London, New York: Verso, 2007), 115–31.

80. Rotundo, *American Manhood*, 44–45; Rotundo, "Boy Culture," 23–24.

81. Haywood, *Victorian West*, 168.

82. See Mary Chapman and Glenn Hendler, eds., *Sentimental Men: Masculinity and the Politics of Affect in American Culture* (Berkeley: University of California Press, 1999), 2–8.

83. Jane Tompkins, *Sensational Designs: The Cultural Work of American Fiction, 1790–1860* (New York: Oxford University Press, 1985), 174–77. Literary scholar Ann Douglas also noted that the best-known male sentimental authors themselves postponed adulthood as long as they could. Ann Douglas, *The Feminization of American Culture* (New York: Alfred A. Knopf, 1979) 236; Camfield, "Moral Aesthetics," 321.

84. Morgan, "Better Than Diamonds," 126.

85. Lewis, *Tapadero*, 108.

86. Interview, Charles Goodnight by J. Evetts Haley, 24 July 1925, Manuscript Interview, PPHM.

87. Woodson Coffee, "Memories, Incidents and Tales," 12, in bound typescript "Papers of Woodson Coffee (1862–1953)," Woodson Coffee Collection, PPHM.

88. David Dary, *Seeking Pleasure in the Old West* (Lawrence: University Press of Kansas, 1995), 124.

89. Philip Ashton Rollins, *The Cowboy: An Unconventional History of Civilization on the Old-Time Cattle Range*, Rev. ed. (1936; reprint, Norman and London: University of Oklahoma Press, 1997), 186–87.

90. Gilliland, *Rincón*, 56–57.

91. Irvin Bell to J. Evetts Haley, 18 March 1927, 13, JEH II J–I, JEH–MLHC.

92. Dary, *Seeking Pleasure*, 124–25; Rollins, *The Cowboy*, 187.

93. Emerson Hough gives a fond account of tarantula fighting among the cowboys in "The Cowboy's Amusements," in Adams, ed., *Best of the Cowboy*, 73.

94. Rollins, *The Cowboy*, 174–75, 180–84; Dary, *Seeking Pleasure*, 126.

95. Gober, *Cowboy Justice*, 61–62.

96. "Trail Life," in Hunter, ed., *Trail Drivers*, 273–74.

97. S. A. Wright, "Adventures of a Texas Cowpuncher," 98–101.

98. Rollins, *The Cowboy*, 187.

99. Dary, *Seeking Pleasure*, 122–24.

100. Rollins, *The Cowboy*, 172–73.

101. Dary, *Seeking Pleasure*, 123–24.

102. Logsdon, "The Cowboy's Music," 140. Logsdon collected songs from two old-timers which included discussion of penis size, virility, venereal disease, and sex with animals. On the earthy nature of cowboy conversation, see also Ramon F. Adams, *Cowboy Lingo: A Dictionary of the Slack-Jaw Words and Whangdoodle Ways of the American West* (1936, 1964, reprint ed., New York: Houghton Mifflin, 2000), 4–8. For the most complete set of bawdy cowboy songs, see Logsdon, ed., *The Whorehouse Bells Were Ringing*. Many of the songs he collected are twentieth-century songs but a few are variants on songs from the nineteenth century (which in turn are sometimes cowboy variants of older bawdy folk songs).

103. Whitlock, *Cowboy Life*, 29.

104. Collins, *Storm and Stampede*, 36.

105. See John J. Baker Narrative, 19, and George L. Flanders Narrative, 16, WPA Life Histories; Rollins, *The Cowboy*, 170, 190.

106. Siringo, *Texas Cowboy*, 3.

107. Elliott J. Gorn, "The Wicked World: The *National Police Gazette* and Gilded Age America," *Media Studies Journal* 6, no. 1 (Winter 1992): 5–6.

108. Guy Reel, "This Wicked World: Masculinities and the Portrayals of Sex, Crime, and Sports in the *National Police Gazette*, 1879–1906," *American Journalism* 23, no. 1 (Winter 2005): 63.

109. David Welky, "'We Are the People!': Idealized Working-Class Society in the *National Police Gazette*, 1880–1900," *Mid-America* 84, nos. 1–3 (Winter/Summer/Fall 2002): 104, 113; Reel, "This Wicked World," 65, 66.

110. Welky, "We Are the People," 108, 113–14.

111. Gorn, "The Wicked World," 12; Welky, "We Are the People," 110.

112. Reel, "This Wicked World," 65; Welky, "We Are the People," 123–24.

113. Whitlock, *Cowboy Life*, 66, 178.

114. John Bratt, "Hazards on the Range," in Adams, ed., *Best of the Cowboy*, 180.

115. Rollins, *The Cowboy*, 87–91, 99.

116. *El Paso Lone Star*, 20 May 1885.

117. Reminiscences # 1, 100–103, Reel 1, Wirt W. White Papers, SC–TTU.

118. Lewis, *Tapadero*, 7, 69, 70.

119. Ibid., 12.

120. Abbott, *We Pointed Them North*, 72–73.

121. J.G.K. McClure, "Among the Cowboys of Texas April 23–May 7 1896," Manuscript Interview, PPHM.

122. J. D. Jackson, "A Tenderfoot from Kentucky," in Hunter, ed., *Trail Drivers*, 536.

123. Todd, *Bones Hooks*, 69.

124. "Derby Caused Stir," *Alpine Avalanche*, 28 June 1962.

125. Undated [possibly 1940] clipping from *Alpine Avalanche*, Crosson, George, Vertical Files, ABB–SRSU.

126. Woods, *British Gentlemen*, 156.

127. Todd, *Bones Hooks*, 61–63.

128. D. D. Singleterry to J. Evetts Haley, 22 September 1927, 73–75, JEH II J–I, JEH–MLHC.

129. Bederman, *Manliness and Civilization*, 23–31.

130. Arnoldo De León, *The Tejano Community, 1836–1900* (1982; reprint, Dallas, TX: Southern Methodist University Press, 1997), 55–56; Durham and Jones, *The Negro Cowboys*, 14.

131. Porter, "Negro Labor," 350.

132. Lewis, *Tapadero*, 54–55.

133. Collinson, *Life in the Saddle*, 16.

134. William Loren Katz, *The Black West* (Garden City, NY: Doubleday, 1971), 144; Barr, *Black Texans*, 58.

135. Durham and Jones, *Negro Cowboys*, 58, 70.

136. Bill Oden to J. Evetts Haley, 9 July 1947, JEH II J–I, JEH–MLHC.

137. Todd, *Bones Hooks*, 28.

138. Abbott, *We Pointed Them North*, 33–34.

139. Durham and Jones, *Negro Cowboys*, 30.

140. Gorn, "The Wicked World," 11.

141. Siringo, *Texas Cowboy*, 4.

142. Todd, *Bones Hooks*, 42.

143. Cook, *Fifty Years*, 8–9.

144. De León, *They Called Them Greasers*, 11–17, 19, 24–29, 63–74.

145. Walter W. Meek to Eliza Duis, 9 September 1888, "Meek Letters," 209, bound typescript, Box 516A, A1989–021.002, Walter Meek Family Papers, South Texas Archives, Texas A & M University, Kingsville, TX.

146. Joe McFarland Narrative, WPA Life Histories, 6.

147. Interview with C.W. (Charlie) Walker, W. W. (Walter) Walker and W. D. (Bill) Walker by J. Evetts Haley, 5 August 1937, 78, Box 2H483, Earl Vandale Collection, CAH–UTA.

148. James Shaw," From Texas to Warbonnet," in Adams, ed., *Best of the Cowboy*, 221–22.

149. De León, *They Called Them Greasers*, 103.

150. Lea, *King Ranch*, 2: 517–18.

151. Villareal, *Vaqueros de Sarita*, 108, 109.

152. Mary J. Jaques, *Texan Ranch Life; With Three Months through Mexico in a "Prairie Schooner"* (1894; reprint, College Station: Texas A & M University Press, 1989), 61.

153. Todd, *Bones Hooks*, 80, 85.

154. Ibid., 30, 69–70, 74–78.

155. Montejano, *Anglos and Mexicans*, 84.

156. McCoy, *Historic Sketches*, 377–78.

157. Mora, *Trail Dust and Saddle Leather*, 165–68.

158. Ibid., 224–27.

159. Montejano, *Anglos and Mexicans*, 84–85.

160. Durham and Jones, *Negro Cowboys*, 8.

161. Lewis, *Tapadero*, 71–73.

162. De León, *The Tejano Community*, 57.

163. William Broyles, Jr., "The Last Empire," *Texas Monthly* 8, pt. 2 (October 1980): 156.

164. Bederman, *Manliness and Civilization*, 27, 29.

CHAPTER 5

1. Nina Baym, *Woman's Fiction: A Guide to Novels by and about Women in America, 1820–1870* (Ithaca, NY: Cornell University Press, 1978), 24–25.

2. Morgan, "Better Than Diamonds," 127, 128, 130.

3. Quoted in Robert Griswold, *Fatherhood in America: A History* (New York: Basic Books, 1993), 30.

4. Will Crittenden Narrative, Federal Writer's Project, Works Progress Administration., 2.

5. Lewis, *Tapadero*, 77.

6. T. E. Hines Narrative, 2, WPA Life Histories.

7. Tompkins, *Sensational Designs*, 145–46. Tompkins argues that men were increasingly irrelevant in this model, as was the public sphere. For example, writers like Harriet Beecher Stowe believed that people needed to change their feelings about slavery and have sympathy for the slaves in order to change the moral environment that created the institution. According to Tompkins, Stowe implied that laws abolishing slavery were useless without a fundamental transformation of sentiment. Ibid., 132–33.

8. Branch Isbell, "Days That Were Full of Thrills," in Hunter, ed., *Trail Drivers*, 573.

9. Amanda Burks, "A Woman Trail Driver," in Hunter, ed., *Trail Drivers*, 296, 303.

10. Atherton, *The Cattle Kings*, 86.

11. Matthew "Bones" Hooks Narrative, WPA Life Histories, 4.

12. Luther A. Lawhon, "The Men who Made the Trail," in Hunter, ed., *Trail Drivers*, 197.

13. Mary Taylor Bunton, *A Bride on the Old Chisholm Trail in 1886* (San Antonio, TX: Naylor, 1939), 27, 39–40.

14. Hunter, ed., *Trail Drivers*, iv.

15. West, *Growing Up*, 258.

16. Bynum, J. K. to J. Evetts Haley, 20 August 1925, Manuscript Interviews, PPHM.

17. Abbott, *We Pointed Them North*, 19.

18. West, *Growing Up*, 165.

19. Gober, *Cowboy Justice*, 31.

20. Atherton, *Cattle Kings*, 80–82.

21. S. A. Wright, "The Adventures of a Texas Cowpuncher, Hunter, and a Rambling Hobo," Typescript, 1937, 2–23/821, Archives and Information Services Division, Texas State Library and Archives Commission, Austin, TX.

22. Abbott, *We Pointed Them North*, 6.

23. Bunton, *Bride on the Chisholm Trail*, 19.

24. Garceau, "Nomads, Bunkies, Cross-Dressers and Family Men," in Basso, McCall, and Garceau, eds., *Across the Great Divide*, 150.

25. Media Cottage Productions, Vaquero, 2003 (produced for Kenedy Ranch Museum, Sarita, TX).

26. Annie Hightower Narrative, WPA Life Histories, 9–10, 15.

27. A. G. Anderson Narrative, WPA Life Histories, 8, 9.

28. Troy B. Cowan Narrative, WPA Life Histories, 7.

29. Dee Garceau, *The Important Things of Life: Women, Work, and Family in Sweetwater County, Wyoming, 1880–1929* (Lincoln: University of Nebraska Press, 1997), 103–105, 110.

30. Douglas, *Cattle Kings*, 186–88.

31. "Cattle Trails: A Romance, Their Honeymoon Trail in 1874" reprinted from the *Kansas Weekly Star*, found in "History of Grazing in Texas: Excerpts from Magazines, Frontier Times 1884-1926, Vol. XII," Historical Records Survey, WPA, 1935.

32. Excerpt reprinted from the *Fort Worth Star Telegram*, 17 March 1927, found in "History of Grazing in Texas: Excerpts from Magazines, *Frontier Times* June 1926-1933-1934, Vol. XIII," Historical Records Survey, WPA, 1935.

33. Atherton, *Cattle Kings*, 90.

34. Sandra L. Myres, *Westering Women and the Frontier Experience: 1800-1915* (Albuquerque: University of New Mexico Press, 1982), 261–62.

35. Tijerina, *Tejano Empire*, 50.

36. "I'm a Cowgirl," Mrs. Ben McCulloch Earl Van Dorn Miskimon Narrative, WPA Life Histories, 3–6, 10.

37. T. C. Davis Interview with R. S. McCracken, undated, Tape # 2, Folder 69, Box 3 Crossen Collection Associated Materials, ABB–SRSU; "Collection Summary" in Guide to the Crossen Ranch Collection 1861–1976, ibid.

38. Elizabeth Maret, *Women of the Range: Women's Roles in the Texas Beef Cattle Industry* (College Station: Texas A & M University Press, 1993), 38.

39. Gressley, *Bankers*, 174–77.

40. Myres, *Westering Women*, 259–61.

41. James W. Mathis Narrative, WPA Life Histories, 4.

42. Quoted in Rebecca Edwards, *New Spirits: Americans in the Gilded Age, 1865-1905* (New York: Oxford University Press, 2006), 91.

43. Katherine Harris, "Homesteading in Northeastern Colorado, 1873-1920," in Susan Armitage and Elizabeth Jameson, eds., *The Women's West* (Norman and London: University of Oklahoma Press, 1987), 170–71. Gender ideals could vary across ethnicities, however. On large Tejano ranches the male patron traditionally went to town and bought food and supplies for his worker families rather than the wife shopping for the household. Tijerina, *Tejano Empire*, 48.

44. T. C. Davis Interview with R. S. McCracken, undated, Tape # 2, Folder 69, Box 3 Crossen Collection Associated Materials, ABB–SRSU.

45. Garceau, *Important Things*, 89–90, 101–2; Garceau, "Nomads, Bunkies, Cross-Dressers and Family Men," 149–52, 165.

46. Susan Lee Johnson, "Bulls, Bears, and Dancing Boys: Race Gender and Leisure in the California Gold Rush," in Basso, McCall, and Garceau, eds., *Across the Great Divide*, 45, 47–48; Johnson, *Roaring Camp*, 102, 115–16, 138.

47. Amy Schrager Lang, "Class and the Strategies of Sympathy," in Shirley Samuels, ed., *The Culture of Sentiment: Race, Gender, and Sentimentality in Nineteenth Century America* (New York and Oxford: Oxford University Press, 1992), 129. For an excellent review of the scholarship on sentimentality in literature as it relates to the feminization of culture, see Chapman and Hendler, eds., *Sentimental Men*, 2–8.

48. George W. Saunders, "A Log of the Trails," in Hunter, ed., *Trail Drivers*, 966.

49. Scholar Elizabeth Maret has argued that women were not scarce in Texas, and that by 1880 there were only a handful of counties in which women made up less than one-third of the population. Indeed, by 1880 the population of El Paso County was nearly 50 percent female, and Nueces County was 53.6 percent. Presidio County in the Big Bend was nearly 40 percent female, and Throckmorton County near the Panhandle had 41.9 percent women. But Wheeler County, which had under its jurisdiction most of the eastern Panhandle, was only 25 percent female in 1880, and with the exception of South Texas, most of the women in the main cattle growing regions lived in town rather than on the large ranches. Maret, *Women of the Range*, 31–32, 121–25.

50. Abbott, *We Pointed Them North*, 8.

51. Tom H. McNelly Narrative, WPA Life Histories, 2.

52. Tom Boone Narrative, WPA Life Histories, 7–9.

53. Branch Isbell, "Days That Were Full of Thrills," in Hunter, ed., *Trail Drivers*, 575.

54. 16 August 1898, "Diary Jan 1 1898–Dec 31, 1898, " Ledger # 4, Box 9, Matador Land and Cattle Company Records, Headquarters Division, SC–TTU.

55. 25 August 1898, ibid.

56. A. W. Capt, "The Early Cattle Days in Texas," in Hunter, ed., *Trail Drivers*, 365.

57. Gober, *Cowboy Justice*, 34.

58. Todd, *Bones Hooks*, 60.

59. Walter W. Meek to Eliza Duis, 12 June 1887, "Meek Letters," 51, bound typescript, Box 516A, A1989–021.002, Walter Meek Family Papers, South Texas Archives, Texas A & M University, Kingsville, TX.

60. C. F. Doan, "Reminiscences of the Old Trails," in Hunter, ed., *Trail Drivers*, 778.

61. Roosevelt, *Ranch Life*, 88–90.

62. George L. Flanders Narrative, WPA Life Histories, 16.

63. John J. Baker Narrative, WPA Life Histories, 19.

64. Holden, *The Espuela*, 158–59.

65. Siringo, *Texas Cowboy*, 70–71.

66. Jack Potter, "Coming Up the Trail in 1882," in Hunter, ed., *Trail Drivers*, 69. In the spirit of full disclosure, the editor noted that Jack was "the most cheerful liar on the face of the earth." Ibid., 71.

67. Bill Arp typescript, 10, 12, in "Oden, Bill Arp," Box 2H479, Vandale (Earl) Collection, CAH–UTA.

68. Jaques, *Texan Ranch Life*, 256

69. Gober, *Cowboy Justice*, 28.

70. Hale, *Twenty-Four Years*, 26, 48, 50.

71. H. C. Williams, "Took Time to Visit His Sweetheart," in Hunter, ed., *Trail Drivers*, 403.

72. F. J. "Sam" Wootan Narrative, WPA Life Histories, 3.

73. Ed Bell Narrative, WPA Life Histories, 2.

74. Abbott, *We Pointed Them North*, 78.

75. Fort Griffin Echo, 24 January 1880.

76. Roy S. Scott, "The Cowboy Dance of the Northwest," in "History of Grazing in Texas: Horses," Historical Records Survey WPA 1935, Box 2R333, Grazing Industry Papers, 1537–1940, 1973, CAH–UTA.

77. Holden, *Rollie Burns*, 87.

78. Jaques, *Texan Ranch Life*, 98.

79. J. G. Mooring Narrative, WPA Life Histories, 11; E. L. Murphy Narrative, WPA Life Histories, 8.

80. Charles W. Holden Narrative, WPA Life Histories, 17.

81. Scott, "The Cowboy Dance of the Northwest"; Jaques, *Texan Ranch Life*, 13–14.

82. Scott, "The Cowboy Dance of the Northwest"; Hine and Faragher, *American West*, 313–14.

83. Garceau, "Nomads, Bunkies, Cross-Dressers and Family Men," 160–61; Allmendinger, *The Cowboy*, 60.

84. Edgar Beecher Bronson, "End of the Trail," in Adams, ed., *Best of the Cowboy*, 286–88.

85. Abbott, *We Pointed Them North*, 111–13.

86. Allmendinger, *The Cowboy*, 59–60.

87. Charles W. Holden Narrative, WPA Life Histories, 17.

88. Ben Mayes Narrative, WPA Life Histories, 8–9; Holden, *Rollie Burns*, 92–93.

89. Holden, *Rollie Burns*, 84–86.

90. Ben Mayes Narrative, WPA Life Histories, 9. See also a slightly more colloquial version of this account in the excerpt from Ben C. Mayes, "The Tom Green County Cow Boy," in History of Grazing in Texas Part IV: Boom Days on the Western Range, 1866–1886, Vol. II, Part E "The Cowboy in Fact and Fiction" Box 2R341, Grazing Industry Papers, 1537–1940, 1973, CAH–UTA.

91. Leigh Eric Schmidt, "The Fashioning of a Modern Holiday: St. Valentine's Day, 1840–1870," *Winterthur Portfolio*, 28, no. 4 (Winter 1993): 209–45.

92. Jaques, *Texan Ranch Life*, 98.

93. Schmidt, "Fashioning," 222.

94. Mary Louise Kete, *Sentimental Collaborations: Mourning and Middle-Class Identity in Nineteenth Century America* (Durham, NC: Duke University Press, 2000), xiv, 53–54.

95. See Gutiérrez, "'Tell Me With Whom You Walk," in Basso, McCall, and Garceau, eds., *Across the Great Divide*, 36, for a discussion of how public possession contributed to ideals of manliness.

96. J. Evetts Haley interview with C. W. (Charlie) Walker, W. W. (Walter) Walker and W. D. (Bill) Walker, 7 August 1937, Box 2H483, Earl Vandale Collection, CAH–UTA.

97. Anne M. Butler, *Daughters of Joy, Sisters of Misery: Prostitutes in the American West, 1865–90* (Urbana and Chicago: University of Illinois Press, 1985), 54, 55.

98. Garceau, "Nomads, Bunkies, Cross-Dressers and Family Men," 159.

99. Abbott, *We Pointed them North*, 51, 79–89.

100. *Jacksboro Frontier Echo*, 19 November 1875.

101. Morgan, "Better Than Diamonds," 130.

102. Garceau, "Nomads, Bunkies, Cross-Dressers and Family Men," 160.

103. Abbott, *We Pointed Them North*, 107. Dee Garceau first used this quote to make a similar argument in Garceau, "Nomads, Bunkies, Cross-Dressers and Family Men," 160.

104. Whitlock, *Cowboy Life*, 194–95.

105. Butler, *Daughters of Joy*, 2–5, 11–16.

106. Whitlock, *Cowboy Life*, 195.

107. J. Evetts Haley interview with C. W. (Charlie) Walker, W. W. (Walter) Walker and W. D. (Bill) Walker, 7 August 1937, 64–66, Box 2H483, Earl Vandale Collection, CAH–UTA.

108. Bud Brown Narrative, WPA Life Histories, 3–4.

109. Abbott, *We Pointed Them North*, 31.

110. S. B. Brite, "A Thorny Experience," in Hunter, ed., *Trail Drivers*, 47.

111. Adams, *Cowboy Lingo*, 230.

112. See Butler, *Daughters of Joy*, 61–62.

113. Mary Murphy," The Private Lives of Public Women: Prostitution in Butte, Montana, 1878–1917," in Armitage and Jameson, ed., *The Women's West*, 195.

114. Gober, *Cowboy Justice*, 90.

115. D. D. Singleterry to J. Evetts Haley, 27 September 1927, 78, JEH II J–I, JEH–MLHC.

116. Abbott, *We Pointed Them North*, 107.

117. Morgan, "Better Than Diamonds," 130, 131–32.

118. Pat Bullis, "Ranging the East Panhandle," in Bullis, (Pat), Box 2H468, Earl Vandale Collection, CAH–UTA.

119. Bullis, "Ranging the East Panhandle."

120. Abbott, *We Pointed Them North*, 108–10.

121. West, *Growing Up*, 152–53.

122. Carroll, *Homesteads Ungovernable*, 87–88.

123. See, for example, the numerous cases of assault against women in the 1890s listed in Criminal Case Files, County Clerk's Office, Reeves County Courthouse, Pecos, TX.

124. Bullis's narrative is one of a number of "unexpurgated" accounts of a bawdy and salacious nature collected by historian J. Evetts Haley and shared among a select circle of friends. A number of these manuscripts are in the Earl Vandale Collection, and undoubtedly there are others in similar collections.

125. Kimmel, *Manhood in America*, 86; Glenda Elizabeth Gilmore, *Gender and Jim Crow: Women and the Politics of White Supremacy in North Carolina, 1896–1920* (Chapel Hill: University of North Carolina Press, 1996), 61–62, 75–76.

126. Villareal, *Vaqueros de Sarita*, 95.

127. Hale, *Twenty-Four Years*, 14–15, 92.

128. Jaques, *Texan Ranch Life*, 65.

129. Douglas, *Cattle Kings of Texas*, 251.

130. D. D. Singleterry to J. Evetts Haley, 22 September 1927, 1–2, JEH II J–I, JEH–MLHC.

131. Hunter, ed., *Trail Drivers of Texas*, xiii–xiv.

132. Laura A. Bush to C. W. Campbell, 1 May 1887, Letters Received by B. H. Campbell, E.1 D.3, XIT Ranch Records, PPHM.

133. Siringo, *Texas Cowboy*, 171–72.

134. Abbott, *We Pointed Them North*, 4–5.

135. George F. Hindes, "The Milk of Human Kindness Is Drying Up," in Hunter, ed., *Trail Drivers*, 398–400.

136. Charlie Weldon Narrative, WPA Life Histories, 2.

137. Todd, *Bones Hooks*, 60.

138. Hastings, *A Ranchman's Recollections*, 116.

139. J. Earle Hodges to Fred Horsbrugh, 4 February 1902, Folder 16, Box 2, Espuela Land and Cattle Company Records, SC–TTU. See also same to same 20 July 1901, and 12 October 1901.

140. Lea, *King Ranch*, 2: 514–15.

141. Holden, *The Espuela*, 123.

142. Duke and Frantz, *6,000 Miles*, 112.
143. Ernest Spann Narrative, WPA Life Histories, 5–6.
144. S. A. Wright, "The Adventures of a Texas Cowpuncher," Box 2R312, CAH–UTA.
145. A. G. Anderson Narrative, WPA Life Histories, 2–3, 9–10.
146. Edward E. Jones Narrative, WPA Life Histories, 2.
147. James E. Schultz Narrative, WPA Life Histories, 10–11.
148. Media Cottage Productions, Vaquero, 2003.
149. Atherton, *Cattle Kings*, 83, 84, 87–88, 90.
150. Stephens, *Taft Ranch*, 37–40.
151. Ed Bell Narrative, WPA Life Histories, 5, 6.
152. John H. Fuller Narrative, WPA Life Histories, 1.
153. F. M. Polk, "My Experience on the Cow Trail," in Hunter, ed., *Trail Drivers*, 146.
154. I draw here on the work of Leslie A. Fiedler. Huck does not want to grow up and be civilized like Tom Sawyer and the widow, neither does he wish to become an outlaw. Yet "he cannot, of course stay where he is in the no-man's land of boyhood. . . . For all his illusion of choice, he is not really free, but imprisoned in his 'independence'; for he is incapable of remaining inside the respectable community." Fiedler, *Love and Death in the American Novel*, 580–82.

CHAPTER 6

1. Earnest Cook Narrative, 8, WPA Life Histories.
2. Stearns, *Be A Man!* 82, 86.
3. Andre Jorgenson Anderson Narrative, 6, WPA Life Histories.
4. For a discussion of the performative aspects of working-class masculinity, see Heron, "The Boys and their Booze," 451.
5. "Aunt Mary Davenport," Nancy Kelley Narrative as told by Emma Kelley Davenport, WPA Life Histories, 8–9.
6. H. D. Gruene, "Made a Long Trip to Wyoming," in Hunter, ed., *Trail Drivers*, 136.
7. William Walter Brady Narrative, WPA Life Histories, 6–7.
8. See for example J. L. McCaleb, "My First Five-Dollar Bill," in Hunter, ed., *Trail Drivers*, 486, 488; George W. Saunders, "Reflections of the Trail," in ibid., 434–35.
9. Dykstra, *Cattle Towns*, 88–90.
10. Siringo, *Texas Cowboy*, 38.
11. Abbott, *We Pointed Them North*, 40.
12. See for example the studio photographs reproduced in J. Frank Dobie, *Cow People* (Austin: University of Texas Press, 1964), 65–73.
13. Dykstra, *Cattle Towns*, 101.
14. Siringo, *Texas Cowboy*, 38, 55, 59–60, 98.
15. Abbott, *We Pointed Them North*, 49, 50.
16. Ann Fabian, *Card Sharps, Dream Books & Bucket Shops: Gambling in 19th-Century America* (Ithaca, NY and London: Cornell University Press, 1990), 41.
17. Peck, "Manly Gambles," in Basso, McCall, and Garceau, eds., *Across the Great Divide*, 77–79.
18. Gober, *Cowboy Justice*, 164–76.
19. Heron, "Boys and their Booze," 412.

20. Paul Michel Taillon, "'What We Want Is Good Sober Men': Masculinity, Respectability, and Temperance in the Railroad Brotherhoods, c. 1870–1890," *Journal of Social History* 36, no. 2 (Winter 2002): 321–22; Rotundo, *American Manhood*, 180.

21. Dykstra, *Cattle Towns*, 101–2.

22. George W. Arrington to Adjt. Gen. J. B. Jones, 15 December, 1880, in L. F. Sheffy, "The Arrington Papers," typescript, Folder 1, George Washington Arrington Papers, PPHM.

23. Edgar Rye, *The Quirt and the Spur: Vanishing Shadows of the Texas Frontier* (1909; reprint, Austin, TX: Steck-Vaugh, 1967), x–xi.

24. Jim B. Wilson to J. Evetts Haley, 1 January 1928, 28, manuscript interview, JEH II, J–1, JEH–MLHC.

25. Carl Coke Rister, *Fort Griffin on the Texas Frontier* (Norman: University of Oklahoma Press, 1956), 196–98.

26. Charles Goodnight, "A Sketch of the First Settlement of the Panhandle," 3, undated typescript, Literary Productions: Miscellaneous written by Charles Goodnight, undated, Box 2Q74, Charles Goodnight Papers, CAH–UTA. For more on Mobeetie and Fort Griffin, see Rathjen, *Texas Panhandle*, 167–68.

27. Rathjen, *Texas Panhandle*, 231.

28. For more on Tascosa and Billy the Kid, see Frederick Nolan, *Tascosa: Its Life and Gaudy Times* (Lubbock: Texas Tech University Press, 2007), 38–51.

29. S. A. Bull to J. Evetts Haley, 27 February 1927, manuscript interview, JEH II, J–1, JEH–MLHC.

30. D. D. Singleterry to J. Evetts Haley, 22 September 1927, 71, JEH II, J–1 JEH–MLHC.

31. Bill Oden to J. Evetts Haley, 9 July 1947, 3, 5–7, manuscript interview, JEH II, J–1, JEH–MLHC.

32. Barry Scobee, "Two Johns, Buckhorn and Haymaker Famous Saloons Here in Early Days," *Alpine Avalanche*, 22 November 1940.

33. Alton Hughes, "Just Musin'," typescript, 20 June 1983, on display in West of the Pecos Museum, Pecos, TX. This museum is housed in one of the old hotels and highlights the wild history of the town by pointing out several bullet holes in the bar and putting plaques on the floor where men were killed. Still, Thomas Beauchamp, who came as an educator to the town in 1883, claimed that the boys were just shooting for fun and the town was not nearly as wild as its reputation. Ibid.

34. Haywood, *Victorian West*, 20.

35. Andre Jorgenson Anderson Narrative, WPA Life Histories, 6.

36. "Frontier Times, Pecos County," undated typescript, Folder 1, Mrs. O. L. (Alice Jack) Shipman Collection, 1855–1956, ABB–SRSU.

37. Abbott, *We Pointed Them North*, 26, 100–101.

38. Peiss, *Cheap Amusements*, 20–21.

39. *Jacksboro Frontier Echo*, 19 November 1875.

40. S. A. Bull to J. Evetts Haley, 6 July 1927, 63, manuscript interview, JEH II, J–1, JEH–MLHC.

41. *Fort Griffin Echo*, 19 July 1879.

42. *El Paso Lone Star*, 3 September 1884.

43. *San Antonio Light*, 29 September 1885, 4 March 1885.

44. *San Antonio Light*, 16 July 1886, 30 July 1886.

45. *Texas Livestock Journal*, 26 July 1884.

46. *Fort Griffin Echo*, 5 February 1881, also reprinted in the *Fort Griffin Fandangle*, 20 April 1968, Scrapbook #8, Reel 1, Watt Reynolds Matthews Scrapbooks, SC–TTU.

47. Abbott, *We Pointed Them North*, 220.

48. "W. E. Oglesby," in Jim Lanning and Judy Lanning, *Texas Cowboys: Memories of the Early Days* (College Station: Texas A & M University Press, 1984), 8.

49. Abbott, *We Pointed Them North*, 22.

50. Ibid., 23–24.

51. *Texas Livestock Journal*, 13 September 1884.

52. *El Paso Lone Star*, 28 February 1885.

53. Durham and Jones, *Negro Cowboys*, 81–82, 99.

54. D. D. Singleterry to J. Evetts Haley, 22 September 1927, 71, JEH J–I, JEH–MLHC. Singleterry also boasted that Bat Masterson had asked for the hat and they had refused him, but this is likely an embellishment! Robert Haywood argues that black on black violence was more common than black on white in Dodge City. Robert C. Haywood, "'No Less a Man': Blacks in Cow Town Dodge City, 1876–1886," *Western Historical Quarterly* 19, no. 2 (May 1988): 161–82.

55. Todd, *Bones Hooks*, 44.

56. *State of Texas v. Monroe Clayton*, 1896, 458, Criminal Case Files, County Clerk's Office, Reeves County Courthouse, Pecos, TX.

57. Dykstra, *Cattle Towns*, 106.

58. Durham and Jones, *Negro Cowboys*, 44–45.

59. Porter, "Negro Labor," 368, 371–73; Katz, *The Black West*, [148]; Bill Oden to J. Evetts Haley, 9 July 1947, 5–6, 11, manuscript interview, JEH II, J–1, JEH–MLHC.

60. *El Paso Herald*, 9 November 1881.

61. Rister, *Fort Griffin*, 126–27.

62. The story has become part of the Wild West legends of Fort Griffin, so Dick emerges as a larger-than-life figure, but his actions are ultimately downplayed as those of a clown because part of the story is that Dick shot his own horse in the head by accident, which is why he was on foot and the posse could catch him. Ibid., 126.

63. Richard E. Nisbett and Dov Cohen, *Culture of Honor: The Psychology of Violence in the South* (Boulder, CO: Westview Press, 1996), xv–xvi, 4, 9. The seminal work on Southern concepts of honor and their impact on Southern culture and behavior is Wyatt-Brown, *Southern Honor*. See also discussion of Scots-Irish herder culture in the South in Forrest McDonald and Grady McWhiney, "The Antebellum Southern Herdsman: A Reinterpretation," *Journal of Southern History* 41, no. 2 (May 1975): 147–66, and McDonald and McWhiney, "Celtic Origins," 165–82. Rowland Berthoff argues that herding practices were less related to ethnicity than geography, and that such behavior is not exclusively Scots-Irish. Berthoff, "Celtic Mist," 523–46. For present purposes, it is the herding culture rather than the ethnicity that makes the difference.

64. Ted Ownby, *Subduing Satan: Religion, Recreation, and Manhood in the Rural South, 1865–1920* (Chapel Hill and London: University of North Carolina Press, 1990), 54.

65. Rotundo, "Boy Culture," 24.

66. Gorn, "Gouge and Bite," 21–22.

67. Gutiérrez, "Tell Me With Whom You Walk," in Basso, McCall, and Garceau, eds., *Across the Great Divide*, 32.

68. Gorn, "Gouge and Bite," 22–23. Historian Mark Carroll's current research on dueling in Missouri in the 1830s suggests that in the early to mid-nineteenth century, middle-class professionals were more likely to duel than aristocrats, and did so both to defend against attacks on their virtue and to show their worthiness for political office. However, he argues that duels themselves were a civilized form of violence. The existence of dueling codes ensured that participants would exhaust all efforts to avoid violence before engaging in combat and that they channeled passions away from more barbaric forms of fighting and rash impulses. Mark Carroll, "Bourgeois Dilemma: Morality, Politics, and the Affair of Honor in Upper Louisiana and Missouri, 1804–1860," paper given at the Mid-America Conference on History, 25–27 September 2008, Springfield, MO.

69. William A. Preist Narrative, WPA Life Histories, 14.

70. Brook Campbell Narrative, WPA Life Histories, 7.

71. Hilory G. Bedford, "Memoirs of H. G. Bedford," 16–17, typescript, 1926, Box 2Q435, Hilory G. Bedford Reminiscences, CAH–UTA.

72. Collinson, *Life in the Saddle*, 125–26.

73. Woodson Coffee, "Autobiography," 18, in bound typescript, "Papers of Woodson Coffee (1862–1953)," Woodson Coffee Collection, PPHM.

74. Cosmo Falconer, "Laurel Leaf Tales,"1–2, from the *Cheyenne Star*, 15 February 1912, typescript, Folder 11, Box 2H463, Earl Vandale Collection, CAH–UTA.

75. Hale, *Twenty-Four Years*, 15, 32.

76. Gorn, "Gouge and Bite," 19, 20, 23.

77. Cosmo Falconer, "Laurel Leaf Tales,"1–2, from the *Cheyenne Star*, 15 February 1912, typescript, Folder 11, Box 2H463, Earl Vandale Collection, CAH–UTA.

78. Dickson D. Bruce, Jr., *Violence and Culture in the Antebellum South* (Austin and London: University of Texas Press, 1979), 98–99.

79. Gorn, "Bite and Gouge," 36, 43.

80. *Fort Griffin Echo*, 29 May 1880.

81. Siringo, *Texas Cowboy*, 187.

82. *Texas v. John Weaver*, 1891, #202, Criminal Case Files, Reeves County Clerk's Office, Reeves County Courthouse, Pecos, TX.

83. Hine and Faragher, *American West*, 308.

84. George Claiborne Harris, "Recollections of a Frontier Merchant," Interview with Cecil Briggs, June 18, 25, 27, 1937, Manuscript Interview, PPHM.

85. See, for example, *Texas Livestock Journal*, 28 June 1884, 26 July 1884, 28 January 1888; *San Antonio Evening Light*, 15 July 1884 and 17 July 1884, found in "History of Grazing in Texas: Excerpts from Newspapers, 1880–1884 Vol. II," Historical Records Survey, Works Progress Administration, 1935, Box 2R 333, Grazing Industry Papers, 1537–1940, 1973, CAH–UTA.

86. George Owens to J. Evetts Haley, 10 January 1927, manuscript interview, JEH II, J–1, JEH–MLHC.

87. Hale, *Twenty-Four Years*, 89–91.

88. Ibid., 82, 85.

89. *Fort Griffin Echo*, 14 June 1879.

90. See for example the charges for the 1887 session and *State of Texas vs. G. W. Arrington*, 8 July 1887, Minutes of the District County Court, 286–87, Civil Record No. 1 District Court of Donely County, County Clerk's office, Donely County Courthouse, Clarendon, TX.

91. McWhiney, *Cracker Culture*, 166–67, 169.

92. District Court Minutes 2 Uvalde County, 187, District Clerk's Office, Uvalde County Courthouse, Uvalde, TX. This is the only duel I found explicitly mentioned in the court records which suggests either that such charges were rare, or that duels were disappearing in a formal sense in Texas after Reconstruction.

93. Murdoch, *American West*, 52–54.

94. Walter W. Meek to Eliza Duis, 1 August 1887, Meek Letters, 81–82, bound typescript, Box 516A, A1989–021.002, Walter Meek Family Papers, South Texas Archives, Texas A & M University at Kingsville, Kingsville, TX.

95. Charles Goodnight, "Autobiography," [1927?], 126, 133–34, Box 2Q74, Charles Goodnight Papers, CAH–UTA.

96. Lea, *King Ranch*, 1: 327–28. Interestingly, historian Lewis Atherton describes the fight as restoring "a sense of harmony and good will, as well as increased respect on both sides." By Atherton's measure, violence again restored order. Atherton, *Cattle Kings*, 121.

97. Charles Goodnight, "A Sketch of the First Settlement of the Panhandle," 3, undated typescript, Literary Productions: Miscellaneous written by Charles Goodnight, undated, Box 2Q74, Charles Goodnight Papers, CAH–UTA.

98. Bronson Edgar Beecher, "End of the Trail," in Adams, ed., *Best of the American Cowboy*, 288–89.

99. Depositions, *Texas v. W. G. Caldwell*, 1890, #465 misfiled (as of June 2008) with County Court Criminal Case Files, County Clerk's Office, Reeves County Courthouse, Pecos, TX. Murder is a felony and thus not in the jurisdiction of county courts, and the case number refers to a District Court case. The jury decisions are in District Court Minutes 1, January 13, 1885–Sept. 8, 1898, 291–94, 317–18, District Clerk's Office, Reeves County Courthouse, Pecos, TX.

100. *State of Texas vs. R. M. Moore*, 15 April 1895, #195, District Criminal Court, County Clerk's Office, Armstrong County Courthouse, Claude, Texas.

101. See Criminal Minutes 1 Guadalupe County, 111, 160, 168–69, 173, 184, District Clerk's Office, Guadalupe County Courthouse, Seguin, TX.

102. *State of Texas vs. W. D. Browning*, 15 May 1891, #23, District Criminal Court, County Clerk's Office, Armstrong County Courthouse, Claude, Texas.

103. J. N. Browning to Fred Horsbrugh, 14 August 1902 and 30 July 1902, Folder 15, Box 2 , J. Earle Hodges to Fred Horsbrugh, 17 September 1902, Folder 16, Box 2, J. N. Browning to Fred Horsbrugh, 30 August 1902 and 19 September 1902, Folder 3, Box 3, Espuela Land and Cattle Company Records, SC–TTU. Characteristically, the Spur disputed paying the doctor's and hotel bills for the 67 days Lindley lingered before his death. Eventually the doctor, noting that the expenses were very high and had been largely "borne by the friends of the poor boy who have manifested such noble traits of character," reduced his bill by $50, but three months after Lindley's death the bill was still in dispute. Quote comes from J. D. Stocking to Fred Horsbrugh, undated, Folder 4, Box 3, ibid. See also J. H. Pirtle to Horsbrugh, 17 September 1902, and W. H. Patrick to Horsbrugh, 3 October 1902, Folder 3, Box 3, and T. W. Carroll to Horsbrugh, 30 December 1902, Folder 15, Box 2, ibid.

104. Dickson Bruce makes this distinction in Bruce, *Violence and Culture*, 99.

105. Stearns, *Be A Man!* 50; Johansen, *Family Men*, 85. Bertram Wyatt-Brown argues that while duels declined and were viewed as oddities after the Civil War, Southern violence to defend "honor" did not entirely disappear, instead it was channeled into lynchings of

blacks. While I agree that violence did not completely lose legitimacy, it was not the elite who were involved in lynchings, as he himself acknowledges. Therefore, I cannot see a correlation between the decline of dueling and the rise of lynchings, or a direct evolution of the idea of honor; only a working-class cooptation of the concept of honor as a justification for racist violence. Bertram Wyatt Brown, *The Shaping of Southern Culture: Honor, Grace, and War, 1760s–1890s* (Chapel Hill and London: University of North Carolina Press, 2001), 270–71, 283–88.

106. For a discussion of the rise of the concept of physical manhood and the importance of organized sports as a way to build up manhood, see Joe L. Dubbert, *A Man's Place: Masculinity in Transition* (Englewood Cliffs, NJ: Prentice-Hall, 1979), 163–75.

107. David I. Macleod, *Building Character in the American Boy: The Boy Scouts, YMCA, and Their Forerunners, 1870–1920* (Madison: University of Wisconsin Press, 1983), 53–54.

108. Rotundo, "Boy Culture," 31–32.

109. Quoted in Haley, *Littlefield*, 77–78.

110. Murdo Mackenzie to J. Evetts Haley, 22 August 1932, 1–2, JEH II J–I, JEH–MLHC; Pearce, *Matador*, 39–41.

111. Hilkey, *Character Is Capital*, 9.

112. *Lampasas Dispatch*, 9 August 1877. This was the infamous Horrells-Higgins feud. See C. L. Sonnichsen, *I'll Die Before I'll Run—The Story of the Great Feuds of Texas*, 2nd ed. (New York: Devin-Adair, 1962), 125–49.

113. Lewis, *Tapadero*, xiii.

114. "Transcript of a Manuscript by Joe Meador brought in March 15, 1955," Joe Meador Papers, SC–TTU.

115. West, *Growing Up*, 26–28, 184–86, 247.

116. Karen R. Merrill, "Domesticated Bliss: Ranchers and Their Animals," in Basso, McCall, and Garceau, eds., *Across the Great Divide*, 171.

117. See for example Hunter, ed., *Trail Drivers*, 20, 25.

118. West, *Growing Up*, 67.

119. Robert L. Griswold, "Anglo Women and Domestic Ideology in the American West in the Nineteenth and Early Twentieth Centuries," in Lillian Schlissel, Vicki L. Ruiz, and Janice Monk, eds., *Western Women: Their Land, Their Lives* (Albuquerque: University of New Mexico Press, 1988), 23.

120. Peck, "Manly Gambles," in Basso, McCall, and Garceau, eds., *Across the Great Divide*, 73.

121. Johnson, "Bulls, Bears and Dancing Boys," in ibid., 51.

122. Garceau, "Nomads, Bunkies, Cross-Dressers and Family Men," in ibid., 153–54.

123. *San Antonio Evening Light*, 5 October 1882, found in "History of Grazing in Texas: Excerpts from Newspapers, 1880–1884 Vol. II" Historical Records Survey, Works Progress Administration, 1935, Box 2R 333, Grazing Industry Papers, 1537–1940, 1973, CAH–UTA.

124. Quoted in Abbott, *We Pointed Them North*, 43.

125. William W. Savage, Jr., ed., *Cowboy Life: Reconstructing an American Myth*, rev. ed. (Niwot: University Press of Colorado, 1993), 110.

126. Criminal Docket District Court B Gonzales County, 76, 80, District Clerk's office, Gonzales County Courthouse, Gonzales, TX.

127. Dykstra, *Cattle Towns*, 115–19.

128. *Fort Griffin Echo*, 26 July 1879, 2 April 1881, 18 May 1881.

129. *Fort Griffin Echo*, 12 March 1881.

130. *El Paso Lone Star*, 10 January 1883. Found in "History of Grazing in Texas: Excerpts from Newspapers, 1880–1884 Vol. II" Historical Records Survey, Works Progress Administration, 1935, Box 2R 333, Grazing Industry Papers, 1537–1940, 1973, CAH–UTA.

131. *El Paso Lone Star*, 18 January 1883.

132. Robert J. Kleberg to "My Dear Little Sister [Mathilde Kleberg?]," 2 October 1881, Letters By Writer: Various Kleberg family Members, 1867–1944 and undated, Box 2J51, Kleberg (Rudolph) Family Papers, CAH–UTA.

133. Bill Oden to J. Evetts Haley, 9 July 1947, 19–20, manuscript interview, JEH II, J–1, JEH–MLHC.

134. 20 September 1870, "Diary of Jonathan Hamilton Baker (1832–1918) of Palo Pinto County 1858–1919, pt II: 1861–1872," 438–39, Box 2Q418, Jonathan Hamilton Baker Diaries, CAH–UTA.

135. 23 September 1870, ibid.

136. Butler, *Daughters of Joy*, 4–5.

137. See *State of Texas vs. Carrie Wilson*, 1889, *State of Texas vs. Willie Reed*, 1889, in Minutes of the District Court, 430–31, Civil Record No. 1 District Court Donely County, Donely County Clerk's Office, Donely County Courthouse, Clarendon, TX.

138. Dykstra, *Cattle Towns*, 104–5, 125–27.

139. John Clay, "Justice on the Range," in Adams, ed., *Best of the Cowboy*, 173.

140. Filene, *Him/Her/Self*, 83, 92; Hilkey, *Character Is Capital*, 148–49.

141. Quoted from advertisements for "Dr. Judd's Electric Belt and Battery," in the *National Police Gazette* in John F. Kasson, *Houdini, Tarzan, and the Perfect Man: The White Male Body and the Challenge of Modernity in America* (New York: Hill and Wang, 2001), 49; "J. H. Reeves Manhood Restored," *Texas Livestock Journal*, 31 January 1885, 7; "Dr. Wassercug," *Texas Livestock Journal*, 13 June 1885, 3; "Dr. Rice," *Texas Livestock Journal*, 11 July 1885, 6; "The Voltaic Belt Company," *Texas Livestock Journal*, 12 July 1884 (a weekly advertiser); Westermeier, "Cowboy Sexuality," 100.

142. Charles Goodnight and D. H. Snyder banned alcohol on the ranches and William Lewis confessed to never really drinking very much, even when in town with fellow cowboys. See chapter 5 and Lewis, *Tapadero*, 98–99, 104–5.

143. Harrison McClure to J. Evetts Haley, 22 September 1935, 2, 27, manuscript interview, JEH II, J–1, JEH–MLHC.

144. *History of the Cattlemen of Texas*, 40.

145. Ownby, *Subduing Satan*, 167–70, 172.

146. Richard Slatta, *Cowboys of the Americas* (New Haven, CT: Yale University Press, 1990, 151.

147. *Handbook of Texas Online*, s.v. "Prohibition," http://www.tshaonline.org/handbook/online/articles/PP/vap1.html (accessed 7 July 2008).

148. George W. Arrington to Adt. Gen. J. B. Jones, 15 December 1880, in L. F. Sheffy, ed., "The Arrington Papers," typescript, Folder 1, George Washington Arrington Papers, PPHM.

149. See for example the many cases dismissed against stores illegally selling intoxicating liquors on Sunday in Armstrong County in 1890. *State of Texas vs. George B. Berry*, 21 August 1890; *State of Texas vs. George Ireland*, 23 May 1890; *State of Texas vs. Jess Gumm*, 23 May 1890; *State of Texas vs. C. M. Johnson*, 12 August 1890; Folders 12–17, Records of the

District Court, County Clerk's Office, Armstrong County Courthouse, Claude, TX. The profusion of cases in that year seems to suggest an attempt to crackdown on such establishments, however.

150. W. B. Mitchell, History Notes, undated typescript, Folder 3, Box 1, W. B. Mitchell Collection, ABB–SRSU.

151. Barry Scobee, "Two Johns, Buckhorn and Haymaker Famous Saloons Here in Early Days," *Alpine Avalanche*, 22 November 1940.

152. Robert J. Kleberg, II to "My dear little sister," 2 October 1881, Letters by writer: Various Kleberg family members, 1867–1944 and undated, Box 2J51, Rudolph Kleberg Family Papers, CAH–UTA.

153. Walter W. Meek to Eliza Duis, 26 August 1887, 27 November 1887, Meek Letters, 84, 104, bound typescript, Box 516A, A1989–021.002, Walter W. Meek Family Papers, South Texas Archives, Texas A & M University at Kingsville, Kingsville, TX.

154. Woods, *British Gentlemen*, 161–63.

155. Johansen, *Family Men*, 155–56. See also David Roediger's discussion of attendance at minstrel shows in Roediger, *Wages of Whiteness*, 120–27.

156. David Hamilton Murdoch discusses the increasing presence of well-bred Europeans among the cowboys as one factor in the improvement of their image, but also notes that they could not act in a stand-offish manner and that "no leopard changes all his spots," so rowdy behavior persisted. Murdoch, *American West*, 55–56.

157. Fabian, *Card Sharps*, 6, 40.

158. J. S. Wynne to J. Evetts Haley, 15 July 1926, 9, Manuscript Interview, PPHM.

159. George W. Littlefield to J. "Will" White, in typescript of letters "September 15, 1860–Dec 12, 1868," 49–51, Reel 1, George W. Littlefield Papers, SC–TTU.

160. *History of the Cattlemen of Texas*, 235. See also ibid., 209.

161. Peck, "Manly Gambles," 79–83.

162. Hatley, *Texas Constables*, 118–19. See also my comments in note 149 above.

163. See 1868–1869 cases in Criminal Docket 1 County Court, 48–82, 1879–1884 cases in Criminal Minutes, County Court, and 1886–1890 cases, Judges Criminal Docket, County Court, County Clerk's Office, Bastrop County Courthouse, Bastrop, TX.

164. Dockets #1619–1634, 1659–1673, 1676–1685, 1686–1786, Judges Criminal Docket, County Court, County Clerk's Office, Bastrop County Courthouse, Bastrop, TX; dockets #2411–2450, 2491–2584, 2622–2673, 2704–2754, 2797–2822, 2893–2930, 3035–3075, Criminal Bar Docket 5 Bastrop County, ibid.; dockets #3142–3157, 3205–3218, 3259–3286, Criminal Bar Docket 6 Bastrop County, ibid.

165. District Court Minutes 1 Uvalde County, 344, 450–55, District Clerk's Office, Uvalde County Courthouse, Uvalde, TX; District Court Minutes 2 Uvalde County, 133–35, 139–40, 165, ibid.; Minute County Court A Uvalde County, 209, 210, 217, 226–27, 230–37, 238–43, 247–54, 259–77, 309–19, 322–23, County Clerk's Office, Uvalde County Courthouse, Uvalde, TX; Minutes County Court 2 Uvalde County, ibid. Of course, the lack of arrests did not necessarily mean a lack of gambling, just a lack of enforcement.

166. Minutes, District Court B Atascosa County, District Clerk's Office Atascosa County Courthouse, Jourdanton, TX, 10, 26–31, 33, 174, 504–5, 553–54.

167. Minutes, County Court No 1 Reeves County, 108–11, 119–25, 232–33, 633, County Clerk's Office, Reeves County Courthouse, Pecos, TX; County Court Criminal Cases 176–360, 1891, and County Court Criminal Cases, 361–530, 1894, ibid.

168. Dykstra, *Cattle Towns*, 121–27. See pages 240–92, for a discussion of illegal businesses' attempts to resist regulation in Kansas cattle towns.

169. Rister, *Fort Griffin*, 160.

170. *Jacksboro Frontier Echo*, 22 February 1878, 12 July 1878.

171. *Fort Griffin Echo*, 9 August 1879. See also ibid., 14 February 1880, for a similar
warning.

172. "The Cowboy's Vacation," *Texas Livestock Journal*, 25 October 1884.

173. *Texas Livestock Journal*, 22 November 1884.

174. "Cow Punchers," reprinted in the *Texas Livestock Journal*, 5 July 1884.

175. Hilory G. Bedford, "Bringing Up the Past to Enjoy It at the Present," 4, 7, typescript,
Box 2Q435, Hilory G. Bedford Reminiscences, CAH–UTA.

176. Abbott, *We Pointed Them North*, 28–29.

177. Quoted in Weston, *Real Cowboy*, 24.

178. *San Antonio Light*, 1 October 1883, found in "History of Grazing in Texas:
Excerpts from Newspapers, 1880–1884 Vol. II" Historical Records Survey, Works
Progress Administration, 1935, Box 2R 333, Grazing Industry Papers, 1537–1940, 1973,
CAH–UTA.

179. There is a growing literature on the racialization of manhood and the attempt to
use whiteness as a way of improving one's own masculine image. See for example Roediger, *Wages of Whiteness*; Bederman, *Manliness and Civilization*; Timothy Tyson, *Radio
Free Dixie: Robert F. Williams and the Roots of Black Power* (Durham: University of North
Carolina Press, 2001).

180. *Fort Griffin Echo*, 19 July 1879. See similar editorials 9 August 1879 and 14 February
1880.

181. *El Paso Lone Star*, 24 June 1885.

182. Abbott, *We Pointed Them North*, 15–16.

183. McCoy, *Historic Sketches*, 10, 137–38.

184. Walter W. Meek to Eliza Duis, 1 May 1887,"Meek Letters, 35, bound typescript, Box
516A, A 1989–021.002, Walter Meek Family Papers, 1845–1981, South Texas Archives, Texas
A & M University, Kingsville, TX.

185. *San Antonio Light*, 28 May 1884, "History of Grazing in Texas: Excerpts from Newspapers, 1880–1884 Vol. II" Historical Records Survey, Works Progress Administration, 1935,
Box 2R 333, Grazing Industry Papers, 1537–1940, 1973, CAH–UTA.

186. *Alonzo Matthews v. The State of Texas*, 1880, 9 Texas Appeals, 138–40.

187. "That Awful Cowboy," *San Antonio Light*, 14 August 1883, found in "History of
Grazing in Texas: Excerpts from Newspapers, 1880–1884 Vol. II" Historical Records Survey, Works Progress Administration, 1935, Box 2R 333, Grazing Industry Papers, 1537–1940,
1973, CAH–UTA.

188. *San Antonio Light*, 23 April 1885, found in "History of Grazing in Texas: Excerpts
from Newspapers, 1885–1886 Vol. III" Historical Records Survey, Works Progress Administration, 1935, Box 2R 333, Grazing Industry Papers, 1537–1940, 1973, CAH–UTA.

189. "Round About Town," *Austin Statesman*, 4 March 1884, found in "History of Grazing in Texas: Excerpts from Newspapers, 1880–1884 Vol. II" Historical Records Survey,
Works Progress Administration, 1935, Box 2R 333, Grazing Industry Papers, 1537–1940,
1973, CAH–UTA.

190. *San Antonio Light*, 1 February 1892, "History of Grazing in Texas: Excerpts from Newspapers, 1890–1894 Vol. V" Historical Records Survey, Works Progress Administration, 1935, Box 2R 334, Grazing Industry Papers, 1537–1940, 1973, CAH–UTA.

191. "A Hero of the Plains," *El Paso Herald*, 19 October 1881. On the importance of ritual boasts see Gorn, "Gouge and Bite," 28–29.

192. "Rather Confusing," in Hunter, ed., *Trail Drivers*, 1031–32.

193. *San Antonio Light*, 19 July 1894. "History of Grazing in Texas: Excerpts from Newspapers, 1885–1886 Vol. III" Historical Records Survey, Works Progress Administration, 1935, Box 2R 333, Grazing Industry Papers, 1537–1940, 1973, CAH–UTA.

194. Jack Potter, "Coming Up the Trail in 1882," in Hunter, ed., *Trail Drivers*, 62–63, 66–68.

195. Hastings, *A Ranchman's Recollections*, 118, 122. For other examples, see George W. Saunders, "Reflections of the Trail," in Hunter, ed., *Trail Drivers*, 451; Jasper (Bob) Lauderdale, "Reminiscences of the Trail," ibid., 404; Annie Hightower Narrative, WPA Life Histories, 5; Hilory Bedford, "Reminiscences," 30–33, Box 2Q435, Hilory G. Bedford Reminiscences, CAH–UTA; S.A. Wright, "Adventures of a Texas Cowpuncher," Box 2R 312, CAH–UTA.

196. "Where Cowboys Are Subdued," *Texas Livestock Journal*, 2 April 1887.

197. "Soothing Syrup for the Cowboys," *Texas Livestock Journal* (monthly edition), April 1887, 23.

198. *Texas Livestock Journal*, 12 September 1885.

199. *San Antonio Light*, 26 March 1884, ibid.

200. J.G.K. McClure, "Among the Cowboys of Texas April 23–May 7, 1896," 19–21, Manuscript Interview, PPHM. McClure, an English visitor to the ranch could not praise the rules highly enough as he said otherwise the cowboys would all gamble and drink, and now they were all really well behaved.

201. J. S. Kenyon, quoted in Duke, and Frantz, *6,000 Miles*, 34.

202. Abbott, *We Pointed Them North*, 74.

203. J. E. Farrington to M. C. Scott, 5 July [188]9, JA Ranch Letterpress, "July 1887 to November 1891," 8, JA Ranch Records, PPHM.

204. See Ownby, *Subduing Satan*, 176–77.

205. Karen Halttunen, *Confidence Men and Painted Women: A Study of Middle-class Culture in America, 1830–1870* (New Haven, CT: Yale University Press, 1982), 193–97.

206. Laura Wexler, "Tender Violence: Literary Eavesdropping, Domestic Fiction, and Educational Reform," in Samuels, ed., *Culture of Sentiment*, 15–16.

207. Robert L. Griswold, "Anglo Women and Domestic Ideology," in Schlissel, Ruiz, and Monk, eds., *Western Women*, 24–25.

208. Bruce Burgett, *Sentimental Bodies: Sex, Gender, and Citizenship in the Early Republic* (Princeton, NJ: Princeton University Press, 1998), 155–59.

209. Stearns, *Be A Man!* 66–70.

210. Morgan, "Better Than Diamonds," 132–33.

211. *San Antonio Daily Light*, 2 March 1887, found in "History of Grazing in Texas: Excerpts from Newspapers, 1887–1889 Vol. IV" Historical Records Survey, Works Progress Administration, 1935, Box 2R 333, Grazing Industry Papers, 1537–1940, 1973, CAH–UTA.

212. Haywood, *Victorian West*, 238–39.

EPILOGUE

1. "The Cowpuncher," Arnot, John, Box 2H 471 Vandale (Earl) Collection, CAH–UTA.

2. Holden, *Rollie Burns*, 53.

3. Wirt W. White, "The Big Trail Herd," 38–39, MS Reminiscences #1, Reel 1, Wirt W. White Papers, SC–TTU.

4. Rita Parks, *The Western Hero in Film and Television* (Ann Arbor, MI: UMI Research Press, 1982), 46. For examples of descriptions of pernicious cowboys see Murdoch, *American West*, 45–49.

5. Garceau, "Nomads, Bunkies, Cross-Dressers and Family Men," 154, 163.

6. Richard Etulain, "Cultural Origins of the Western," in Jack Nachbar, *Focus on the Western* (Englewood Cliffs, NJ: Prentice-Hall, 1974), 20–21.

7. Roosevelt, "National Duties," in Roosevelt, *Strenuous Life*, 280.

8. Bold, *Selling the Wild West*, 41.

9. Jane Tompkins, *West of Everything: The Inner Life of Westerns* (New York and Oxford: Oxford University Press, 1992), 43–44.

10. Paul Reddin, *Wild West Shows* (Urbana and Chicago: University of Illinois Press, 1999), 68–69, 70; Dary, *Seeking Pleasure*, 145; Louis S. Warren, *Buffalo Bill's America: William Cody and The Wild West Show* (New York: Vintage Books, 2005), 215, 233–35.

11. Reddin, *Wild West Shows*, 64.

12. Warren, *Buffalo Bill's America*, 217, 220–21, 238, 243–50, 319, 400.

13. Michael Allen, "Real Cowboys? The Origins and Evolution of North American Rodeo and Rodeo Cowboys," *Journal of the West* 37, no. 1 (January 1998): 70, 71, 73; Slatta, *Comparing Cowboys and Frontiers*, 77.

14. Beverly J. Stoeltje, "Rodeo: From Custom to Ritual," *Western Folklore* 48, no. 3 (July 1989): 245–46, 250–52.

15. *Texas Livestock Journal*, 23 August 1884.

16. *San Antonio Light*, 1 September 1884, "History of Grazing in Texas: Excerpts from Newspapers, 1880–1884 Vol. II" Historical Records Survey, Works Progress Administration, 1935, Box 2R 333, Grazing Industry Papers, 1537–1940, 1973, CAH–UTA. This group might have been a troupe organized by A. B. Grady of Lockhart, Texas who established a Wild West type show in 1883. His cowboys were fitted out with "silver-banded Mexican hats, fringed leather jackets, Angora chaps, and great-roweled Mexican spurs." Mari Sandoz, *The Cattlemen: From the Rio Grande Across Far Marias* (New York: Hastings House, 1958), 490.

17. *San Antonio Light*, 3 April 1885, ibid.

18. B. R. Pearson Narrative, WPA Life Histories, 4–6. Pearson's narrative reads much like a tall tale but true or not emphasizes the view of the cowboy as spectacle.

19. Beverly J. Stoeltje, "Power and Ritual Genres: American Rodeo," *Western Folklore* 52, nos. 2, 3, 4 (April, July, October 1993): 146.

20. Warren, *Buffalo Bill's America*, 400.

21. Reddin, *Wild West Shows*, 64; Warren, *Buffalo Bill's America*, 399.

22. Stoeltje, "Power and Ritual Genres," 152.

23. Daryl Jones, *The Dime Novel Western* (Bowling Green, OH: Popular Press, Bowling Green State University, 1978), 5–8, 14.

24. Edward Buscombe, ed., *The BFI Companion to the Western* (London: Andre Deutsch/BFI Publishing, 1988), 18. The best sources to discuss the frontier as metaphor

in fiction, particularly in film, are Jim Kitses, *Horizons West: Directing the Western from John Ford to Clint Eastwood* (1970, rev. ed. London: BFI Publishing, 2004), 12–13; and John Cawelti, "Savagery, Civilization and the Western Hero," in Jack Nachbar, *Focus on the Western* (Englewood Cliffs, NJ: Prentice-Hall, 1974).

25. Jones, *Dime Novel Western*, 38–46, 56–61, 64–72.

26. Ibid., 109.

27. Richard Etulain, *Telling Western Stories: From Buffalo Bill to Larry McMurtry* (Albuquerque: University of New Mexico Press, 1999), 72–73.

28. Owen Wister, *The Virginian: A Horseman of the Plains* (1902; reprint, New York: New American Library, 1979), 26, 137, 250, 258.

29. Buscombe, ed., *BFI Companion*, 18; Parks, *Western Hero*, 69–70.

30. Adams, *Charles M. Russell*, 70.

31. Murdoch, *American West*, 73; Bold, *Selling the West*, 45–52.

32. Ibid., 57–58.

33. Murdoch, *American West*, 72–73.

34. Buscombe, ed., *BFI Film Companion*, 10, 1, 21–25, 36.

35. Ibid., 24–25, 28–31, 35–36.

36. Ibid., 10, 26–28, 32.

37. Lee Clark Mitchell, *Westerns: Making the Man in Fiction and in Film* (Chicago and London: University of Chicago Press, 1996), 166, 167, 183.

38. Parks, *Western Hero*, 56–57; Tompkins, *West of Everything*, 128.

39. See for example "Cowboys Are Real Men" by J. Frank Dobie from Dallas *News* 7/11/26[?] also *Frontier Times* 3:11(Aug. 1926) from partial typescript, in "History of Grazing in Texas: Excerpts from Magazines, *Frontier Times*, 1934–40, Index-Undated, Volume XIV, Historical Records Survey, Works Progress Administration, 1935, Box 2R338, Grazing Industry Papers, CAH–UTA.

40. Allen, "Real Cowboys," 76.

41. Reddin, *Wild West Shows*, 177.

42. "The National Old Time Cowboys' Association," leaflet, [1939], Old Time Cowboy's Association Collection, Folder 1, ABB–SRSU.

43. Reddin, *Wild West Shows*, 150, 159–60.

44. Warren, *Buffalo Bill's America*, 209.

45. Reddin, *Wild West Shows*, 163–64.

46. Stoeltje, Beverly June Smith, "Rodeo As Symbolic Performance" (PhD diss., University of Texas at Austin, 1979), 462–63.

# Index

Abbott, E. C. "Teddy Blue," background, 8, 111; clothing, 170; cross dresses, 154; foolish bet, 80; hero worship, 51, 53; injured, 78; job mobility, 77, 103; marriage, 163; reckless spending, 170; resists parental restraint, 57; restricted behavior, 201; sabotage, 99–100; saloons, 173, 175; sentiment, 120, 144; suffers abuse, 46–47; surrogate fathers, 49; treats other men, 63–64; and women, 149, 156, 160
Adair, Bill, 48
Adair, John, 31, 37, 85
African Americans: earn respect through skills, 40, 70, 71; horse wranglers, 58; lack of narratives, 9; masculinity, 134; numbers of, 40; poverty, 59; race relations, 10, 134–36; ranchers, 23; slaves, 29; soldiers, 41. *See also* racism
Alpine Cattle Company, 33
Anderson, A. G., 164
Armour packinghouse, 25
Arrington, George W., 191
artists, 210–12
Ashworth, Aaron, 23
Atascosa County, TX, 105
Austin, Stephen F., 29
Autry, Gene, 213

bachelor camps, 124
Baker, Jonathan Hamilton, 24, 114, 188
barbed wire, 25–27
Barton, Bell Vanderver, 146
Bastrop County, TX, 104
Bedford, Hilory G., 178, 196
blizzards, 28

Boyce, A. G., 89, 114
Boys: aggressive behavior encouraged, 20, 44; develop independent identities, 45, 63; false bravado, 64, 82; friendships, 116–17; hero worship, 50–53; homesick, 62; leave home, 67; leniency toward, 53; and mothers, 44–45; parenting strategies, 43–45; see schools as restriction, 56–57; suffer abuse, 46–47; use of term, 5–6
branding chutes, 94–95
Britton, A. M., 32, 37, 88
Broncho Billy, 213
Bugbee, Thomas, 32
Bullis, Pat, 159
Bunton, Mary Taylor, 143–44, 145–46
Burks, Amanda, 143, 145–46
Burnett, Samuel Burk, 4
Burns, Rollie C., 50, 69, 152–53, 154

Caldwell, C. G., 184–85
Campbell, B. H. "Barbecue," 88–89, 114–15
Campbell, Brook, 52–53, 178
Campbell, H. H., 37, 81, 88, 95, 133
cattle drives: Chisholm Trail, 24; closing of the trails, 28; numbers of cattle, 24; origins of, 23–24; quarantine laws, 24, 27; as rite of passage, 61–63; Western Trail, 24; women on, 145–46
cattle industry, in Big Bend region, 33–34; Big Die-Up, 28; breeding techniques, 29, 34; cattle prices, 25, 28; corporatization of, 34–35, 85, 87–90; de-skilling of work, 94–95; early development of, 2, 22–23; general trends 1870–1900, 34–35; on Gulf Coast, 28–29; and honor culture, 177;

# About the Author

JACQUELINE M. MOORE is Professor of History at Austin College in Sherman, Texas. She is the author of several books on the Gilded Age and Progressive Era, including *Booker T. Washington, W.E.B. Du Bois and the Struggle for Racial Uplift*. In the process of researching this book, she drove over 4,000 miles without once leaving the state of Texas.

CPSIA information can be obtained at www.ICGtesting.com
Printed in the USA
LVOW11*1304110816

499989LV00001B/2/P